TRAVEL MEDICINE:
TALES BEHIND THE SCIENCE

ADVANCES IN TOURISM RESEARCH

Series Editor: **Professor Stephen J. Page**
University of Stirling, UK
s.j.page@stir.ac.uk

Advances in Tourism Research series publishes monographs and edited volumes that comprise state-of-the-art research findings, written and edited by leading researchers working in the wider field of tourism studies. The series has been designed to provide a cutting edge focus for researchers interested in tourism, particularly the management issues now facing decision-makers, policy analysts and the public sector. The audience is much wider than just academics and each book seeks to make a significant contribution to the literature in the field of study by not only reviewing the state of knowledge relating to each topic but also questioning some of the prevailing assumptions and research paradigms which currently exist in tourism research. The series also aims to provide a platform for further studies in each area by highlighting key research agendas, which will stimulate further debate and interest in the expanding area of tourism research. The series is always willing to consider new ideas for innovative and scholarly books, inquiries should be made directly to the Series Editor.

Published:

Benchmarking National Tourism Organisations and Agencies
LENNON, SMITH, COCKEREL & TREW

Extreme Tourism: Lessons from the World's Cold Water Islands
BALDACCHINO

Tourism Local Systems and Networking
LAZZERETTI & PETRILLO

Progress in Tourism Marketing
KOZAK & ANDREU

Destination Marketing Organisations
PIKE

Indigenous Tourism
RYAN AND AICKEN

An International Handbook of Tourism Education
AIREY & TRIBE

Tourism in Turbulent Times
WILKS, PENDERGAST & LEGGAT

Taking Tourism to the Limits
RYAN, PAGE & AICKEN

Tourism and Social Identities
BURNS & NOVELLI

Micro-clusters & Networks – The Growth of Tourism
MICHAEL

Tourism and Politics
BURNS & NOVELLI

Tourism and Small Businesses in the New Europe
THOMAS

Hospitality: A Social Lens
LASHLEY, LYNCH & MORRISON

The Critical Turn in Tourism Studies
ATELJEVIC, MORGAN & PRITCHARD

Forthcoming:

Tourism Research
AIREY & TRIBE

For other titles in the series visit: www.elsevier.com/locate/series/aitr

Related Elsevier Journals — sample copies available on request
Annals of Tourism Research
International Journal of Hospitality Management
Tourism Management

TRAVEL MEDICINE: TALES BEHIND THE SCIENCE

EDITED BY

ANNELIES WILDER-SMITH

Travellers' Health and Vaccination Centre, Singapore

ELI SCHWARTZ

The Chaim Sheba Medical Centre, Israel

MARC SHAW

WORLDWISE Travellers Health Centre, New Zealand

ELSEVIER

Amsterdam • Boston • Heidelberg • London • New York • Oxford
Paris • San Diego • San Francisco • Singapore • Sydney • Tokyo

Elsevier
Linacre House, Jordan Hill, Oxford OX2 8DP, UK
Radarweg 29, PO Box 211, 1000 AE Amsterdam, The Netherlands

First edition 2007

British Library Cataloguing in Publication Data
A catalogue record for this book is available from the British Library

Library of Congress Cataloging-in-Publication Data
A catalog record for this book is available from the Library of Congress

ISBN: 978-0-08-045359-0

For information on all Elsevier publications
visit our website at books.elsevier.com

Printed and bound in The Netherlands

07 08 09 10 11 10 9 8 7 6 5 4 3 2 1

Contents

Section 4: Malaria Drugs and Infections of Adventure

Section 5: Personal Tales: Travel Medicine Practitioners Share Their Stories

Section 6: Tales Behind the Research in Travel Medicine

List of Figures and Maps

List of Tables

Contributors

Francis E. Andre is currently 'retired' but keeps himself busy as a part-time consultant in vaccinology, a science he has dabbled in for most of his professional career.

Paul M. Arguin, Chief of the Domestic Response Unit in the Malaria Branch at the U.S. Centers for Disease Control and Prevention in Atlanta, Georgia. Paul is also an editor of Health Information for International Travel, also known as CDC's Yellow Book. His research interests include the prevention and treatment of infectious diseases associated with international travel, including malaria and zoonoses.

Gabriela Buck is a resident doctor at the WHO Collaborating Center for Travel Medicine, Institute of Social and Preventive Medicine, Zurich, Switzerland.

Santanu Chatterjee graduated in medicine from Calcutta. His major interests in travel medicine include health risks in the tropics, emergency medical care and the impact of travel on host countries. He is currently President of the Asia-Pacific Travel Health Society and on the Editorial Board of the Journal of Travel Medicine. He is also a contributing author in the 'Textbook of Travel Medicine and Health', in 'Travel Medicine and Migrant Health', in the 'Pocket Guide to Cultural Health Assessment', in 'Tourism and Health', and in the 'Guide to Healthy Living in Thailand and South East Asia'.

Chen Collins is a specialist in public health with an interest in travel health and immunization and the history of tropical diseases. He has worked as a Medical Officer in Zambia, medical advisor in travel health clinics in Jerusalem and Tel Aviv, immunization coordinator and medical advisor in NW London, Medical Officer at the Health Control Unit at London's Heathrow Airport and is currently working as a Consultant in Public Health at the Tel Aviv District Health Office in Israel.

Larry DeLucas is a Professor in the Center for Macromolecular Crystallography at the University of Alabama at Birmingham. He serves as the Director of the Center for Biophysical Sciences and Engineering. Dr. DeLucas flew as a payload specialist on the United States Microgravity Laboratory-1 flight, Mission STS-50, in June 1992.

Michel J. Deprez has partially retired from legal practice after 45 years of working on the Bar of Liège, Belgium. He has an enduring interest in Christian traditions and religion, which he now has the time to explore more fully. He has made pilgrimages to Rome, Santiago de Compostella, Notre Dame de Lourdes, Assisi, and plans many more.

Eran Dolev, Professor of Internal Medicine and History of Medicine at Sackler School of Medicine, Tel-Aviv University, Israel. Retired Surgeon General, the Israel Defense Forces Medical Corps. Main research subjects: Interrelations between wars and epidemic diseases. His book concerning military medicine during the Palestine Campaigns, 1917–1918, will be published in March 2007.

Yoel Donchin is a Professor at Hadassah Hebrew University Medical School in Jerusalem, Israel (1971). Yoel completed his fellowship in anesthesia and intensive care medicine, at the Hadassah Hospital. He serves as a special adviser to the surgeon general of the Israeli army on trauma, having built the first trauma unit in Israel. Currently he heads the Cardio-pulmonary resuscitation school. In the last 10 years his main interest is 'human factors in the medical domain' and since 2004 has served as the director of the Hadassah patient safety center.

Charles D. Ericsson graduated from Harvard Medical School in 1970, did his internal medicine residency training at the University of Minnesota hospitals and his infectious diseases fellowship at the University of Texas Medical School at Houston, where he has remained on the faculty since 1976. An infectious diseases consultant, Professor, hospital epidemiologist and antibiotic steward, his research interests in travelers' diarrhea led to an abiding interest in travel medicine. He is director of the University of Texas Travel Medicine Clinic in Houston. He is the past President of the International Society of Travel Medicine (ISTM). He was founding editor of the *Journal of Travel Medicine* and presently is the chair of the ISTM Publications Committee.

David O. Freedman is Professor of Medicine and Epidemiology at the University of Alabama at Birmingham (UAB). David is also Director of the UAB Travelers' Health Clinic, Director of the Gorgas Course in Clinical Tropical Medicine (Lima, Peru), Executive Board Member of the International Society of Travel Medicine, co-Editor of the textbook, Travel Medicine, and served as Chair Advisory Panel on Parasitic Diseases of the US Pharmacopeia 1995–2000. For the past 10 years he has been Director of the global GeoSentinel Surveillance Network which he co-founded, and which currently maintains the largest database of ill travelers available. His research focuses on clinical tropical medicine and immuno-parasitology, including the development of surveillance networks to characterize infectious disease morbidity in travelers and migrants.

Steven Friedman is qualified in emergency medicine at the University of Toronto and McMaster University, and in Public Health from Harvard in 1996. Dr. Friedman is Assistant Professor of Medicine at the University of Toronto. He practices emergency medicine at University Health Network, where he is Director of the Emergency Medicine Research Program there. Dr. Friedman is Editor-in-Chief of the Israeli Journal of Emergency Medicine.

Laragh Gollogly is qualified in medicine from the University of Liege, Belgium. She has a BA from the University of Tasmania, and an MPH from the University of Queensland. Laragh was employed by Paramount Pictures as a Unit Doctor while working at the Radcliffe Hospital in Oxford, and is currently working for the World Health Organization in Geneva.

Brian Gushulak is a Canadian physician whose career has focused on the relationships between health and international travel. He has held positions in the federal health where he managed the national travel medicine unit, and immigration departments and in the late 1990s was the Director of Migration Health Services of the International Organization for Migration in Geneva where he was involved in refugee and complex humanitarian emergencies in Eastern Europe, the Balkans, Asia, and Africa. He is now engaged in research and consulting in the area of health and population mobility where his research interests include migration health and population mobility, international disease control, and the history of quarantine practices. He has recently co-authored a textbook dealing with health and migration.

Max Hardiman is qualified in medicine from Sheffield University, UK in 1981. Following specialist training in General Practice he worked as a general physician in Tansen Hospital in Western Nepal. Returning to the UK he trained in public health medicine in the East Anglian region and in 1997 he moved to the World Health Organization Headquarters in Geneva to work in the area of epidemic disease. In 2003 he was part of the Management Group overseeing the response to SARS by WHO Headquarters. More recently Dr. Hardiman led the WHO project to revise the International Health Regulations (IHR), which was successfully concluded by the adoption of the IHR (2005) by the World Health Assembly in May 2005. Dr. Hardiman is currently the Coordinator of the IHR Secretariat in the Department of Epidemic and Pandemic Alert and Response.

Nancy Piper Jenks is currently the Director of travel and immigrant medicine at Hudson Community Health in Peekskill, NY. She has lived and worked on four continents, including 2 years at CIWEC Clinic in Kathmandu. She has published in the peer-reviewed medical literature on topics including Hepatitis E in travelers and Lyme disease in migrants. Her current focus is delivering primary health care to a largely undocumented migrant population, with research interests including chronic and infectious diseases among this population. She is a site director for the GeoSentinel network and a member of the ISTM Executive Board.

Jay S. Keystone is a Professor of Medicine, Department of Medicine, at the University of Toronto. He is also a staff physician in the Tropical Disease unit at the Toronto General Hospital and Director of the Medisys Travel Health Clinic, Toronto. He is a past president of the International Society of Travel Medicine. Dr. Keystone is a renowned lecturer in the fields of travel and tropical medicine. He has spoken on several continents and has been incontinent. His research interests are in leprosy, traveler's diarrhea, delusional parasitosis and traveler's health.

Phyllis Kozarsky is a Professor of Medicine and Infectious Diseases at Emory University School of Medicine and a consultant at the Centers for Disease Control and Prevention (CDC). Originally having planned to study languages and travel, Phyllis changed courses to become a doctor and trained at the Albert Einstein College of Medicine in New York. After internship and residency, she moved to Atlanta, fellowship training in infectious diseases, and then joined the Emory faculty. She became Chief of Travelers' Health at CDC and now remains in the Division of Global Migration and Quarantine as an expert consultant. She was the co-organizer of the Atlanta Travel Medicine meeting in 1991 and a founding member of the International Society of Travel Medicine. Since then she has played many roles within the ISTM including Chair of the Professional Education Committee, President-Elect, and is now Chair of the Examination Committee. She is a co-director of the GeoSentinel surveillance project and is director of tropical and travel medicine at Emory. She cares for a diverse group of people including CDC personnel; numerous leisure and business travelers; missionaries and volunteers; travelers for international corporations, airline personnel, newscasters, as well as immigrant and refugee populations.

Ted Lankester is a family doctor who has had an involvement in travel medicine since living in India in the 1980s. In 1989 Ted co-founded InterHealth, where he now is Director of Health Care. InterHealth is a medical charity and international health center, which acts as travel health advisor to over 300 organizations, mainly international NGOs both secular and faith based. His areas of special interest are the travel and occupational health needs of those working internationally, especially in the relief and development sector and in faith-based organizations. An author, Ted has written several books including 'The Travelers Good Health Guide', 3rd Edition, Sheldon Press UK, 2006.

Peter A. Leggat is Professor and Acting Director of the Anton Breinl Centre for Public Health and Tropical Medicine, James Cook University, Australia, and Visiting Professor, School of Public Health, University of the Witwatersrand, South Africa. He has coordinated the Australian postgraduate course on travel medicine since 1993 and has assisted with the development of travel medicine courses in other countries. Professor Leggat is currently the President of The Australasian College of Tropical Medicine. He was a Member of the Executive Board of the International Society of Travel Medicine from 2003–2005.

Anne E. McCarthy is an Associate Professor of Medicine at the University of Ottawa and a member of the Division of Infectious Diseases at the Ottawa Hospital. She is actively involved in Tropical Medicine and International Health including the development of prevention and treatment strategies for malaria and recommendations for travel related vaccine preventable diseases. Dr. McCarthy is the National Coordinator of the Canadian Malaria Network in collaboration with the Public Health Agency of Canada's Travel Medicine Program and chairs the malaria subcommittee of the Committee to Advise on Tropical Medicine and Travel. Her educational interests include undergraduate and postgraduate medical teaching in infectious disease, travel medicine, tropical medicine and international health. Her research interests include infections in compromised hosts, implementation of vaccine delivery programs within a healthcare setting, studies on antimalarial drugs, and compliance with travel medicine recommendations.

Eyal Meltzer works in the Center for Geographic Medicine and the infectious disease unit at the Sheba medical center in Israel. A specialist in infectious diseases, his major interests are in travel medicine and tropical diseases.

Ziad A. Memish is the Director of the Gulf Cooperation Council States Center for Infection Control, and Head of Infectious Diseases in the Department of Medicine — King Abdulaziz Medical City Riyadh, Kingdom of Saudi Arabia. Ziad is a Council member of the Asia Pacific Travel Medicine Society, a member of the editorial board of Journal of Travel Medicine, and has a special interest in 'large gathering' medicine.

Karl Neumann is a pediatrician, travel medicine practitioner, and a journalist. He is Clinical Associate Professor of Pediatrics at Weill Medical College of Cornell University and Clinical Associate Attending Pediatrician at New York Presbyterian Hospital/Cornell Medical Center. Karl is editor of the newsletter of the International Society of Travel Medicine and co-editor of the International Child Health Newsletter of the American Academy of Pediatrics. He has written chapters on pediatric travel medicine for textbooks, articles and columns for major newspapers and magazines, and edited and published a popular newsletter. He is Editor Emeritus of the Publication Committee of the Wilderness Medical Society and lectures frequently around the world.

Nicole F. Oechslin, Ed. D. Nicole is an Associate Professor of Education and Advisor in the Adult Degree Program at Mary Baldwin College in Staunton, Virginia. A well-vaccinated traveler herself, Nicole also teaches research, reading, and writing, including travel stories, to adult students. Nicole's current research projects include an exploration of instructional design and student success in high-stakes testing environments and evolutions in the native recipes of the Caribbean Diaspora.

Steve Ostroff, until 2005, Steve was Deputy Director of the National Center for Infectious Diseases at the Centers for Disease Control and Prevention (CDC) in Atlanta. In that position he played a coordinating role in many of the CDC emerging infectious disease investigations during the 1990s and early 2000s. He is currently Director of the Bureau of Epidemiology for the Pennsylvania Department of Health.

Prativa Pandey, a Nepali, is an American Board certified internist practicing travel medicine in Kathmandu, Nepal at the CIWEC Clinic Travel Medicine Center. She has been the medical director of the clinic since 1998 and has been site director for the GeoSentinel project. She is the current President of the International Society of Travel Medicine from 2005. Her research interests include health problems in travelers particularly for those traveling in Nepal.

Galia Sabar is the Chair, African Studies, Tel Aviv University Israel. Galia's main Research interests are: African Migrants in the West, Religion and Migration, Feminization of migration, socio-political aspects of HIV/AIDS prevention education amongst migrants in Israel. Galia is a board member of the 'Hotline for Migrant Workers, Israel'.

Patricia Schlagenhauf-Lawlor is a Senior Lecturer and Scientist at the University of Zuerich Travel Clinic, Switzerland. Her research focuses on anti-malaria strategies for travelers including the evaluation of chemoprophylaxis tolerability and the emergency self-treatment approach and the use of malaria rapid dip-stick tests. Other studies examine the epidemiology of imported malaria in non-endemic countries to identify risk groups and to formulate evidence-based approaches to the prevention of malaria in travelers. Dr. Schlagenhauf-Lawlor serves as temporary advisor on malaria issues to the WHO. She is editor of the book *Travelers' Malaria* (BC Decker 2001) and author of the handbook *PDQ Handbook of Travelers' Malaria* (BC Decker 2005) and has published more than 50 papers on travel medicine.

Eli Schwartz is Associate Professor at Sackler Faculty of Medicine, Tel Aviv University, and the Director of the Center for Geographic Medicine and Tropical diseases, Sheba Medical Center, Tel Hashomer, Israel. Eli is currently the President of the Israeli society of Parasitology and Tropical diseases, and has been involved in Tropical and Travel Medicine since 1980. He has gained much experience in the field whilst working in Asia and Africa for several years, and whilst treating pre- and post travel patients. Eli has published significantly in the peer-reviewed medical literature on travel and tropical diseases among returning travelers. Eli is an Executive Board Member of the International Society of Travel Medicine (ISTM), and served as Chair of the Professional Education Committee of the ISTM. Currently he is the President-Elect of the Asia Pacific Travel Health Society.

Marc Shaw is Associate Professor and a doctor, traveler, actor and director, and observer of fine humor. A member of International Society of Travel Medicine with the Diploma of Travel Medicine from Glasgow, he is also a Fellow of the Australasian College of Tropical Medicine and a Fellow of the Faculty of Travel Medicine from the same College. He has research interests in infectious diseases, expedition medicine, and the safety and security of travelers abroad. Other medical interests include Medicine and the Media, and the Art in Medicine. He has traveled extensively, including recently to the Pitcairn Islands and on Expeditions to Namibia and Mongolia, and as the Team Doctor with Sir Peter Blake to the Amazonas of South America.

David R. Shlim was the medical director of the CIWEC Clinic Travel Medicine Center in Kathmandu, Nepal from 1983 to 1998. David has published significant original research papers on diseases and risks associated with travel. He has contributed numerous chapters to travel medicine textbooks, and serves on the editorial boards of the *Journal of Travel Medicine*, *Wilderness and Environmental Medicine*, and *High Altitude Medicine and Biology*. He is the only person to have received awards for research from both the International Society of Travel Medicine, and the Wilderness Medical Society. In 2004, he published a book in collaboration with Chokyi Nyima Rinpoche entitled: *Medicine and Compassion: A Tibetan Lama's Guidance for Caregivers*.

Robert Steffen was the first worldwide Professor of Travel Medicine, at the University of Zurich, Switzerland. There, he heads the Division of Epidemiology and Prevention of Communicable Diseases and he is also Director of the World Health Organization Collaborating Center for Traveler's Health. Robert is a trained internist and flight surgeon, and as he started to conduct small-scale travel medicine research in 1972 became interested in extending the field. He subsequently organized the First 'Conference on International Travel Medicine' in 1988. He was a co-founder of the International Society of Travel Medicine and is the Editor of the Journal of Travel Medicine. He is editor/author of several books and more than 200 publications related to travel medicine.

Stephen Toovey established and ran the first travel clinics in Africa. He has worked in a number of African countries in the preventive, curative, and research fields. His research interests are in the treatment of tropical diseases, especially in parasitic diseases, and the neuropharmacology of anti-infectious agents. He teaches travel medicine at the University College and Royal Free Medical School, London, United Kingdom.

Annelies Wilder-Smith is the Head of the Travelers' Health and Vaccination Center, Tan Tock Seng Hospital, Singapore, and Associate Professor at the Department of Community, Occupational and Family Medicine, National University Singapore. She is Editorial Consultant to the Lancet, Advisor to GeoSentinel, on the Editorial Board for the Journal of Travel Medicine, Fellow of the Australasian College of Tropical Medicine and a Fellow of the Faculty of Travel Medicine from the same College, as well as Medical Director of a Community Health Project in Southern India. Her research interests are meningococcal disease, the Hajj pilgrimage, dengue, SARS and travel health. She is co-editor of the 'Manual of Travel Medicine and Health'.

Ken Zafren lives in Anchorage, Alaska, USA, and is Associate Medical Director of the Himalayan Rescue Association (Nepal). He practices emergency medicine at the Alaska Native Medical Center in Anchorage and also at Stanford University Medical Center in Palo Alto, California, where he holds a clinical faculty appointment in the Division of Emergency Medicine. His primary research interest is high altitude medicine. Ken became a teetotaler in the Everest Region of Nepal after tracing multiple episodes of giardiasis to a beverage called 'chang' — the local equivalent of beer.

Introduction

Annelies Wilder-Smith, Eli Schwartz and Marc Shaw

"The reasonable man adapts himself to the world; the unreasonable man persists in trying to adapt the world to himself; therefore, all progress depends upon the unreasonable man." (George Bernard Shaw)

Every year, close to a billion people cross international frontiers. They do so perhaps because of the innate nomadic nature of mankind, or perhaps because of a restless spirit that makes it hard to stay in one place too long, or possibly even because of a thirst for new knowledge and better pastures. The earliest hominids evolved through migrations and along the way their descendants discovered new expanses. They forged new trading links whilst traveling to all corners of the globe. So, humans travel, and move, and they migrate. There is a difference, however, between moving, traveling and migrating. *Moving* means roving in a familiar space without losing sight of one's familiars. *Traveling* alludes to exploring unknown territories beyond the reassuring signs and landmarks, and by extension pushing toward mysteries and different climes. *Migrating* is journeying with the mesmeric promise of a better life.

Classical myths are based on the nomadic hero like Hercules and the great traveler Marco Polo, humanity's most lauded global traveler. Today, as a result of our forefathers' evolution and learned experience, we can travel with relative safety and knowledge to most places for a variety of reasons. Mankind, in all its myriad forms, travels for research and study, faith and pilgrimage, for experiences for our souls and to seek sensations created by romantic and exotic routes.

The enormous global mobility increasingly brings with it an increase in health risks for travelers and host populations alike, together with greater risks for the environment and for the cultural identity of the peoples of the world. How lucky we are to be part of this global movement. How lucky we are to be in at the beginning of a new specialization within medicine. It is this fact that guides us into wanting to know just who we are going along this 'new path' with, and what their history and their humanity are. For, we contend, that it is only by knowing these facts that we can fully see the extensions and ramifications of this exciting field in which we move. It will be *then* that we will see how we and our skills fit best into the 'travel and health' network.

It is because of travel, and our overwhelming interest in it and its ramifications, that we have developed and edited this tome. It is different from other texts in travel medicine.

Travel Medicine: Tales Behind the Science
Copyright © 2007 by Elsevier Ltd.
All rights of reproduction in any form reserved.
ISBN: 0-08-045359-7

It is not purely a scientific book, but rather a collection of stories, histories, anecdotes, personal experiences, and some dreams into our future. All contribute to the understanding of travel medicine.

Section 1 describes the evolution of travel medicine as a specialty. The early masters in travel health epidemiology and the founders of travel medicine are described to provide an understanding of the history of travel medicine. This is followed by Section 2 which covers the 'education in travel medicine'. An increasing specialization in travel medicine means that its education needs to be standardized and constantly revised. The 'Ten Commandments for Healthy Tropical Travel' reflect a humorous approach to educating travelers prior to travel to the tropics.

Section 3 is dedicated to vaccinations, for they play an integral part in travel medicine. Some vaccines that have evolved specifically with the traveler in mind, are now moving toward more global usage, such as the example of hepatitis A. Other 'old diseases' have new vaccines and new twists in their prevention. Yet we also need to consider how routine vaccinations have developed, for they are efficient and effective public health interventions in the fight against global disease.

As travel to certain magical places may also attract other uninvited hazards like mosquitoes, we elaborate in Section 4 how mankind has struggled to defeat malaria with drugs that vary from those made from cinchona, to the qinghaosu-based drugs of today. Furthermore, as travel expands the locales, the chances of other exotic, yet fascinating diseases increase. To visit beaches beside enchanting oceans is what travel is all about. Yet it has its attendant risks, and many infections can accompany recreational pursuits in the sea or in the freshness of a stilled lake or flowing stream.

We believe that the best lessons are learned from personal stories. Section 5 includes a collation of narratives, anecdotes and personal tales that relate to travelers' health as experienced by travel medicine practitioners.

Behind every piece of research in travel medicine, there are stories that remain untold in the scientific literature. Section 6 has some 'real life' tales that unravel the science behind travel medicine.

Not every travel experience is for fun. Section 7 expresses this. Some travel is for a cause, be it religious or humanitarian, or be it to escape certain political systems. We describe the tragedies of so called 'undocumented refugees' — the dominant movement of women migrants who have to live between the values of their old world and the values of their new world. We have included a number of wonderful moments where our colleagues have found their work abroad useful, for example relief work in Haiti and Rwanda. Pilgrimages attract large numbers of 'travelers'. Colleagues describe the pearls and perils of the Muslim, Hindu, Buddhist and Christian pilgrimages.

Travelers travel, and diseases travel with them. Section 8 describes the spread of diseases worldwide via globalization, migration and military campaigns. For all travel medicine practitioners who struggle to understand the implications of the revised international health regulations, we have included a chapter on "What does the travel medicine practitioner need to know about the international health regulations?"

In the next millennium our world will have inherited further global movement, momentum and government. It may even include travel through the universe. The epilogue re-awakens our old dreams — the last frontier, aerospace…

Annelies Wilder-Smith

Eli Schwartz

Marc Shaw

SECTION 1:

HISTORY OF TRAVEL MEDICINE

Chapter 1

History of the Development of Travel Medicine as a New Discipline

Gabriela Buck and Robert Steffen

From Antiquity to Shakespeare

Travel medicine as an interdisciplinary concept is not new. Already Seneca (4 BC–65 AD) criticized sex tourism in Canopus, the sunken city north in the Aboukir Bay recently redis-covered by the underwater explorer Franck Goddio. Six kilometers north of Alexandia in Egypt, it had the infamous prestige of antiquity's Las Vegas. Having realized that rich men and young women had come from far for paid sex, Seneca commented in a letter to Lucilius "the wise and upright man, … or he who is on the way toward wisdom … will not select Canopus, nor Baiae either; for both places have begun to be resorts of vice. At Canopus luxury pampers itself to the utmost degree …"

Alexander the Great — responsible for the spread of Greek culture in the ancient world — died in Babylon in 323 BC, at the age of 33. Possible explanations for his death have included alcoholic liver disease since he regularly enjoyed great drinking parties. However, based on the description of his final illness in the royal diaries, the conqueror of large parts of the world of those days most likely died from malaria or typhoid fever, both classical travelers' infections (Cunha, 2004). The medical doctor and philosopher Peter Bamm wondered what would have happened to ancient history if Alexander had not been bitten by an infected mosquito, or if he would have been cured of his infection (Bamm, 1963).

Shakespeare asked the relevant question relating to epidemiology for travelers:

> Alas, what danger will it be to us,
> Maids as we are, to travel forth so far
> (*As You Like It I*, iii, pp. 104–105).

Elsewhere he concluded on the need for prevention:

> O God! — O nurse, how shall this be prevented?
> (*Romeo and Juliet*, III, v, p. 206).

and he also gave very specific advice:

> Leave thy drink and thy whore
> And keep in-a-door
> (*King Lear*, I, iv, p. 118).

Introduction of Quarantine

Coastal cities in the 14th century, in an effort to protect themselves from plague, requested that ships arriving from an infected port sit at anchor before landing. The original document from 1377, which is kept in the Archives of Dubrovnik, states that before entering the city, newcomers had to spend 30 days in a restricted location (originally nearby islands) waiting to see whether the symptoms of plague would develop. Later on, isolation was prolonged in Venice to 40 days and was called quarantine (from Medieval French: *une quarantaine de jours*, a period of 40 days, or Italian: *quaranta giorni*).

Explorers and Military Medicine

During Admiral Vernon's expedition 1740–1741 to Jamaica, more than 11,000 of 15,000 seamen and marines were sent to the hospital, and of these one in seven died (Scott, 1942). Typically, more seamen and marines died of diseases than were killed in battle; thus the importance of precautions for preventing and avoiding sickness was gradually realized. Improving hygiene was the major focus. The supply of soap in 1782, fumigation and better nutrition were initial steps (Scott, 1942).

The Scottish physician Sir Gilbert Blane (1747–1834) declared not merely the advantages but also the necessity for cleanliness on board and the need of regular inspection. Officers should inspect the men and their clothing weekly. There also should be a supply of fruits, and wine had to be supplied in place of rum (Scott, 1942). He suggested that the government should supply particularly Peruvian bark (a source of quinine) free of charge, and that the surgeons accompanying the troops should be allocated a certain amount of money to be spent as they wished. Having observed that treatment on board under crowded conditions was risky, he proposed that onshore hospitals should be established and that there should be a spacing of beds; specifically infectious patients should be separated. Blane's *Memorial to the Admiralty* had an impact, and he noted with satisfaction that from December 1781 to May 1782 no man died of disease and only 13 were sent to hospitals whose complaints were smallpox and ulcers (Scott, 1942).

Captain Cook was an example of an apt and humane commander. During his second voyage, he distributed sweetcorn to crewmembers to prevent scurvy. He also had scurvy grass, celery and other vegetables cooked in a soup that was served every morning for breakfast and for dinner. As a result only one man on board had scurvy. Every effort was made to keep the men, their clothes, hammocks and bedding dry. Weekly or even twice a week, the ship was aired with fires. At the end of the second voyage Cook said: "Our having discovered the possibility of preserving health amongst a numerous ship's company for such a length of time, in such varieties of climate and amidst such continued hardships and fatigues, will make this voyage remarkable". During Captain Cook's last and third voyage

(1776–1780) another experiment, the preservation of food by bottling and tinning, was carried out. Biscuit, flour, peas, oatmeal etc. had been sealed in small casks lined with tinfoil. All food except the peas was found to be in much better state than it could have been expected in the usual manner of package (Scott, 1942).

Further progress was minimal in the beginning of the 19th century. Thomas Trotter was one of the few who worked hard to improve the health of the seamen. In his three volumes of *Medica Nautica* he suggests that men to be appointed to a ship should be examined so that infectious recruits could be excluded. He had not much faith in fumigation, for him the immediate separation of those who were infected was a more dependable measure (Scott, 1942).

In those days little was known of tropical diseases. Sir William Burnett (1779–1861), Medical Director-General of the Navy, requested Bryson to publish in 1847 an epidemiological account on the "Climate and Principal Diseases of the African Station". Bryson, for the 1825–1845 period, reported a mortality rate of 54·4 per 1000, as compared to 7·7 in South America, 9·3 in the Mediterranean, 15·1 in the East Indies and 18·1 in the West Indies. Although Sir William Burnett had made arrangements for the instruction of medical officers in the Navy in 1827, it took more than another half-century until a school at Haslar started teaching naval hygiene and tropical diseases.

There were two physicians named James Lind, both famous and contemporaries. One was a physician at the Royal Naval Hospital Haslar (1716–1794) who published a treatise on scurvy (1754) and on tropical medicine, although he had no experience abroad. The other (1736–1812), was physician at the Royal Household at Windsor, and had been in Bengal in 1762. The former Lind was an enthusiast for prevention, who made recommendations on empirical grounds. The results of his observations found scientific confirmation often only a century or more later. In spite of his urge with respect to the prevention of scurvy and also of the success of his methods applied by Captain Cook in 1772–1775, lemon juice was made compulsory in the British Navy only in 1844.

Wiliam Osler, born in 1849 in Ontario, was one of the most famous physicians at the turn to the 20th century. The father of the modern medicine describes in the *The Story of the Panama Canal* how he reduced mortality among the workforce from 177 per 1000 in September 1885, most resulting from yellow fever, malaria and dysentery, to 8 and 44, respectively, amongst the white and black communities by 1905. Osler claimed this first important example of occupational travel medicine as "a marvellous history of sanitary organisation" (Cook, 1995).

The Early Masters of Travel Health Epidemiology, Microbiology and Prevention

Kendrick, in 1972, distributed 87,000 postcards to passengers arriving at the U.S. airports and noted that 22% reported some illness, including many with travelers' diarrhoea, and few with hepatitis (Kendrick, 1972). Gsell in Basel, Wiedermann in Vienna and Mohr in Hamburg, in the 1970s, published accounts on imported infections in German, based on notification and anecdotal observations. Schulz and Gangarosa were the first to publish broad surveys in English (Gangarosa, Kendrick, Loewenstein, Merson, & Mosley, 1980; Schulz, 1977). Mike Schulz from Centers for Disease Control and Prevention (CDC) already realized in 1977 that there were "high risk travelers", and suggested at that time the prevention "by the use of commonsense measures". With respect to returning travelers he stresses that the "biggest pitfall was … failure to connect a history of travel with signs and symptoms".

Ben Kean investigated travelers' diarrhoea not only in Mexico, but also elsewhere, including at a medical convention in Teheran (he became later one of the physicians consulted by the Shah of Iran). To our knowledge he was the first to conduct prophylactic studies, using a variety of agents such as phthalylsulfathiazole and neomycin sulphate (Kean, 1963, 1986). Not only was his interest limited to diarrhoea, but he also published, for example, on malaria in travelers.

As a leader of a whole generation of investigators in Houston, Herbert L. 'Bert' DuPont was the first one interested in the microbiology and pathogenesis mainly of travelers' diarrhoea (DuPont et al., 1971). Still very active, he has almost 400 publications that describe epidemiological, prophylactic and therapeutic trials in travelers' diarrhoea (DuPont, Sullivan, Pickering, Haynes, & Ackerman, 1977) and other — mainly travel-related — infections. For his oeuvre he has been awarded an honorary doctorate at the University of Zurich.

The "Creation" of Travel Medicine

In the late 1970s there was somewhat an explosion of interest in the health, illness and injury of travelers both in Europe and in North America. In Canada, Krass and White investigated the use of emergency departments by travelers and trends in immigration data (Krass, 1976; White, 1977). In the United Kingdom hospital records of the traveling population were analyzed (Geddes & Gully, 1981), while a Finnish group concentrated on behavioral aspects resulting in infections (Peltola, Kyrönseppä, and Hölsä, 1983). Germans investigated imported infections in refugees and tourists (Feldmeier, Feldheim, Rasp, & Bienzle, 1981; Diesfeld, 1980), and a very active Scottish group evaluated mainly package tourists (Reid, 1983); it would in 2006 create the first Faculty of Travel Medicine in Glasgow. A single researcher associated with the World Health Organisation (WHO) assessed health problems in mass tourism (Velimirovic, 1973). Although the WHO never considered travel medicine a priority, it had a tradition to publish *Vaccination Certificate Requirements for International Travel and Health Advice for Travelers*, later to become the annual publication *International Travel and Health* (WHO, 2007). As early as in April 1982 the WHO devoted an issue of its journal *World Health* to "Travel and Health".

Robert Steffen, the President of the International Federation of Medical Student Associations from 1967 to 1969, had to visit the 200,000 members in almost 50 countries worldwide. He realized vast contradictions in travel health advice, for example the British *Manson's Tropical Diseases*, 15th edition in 1961 recommending inoculations "about four weeks before departure against typhoid and paratyphoid, … cholera and typhus". In contrast, American sources recommended such measures only for those "off the beaten track". This stimulated him to systematically assess health problems in travelers. His initial survey was based on self-administered interviews in almost 12,000 charter flight passengers returning to Switzerland, a later follow-up study included again 10,000 subjects (Steffen, van der Linde, & Meyer, 1978; Steffen, Rickenbach, Wilhelm, Helminger, & Schar, 1987). Interested in evidence to base vaccination recommendations upon, he initially concentrated on the epidemiology of vaccine preventable infections (Steffen, 1977, 1982; Morger, Steffen, & Schar, 1983; Kubli, Steffen, & Schar, 1987).

Invited by Roche Pharmaceuticals to contribute to the investigations on severe cutaneous adverse reactions associated with Fansidar (Miller et al., 1986), Steffen met Hans Lobel from the Malaria Branch at CDC. They not only started scientific collaboration but also organized the first International Conference on Travel Medicine in April 1988 in Zurich attended by some 400 health professionals. A 2nd conference was organized in Atlanta in 1991 with the assistance of Phyllis Kozarsky. DuPont, who had collaborated with Steffen in many joint studies on diarrhoea, joined the two in drafting the by-laws for the foundation of the International Society of Travel Medicine (ISTM) on this occasion. He served as the Society's first president and was instrumental to set up the *Journal of Travel Medicine* with Charles D. Ericsson being the first editor-in-chief.

Meanwhile, 2000 doctors, nurses and other health professionals have joined the Society and the 10th conference of the International Society of Travel Medicine is scheduled to take place in May 2007.

References

Bamm, P. (1963). *Alexander der Grosse oder die Verwandlung der Welt*. Zurich: Droemer.

Cook, G. C. (1995). Williams Osler's fascination with diseases of warm climates. *Journal of Medical Biography, 109*, 7–11.

Cunha, B. A. (2004). The death of Alexander the Great: Malaria or typhoid fever? *Infectious Disease Clinics of North America, 18*(1), 53–63.

Diesfeld, H. J. (1980). Einschleppung von Tropenkrankheiten und Prophylaxe im internationalen Reiseverkehr. *Öffentliches Gesundheitwesen., 42*, 497–502.

DuPont, H. L., Formal, S. B., Hornick, R. B., Snyder, M. J., Libonati, J. P., Sheahan, D. G., LaBrec, E. H., & Kalas, J. P. (1971). Pathogenesis of *Escherichia coli* diarrhea. *The New England Journal of Medicine, 285*, 1–9.

DuPont, H. L., Sullivan, P., Pickering, L. K., Haynes, G., & Ackerman, P. B. (1977). Symptomatic treatment of diarrhea with bismuth subsalicylate among students attending a Mexican university. *Gastroenterology, 73*, 715–718.

Feldmeier, H., Feldheim, W., Rasp, F., & Bienzle, U. (1981). Das Krankheitsspektrum von Flüchtlingen aus Südostasien. *Deutsches Ärzteblatt, 17*, 817–823.

Gangarosa, E. J., Kendrick, M. A., Loewenstein, M. S., Merson, M. H., & Mosley, J. W. (1980). Global travel and travelers' health. *Aviation, Space, and Environmental medicine, 51*, 265–270.

Geddes, A. M., & Gully, P. R. (1981). The returning traveller. *Journal of the Royal College of Physicians of London, 15*, 124–128.

Kean, B. H. (1963). The diarrhea of travelers to Mexico. Summary of a five-year study. *Annals of Internal Medicine, 59*, 605–614.

Kean, B. H. (1986). Travelers' diarrhea: An overview. *Reviews of Infectious Diseases, 8*(Suppl 2), S111–S116.

Kendrick, M. A. (1972). Summary of study on illness among Americans visiting Europe, March 31, 1969–March 30, 1970. *Journal of Infectious Diseases, 126*, 685–687.

Krass, M. E. (1976). Patterns of local and tourist use of an emergency department. *Canadian Medical Association Journal, 115*, 1230–1233.

Kubli, D., Steffen, R., & Schar M. (1987). Importation of poliomyelitis to industrialised nations between 1975 and 1984: Evaluation and conclusions for vaccination recommendations. *British Medical Journal (Clinical Research Ed.), 295*(6591), 169–171.

Miller, K. D., Lobel, H. O., Satriale, R. F., Kuritsky, J. N., Stern, R., & Campbell, C. C. (1986). Severe cutaneous reactions among American travelers using pyrimethamine-sulfadoxine (Fansidar) for malaria prophylaxis. *The American Journal of Tropical Medicine and Hygiene, 35*, 451–458.

Morger, H., Steffen, R., & Schar, M. (1983). Epidemiology of cholera in travellers, and conclusions for vaccination recommendations. *British Medical Journal (Clinical Research Ed.), 286*(6360), 184–186.

Peltola, H., Kyrönseppä, H., & Hölsä, P. (1983). Trips to the south — A health hazard. Morbidity of Finnish travellers. *Scandinavian Journal of Infectious Diseases, 15*, 375–381.

Reid, D. (1983). Some Medical Aspects of Travel. *Australian Health Review, 6*, 47–51.

Schulz, M. G. (1977). Exotic diseases. Ounce of prevention or pound of cure? *Postgraduate Medicine, 62*, 121–125.

Scott, H. H. (1942). *A history of tropical medicine* (Vol. 1). Baltimore: Williams & Wilkins.

Steffen, R. (1977). Tourist hepatitis. *British Medical Journal, 2*(6101), 1543.

Steffen, R. (1982). Typhoid vaccine, for whom? *Lancet, 1*(8272), 615–616.

Steffen, R., Rickenbach, M., Wilhelm, U., Helminger, A., & Schar, M. (1987). Health problems after travel to developing countries. *Journal of Infectious Diseases, 156*, 84–91.

Steffen, R., van der Linde, F., & Meyer, H.E. (1978). Risk of disease in 10,500 travelers to tropical countries and 1,300 tourists to North America. *Schweizerische Medizinische Wochenschrift, 108*, 1485–1495. (German).

Velimirovic, B. (1973). Mass travel and health problems (with particular reference to Asia and the Pacific Region). *Journal of Tropical Medicine and Hygiene, 76*, 2–7.

White, F. M. M. (1977). Imported diseases: An assessment of trends. *Canadian Medical Association Journal, 117*, 241–245.

WHO. (2007). *International Travel and Health.* Geneva: WHO.

SECTION 2:

EDUCATION IN TRAVEL MEDICINE

Chapter 2

Education in Travel Medicine

Phyllis Kozarsky

I have just completed rummaging through this week's *New England Journal of Medicine* where there is the announcement of a new series in the journal on medical education. In fact, the first in the series was right there written by Cooke and colleagues summarizing the chaotic and ever-changing world of medical education over the past 100 years.

It was indeed almost a century ago when Abraham Flexner, a research scholar, wrote his treatise on the state of medical education in the United States. It was not a pretty picture, and it very much stressed upon the need for a scientific basis for the practice and teaching of medicine. How history repeats itself. Vast changes were to occur soon after, and still, vast changes are occurring, worldwide. The authors state that the key goals in professional education are several: "to transmit knowledge, to impart skills, and to inculcate the values of the profession." True, true, and true.

To some extent, the challenges of professional education in travel medicine are far simpler than those of teachers in medical schools; in some ways, however, they are far more challenging.

In 1988, having recently completed post-graduate training in infectious diseases, my mind and days were over-filled with new information about HIV, its opportunistic infections, and their management; the new third generation of cephalosporins and their many uses; and the growing resistance of Staph aureus to our armamentarium of antibiotics.

I also had an urge: to travel, to care for those in other settings and those who returned from such settings. A dear friend and colleague, Eileen Hilton, had done something innovative combining her academic infectious diseases practice and her wanderlust. She started a travel clinic at the Long Island Jewish Hospital in New York. She and her partners counseled individuals and groups prior to traveling to the developing world, and cared for those who were ill on their return from travel. After visiting the clinic, I decided that such a practice would be just perfect for the lazy little parochial southern town known at Atlanta, Georgia, where college-educated people had no clue where Tyland is, let alone its correct spelling, and where they pronounce the word "cement" with the accent on the first syllable. Enough said.

At the same time I heard from Eileen about a travel medicine meeting being held in Zurich, Switzerland. A Robert Steffen, who had published scientific papers on travelers' diarrhea and other such ailments, was the host; and his co-host was Hans Lobel, a malaria expert from down the block and around the corner at the other ivory tower in Atlanta, the Centers for Disease Control.

I showed up in Zurich and took notes on anything and everything I heard — from malaria chemoprophylaxis to vaccinations — and found myself infected with the travel medicine bug. I was lucky to begin some (hopefully) life-long friendships with very gifted people such as Robert, Jay Keystone, and Elaine Jong, who would become my teachers.

Midst my travels over the next years and serving apprenticeship to Jay in India, Hans came to the clinic and suggested that we host another travel medicine meeting in Atlanta. There began what I never would have believed could be accomplished: years of planning and the culmination, a conference in 1991 that attracted 850 participants from 45 countries, still the largest continuing education meeting that our medical school has ever hosted. It was there that the International Society of Travel Medicine (ISTM) was founded and it was there that I became a counselor of the Society and the first Chair of the Professional Education Committee.

Not quite sure what we should be doing, but knowing that education would naturally be one of the major missions of the new Society, we began to have meetings. And biblically speaking, of course, meetings beget more meetings. About 20 of us from around the globe began to talk and to network. We opened our practices to one another; we discussed our methods of practice, how we counseled travelers, what science existed in the field, and what research there was to be done. We helped plan conferences and worked with the scientific program committees of each conference to insure that what we thought should be included on the agenda were indeed part of the conferences. We worked with Emory University's office of Continuing Medical Education to insure that continuing medical education credits were awarded to those who would benefit and, much later, learned that obtaining similar credits for our nurses was important as well.

That piece was and is far simpler than dealing with medical education as a whole. The difference is as follows: People who decide they want to be educated in travel medicine realize its importance as a subspecialty and must make a special effort to find that training. In fact, it was Robert who pointed out that it is rather a subspecialty of a whole lot of specialties: internal medicine, primary care, infectious diseases, occupational health, pediatrics, emergency medicine, and tropical medicine, just to name a few. Those who choose to dabble or delve into it are typically the more adventuresome, and because they travel, tend as well to be those committed to knowing and learning more about the social, political, and economic problems surrounding health care issues and systems in various parts of the world. Also, most practitioners realize that it is far (indeed, quite far) from the most lucrative subspecialty to choose. Thus the commitment to the educational process for the sake of education alone may be stronger than elsewhere in medicine. My bias.

The ISTM and the success of the Atlanta conference sent a strong message to the medical community that the cottage industry had indeed turned the corner and was now a legitimate specialty in medicine. No longer was it acceptable to call a provider friend and ask what yet another friend needs (shots? pills?) for a trip to Africa. A consultation was appropriate with education and provision of items such as immunizations, malaria chemoprophylaxis, and self-treatment medications for travelers' diarrhea, to name just a few.

As clinics assisting travelers were popping up around the globe, the need for more available education in the field continued to rise. Biennial meetings of the ISTM were well attended and a rise in the number of national societies and their membership was witnessed. Well-established clinics became resources for information about how to practice travel medicine, and it was not uncommon to host hopeful practitioners from afar who were eager to learn all they could about travel medicine and starting a clinic.

Experimentation with some of the new and innovative approaches to the teaching of medicine was found to be very successful and popular for teaching travel medicine. With the understanding that it is always better to engage students rather than talk to them, "workshops" were designed and became a very popular mode of teaching during the conferences. This problem-based approach that uses real-life cases has been used both at the beginner level (termed the "A, B, C's of Travel Medicine") and for the more sophisticated practitioner.

In late 1998 at the Executive Board meeting of the ISTM, the then president of the Society, Dr. Michel Rey, asked the Education Committee to investigate the interest and feasibility of a Certificate of Knowledge Examination in Travel Medicine. There was a general feeling within the Executive Board, as there is in most of medicine and teaching, that review and evaluation foster learning and elevate the standard of care. The benefits of such an exam (and those already acknowledged by current holders of the Certificate in Travel Health [CTH]) would be — enhanced professional development, enhanced professional credibility, and personal satisfaction.

It is an overwhelming task to envision a new subspecialty embarking on an initiative to have an exam to assess competence, but the idea of doing this on an international basis was truly novel. All of us were aware of the variety of specialties involved in travel medicine, the various cultures, practice modes, and the different availability of vaccines and preventive medications worldwide. These differences imposed on a background of philosophical differences in the practice of medicine, the use of medicines, the overabundance of lawyers in some areas, and patient expectations were enormous issues to overcome. Also, consideration of the credential, though the key focus, was sometimes overshadowed by issues such as governance and committee structure, business aspects of the program, psychometric issues of the exam, legal concerns, and issues related to marketing and strategic planning.

We found assistance through a professional education and testing firm in Princeton, New Jersey. Experts in every way in the crafting and administration of professional tests, they have been the foundation for the ISTM in the development of this exam process. First, a needs assessment survey of Society members and participants attending the ISTM's Montreal meeting showed substantial interest in the certificate exam. The next challenge was to determine what the scope of the content of travel medicine actually is so that we could have fundamental agreement about the material on which practitioners could be tested. After all, it is easier to write a test when you know what the body of knowledge is. Our charge then during a meeting in the spring of 1999 was to develop a Body of Knowledge for the Practice of Travel Medicine (BOK). Sounds easy, but it is not as straightforward as what constitutes Geometry I. It took days of sequestered meeting, small focus groups, larger discussions, and endless brainstorming to come up with lists of items that were important for the travel medicine practitioner to know. The next step was to send this list to a different group of 110 practitioners worldwide and ask them to rank the items in terms of their importance. Almost by magic a document arose with a listing of items, the scope of the specialty by the topics' relative "importance" to the travel medicine practitioner. The BOK has been used as a guide to the development of conferences, curricula, training programs, and the professional development of individuals practicing travel medicine. In addition, it has served as the vehicle for establishing the content of the credentialing process.

Time to write test questions — the details of this chore are beyond the scope of this essay, but suffice it to say that learning to write valid and reliable questions is an art in itself. One challenge not faced by teachers in medical schools or by teachers of most specialties in medicine has been the need to "globalize" questions and answers. Because of philosophy and culture, there may be several ways to interpret scientific data so that it can support more than one set of recommendations. Though many of us have come to appreciate the differences in guidelines among nations, it can be quite frustrating to understand how complex these are and how they have developed over time. For example, practitioners from country A may prescribe one antimalarial for trips to India, while those from country B may prescribe one of the three other options. At the same time, country A may not have the availability of a vaccine that country B has. These complexities aside, the exam committee, made up of over 20 from various regions of the world and various practice patterns, and without testing firm at its side, has found the means to stay within the territory of mutual agreement. We should have a seat at the United Nations. The time, energy, and effort placed in the development and continued exam process has been a learning experience for all involved. And yes, just in case you are wondering, we did have a lawyer read all of the exam documents to make sure our "I's were dotted and T's were crossed."

Those who pass the exam are awarded an ISTM Certificate in Travel Health, and the CTH designation has even been trademarked. The exam process has proven overwhelmingly successful and the exam has been administered twice, the first time in New York City in 2003 where the examinees filled the grand ballroom at the Marriott Marquis Hotel in Times Square — a site to behold for a medical society only 12 years of age. The next exam will be given in Vancouver in 2007. Four hundred and seventy-five currently have their certificates and the Canadian Public Health Department is considering making the certificate exam mandatory for those who administer the yellow fever vaccine, an outstanding move in the direction of elevating the standard of care. There are proposals to consider administering the exam annually, and in the future to consider giving it at several venues around the world and perhaps even to administer it electronically — just a few years and several thousand more Euros down the line.

Meanwhile, around the world greater numbers of national meetings are held, and regional conferences are attracting an international group of attendees to places such as Hong Kong and Johannesburg. Switzerland remains a popular destination for clinical training, while both short and long courses in travel medicine are being hosted in Scotland, Australia, New Zealand, and elsewhere around the globe.

Other activities are being held in parallel to the exam development and should not be overlooked as they represent some of the meat of the educational process. Because of the intensity of the exam development process, this group split from the Professional Education Committee, which is quite active with other initiatives. The committee under the leadership of Michele Barry has been highly productive having developed exam review courses that will be given for the first time in 2007, creating slide sets that are now available to ISTM members for teaching and crafting clinical vignettes that are posted on the ISTM website for discussion by practitioners. The ISTM listserv, under an ever energetic David Freedman, is more active than most and involves daily discussion by travel medicine professionals around the world seeking to help one another better understand this ever-changing field. The Research Committee serves as a catalyst by encouraging and funding those in training or newer practitioners to investigate those areas where knowledge is lacking. Though the fund of knowledge and evidence base for travel medicine has certainly increased in the last two decades, this is still a fledgling subspecialty. Yet another aspect of education is that of the public and the travel industry — at the outset quite an uphill battle tackled by Brad Connor, and still a formidable challenge.

Though the ISTM has, as any new organization, suffered from growing pains, its accomplishments are many. The Society is maintaining and building on its mission of promoting safe and healthy travel through education. Areas unexplored in travel medicine are many and there are a multitude of talented and interested practitioners whose job is and will be to continue to fulfill the mission and do the necessary research to expand our evidence base. For us older generation, mentoring — the imparting of this new knowledge along with the clinical skills to our younger colleagues — is what will sustain and grow the field. But most important, it is the compassion with which we practice that serves to define our roles.

Reference

Cook, M., Irby, D. M., Sullivan, W., & Ludmerer, K. M. (2006). American Medical Education 100 years after the Flexner Report. *The New England Journal of Medicine*, *355*(13), 1339–1344.

Chapter 3

The Gorgas Course: Learning Travel Medicine While Traveling

David O. Freedman

"To study the phenomena of disease without books is to sail on uncharted seas, while to study books without patients is not to go to sea at all."

Sir William Osler

The Gorgas Course in Clinical Tropical Medicine is a 9-week entry-level English-language diploma course that has as its motto "Learn Tropical Medicine in the Tropics." The philosophy encompasses seeing patients *in situ* in the tropics on a 36-bed tropical disease unit and experiencing the milieu of the tropics in addition to standard classroom and book learning featured by traditional courses. The Gorgas Memorial Institute also runs The Gorgas Expert Course, a 2-week clinical-rounds-only course, to allow graduates of our course and other diploma courses, as well as individuals with demonstrated high-level skills in tropical medicine, a hands-on refresher course. While the focus of these courses is tropical and parasitic diseases, travel medicine is included in both curricula. Along the way, we have developed several field teaching trips in travel medicine that even the most experienced travel medicine practitioners amongst our course enrollees have found highly instructive in a way that, they have told us later, would alter the way they counsel and deliver travel medicine advice. These Gorgas Course experiences have led me to become a very strong believer that no training can match hands-on travel experience in a developing world setting in order to attain maximum proficiency in the field of travel medicine. Two of our field experiences will be described here.

Introduction to the Gorgas Course

American General William Crawford Gorgas, a tropical medicine pioneer and native Alabamian, is credited with the elimination of yellow fever and malaria that allowed the

Travel Medicine: Tales Behind the Science
Copyright © 2007 by Elsevier Ltd.
All rights of reproduction in any form reserved.
ISBN: 0-08-045359-7

Panama Canal to be built. For over 60 years, until the loss of congressional funding in 1990, the Gorgas Memorial Institute (GMI) operated the Gorgas Laboratories in Panama. The GMI was moved to my institution, the University of Alabama at Birmingham (UAB), in 1992 in order to carry on its tradition of research, service, and training. At its 1995 Board of Directors meeting, the GMI approved resumption of the Gorgas Course as an English language train-ing initiative to serve the international community. From 1996–2007, 405 graduate physicians and nurses from 50 countries have graduated from the Gorgas Diploma Course. An additional 100 more experienced individuals including faculty from many tropical and infectious dis-eases departments from around the world have completed the Gorgas Expert Course. Gorgas teaching faculty are drawn from the *Universidad Peruana Cayetano Heredia* (UPCH) that actually run the courses on a day-to-day basis, UAB, and the United States Navy which has an overseas laboratory in Lima. Guest faculty rotate each year from the US, Canada, and Africa but have included Brian Ward and Evelyne Kokoskin (McGill), David Warrell (Oxford), Srikant Bhatt (University of Nairobi), Alan Magill (Walter Reed), Jaime Torres (Tropical Institute Caracas), Raul Isturiz (Caracas), Christoph Hatz (Swiss Tropical Institute), Sten Vermund (Vanderbilt), Richard Guerrant (Virginia), Herbert Dupont (Texas), and Stephen Hoffman (US Navy).

Since its founding in 1968, the *Instituto de Medicina Tropical "Alexander von Humboldt"* (IMT) has risen to international stature in service, research, and training in infectious diseases and tropical medicine. Eduardo Gotuzzo, the institute Director and Co-Director of all the Gorgas Course, is a Past-President of the International Society of Infectious Diseases and the Pan American Infectious Disease Society and is President-Elect of the International Federation of Tropical Medicine. The faculty teaches extensively in English and in Spanish, in the classroom and at the bedside, in Lima and at field sites. An unusually rich diversity of diseases present on the wards and in the outpatient department. In addition to the complete range of common ubiquitous tropical enteric, respiratory, and viral exanthematous diseases, the following is a partial list of infectious agents presenting to the IMT: malaria, yellow fever, leishmaniasis, Chaga's disease, cyclosporiasis, brucellosis, leprosy, plague, free-living ame-bas, HTLV-1, strongyloidiasis, chancroid, viral hepatitis (A,B,C, and D), oropouche virus, bartonellosis, leptospirosis, cholera, anthrax, cysticercosis, diphyllobothriasis, paragonomia-sis, fascioliasis, tetanus, typhus, diphtheria, paracoccidiomycosis, rabies, echinococcosis, and chromomycosis. Eighty percent of the inpatients are current residents of the impoverished "Northern Cone" of Lima. There are just three hospitals of under 500 beds each to serve three million people, and UPCH has the only infectious diseases unit. The rest of the patients are migrants from throughout the tropical zones of the country drawn by the unit's reputation.

A Field Trip to the Andes: Sea Level to 4800 m and Down in Time for Lunch

Peru is a land of great geographic, topographic, and ecologic diversity. The coastal strip, only a few kilometers wide in many places, is arid desert. Measurable rain does not occur in Lima. The roofs are all flat and no house needs any drainage system built into it. The Andes rise quickly and are equally arid on their western slope. Over the crest, the lush eastern slope is called the high jungle and drops down into the low jungle forming the Amazon basin.

The Central Highway, beginning from Lima at sea level, reaches the highest point on the road at a crossing called Ticlio at 4818 m above sea level in just 132 km of winding but wide and well paved road. Our bus takes just a few hours to rapidly achieve this altitude in order to help course participants experience first hand both the hypoxia at this altitude as well as the rapidity of its onset. Twenty kilometers beyond Ticlio, the road descends slightly and forks left and right to run north and south along the crest of the Andes. The railway tracks at Ticlio, which parallel the road, formed, until July 2006, the highest standard gauge railway crossing in the world. When the new Tibetan railway opened, with several long stretches over 5000 m, Ticlio lost its title but it remains to be seen whether these new tracks in the Far East will survive the permafrost into which they were built. The tracks through the Andes were considered one of the engineering wonders of the world when completed in the 1870s and many of the original bridges on the route are still in use today.

The first purpose of the Ticlio bus trip is to view and experience the so-called inter-Andean valleys and the endemic environment for both leishmaniasis and bartonellosis, which occur at moderate altitudes on the way up. Both diseases are transmitted by *Lutzomyia* sp. sandflies. The sandflies hide under rocks during the days and become active at about 5 pm. A quick reminder of this has turned out to be a wonderful way to get course participants back in the bus in time to return to Lima by 6 pm after the wonderful traditional Incan feast of *Pachamanca* and beer, for which we always stop on the way down. Bartonellosis is a tiny bacteria that lives within red blood cells and causes fever and anemia due to the rupture of infected red cells. It is only transmitted between 800 and 3200 m in inter-Andean valleys, and these valleys begin soon after leaving Lima. The arid environment is inhospitable to the *Anopheles* mosquitoes that transmit malaria. Thus the bartonellosis endemic areas do not overlap with the jungle areas where malaria is transmitted. The visual images of the arid valleys during this brief ride are easily retained in a way that cannot be portrayed in textbooks. A patient with fever and anemia returning from Peru, who was in the jungle, likely has malaria, a patient with fever and anemia who visited only inter-Andean valleys likely has bartonellosis. The distinction may be life saving. Bartonellosis is exquisitely sensitive to a single dose of essentially any anti-bacterial drug. A febrile traveler returning from Peru who is empirically treated with anti-malarial drugs even when no malaria parasites can be found on the blood film could easily die of bartonellosis for lack of a single dose of oral penicillin.

The second component of this field exercise involves each participant measuring their own blood oxygen saturation at sea level, at 3000 m, and at 4818 m (15,600 feet) using portable pulse oximeters that we carry with us. These devices measure oxygen saturation using a simple probe that clips on to the end of any finger. We then plot the results and show them back to the group. This exercise allows participants to understand the degree to which an individual's blood oxygenation drops at altitude and also to be able to experience first hand the correlate of a specific oxygen saturation level with a corresponding level of decreased physical and mental functions. The most vivid demonstration is with respect to the wide and presumably genetically programmed range of tolerability to altitude that occurs between individuals. It becomes apparent in the group setting that this variation is totally unpredictable based on age, size, or physical fitness. While almost everyone in our groups records oxygen saturations over 97% at sea level, at 4800 m the range was from 62 to 90% in one group. Most people do feel quite poorly and light-headed and those at the lower end of the oxygenation range are usually sick with headache, nausea, vomiting, and decreased mentation. This demonstrates the need for the adaptation to higher altitude, which naturally occurs in most people after several days, though some people never adapt above a certain altitude and must descend. No one lives permanently at Ticlio as it is simply too high for almost anyone to adapt to. For those feeling energetic at this altitude, we encourage some mild exercise to demonstrate how easy it is to rapidly desaturate when one is not compensated. The occasional participant has attempted to vigorously exercise and the record low oxygen saturation of 49% is shown in Figure 5.

The final and most valuable lesion is the extremely powerful effect of descent as the primary treatment of altitude illness. This is the most important message that can be delivered to any patient being counseled on altitude. On the paved highway, we can descend 1000 m in 30 minutes and 2000 m in 1 hour. After a 1000 m descent, those few that were disoriented, vomiting, and unable to ambulate at 4800 m exhibited none of those symptoms. Most remarkably, by the time we get back down to 1000 m to stop for the luncheon feast, people that had been nauseated and vomiting a couple of hours earlier are completely recovered and ask for lunch.

A Trip Down the Amazon

Each year the Gorgas Course spends its final week in Iquitos in the Peruvian Amazon. Iquitos, with a population of around 500,000, is the largest city in the world that is not connected to the outside world by road. While a few roads branch out from the city for short distances, the nearest road connection to the rest of the world ends 450 km away. The only way in or out is by river taxi — 5 days travel from where the road ends, or by air. The course itself stays in the city and in the local hospitals, which presents few real health risks. The city center is quite built up and without malaria transmission, though dengue is a risk most years. However, in the mid-to-late 1990s, together with a major tour operator we ran for a few years only a series of 1-week long Amazon Travel Medicine courses where we did venture out into the primary jungle itself.

Because very few had been to the Amazon at the time, we were able to attract the top names in travel medicine as both faculty and participants on these courses. Because all these individuals themselves are opinion leaders and teachers of many others, I believe that much of the travel advice and teaching about Amazon travel today emanates from those few short hands-on courses. Up until then, few travelers ventured to the Amazon and many countries did not recommend any continuous malaria prophylaxis for anywhere in Latin America. A quick inspection of the many typical *Anopheles* breeding areas around any of the jungle lodges and a visit to the regional malaria laboratory in Iquitos where a thousand positive malaria smears a day were coming in was quite instructive.

We also experienced first hand how difficult it is to follow our own personal protection advice in a hot humid jungle environment. Liquid repellents, especially of the lotion-based variety, are extremely effective at obstructing the sweat glands — a mostly intolerable side effect when one is in the jungle. Bed nets quite effectively prevent spontaneous circulation of air, so that when there is no electricity and no fans, bed-net compliance is easier said than done. Finally, chigger mites abound in grassy areas of the Amazon and will get on any low-lying exposed skin. Thus, stay on the path and out of the grass if one is to wear sandals or open shoes. Chigger saliva is highly allergenic and slow to decay; two weeks of incessant itching without obvious hives are guaranteed even after the chiggers are long gone. This usually results in 2 weeks sleeping on the sofa upon return home for those with spouses who are pretty sure that there is nothing in the jungle that is not potentially contagious.

Ten Years of Gorgas

Eduardo Gotuzzo and I together with our incredibly talented group of Peruvian faculty have just celebrated 10 years of this unique tropical and travel medicine training initiative. We have been privileged to be able to impact so far over 500 physicians and health professionals from around the world and to now have friends and colleagues in so many places. More information and a pictorial history of the Gorgas Course can be found at www.gorgas.org. For those that cannot get away to attend a course, we post for free 12 teaching cases per year on the website using patients seen by our course participants that year.

Image 3.1. **Typical inter-Andean valley**. David O. Freedman and Ciro Maguina in an arid Andean valley at about 1,000 m above sea level. This is a typical endemic area for leishmaniasis and bartonellosis. In Peru, malaria transmission occurs primarily in the jungle regions so that there is no overlap between the two diseases. Ciro Maguina is a leading authority on *Bartonella bacilliformis* and his reviews in the medical literature should be consulted for those interested in the disease.

Image 3.2. **Coca Tea and Altitude illness prevention**. Ciro Maguina with a coca leaf and the author showing the traditional Peruvian prophylaxis for mountain sickness. On the Gorgas Course field trip, a Coca-tea stop is always made at San Mateo at about 3,000 m just before reaching medically significant altitudes. The active and notorious ingredient in coca leaves is not water soluble, so it is not present in the tea. The taste is pleasant, and even if no scientific study has shown any benefit of the tea, the stop needed to rest and drink the tea before ascending is likely a main benefit.

Image 3.3. **Oxygen Saturation Measurement**. Yae-Jean Kim (South Korea) after measuring her oxygen saturation at San Mateo during the second of three readings done by each course participant, and recording her Lake Louise score. Paul Southern looks on.

Image 3.4. Ticlio — **Highest Point on the Road and Railway**. From Left, Ted Kuhn (Medical College of Georgia, USA), Joseph Kolars (Mayo Clinic, USA), Susan Mcllelan (Tulane University, USA), and Annelies Wilder-Smith (Tan Tock Seng Hospital, Singapore) after the rapid ascent over a few hours from sea level to the sign showing what was in 2001, the highest railway tracks in the world at 4,818 m (15,600 feet).

Image 3.5. **Rapid De-Saturation with Exercise at Altitude**. Anne McCarthy (Ottawa) at Ticlio after 1 min of vigorous exercise. The oxygen saturation of 49% was the lowest we have recorded and fortunately climbed quickly with the ensuing reflex hyperventilation.

Image 3.6. **Gorgas Expert Group 2005 After Pachamanca (Incan feast) Lunch**. After descent to a comfortable altitude, the Gorgas groups can sit down and share experiences of tropical and travel medicine with colleagues from all over the world in an inter-Andean valley. Pictured from left to right are: Peter Leutscher (Denmark), Jetmund Ringstad (Norway), Paul Southern (USA), Judy Stone (USA), Micheal Parry (USA), Yae Jean Kim (South Korea), Ashley Watson (Australia), Leigh Grossman (USA), Poh Lian Lim (Singapore), Theresa Schlager (USA), Soren Thybo (Denmark), Debbie Heit (USA), Leif Dotevall (Sweden), Cathy Suh (Canada), David Freedman (USA, Faculty), Michael Barnish (USA), Anne McCarthy (Canada), David Roesel (USA), Issa Ephtimios (Canada), Kathy Hernandez (Peru, Faculty), Ciro Maguina (Peru, Faculty).

Image 3.7. **Dr Alan Magill (Walter Reed Army Institute of Research) Leading a Field Trip to a Malarious Amazonian Village**. Pictured are some members of the Diploma Class of 1999 from left to right: Judy Streit (USA), Jeff Chapman (USA), Mario Onagan (Philippines), Ali Al-Barak (Saudi Arabia), Alan Magill, Monica Guardo (Colombia).

Image 3.8. **First Amazon Travel Medicine Course, 1997**. Robert Steffen (Zurich), the father of travel medicine, conducting a malaria workshop exactly in context in the Amazon rainforest.

Image 3.9. **Time-off During the Amazon Travel Medicine Course**. Elaine Jong (University of Washington) trying her hand with a traditional hunting implement loaded with blanks and not "live" curare tipped ammunition.

Image 3.10. **Familiarization Cruise on La Turmalina, 1997**. During the first Amazon Travel Medicine course, the owner of a fleet of luxury cruise boats in the burgeoning Amazon cruise business recognized the potential influence of this group and invited us on board for the day. Pictured from left to right are: Nancy Bennett, Karl Neumann, Robert Steffen, Assunta Marcolongo, Vernon Ansdell, Ed Cupp, Dominique Tessier, Elaine Jong, Charlotte deFrances, Tom Nutman, David Freedman, Unknown, Linda Casebeer. Robert Steffen and his wife Eve would later return to enter the 21st century on the special Millenium Cruise aboard La Turmalina.

Chapter 4

The Ten Commandments for Healthy Tropical Travel

Jay S. Keystone

Someone once said that you can do everything wrong and remain healthy, and every-thing right and become ill. Staying healthy during travel is more often the result of one's knowledge of local health risks, food and water as well as insect bite precautions, common sense, and good luck. My approach to educating the public and health care providers about travel health is to use the format of the "10 Commandments for healthy travel." Why the 10 Commandments? Because some of my best friends are Jewish ... and all of my relatives.

Commandment #1: "Thou Shalt Seek Advice from Your Health Care Provider"

Why should travelers come to *me* for advice? In my case, now that I am single again, I need to be able to support my five children in the style to which they have become accustomed. I can now appreciate what Rod Steward once said: "Instead of getting married again, I'm going to find a woman I don't like and just give her a house." We split the house.

The most important reason to seek travel advice, apart from the fact that health care providers need to make a living, is to obtain immunizations. A number of years ago, Elaine Jong from Seattle Washington coined the expression the "three R's" for travel immuniza-tions: 1. *Routine* (childhood or adult immunizations such as tetanus, polio, and diphtheria); 2. *Required* (immunizations required to cross international borders such as yellow fever and meningococcal meningitis); and 3. *Recommended* (immunizations according to risk of infec-tion). It is important to understand that travel health recommendations are based on an *indi-vidual* risk assessment carried out by the travel medicine practitioner. He or she then develops a risk management strategy that might include immunizations, antimalarial pills and advice for the self-treatment of travelers' diarrhea. We immunize not only according to the country to which one is traveling, but also according to an individual's risk of infection; the latter is determined by a number of factors including the style and activities of travel, exact itinerary, season, purpose and duration of travel, and underlying health problems.

The most frequent vaccine-preventable infections include, in order, enterotoxigenic *E. coli* (the most frequent cause of travelers' diarrhea), influenza, hepatitis A, hepatitis B, typhoid fever, and cholera. Of the recommended vaccines, hepatitis A and B are most important for the average traveler, whereas typhoid vaccine is most important for those going off the usual tourist routes, and especially for immigrants returning home to developing countries to visit friends and relatives (VFRs is the current nomenclature for this group).

Hepatitis A is acquired by ingesting contaminated food and/or water. I used to think that hepatitis A was a benign disease causing yellow jaundice. I assumed that infected patients would go to a local department store to buy something that matched yellow for a few weeks, and then all would be well. I was wrong. Unfortunately, for the older people like me (and the editors of this book) hepatitis A is potentially a serious disease with a mortality rate of 2–3% over the age of 50.

Hepatitis B, on the other hand, is acquired by such activities as sharing of secretions (mostly sex), injections, blood transfusions, piercing, and tattooing. I used to believe incorrectly that most older married couples were not at risk of acquiring the infection because they were unlikely to be sexually adventurous during travel (having sex after 20 years of marriage is improbable anyway). That was until I read a scientific paper showing that 17% of travelers who sought medical attention in the developing world received an injection. No big deal I thought, until the World Health Organization published a study showing that up to 75% of injections given in the developing world were administered with unsterile equipment. This is not a minor issue! For this reason, I am now convinced that *all* travelers should be immunized against both hepatitis A and B. Since these immunizations provide lifetime protection, they are an excellent investment, especially since 97% of international travelers have been shown to travel repeatedly.

It is interesting to note that almost 80% of all the typhoid fever cases diagnosed in North America and Europe occur in VFRs newly returned from their country of birth. Hence, typhoid immunization is a must for VFRs, especially those traveling to South Asia. Other vaccines such as meningococcus, Japanese encephalitis, rabies, and cholera are recommended for specific areas of the world and for particular types of travelers. For example, meningococcal vaccine is recommended for travel to sub-Saharan Africa, while rabies vaccine is recommended for young children traveling for prolonged periods in rabies endemic areas. My children were immunized against rabies, mostly to protect the neighbors.

Commandment #2: "Thou Shalt Acclimatize Thyself"

Acclimatization in warm climates includes the need to use sun block with a minimum SPF (sun protection factor) of 30, and to maintain adequate hydration and salt replacement to make up for that lost due to sweating. When traveling to high altitudes, greater than 2500 m, it is advisable to ascend slowly, less than 300 m per day. When rapid acclimatization is required, acetazolamide (Diamox) is often recommended; unfortunately, the drug makes carbonated beverages taste horrible. To a diet cokeaholic like myself, this problem is unbearable, almost as upsetting as acute mountain sickness itself.

Commandment #3: "Thou Shalt Protectest Thyself from Insects"

You want to believe that there are some very large and disease-carrying insects found in the tropics. The most effective and safest insect repellents contain DEET (*N,N*-diethyl-3-methylbenzamide). The concentration of DEET in most formulations determines the duration of action and not the effectiveness. For example, 30% DEET protects for 4–6 hours whereas 99% DEET protects for 10–12 hours. Citronella is effective for about 30–60 minutes at most. Therefore, should you choose to use the latter, be prepared to have someone carry a backpack and spray you down every hour. Thirty percent DEET is now recommended for children down to two months of age, and has been shown to be safe in pregnant women. DEET *must* be safe in pregnancy given the amount used by my spouse who was constantly pregnant. For some reason, I had "recreation" confused with "procreation"; they sounded alike, but the consequences were clearly different. It took me 12 years and 5 kids to figure out what I was doing wrong. It is important to remember that insect repellent use should be determined by the biting time of the insect one wishes to avoid. For example, malaria is transmitted by a night-biting mosquito for which repellent use is required *between* dusk and dawn to avoid infection. On the other hand, to prevent dengue, an urban, viral infection transmitted by a day-biting mosquito, repellents must be used at dusk and dawn. Maximum protection is achieved when DEET applied to skin is combined with permethrin (an insecticide) soaked in or sprayed on clothing. In high risk areas, permethrin-impregnated bed nets should be considered.

Commandment #4: "Thou Shalt Purify the Water that Thou Drinks Including by Cubes of Ice"

Apparently, Keystone beer from Colorado is very good and safe to drink. However, I wouldn't know because I don't drink alcohol (no one will let me drink because I am so obnoxious even when I am sober!). This commandment reminds all travelers to drink only commercially bottled beverages or those that have been purified. Ice cubes, unless made by purified water, are to be avoided because microorganisms remain viable in a frozen state. Bummer!

Commandment #5: "Thou Shall Cook Well Thy Food and Peel Thine Fruits and Vegetables"

Although the standard dictum in travel medicine is to "boil it, peel it, cook it or forget it," it has become eminently clear that the saying is "easy to remember, but impossible to do." As David Shlim, an excellent travel medicine practitioner, once opined, "travelers' diarrhea will always be a problem as long as travelers are in a position to eat other people's stool." We generally advise travelers to avoid street vendors and salads, as well as unpasteurized milk products. However, the medical literature has shown that 97% of travelers make any food or beverage "*faux pas*" within the 72 hours of arrival in the tropics. This of course brings me to the next obvious commandment …

Commandment #6: "Thou Shal Carry an Antibiotic for Self-Treatment of Travelers' Diarrhea"

Along with an American Express card, one should never leave home without loperamide (Imodium) and an antibiotic for self-treatment of travellers' diarrhea. Except for Thailand and Nepal, where considerable antibiotic resistance has been documented recently, the antibiotic of choice is a quinolone such as ciprofloxacin, ofloxacin, or levofloxacin. The medical literature shows that a single dose of antibiotic, especially when used with loperamide, is often as effective as three daily doses. Therefore, it is appropriate to tell the traveler that if the first dose solves the problem, additional doses are unnecessary. It is interesting to note that many health care providers feel that medications should not be used to stop travelers' diarrhea, because "diarrhea is nature's way of getting rid of intestinal pathogens." These same practitioners have probably never been stuck on a bus in Mexico that does not stop for 3 hours. Furthermore, as David Shlim once said: "isn't it interesting how cavalier health care providers are about other people's diarrhea" ... except of course, about their own. To be complete, it is worth mentioning that rifaximin, a new, safe, nonabsorbable antibiotic, has been shown to be very effective in the treatment of *E. coli*-induced diarrhea, the most frequent cause of travelers' diarrhea. Antibiotic prophylaxis with these same drugs should be reserved for those who cannot afford to be dehydrated, such as those with diabetes mellitus, renal disease etc.

Commandment #7: "Thou Shalt Wear and Carry Thy Prophylactics"

Martin Haditch from Austria once declared to those planning to have casual sex during travel: "if it's wet, and not yours ... don't touch it!" When it comes to prophylactic use to prevent sexually transmitted infections, each and every (casual) sexual encounter during travel must be protected using a condom, whether one is the donor or recipient of the sexual organ.

The other prophylactics that are crucial during travel are the drugs use to prevent malaria. The choice of a particular drug will depend on the resistance pattern of malaria in the country or countries to be visited. In several countries of Europe, malaria chemoprophylaxis has been abandoned for travel in low-risk areas such as Latin America, India, and Southeast Asia. Instead, insect protection measures are recommended along with a self-treatment regimen to be carried and used when fever occurs and medical care is not readily accessible.

The prophylactic drugs of choice for chloroquine-resistant areas of the world (almost everywhere except for Central America, the island of Hispaniola, parts of the Middle East and central China where chloroquine may still be effective) are mefloquine (Lariam), doxycycline, and atovaquone/proguanil (Malarone). The choice of antimalarial is determined by drug efficacy, potential adverse events, convenience, contraindications, and cost. Even newborns who are being breastfed require antimalarials because not enough drug crosses into breast milk. I recall some years ago that my wife telephoned me from Indonesia to tell me that the antimalarial that my children were taking was causing them to be irritable, and therefore she was stopping it. Without hesitation I asked, "How would you know if it was the drug causing the problem? They were irritable before they left Canada?"

The problem with traveler acceptance of antimalarial drug side effects is that they start off healthy and are unwilling to tolerate even the mildest of adverse events. On the other hand, when they are ill, they are willing to accept significant side effects of therapeutic drugs. What travelers need to remember is that antimalarial pills are used to prevent a potentially fatal infection, keeping in mind that death is usually a life-ending event, unless one believes in reincarnation. Travelers should always buy their antimalarials at home, since poor-quality and counterfeit drugs are all too often available for sale in the developing world. Better to have expensive malaria protection, than no protection at all.

Commandment number #8: "Thou Shalt Not Swim in Freshwater Nor Walk in Thy Bare Feet"

It is advisable not to swim, wade, or walk in or on (if you can do the latter) slow moving freshwater rivers or lakes in many parts of the developing world because of the risk of schistosomiasis (Bilharzia). This infection is acquired when a microscopic worm penetrates the unbroken skin during freshwater exposure and enters the veins of the bowel or bladder. Because hookworms and other nasty parasites can penetrate the unbroken skin of the feet and wind up in one's bowels, footwear should be worn at all times.

Commandment #9: Thou Shall Be Concerned about Thy Security

In general, travelers should not wear expensive jewelry or flash a roll of dollar bills … unless they are Canadian. Also, we remind travelers to wear a Canadian pin on their lapel, especially if they are American. Finally, travelers should not travel alone at night, especially women. Not that they are the weaker sex, but are more likely to be assaulted! When it comes to travel safety, I recall with fondness the T-shirt worn by a bomb disposal expert that said, "If you see me running … try to keep up."

Commandment #10: Be Wary of By Conveyance

This tenth commandment reminds me of my son David who once said, "If you don't like the way I drive … get off the sidewalk." If one looks at statistics on the causes of death of travelers, fewer than 1% die of infection, whereas 40% die in motor vehicle accidents. From my perspective, of all the health information that I give to a traveler, avoidance of motor vehicle accidents is by far the most important. For young travelers especially, I recommend that they not drive a motorcycle in the developing world, even though I've done it myself and enjoyed it thoroughly (unfortunately, there is no lifeguard for the gene pool!). For all travelers, I tell them "Don't even *think* about traveling by a road in rural areas after dark in the developing world." The roads are bad, the drivers are worse, and the vehicles are poorly maintained.

In spite of the many "Do's' and 'Don'ts" in the 10 commandments travel medicine practitioners recommend in order to maintain one's health, travel is for most a safe and enjoyable pastime. As Rudyard Kipling once wrote in his poem about how travel might change our view of those from other cultures and countries: "You might just look on 'we,' as only a sort of 'they'."

For those with a short attention span and memory, let me close by giving you my CNN version on how to stay healthy during travel (borrowed from Dr. David Smith of Toronto). Clarifications are noted in brackets: Don't get hit (motor vehicles), Don't get bit (animals), Don't get "lit" (drunk), Don't do "it" (casual sex), and don't eat shit ("Do-do" according to George Bush Senior)! What could be more common sense than this?

SECTION 3:

EVOLUTION OF TRAVEL VACCINES

Chapter 5

Routine Vaccinations and Travel

Peter A. Leggat

Introduction

Vaccination is one of the population health interventions that have had the greatest impact on global health. Since the ground-breaking development of vaccines by scientists such as Jenner and Pasteur, millions of deaths and serious illnesses have been avoided every year through the implementation of routine vaccination programs and improved vaccination coverage. The approximate timeline of early vaccine development is given in Table 5.1. Following the success of the smallpox eradication programme, the World Health Organization (WHO) and the United Nations Children's Fund (UNICEF) have introduced various initiatives to maximize routine vaccination coverage, including the Expanded Program on Immunization and the Global Immunization Vision and Strategy (WHO\UNICEF, 2005).

Immunization is also a key part of the pre-travel consultation and can play a major role in the reduction of risks from vaccine preventable infectious diseases commonly found abroad. Travel vaccines generally include both mandatory travel vaccinations and other travel vaccinations for particular geographic or other risks. The pre-travel consultation is also an excellent opportunity to review the status of routine immunizations (Jong, 1999), which constitutes a country's national immunization schedule. Many of these vaccines are administered during childhood and may need to be updated or boosted. The WHO (2005) provides a generic list of these routine vaccinations, which may, of course, differ slightly from country to country (see Table 5.2).

Benefits of Reviewing Routine Vaccination

There are several benefits of reviewing and updating travelers' routine vaccinations during the pre-travel health consultation and perhaps completing vaccine schedules on return. These include:

- protecting travelers against the infectious diseases whilst abroad;
- protecting travelers against the infectious diseases when they come back home;

Table 5.1: Approximate timeline of early development of human vaccines.[a]

1798	Smallpox
1885	Rabies
1897	Plague
1923	Diphtheria
1926	Pertussis
1927	Tuberculosis (BCG)
1927	Tetanus
1935	Yellow Fever
1955	Injectable Polio Vaccine (IPV)
1962	Oral Polio Vaccine (OPV)
1964	Measles
1967	Mumps
1970	Rubella
1981	Hepatitis B

[a]After Plotkin and Plotkin (2004).

- protecting host populations against carriage of the infectious diseases during travel; and
- improving the herd immunity of the travelers' home countries against the infectious diseases.

One of the issues over the past few decades has been a variable rate of routine vaccination amongst children and adults for national schedule vaccinations and certainly vaccination rates for some routine immunizations remain well under 90% for about half of the world's countries and in some cases well under 50% (WHO, 2006). All vaccinations given should be documented in the travelers' vaccination booklet and a duplicate record kept, if possible in a separate but accessible location.

Risk Assessment

The approach to determine what routine vaccinations should be given will depend on a detailed risk assessment, which is described in detail elsewhere (Leggat, 2006). It is dependent on several factors, which include:

- the itinerary of the traveler, including the epidemiology of the potential infectious diseases and other hazards at the destination;
- the medical profile and history of the traveler;
- the time available before trip departure and personal circumstances of the traveler; and
- the adverse events and contraindications associated with each vaccine, particularly in the light of the medical profile and history of the traveler.

In addition, when immunization is clearly indicated during pregnancy, the risk to mother and foetus from the infectious disease itself must be balanced against the risk to both from

Table 5.2: Routine vaccinations to be reviewed in the pre-travel health consultation (after WHO, 2005).

Vaccine preventable disease	Type of vaccine[a]
Routine vaccinations	
Diphtheria/tetanus/pertussis (DTP)	
Diphtheria	Toxoid vaccine
Tetanus	Toxoid vaccine
Pertussis	Inactivated vaccine
Hepatitis B virus (HBV)	Inactivated vaccine
Hemophilus influenzae type b (Hib)	Inactivated vaccine
Measles, mumps, rubella (MMR)	
Measles	Live vaccine
Mumps	Live vaccine
Rubella	Live vaccine
Poliomyelitis	
Oral Poliomyelitis Vaccine (OPV)	Live vaccine
Inactivated Poliomyelitis Vaccine (IPV)	Inactivated vaccine
Routine vaccinations for special groups	
Influenza	Inactivated vaccine
Pneumococcal disease	Inactivated vaccine

[a]After Zuckerman, 2001.

immunization (Thanassi & Weiss, 1997). As a general rule, immunization should be avoided during the first trimester, and live vaccines are contraindicated throughout pregnancy (Jothivijayarani, 2002). However, it is always safer to be immunized against certain diseases than to run the risk of contracting a serious, possibly life-threatening infection (Jothivijayarani, 2002).

Children often accompany adults, who are traveling from developed countries to developing countries and vice versa for work, business, pleasure and/or visiting friends and families. In addition, an increasing number of children and adolescents travel on their own to join parents or as part of exchange, scouting, school or summer camp activities. There may be additional requirements for children traveling to countries for extended periods of time, with or without their parents, particularly on exchange scholarships.

Tetanus

Tetanus vaccination is generally regarded as safe. Although tetanus vaccination has not been reported in travelers, it may be hidden in national surveillance data (Steffen, Baños, & deBernardis, 2003). Tetanus boosters are recommended for travelers where post-exposure tetanus immunization might be unavailable and/or a booster is required (ACIP, 1991). In pregnancy, it should be administered after the first trimester (Jothivijayarani, 2002).

Diphtheria

Diphtheria vaccination is generally regarded as safe. As demonstrated by a large epidemic in the former Soviet Union 1990–1997, diphtheria may flare up under specific circumstances (Galazka, 2000). This epidemic resulted in dozens of importations to Western Europe and North America and some travelers died while still in Russia. The far less serious form of cutaneous diphtheria is occasionally imported, mainly from developing countries (Anonymous, 1998). In pregnancy, the diphtheria vaccine should be administered after the first trimester (Jothivijayarani, 2002).

Polio

A global eradication program against poliomyelitis has been underway for sometime and, although significant progress has been made in most parts of the world, it may rarely still be associated with virus imported by asymptomatic persons, as demonstrated fairly recently in Bulgaria and China (Anonymous, 2000, 2001). In travelers, poliomyelitis has not been observed since the 1990s. Polio remains endemic in seven countries: India, Nigeria, Pakistan, Egypt, Afghanistan, Niger and Somalia (Anonymous, 2003), although there are some areas where polio outbreaks have reoccurred in areas thought to be free of polio from the global immunization program. Travelers to these countries are advised to receive a single booster of inactivated polio vaccine (IPV) if the primary doses have already been administered. In pregnancy, IPV is preferred, but the oral polio vaccine may be considered if IPV is not available, after the first trimester (Jothivijayarani, 2002).

Measles, Mumps, Rubella

Hardly any data exist on measles, mumps and rubella in travelers. Because of suboptimal compliance with vaccination, European, African and Asian travelers are responsible for outbreaks on the American continent, where vaccine uptake has been higher (Rota, Rota, & Redd, 1998). Measles is endemic in many developing nations, and a booster of measles-mumps-rubella (MMR) vaccine is warranted for any person born after 1956, who does not have documentation of two doses of the vaccine or immunity by serum antibody testing (Watson, Hadler, Dykewicz, Reef, & Phillips, 1998). Children 6–11 months of age should receive one dose of MMR vaccine if traveling to highly endemic areas, but they still must receive two doses of the vaccine after 12 months of age to be considered fully immunized (Watson et al., 1998).

Vaccination against measles, mumps and rubella during pregnancy is contraindicated because of possible harm to the foetus from this live viral vaccine. Measles and rubella can cause an adverse effect on the developing foetus. Measles can also cause severe illness in the mother. It is important to check for immunity to these diseases. Non-immune travelers should defer travel to less-developed countries, where the vaccine coverage is poor and the risk of disease is higher (Jothivijayarani, 2002).

Varicella

There is little published literature concerning varicella (chickenpox) in travelers. In travelers, immunity should be reviewed and, if needed, children 1 through 12 years of age should receive a single dose of vaccine, while those 13 years and older should receive two doses of vaccine administered 4–8 weeks apart (ACIP, 1999; Jong, 1999; Wilson, 2001; CDC, 2006). In particular, this vaccine should be considered for women of childbearing age who do not have documented varicella disease before vaccination or antibody titres.

Hepatitis B Virus

Hepatitis B virus (HBV) infection remains an important problem for travelers. The monthly incidence of HBV is 25/100,000 for symptomatic infections and 80–420/100,000 for all infections in travelers (Lőscher, Keystone, & Steffen R, 1999). Transmission requires only a very small number of HBV particles. HBV is now a routine immunization for children in most industrialized and developing countries; however, there will be a number of adult travelers who may never have been immunized. WHO recommendations for HBV immunization and risks of HBV for travel are given in Table 5.3.

HBV and other viruses can be transmitted in a number of developing country settings for travelers, including through casual sex and noscominal transmission (Simonsen, Kane, & Lloyd, 1999). Travel health advisors should ensure that HBV vaccination does not engender complacency to the risks of other similarly transmitted disease causing viruses such as human immunodeficiency virus and hepatitis C virus, where there is no vaccination at present.

While expatriates and other travelers living close to the local population are probably most at risk, surveys have suggested that 10–15% of travelers voluntarily or involuntarily expose themselves to blood and body fluids while abroad in high-risk countries (Zuckerman & Steffen, 2000; Correia, Shafer, & Patel, 2001). HBV vaccination status should be checked in children and pregnancy is not a contraindication to vaccination (CDC, 2006).

Table 5.3: Recommendations for Hepatitis B vaccination based on potential risks for travelers (after WHO, 2005).

Those travelers with moderate to high risk of infection:

- Travelers involved in accidents and trauma abroad
- Those who expose themselves to potentially infected blood or blood-derived fluids, or who have unprotected sexual contact

Principal risky activities include:

- health care (medical, dental, laboratory or other) that entails direct exposure to human blood;
- receipt of a transfusion of blood that has not been tested for HBV; and
- dental, medical or other exposure to needles (e.g. acupuncture, piercing, tattooing or injecting drug use) that have not been appropriately sterilized.

A combination of hepatitis A and B vaccine is available for use in adults older than 18 years. It is as efficacious and safe as each of the monovalent vaccines (Murdoch, Goa, & Figgitt, 2003; Woo, Miller, & Ball, 2006). Primary immunization occurs at zero, one and six months. HBV vaccination is generally safe in pregnancy and can be administered to travelers at risk. Testing for HBV antigen should be performed in all pregnant women (Jothivijayarani, 2002).

Hemophilus Influenzae Type B (Hib)

Hemophilus influenzae type B is a common cause of bacterial meningitis and other potentially life-threatening conditions (WHO, 2005). Hardly any data exist on pertussis or *Hemophilus influenzae* type B in travelers, but it would be considered a risk for unprotected children who may be traveling, at least till the age of 5 (WHO, 2005), especially when children are going from low-risk to high-risk areas.

Pneumococcal Vaccine

The pneumococcal vaccine should be considered for travelers who are older than 65 years as well as younger adults with chronic diseases such as chronic cardiopulmonary disease, asplenia, cirrhosis or diabetes mellitus (CDC, 2006; ACIP, 1997).

Influenza

Influenza has rapidly overtaken hepatitis A virus as one of the most common vaccine preventable diseases of travelers (Steffen et al., 2005). In addition to the special groups that are considered for the pneumococcal vaccine, the influenza vaccine should be considered in all international travelers during influenza season. Influenza usually peaks during the months of November to March in the northern hemisphere and from April until September in the southern hemisphere. Travelers should receive the most current vaccine available (WHO, 2005).

Conclusions

Travel health advisors should use the pre-travel health consultation as an opportunity to evaluate travelers' routine vaccination status, according to their national schedule. The need for vaccination should be based on a thorough risk assessment. It is important that travelers are made aware of the potential adverse events and contraindications associated with each routine vaccine, and document all vaccinations given. Travelers should continue to take measures to reduce their exposure to vaccine and non-vaccine preventable diseases of travel.

References

ACIP. (1991). Diptheria, tetanus, and pertussis: recommendations for vaccine use and other preventive measures. Recommendations of the Immunization Practices Advisory Committee (ACIP). *MMWR Recomm. Rep.*, *40*(RR-10), 1–28.

ACIP. (1997). Prevention of pneumococcal disease: Recommendations of the Advisory Committee on Immunization Practices (ACIP). *MMWR Recomm. Rep.*, *46*(RR-8), 1–24.

ACIP. (1999). Prevention of varicella. Update recommendations of the Advisory Committee on Immunization Practices (ACIP). *MMWR Recomm. Rep.*, *48*(RR-6), 1–5.

Anonymous. (1998). Diphtheria in visitors to Africa. *CDR Wkly*, *8*, 289.

Anonymous. (2000). Wild poliovirus imported into Qinghai province, China. *WHO Wkly Epidemiol. Rec.*, *75*, 55–57.

Anonymous. (2001). Imported wild poliovirus causing poliomyelitis, Bulgaria. *WHO Wkly Epidemiol. Rec.*, *76*, 332–335.

Anonymous. (2003). Progress toward global eradication of poliomyelitis, 2002. *MMWR Morb. Mortal. Wkly. Rep.*, *52*, 366–369.

Centres for Disease Control and Prevention (CDC, USA). (2006). *Health information for international travel, 2006–2007.* Atlanta, Ga.: CDC. URL. http://www.cdc.gov/travel (accessed 1 November 2006).

Correia, J. D., Shafer. R. T., Patel, V., Kain, K. C., Tessier, D., MacPherson, D., & Keystone, J. S. (2001). Blood and body fluid exposure as a health risk for international travelers. *J. Travel Med.*, *8*, 263–266.

Galazka, A. (2000) The changing epidemiology of diphtheria in the vaccine era. *J. Infect. Dis.*, *181* (Suppl 1), 2–9.

Jong, E. C. (1999). Travel immunizations. *Med. Clin. North Am.*, *83*, 903–922.

Jothivijayarani, A. (2002). Travel considerations during pregnancy. *Prim Care Update for Ob./Gyns.*, *9*, 36–40.

Leggat, P. A. (2006). Risk assessment in travel medicine. *Travel Med. Inf. Dis.*, *4*, 126–134.

Löscher, T., Keystone, J. S., & Steffen, R. (1999). Vaccination of travelers against Hepatitis A and B. *J. Travel Med.*, *6*, 107–114.

Murdoch, D. L., Goa, K., & Figgitt, D. P. (2003). Combined hepatitis A and B vaccines: A review of their immunogenicity and tolerability. *Drugs*, *63*(23), 2625–2649.

Plotkin, S. L., & Plotkin, S. A. (2004). A short history of vaccination. In: S. A. Plotkin, & W. A. Orenstein (Eds), *Vaccines* (4th ed., pp.1–15). Philadelphia: WB Saunders.

Rota, J. S., Rota, P. A., Redd, S. B., Redd, S. C., Pattamadilok, S., & Bellini, W. J. (1998). Genetic analysis of measles viruses isolated in the United States, 1995–1996. *J. Infect. Dis.*, *177*, 204–208.

Simonsen, L., Kane, A., Lloyd, J., Zaffran, M., & Kane, M. (1999). Unsafe injections in the developing world and transmission of bloodborne pathogens: A review. *Bull. WHO*, *77*, 789–800.

Steffen, R., Baños, A., & deBernardis, C. (2003). Vaccination priorities. *Int. J. Antimicrob. Agents.*, *21*, 175–180.

Steffen, R., Dupont, H. L., & Wilder-Smith, A. (2007). Manual of travel medicine and health. Hamilton, Canada: Decker publication.

Thanassi, W. T., & Weiss, E. L. (1997). Immunizations and travel. *Emerg. Med. Clin. North Am.*, *15*, 43–70.

Watson, J. C., Hadler, S. C., Dykewicz, C. A., Reef, S. & Phillips, L. (1998). Measles, mumps, and rubella-vaccine use and strategies for elimination of measles, rubella, and congenital rubella syndrome and control of mumps: Recommendations of the Advisory Committee on Immunization Practices (ACIP). *MMWR Recomm. Rep.*, *47*(RR-8), 1–57.

Wilson, M. E. (2001). Travel-related vaccines. *Infect Dis. Clin. North Am.*, *15*, 231–251.

Woo, E. J., Miller, N. B., & Ball, R. (2006). Adverse events after hepatitis A B combination vaccine. *Vaccine*, *24*, 2685–2691.

World Health Organization. (2005). *International Travel and Health*. Geneva: WHO. URL. http://www.who.int/ith (accessed 1 November 2006).

World Health Organization. (2006). *WHO Immunisation Highlights, 2005*. Geneva: WHO. URL. http://www.who.int/immunization/WHO_Immunization_highlights2005.pdf (accessed 1 November 2006).

World Health Organization/United Nations International Children's Fund (2005). Global Immunisation Vision and Strategy 2006–2015. Geneva. URL. http://www.who.int/vaccines-documents/DocsPDF05/GIVS_Final_EN.pdf (accessed 10 January 2007).

Zuckerman, J. N., & Steffen, R. (2000). Risk of hepatitis B in travelers as compared to immunization status. *J. Travel Med.*, *7*, 170–174.

Chapter 6

Recommended Travel Vaccines: From "Travel Vaccine" to Universal Vaccination — The Hepatitis A Story

Francis E. Andre

Introduction

Jaundice, because of its distinctive sign — yellow skin — must have been a feared malady since pre-historic times. Historically, Hippocrates is credited to have been the first to surmise that it had something to do with the liver. Epidemics of jaundice have been known throughout history to be the bane of military campaigns. What was almost certainly hepatitis A was, at first, called the jaundice of camps. Many battles and wars have been lost because soldiers went "yellow". The first records of outbreaks of jaundice in Europe date back to the 17th and 18th centuries. Between 1802 and 1874 more than 50 epidemics occurred.

In the USA the earliest recorded epidemic was in 1812. During the Civil War, Union troops were the main victims. Early in the 20th century it was recognized that sporadic and epidemic jaundice were the same disease probably caused by a virus. The military, because of the ravages wrought among its fighting men, have always taken a special interest in the condition, and looked for ways to prevent it. In the late 1930s, with proof of the efficacy of serotherapy for pneumococcal pneumonia and measles — and the fact that soldiers who recovered from an attack of jaundice were spared further trouble of that sort — prevention by the use of pooled gamma globulin was not only attempted but proven to be effective when administered before exposure or during the incubation period of the disease. Challenge experiments during the Second World War in the American and the British armies established that, what at the time were identified as "infectious hepatitis" and "serum hepatitis" were caused by different viruses that had "short" and "long" incubation periods. After the war, the Report No. 273 of the (British) Medical Research Council, published in 1951, suggested to call the two responsible viruses hepatitis A and B, respectively. Subsequently, other hepatitis viruses have been identified and, today, we talk about an alphabet of them being constructed, although this may be a slight exaggeration.

Aetiology of the Problem and the Response of Mankind

The cause of the hepatitis A problem was discovered in 1973, as the responsible virus had been finally visualized in the stools of a patient by immune electron microscopy. That discovery took a long time, although, in cosmic terms, that was only the flutter of an eyelid. Immediately after identification of the culprit, efforts to develop a vaccine started. Enough was known about immunity to hepatitis A to be reasonably certain that a vaccine was possible. The problem was that the virus could not be grown in tissue culture, the technique that had allowed the development, just before, of other vaccines like polio, measles, rubella and mumps. The only way at the time to replicate the virus was in humans or marmosets.

An attempt to develop a vaccine from the liver of infected marmosets was even started. But the major breakthrough came when scientists from Merck Sharpe and Dohme (MSD) managed, in 1979, to grow the virus in tissue culture. But the battle was only partly won, as the virus did not replicate efficiently enough to give sufficient yields of virus to make a potent vaccine. They, the MSD scientists, had then to make a choice between working on an inactivated or live vaccine. They decided to work on both approaches, as did some other groups, since with a similar virus, the poliovirus, both the Salk injectable (inactivated) vaccine (IPV) and the Sabin live (oral) vaccine (OPV) had been shown to be safe and effective after widespread use worldwide.

Rapid progress was made, since in May 1985 I heard a presentation on the first clinical results on an inactivated hepatitis A vaccine prepared by MSD. At the time, I was working for what is now GlaxoSmithKline Biologicals (GSK). They had also started work on the development of an inactivated vaccine. The first clinical study on the first candidate — based on the CLF strain (in the end abandoned) — of that manufacturer started in April 1988. The company then decided to switch to another strain — the HLM75 strain (it is not appropriate to go into the reasons of that decision here) — and the first administration of that vaccine to humans occurred in December 1988 in Leuven, Belgium. Just over 3 years later, at an international symposium held in Vienna, I had the privilege to announce, in front of most scientists who had made significant contributions, that the first vaccine against hepatitis A was available for use to prevent an ancient scourge of Man. The live vaccine approach was abandoned (except in China where a live vaccine — given by injection and not orally like the Sabin polio vaccine — is now widely used) when it was shown that the inactivated vaccine was not only safe but also highly efficacious. Four manufacturers currently produce that vaccine. Before going any further into the story of vaccine development and its use, and in order to set the scene, a description of the scientific background to that saga — the virology, epidemiology and immunology of the hepatitis A virus (HAV) — would be useful.

Virology and Epidemiology of HAV

HAV is a picorna virus that has been classified in its own genus, named Hepatovirus, because of some unique properties that differentiate it from other enteroviruses. Although wild HAV may replicate in a variety of human and other primate cells it grows to any extent only in human hepatocytes. From there, it gains entry, through the bile duct, to the gut and is then shed in faeces. Human faeces constitute the reservoir that is epidemiologically relevant. HAV is remarkably resistant to physicochemical inactivation. It can survive for many weeks in the environment. When it reaches the sea it can be concentrated in shellfish. The huge epidemic — there are more than 300,000 cases — that occurred in Shanghai during January 1988 was caused by the consumption of raw or inadequately cooked contaminated hairy clams. Inactivation of HAV by heat requires a temperature of 85°C for at least one minute. It will survive for weeks in dried faeces.

Although genetic heterogeneity has allowed delineation of four distinct genotypes, only one serotype exists. Thus only one strain of the virus is needed in a vaccine. Infection with HAV occurs when a non-immune individual ingests food, water or fomites contaminated by faeces from a person in the shedding phase of an HAV infection. Very rarely, it can also be transmitted iatrogenically through inoculation of blood products. However, spread of the virus in a population is essentially by the faecal–oral route or close contact with an infectious person since the main natural source of the virus is human faecal matter. Virus transmission is facilitated by poor sanitation and unhygienic practices and is therefore rampant in socio-economically underprivileged nations, communities and situations where human faeces are disposed in ways that allow contamination of food and drinking water. In such environments, exposure to the virus is almost inevitable and most children are infected, in most cases sub-clinically, before they reach the age of five. They become immune, as evidenced by the appearance of serum HAV antibodies that persist for life. These antibodies confer protection when administered as immune globulin. Naturally acquired immunity against re-infection is probably for life. Second attacks of the disease do not occur. Populations who live under circumstances where infection is highly endemic have a high level of natural immunity in all age groups. In communities with very good sanitation and hygienic habits, exposure to the virus may not happen until adult life. At that stage, exposure and infection may occur when a non-immune individual travels to a highly endemic area for pleasure or business. In populations with low levels of natural immunity until early or late adult life (which usually reflects infection in a distant less affluent past) the main route of infection is through close direct or indirect contact with an infected person, and only rarely by consumption of contaminated food or water. In the rest of the world, where infection occurs gradually with increasing age through both ingestion of contaminated food and water and close personal contact with persons excreting infectious virus the endemicity is described as being intermediate. Maps of the world showing, in different colors, areas of the world with "very low", "low", "intermediate" and "high" endemicities have been produced. However, this is an oversimplification of the real world where low and high endemicities may coexist next to each other in different communities of the same country. Furthermore, the situation has been changing rapidly in the last few decades and, because of improving socioeconomic conditions, many less developed countries are shifting from "high" to "intermediate" endemicities. A recent review of global anti-HAV seroprevalence shows that, apart from the poorest countries in Africa, levels of natural immunity are declining in all parts of the world. The socioeconomically privileged in many developing countries are already experiencing "intermediate" or even "low" endemicities. This trend, paradoxically, is bringing with it new dangers that plead in favour of more extensive immunization programs in countries or communities that can afford it.

Disease Burden

From seroprevalence surveys of anti-HAV it can be deduced that hepatitis A is one of the most prevalent viral infections in the world. On average, about 1.5 million cases are estimated by the World Health Organization to occur annually. However, because of under-reporting, the true disease incidence is undoubtedly very much higher. In the United States (US) a thorough study, which used a sophisticated mathematical model to estimate case incidence from observed age-adjusted seroprevalence rates, came to the conclusion that between 1980 and 1999 the true case incidence was 10.4 times that actually reported. In other parts of the world, the degree of under-reporting is unlikely to be lower. Estimation of global disease incidence is rendered difficult by the fact that infection results in clinical disease at very different frequencies depending upon age at infection. In childhood infection generally is asymptomatic, sub-clinical or mild. With advancing age infection more frequently causes disease of increasing severity and death, from fulminant hepatitis or complications, is no longer exceptional. The case-fatality rate for those above 40 years was 1% in 1995 in the USA. Clinical hepatitis A typically manifests itself 28 days (range: 15–50) after infection. It is an acute disease, characterized by the rapid onset of increasing fatigue, malaise, nausea, anorexia, vomiting, fever, myalgia and diffuse abdominal pain and diarrhoea (in children). This may be followed, within a few days to a week, by the appearance of dark urine, pale stools and jaundice. This symptomatology is no different from that experienced by patients suffering from other forms of hepatitis (B, C, D, E etc), and a specific laboratory diagnosis (detection of serum anti-HAV IgM) is necessary. The natural course of the disease varies but most patients start feeling better within a few weeks. Most will recover fully, although sometimes, after a convalescence of many months. In the 1988 epidemic in Shanghai, only 47 deaths occurred among 310,746 reported cases in mainly adolescents and young adults. Hepatitis A infection never leads to a chronic state but can progress to usually benign complications such as cholestatic jaundice, relapsing hepatitis and other rare extra-hepatic disorders. The most dreaded complication, with a high case-fatality rate, is fulminant hepatitis (which develops at an average rate of 1 per 10,000; with a wide range depending upon age in different series) that often requires heroic interventions like liver transplantation to save life. Hepatitis A has been identified as the predominant aetiology of acute hepatitis and fulminant hepatic failure in Argentina. In Latin America hepatitis A is recognized as a major cause of acute liver failure. A trustworthy estimate of deaths caused worldwide by HAV is not available. In future, the ongoing improvement of sanitation and hygiene in most parts of the world, will, paradoxically, result in a greater disease burden. This, in turn, will increase the need for more widespread vaccination.

Vaccine Development

As I was intimately involved in the development of the GSK hepatitis A vaccine — I was responsible for its clinical assessment — I will briefly recount how it was done. Work started in the early 1980s. It consisted mainly in selecting strains of the virus for their ability to replicate in tissue culture. They were adapted to grow in the MRC-5 cell line by serial passaging. The HM175 strain was finally chosen since adaptation had resulted in a satisfactory increase in antigen yield and a speeding up of the growth cycle. This crucial laboratory work to obtain suitable vaccine for the clinical testing of its safety and efficacy took about 6 years. The final vaccine is akin to IPV: it is a purified whole-virion aluminium-hydroxide-adsorbed preparation initially containing, for adults, 720 Elisa Units (El.U) of antigen and, for children, 360 El.U. These concentrations were subsequently doubled to allow the vaccination schedule to be reduced to two administrations from the three-dose schedule initially recommended. Commercial production of the vaccine is done in a purpose-built dedicated GMP facility.

Clinical testing of the HM175-based vaccine started in December 1988 with the following specific objectives:

- preliminary assessment of the clinical tolerance and immunogenicity of pilot lots of vaccine;
- recording of the frequency, severity and duration of solicited local and general signs and symptoms as well as spontaneously reported (unsolicited) signs and symptoms;
- evaluation of the "safety" of the vaccine, particularly with regard to the risk of hypersensitivity;
- assessment of the effect of aluminium hydroxide content (0.5 or 1.0 mg aluminium) in a vaccine dose on reactogenocity and immunogenicity;
- choice of an appropriate quantity of antigen per vaccine dose;
- comparison of different commercial scale vaccine lots in terms of reactogenicity and immunogenicity in order to confirm consistency of vaccine manufacture;
- evaluation of the serum anti-HAV response in terms of seroconversion rates and antibody levels attained using different vaccination schedules;
- determination of whether the vaccine can be administered simultaneously (at a different site) with Ig or hepatitis B vaccine;
- obtainment by indirect evidence, based on an analysis of the qualitative and quantitative aspects of the immune response, that the vaccine will protect at least as well as Ig;
- demonstration of the protective efficacy of vaccine in controlled randomized prospective field evaluation;

The clinical development program proceeded smoothly and quickly.

Satisfactory information was obtained regarding all objectives, and a registration dossier was submitted in mid-1991. The first country to grant a marketing authorization was Switzerland, in December 1991. At the launch symposium of the vaccine in Vienna, held on 27–29 January 1992, I reported that:

> Since December 1998…a total of 67 studies in 18 countries have been initiated. A total of 47,147 subjects, including 20,586 controls receiving hepatitis B vaccine or Ig, were recruited into these [ongoing] studies during which 55,259 doses of HM175-derived hepatitis A inactivated vaccine have, so far, been administered.

The vaccine was subsequently registered for sale in "many" countries. Below is a description of the properties of all registered hepatitis A vaccines and their policies in different parts of the world.

Vaccine Properties and Vaccination Policies

Protection conferred against infection by killed hepatitis A vaccine is mainly mediated by neutralizing antibodies. It is expected to last at least 25 years because of the slow decline of vaccine-induced antibodies and much longer — possibly for life — due to the induction of immunological memory and the long incubation period of the disease. Booster doses are thought to be unnecessary to maintain disease immunity. The response to the vaccine is blunted by the presence of pre-existing serum antibodies acquired from passive immunization with immunoglobulin or through the placenta. Consequently, the vaccine is licensed only after one year of age (2 years in the US) when maternally acquired antibody has largely disappeared. However, immunological memory is elicited even in the presence of maternal antibodies and the vaccine would, no doubt, be effective in infancy in environments where natural immunity is rare in women of childbearing age.

Vaccination policies can range from banning vaccine use to mandatory inoculation of everybody. The efficient strategy is to aim for maximal disease reduction with a minimum financial outlay. Any policy must also take into consideration other perceived needs, available resources and other possible beneficial interventions. However, given the availability of a safe and efficacious vaccine, it is obvious that reason dictates that it should be used as effectively as possible. In order to maximize the efficiency of a vaccination program, it is important to know the predominant ways in which the pathogen is spread within and between age groups and other sub-sections in a population, the period during which a pathogen is transmissible and its infectiousness. Age-related disease burden and peak incidence are also relevant parameters that influence what constitutes the most efficient policy. Characteristics of the vaccine that are critical include the duration of vaccine-induced protection, the earliest age at which it is efficacious and practical considerations like ease of administration and cost of delivery. Clearly it is not easy to choose an "optimal" policy. Computer-assisted modeling of epidemiological and economic parameters should, in defined situations, help to make an objective choice between possible policies. In the end, any recommended policy is a socio-political decision informed by economic considerations. Economic reasons were, no doubt, at the root of the timid policy of all public health authorities of restricting vaccine use to some population groups (like presumed non-immune travelers to high-endemicity regions, men who have sex with men, drug addicts, food-handlers who may spread the virus to their clients and individuals — such as patients with chronic liver disease — who may suffer more severe illness) and others deemed to be at high risk in spite of the fact that such high-risk groups were known to contribute, in total, only a minority of the cases in the general population.

Hepatitis A Vaccine and Travel

When first introduced, the vaccine was predominantly perceived as one for travelers from industrialized to developing countries, because they were likely to be non-immune and could afford to pay for it. Furthermore, hepatitis A had been identified through the work of prominent members of the Travel Medicine community as the most common vaccine-preventable disease in travelers. The vaccine manufacturers saw this as an easy and lucrative market to conquer and initially directed their promotional campaigns to that market segment. However, from the public health point of view, travelers represent a relatively small problem in most countries. For example, in the US, traveling abroad was the risk factor in <5% of indigenous cases. In Scandinavian countries the percentage was much higher. It was clear that, just as it had been shown for hepatitis B, the policy of immunizing only persons belonging to so-called high-risk groups would have a limited impact on disease incidence in a country, although those travelers who were at risk and wise enough to get themselves vaccinated obviously derived benefits.

Beginnings of Policy Change

It took some time and well-conducted epidemiological studies to establish the now generally accepted message that "sustained nationwide reductions in incidence are more likely to result from routine childhood vaccination than from targeted vaccination of high-risk groups", a simple truth that was also learnt slowly in the case of hepatitis B. In the case of hepatitis A, this conclusion is even more justified since the evidence that children are the main spreaders of the virus in the general population has gradually become more persuasive. An obvious hypothesis that begged to be tested is that interruption of virus circulation, through vacci-nation as early as possible in childhood, would result in a major reduction of virus trans-mission — and thus disease incidence — in the whole population, not by producing classical herd immunity but rather through the mechanism of "source drying".

Early Demonstration Projects

The protective efficacy of inactivated hepatitis A vaccine has been clearly demonstrated in two randomized double-blind field trials. The first hint that vaccine-induced community immunity could play a major role in overall reduction of hepatitis A disease incidence came in the demon-stration project in Slovakia where a large community-wide outbreak, which started in two villages in December 1991, was terminated by vaccination — in December 1992 — of pupils attending the common school. A more extensive proof of the effectiveness of vaccination was provided by the rapid state-wide elimination of hepatitis A in Alaska by the inocula-tion — between April and May 1993 — of only a single dose of vaccine.

Planned Mass Prevention Programs Carried Out

After the scientific proof of the wisdom of mass vaccination against hepatitis A was provided, several jurisdictions realized it was their socio-political duty to implement that strategy of control where local epidemiological and economical data — not to mention political motives — justified it. What follows is a chronological record of what has been done and achieved in the recent past.

Puglia, Italy

Puglia, a region in the southeast of Italy with a population of four million, experienced inter-mediate HAV endemicity until the 1990s. The main mode of transmission was identified as the consumption of shellfish. There were large epidemics in 1992 and 1996–1997. As from the end of 1997, a dose of hepatitis A vaccine at 15–18 months (simultaneously with MMR vaccine) and three doses at 12 years of the bivalent hepatitis A + B vaccine were administered. Epidemics have not occurred since and cases are now rare in the region. On the other hand, in an adjacent region, Campania, where routine vaccination was not performed, an outbreak with 615 cases occurred in 2004.

Catalonia, Spain

Catalonia, an autonomous province of Spain with 6 million inhabitants, started a program of vaccination against hepatitis B in schools in 1990. This program proved very successful since the coverage rate attained was >90% and it resulted in a reduction of ~80% in the incidence of hepatitis B in the 10–19 year age group over an 8-year follow-up. In Catalonia, the main mode of HAV transmission that has been identified in reported cases is person-to-person contact (31%) and ~50% of the cases were of unidentified source.

As the main brunt of the HAV disease burden is borne by adolescent and young adults and the initial recommendation of vaccinating only those individuals in high-risk groups (travelers, day-center staff, male homosexuals and others) would prevent at most 16% of cases, it was obvious to think of replacing the monovalent hepatitis B vaccine with the bivalent A + B vaccine. In September 1998, the switch-over was made, at first in pilot mode and later throughout the province. The outcome of this initiative has been shown to be highly beneficial. The reduction in disease incidence observed in the three years before (1996–1998) and after (1999–2001) the program started was statistically significant in all age groups of the population except the >60-year olds.

North Queensland, Australia

In the 1990s, hepatitis A reached the status of a "major public health problem" in North Queensland because two large epidemics occurred during the decade. It was only from 1996 that an enhanced surveillance system allowed the clear demonstration that indigenous people had a much higher incidence of disease than the non-indigenous (110 vs. 25 per 100,000 in 1996–1999). Three indigenous children had died of fulminant hepatitis A between 1993 and 1998. This situation demanded action. Starting in February 1999, free hepatitis A vaccine was offered at 18 and 24 months of age to indigenous children and a catch-up vaccination, up to their sixth birthday was carried out. In 2000–2003 the incidence rate dropped to 4.0 and 2.5 per 100,000, respectively, in the indigenous and non-indigenous populations of the region. The conclusion was that "a hepatitis A vaccination program targeting a high-risk population within a community can reduce disease incidence in the broader community".

Israel

In that country, epidemiologists convinced themselves that toddlers, most of whom attended day-care centers, were not only the nursery of HAV but also the main direct or indirect source of the virus for others in the whole population. Stopping virus transmission in that group could have a major impact on disease incidence in the country. In late 1996, an extended epidemic of hepatitis A had been halted by the vaccination of children aged 1–6 years. The government therefore decided to embark upon a national program to test the validity of the hypothesis since, furthermore, a pharmacoeconomic study had highlighted its financial advantages. On 1 July 1999, a free-of-charge program of mass vaccination for all toddlers aged 18 months — with a second dose scheduled at 24 months — started in the whole country. No vaccine was offered to the rest of the population who were therefore faced with having to pay privately for protection, a prospect that only a few relished. The implementation of the program was exemplary since the coverage attained in the target group was ~90%. Less than 10% of individuals in the rest of the population received vaccine. The outcome was stupendous. Three years after the start of the program, disease incidence had fallen to <5/100,000 in the whole population whereas before the program it had been at an average of 37.2 and 57.8 per 100,000 in, respectively, the Jewish and non-Jewish communities. The drastic disease reduction occurred not only in the vaccinated cohort but also in all age groups supporting the hypothesis that toddlers were the major transmitters of HAV in Israel.

United States

Inactivated hepatitis A vaccine became available in 1995 in the US. In 1996, the Advisory Committee on Immunization Practices (ACIP) recommended that it should preferentially be given to individuals at high risk of infection (travelers to countries with high or intermediate endemicity, men who have sex with men, injecting-drug users, patients with clotting-factor disorders) and patients with chronic liver disease who are prone to develop fulminant hepatitis A. It was also recommended to vaccinate children in communities with high rates of disease (Alaska Natives, American Indians, selected Hispanic and religious communities). On 1 October 1999, updated recommendations of ACIP were published. In addition to the 1996 recommendations it was stated that "children in states, counties, and communities with rates twice the 1987–1997 national average [20 per 100,000] or greater" should be vaccinated routinely, 11 states fell in that category. Whereas for those living where rates are between 10 and 20 per 100,000 — 6 states — routine vaccination should be "considered". The impact of these two successive ACIP recommendations on disease incidence in children and their communities has been well documented. First, among American Indians and Alaska Natives the hepatitis A rates "declined dramatically coincident with implementation of routine hepatitis A vaccination". Nationally, hepatitis A has declined to "historically low rates" and a thorough analysis of the vaccine coverage and disease notification data from vaccinating and non-vaccinating areas in the US have supported the conclusion that "much of the recent reduction of hepatitis A rates is attributable to immunization and that immunization has been associated with a strong herd immunity effect".

Is Elimination or Even Eradication of Hepatitis A Possible?

This possibility was discussed at the 1992 Vienna symposium but, at the time, all participants felt it was too early to consider it seriously. Elimination has probably been already achieved in Alaska and is within sight in some other parts of the world. Although it could be argued that elimination worldwide or even eradication is theoretically possible, the sensible position to take is not to "dream the impossible dream" and only hope that the disease will be gradually controlled "by improving living conditions in the developing world and the wise application of the existing vaccines in other areas". It is interesting to point out that a vaccine that started as one recommended essentially for non-immune travelers from developed to less-developed countries is now increasingly used for universal vaccination of whole birth cohorts.

References

André, F. E., Hepburn, A., & D'Hondt, E. (1990). Inactivated candidate vaccine for hepatitis A. *Prog. Med. Virol.*, *39*, 72–95.

André, F. E., D'Hondt, E., Delem, A., & Safary A. (1992). Clinical assessment of the safety and efficacy of an inactivated vaccine: rationale and summary of findings. *Vaccine*, *10*(Suppl.1), S160–S168.

André, F. E. (1995). Approaches to a vaccine against hepatitis A: Development and manufacture of an inactivated vaccine. *J. Infect. Dis.*, *171*(Suppl. 1), S33–S39.

André, F. E., Van Damme, P., Safary, A., & Banatvala, J. (2002). Inactivated hepatitis A vaccine: immunogenicity, efficacy, safety and review of official recommendations for use. *Exp. Rev. Vaccines*, *2002*, *1*(1), 9–23.

Banatvala, J. (1996). Epidemiology of hepatitis A (HAV) in Europe and its relationship to immunisation. In: Y. Buisson, P. Coursaget, & M. Kane (Eds), *Proceedings of the International Symposium on enterically-transmitted hepatitis viruses* (pp. 72–77). Tours, France: La Simarre.

Bell, B. P., & Feinstone, S. M. (2004). Hepatitis A vaccine. In: S. A. Plotkin, W. A. Orenstein (Eds), *Vaccines* (4th ed., pp. 269–297). Pennsylvania, USA: Elsevier Inc.

Dagan, D., Leventhal, A., Anis, E., Slater, P., & Shouval, D. (2005). Incidence of hepatitis A in Israel following universal immunization of toddlers. *JAMA*, *294*, 202–210.

Dominguez, A., Salleras, L., Carmona, G., & Batalla, J. (2003). Effectiveness of a mass hepatitis A vaccination program in preadolescents. *Vaccine*, *21*, 698–701.

Hanna, J. N., Hills, S. L., & Humphreys, J. L. (2004). Impact of hepatitis A vaccination of indigenous children on notifications of hepatitis a in North Queensland. *Med. J. Aus.*, *181*, 482–485.

Hilleman, M. R. (1993). Hepatitis and hepatitis A vaccine: A glimpse of history. *J. Hepatol.*, *18*(Suppl. 2), S5–S10.

Hollinger, F. B., André, F. E., & Melnick, J. (Eds). (1992). Proceedings of International Symposium on active immunization against hepatitis A. *Vaccine*, *10*(Suppl.1), S1–S176.

Innis, B. L., Snitbhan, R., Kunasol, P. et al. (1994). Protection against hepatitis A by an inactivated vaccine. *JAMA*, *271*, 28–34.

McMahon, B.J., Beller, M., Williams, J., et al. (1996). A program to control an outbreak of hepatitis A by using an inactivated hepatitis A vaccine. *Arch. Pediat. Adolesc. Med.*, *150*, 733–739.

Prikazsky, V., Olear. A., Cernoch, A., Safary, A., & André, F. E. (1994). Interruption of an outbreak of hepatitis A in two villages by vaccination. *J. Med. Virol.*, *44*, 457–459.

Steffen, R., Kane, M. A., Shapiro, C. N., et al. (1994). Epidemiology and prevention of hepatitis A in travellers. *JAMA*, *272*, 885–889.

Van Damme, P., Banatvala, J., Fay, O., et al. (2003). Hepatitis A booster vaccination: Is there a need? *Lancet*, *362*, 1065–1071.

Wasley, A., Samandari, T., & Bell, B. P. (2005). Incidence of hepatitis A in the United States in the era of vaccination. *JAMA, 294*, 194–201.

Wertzberger, A., Mench, B., Kuter, B., et al. (1992). A controlled trial of a formalin-inactivated hepatitis A vaccine in healthy children. *N. Eng. J. Med., 327*, 453–457.

Zuckerman, A. J. (1983). The history of viral hepatitis from antiquity to the present. In: F. Deinhardt, J. Deinhardt (Eds), *Viral hepatitis: Laboratory and clinical science* (pp. 2–32). New York: Marcel Decker.

Chapter 7

Required Travel Vaccinations: Yellow Fever — The Disease and the Vaccine

Chen Collins

Yellow fever (YF) is a viral disease endemic in Africa and the Americas, and is transmitted to monkeys or humans by infected mosquitoes of the *Aedes* (known also as the "Tiger" mosquito) and *Haemagogus* species. The natural YF cycle is mosquito-monkey-mosquito. The virus is taken up by the mosquito that feeds on susceptible monkeys or man. These mosquitoes are daytime biters. There are three types of transmission cycle: sylvatic (jungle), intermediate (humid savannah) and urban. All three cycles exist in Africa, but in South America, only sylvatic and urban YF occur.

Yellow fever is one of the three diseases notifiable under current International Health Regulations (IHR). YF is considered a public health emergency of international concern. IHR stipulate that member states are obliged to officially notify YF cases to the World Health Organisation. The registration of YF official cases began in 1950.

A YF vaccination certificate is now the only vaccination certificate that is required by IHR for international travel. Many countries require a valid international certificate of vaccination from travelers, arriving from infected countries or areas, including those in transit. Some countries require a certificate from all entering travelers, even those arriving from countries where there is no risk of YF. Although this exceeds the provisions of IHR, travelers may find that it is strictly enforced, particularly for people arriving in Asia from Africa or South America. The actual areas of YF virus activity far exceed the officially reported infected zone. IHR enforcement is based upon the severity of disease, the high degree of protection in vaccinated individuals and fear of introduction of YF to non-affected countries associated with international travel.

Symptoms

Most infected individuals remain asymptomatic while disease typically ranges from flu-like symptoms to severe hepatitis, hemorrhagic fever or death. Following an incubation period of

Travel Medicine: Tales Behind the Science
Copyright © 2007 by Elsevier Ltd.
All rights of reproduction in any form reserved.
ISBN: 0-08-045359-7

3–6 days, initial symptoms consist of fever, chills, headache, myalgia, backache, loss of appetite, nausea and vomiting. These symptoms usually subside within three to four days.

Approximately one person in six then enters a second, "toxic phase" characterized by recurrent fever, vomiting, listlessness, jaundice, kidney failure and profuse bleeding with up to half of these cases resulting in death. Fever is paradoxically associated with a slow pulse (Faget's sign). Bleeding can occur from the mouth, nose, eyes and/or stomach with blood appearing in vomit and faeces. Kidney function deteriorates with decreased urine output, which may be fatal. The mortality rate from the disease is approximately 10%, but during epidemics case fatality rates have reached as high as 50%. There is no specific treatment for YF except supportive care. There is, however, long lasting immunity in survivors.

Yellow fever is often difficult to diagnose and symptoms may be confused with malaria, typhoid, rickettsial diseases, other hemorrhagic viral fevers (e.g. Lassa), arboviral infections (e.g. dengue), leptospirosis, viral hepatitis and poisoning (e.g. carbon tetrachloride). Laboratory tests (serology) can detect YF antibodies that are produced in response to infection to confirm the diagnosis.

Epidemiology

Five hundred and eight million people in 33 countries from 15°N to 10°S of the equator are at risk of YF in Africa. Yellow fever is endemic in nine South American countries and in several Caribbean islands. Bolivia, Brazil, Colombia, Ecuador and Peru are considered at greatest risk. The disease is more prevalent during months with high rainfall, humidity and temperature, due to mosquito breeding cycles. In Africa, the incidence of disease is greatest at the end of the rainy season and early into the dry season.

There are 200,000 estimated cases of YF and 30,000 deaths annually. The actual number is likely to be higher due to misdiagnosis, poor surveillance and under-reporting. The YF virus (of the flavivirus group) is endemic (low levels of infection) in tropical areas of Africa and the Americas. The disease has not been reported in Asia for reasons that are still not clear but previous exposure to or infection with dengue appears to confer some protection against YF. However, this region is at risk because of the presence of appropriate primates and mosquitoes.

Outbreaks and Control

During YF epidemics, outbreak response vaccination campaigns are carried out with minimum delay in order to limit the spread of the disease. To prevent an epidemic in a country, at least 80% of the population must have immunity to YF. During the last 20 years the number of YF epidemics has risen and more countries are reporting cases. Mosquito numbers and habitats are increasing; and overseas travel to infected areas has become more common. In both Africa and the Americas, there is a large susceptible, non-immune population. Eighteen African nations have agreed to incorporate YF vaccine in their routine national vaccination programs where YF is endemic. This is more cost effective and prevents more cases (and deaths) than when emergency vaccination campaigns are carried out to control an epidemic.

History of the Disease

Yellow fever probably existed in Africa for thousands of years, being transmitted between monkeys and mosquitoes with man becoming infected as he explored and settled in tropical regions where the virus was present. When Europeans began to colonize western Africa, YF killed hundreds of settlers and the area became known as the "white man's grave". Expanding international trade along maritime routes facilitated the spread of the virus to other continents. Trade between Europeans and the West Indies with ships that contained cisterns of water and crowded conditions provided a natural habitat for the mosquito vector and the transmission of the virus.

Yellow fever epidemics occurred in almost every major port on the east coast of the United States for three and a half centuries and had a severe impact on several European cities. The earliest epidemics described were in Guadeloupe and in Yukatan in 1648. However, during the previous year scores of people died in Barbados in what was thought to be an outbreak of YF. An outbreak of YF is believed to have occurred in Havana in 1649 with severe mortality and in 1665 approximately 1,500 French troops died from the disease on the Caribbean island of St. Lucia.

During the slave trade in the 17th century the disease was brought from West Africa to Spanish–Portuguese America. "Yellow Jack" was described as one of the most dreaded diseases of the Atlantic shipping trade routes and was recorded by Sir Walter Scott in the legend of the "Flying Dutchman": "a yellow fever infected vessel was doomed to haunt the seas around the Cape of Good Hope as no port would allow the ship to dock and all the crew perished".

Yellow fever was a major cause of morbidity and mortality in Jamaica during the same period as described by Mary Manning Carley in Jamaica in her book, the "Old and the New": "The chief curse of Jamaica, yellow fever, which made the island a by-word for generations as a real 'white man's grave', was introduced with the slave trade from Africa, but was at its most virulent during the 18th century". Sir Frederick Treves in "The Cradle of the Deep," describes Admiral Venon's attack on Fort San Lazar in Cartagena in 1741 in which 179 were killed and 459 wounded but when YF broke out it left 500 of his sailors dead and 1,000 sick.

Admiral James Lind, a British naval physician and better known for his work on scurvy describes a case of fever aboard a naval vessel off the coast of Senegal in 1782, is thought to be the first recognized report of YF in Africa. The first clinical report on YF was published by Schotte in 1782 on the "Synochus Atrabiliosa" in Senegal in 1778.

Epidemics occurred in the 1700's in Italy, France, Spain and England. Between 1801 and 1821, there were nine epidemics in Spain, leading to 130,000 deaths. The West Indies, Central America and southern United States experienced repeated epidemics decimating populations and with severe implications on industry and trade.

Philadelphia

In 1793, Philadelphia experienced the largest YF epidemic in American history with approximately 5,000 deaths, amounting to approximately 10% of the population. Philadelphia was at that time the largest port city in the United States and the seat of the US Government.

Increasing numbers of political refugees from the Caribbean had recently arrived and thousands of Philadelphians, including prominent government officials like George Washington and Alexander Hamilton fled the city in the midst of the epidemic.

Dr. Benjamin Rush conferred with two other local doctors about a disease that he had observed over the last two weeks with symptoms that included fever, nausea, skin eruptions, black vomit, incontinence, jaundice and finally death. However, he noted that in many patients, symptoms resolved leading them to believe that they were cured. The remission of fever two to three days after the on-set of symptoms sent some people back to their jobs and into the streets only to drop dead later. The implications of YF infection were extremely demoralizing and as in the more recent AIDS epidemic, struck adults in their prime, victimizing many heads of families. Rush, however, noted that YF went on to affect persons of all ages and sectors of society and recorded the varieties, stages and severity of the disease.

Strong quarantine measures were instituted in New York and in other US cities against people fleeing from Philadelphia, turning them away at gunpoint in some places. Yellow fever epidemics occurred as far north as Portsmouth, N.H. and Charleston, S.C., which suffered more than 20 epidemics in as many summers, during the 18th century.

Maritime entrepreneur, Stephen Girard organized a fever hospital established at Andrew Hamilton's estate on Bush Hill, just outside Philadelphia. Matthew Carey published an account of the epidemic in: *A short account of the Malignant Fever, Lately Prevalent in Philadelphia*. Richard Allen and Absalom Jones of the African American community in their efforts to stem the epidemic wrote a pamphlet, *Narrative of the Proceedings of the Black People, During the Late Awful Calamity in Philadelphia*, which detailed the contributions of the African Americans during the epidemic.

Norfolk

A ship carrying persons infected with the YF virus arrived in Hampton Roads in southeastern Virginia in June of 1855. The disease spread quickly through the community, eventually killing over 3,000 people, mostly residents of Norfolk and Portsmouth. After two seamen died of YF during the voyage, the steamship *Ben Franklin* docked at Norfolk, Virginia. The port doctor, unaware of these deaths, allowed the ship to dock for repairs which resulted in 10,000 residents falling ill from the virus and 2,000 deaths. The military director of New York harbour, Dr. Lafayette Guild noted that isolating patients alone did not prevent the spreading of this infection, leading him to believe that YF was transmitted by a vector.

In 1878 there were 17,600 cases and 5,150 deaths from YF in Memphis Tennessee and during the same year, the Quarantine Law was signed by President Hayes giving the Marine Hospital Service authority to implement quarantine, intended to prevent entry of infectious diseases into the country via the ports.

New Orleans

About 2,000 of the 6,700 emigrants who sailed from France between 1717 and 1721 died shortly after arriving in Louisiana as a result of malaria, YF and dysentery. Yellow fever in Louisiana first appeared between 1769, when Governor-General Alejandro

Benjamin Rush

Image 7.1. Dr. Benjamin Rush.

O'Reilly' of Spain first claimed the land and 1796, the year of New Orleans's first major YF epidemic.

Yellow fever became known as the "black vomit" or the "saffron scourge," causing the deaths of over 8,000 people in 1853 in New Orleans or 1 out of every 15 people living there making it the one of the most devastating disasters ever to strike Louisiana. Early in the 19th century British visitor Thomas Ashe condemned misleading information that lured thousands to Louisiana "in search of a paradise only to find a grave, while those who survived suffered from a shattered constitution and debilitated frame."

Yellow fever invaded 132 towns in the United States, producing a loss of 15,932 lives and a cumulative number of cases of more than 74,000.

Cuba

In 1848, Josiah Clark Nott (1804–1973) of Alabama suggested that YF was spread by mosquitoes. Professor Stanford E. Chaille led the first investigatory commission to Havana, Rio de Janiero and the West Indies. George Miller Sternberg who became Surgeon General of US army and Juan Guiteras who later became director of Public Health for Havana concluded that the causative agent for YF was an environmental factor and consulted with the Cuban physician and epidemiologist C. J. Finlay (1833–1915). Giuseppe Sanarelli, an Italian scientist had earlier proposed in 1897 that Bacillus Iteroides was the causative agent of YF but epidemiological findings did not support this. Finlay wrote in 1881: "The mosquito hypothetically considered as the transmitting agent of yellow fever" which did not gain widespread support when presented at the Havana Academy of Sciences. However, Walter Reed later produced experimental evidence in human volunteers, in a controlled setting at Camp Lazear in Cuba. Jesse William Lazear and Clara Maass deliberately allowed themselves to become infected with the virus and died as a result of the disease.

The American Yellow Fever Commission headed by army surgeon Major Walter Reed (1851–1902), acting assistant Surgeons Major James Carroll, Major Jesse W. Lazear and Major Aristides Agramonte, was set up in Cuba during the Spanish–American war. In September 1900, the Reed Commission proved conclusively that (a) the mosquito was the vector of YF, (b) there was an interval of about 12 days between the time that the mosquito took an infectious blood meal and the time it could convey the infection to another human being, (c) YF could be produced experimentally by the subcutaneous injection of blood taken from the general circulation of a infected patient during the 1st and 2nd days of his illness; and (d) YF was not transmitted by fomites.

The Cuban capital of Havana benefited from an extremely aggressive effort by the US forces stationed there. Stagnant puddles and ponds, where the mosquito larvae mature were drained or treated with oil to kill the larvae. Not only was YF eliminated, but malaria transmission was also greatly reduced.

Image 7.2. Dr. Reed's bold experiments proved that YF was indeed spread by the bite of the mosquito *Aedes aegypti*.

Reed proposed that YF could be most efficiently controlled by anti-mosquito measures. The commission also demonstrated for the first time that a filterable virus caused a specific human disease.

The Reed Commission findings were applied in 1900 by Colonel William Crawford Gorgas (then chief sanitary officer for the department of Cuba) to end long standing epidemics in Havana and Panama. There were 310 YF deaths in 1900 and 18 in 1902. While YF had been eliminated in Cuba it was still present in the southern United States. Certain Central American countries have responded well to outbreaks of YF, with intense mosquito control while environmental concerns about the use of pesticides make it difficult to conduct the wide-scale aerial spraying and mosquito control in the southern United States.

A century before the disease was defeated in Cuba, it had defeated Napoleon. When slaves led by Toussaint L'Ouverture revolted on the island of Santo Domingo, Napoleon sent a force of 33,000 to put it down. Within a few months, YF had killed 30,000 French soldiers, leading to the foundation of independence of Haiti and forced Napoleon to give up his ambitions for the Americas.

Panama Canal

The Panama Canal is around 80 km long and links the Pacific and Atlantic Oceans, running across the center of Panama. Locks at the Pacific and Atlantic ends of the canal either lower vessels to sea level or raise them up to the canal.

The construction of the Panama Canal was the miracle of the beginning of the 20th century but only succeeded once malaria and YF control based on an integrated mosquito control program were enforced by the military. The Panama Canal construction project was abandoned by the French in 1889 after expending about $26 million and losing more than 22,000 lives to the YF mosquito. The Isthmus of Panama was an ideal environment for mosquitoes. The high temperature varies little during the year. The rainy season lasts for 9 months and the interior of the Isthmus is tropical jungle, ideal for mosquito breeding. An integrated program of mosquito control was installed with an emphasis on drainage, bush and grass cutting and oiling.

Image 7.3. Colonel William Crawford Gorgas.

Image 7.4. Screening and isolation of malaria and YF patient in the Panama
Canal region.

The United States began its effort to construct the Panama Canal in May 1904, after
signing a treaty with the newly formed nation of Panama and buying out the French for
40 million dollars. The Sanitary Department was formed and headed by Colonel Gorgas.
The canal was completed and officially opened in 1914. There are presently approximately
14,000 ships traveling through it every year. The total financial cost to the American
government was around $375 million, but with approximately 25,000 deaths (mainly due
to malaria and YF) during the construction period.

Vaccine Developments and Control of Epidemics

In 1927, Dr. A. F. Mahaffy managed to transmit YF to an animal other than man using blood
from a YF patient into a rhesus monkey confirming that the infection was transmitted from
monkey to monkey, or from man to monkey by *Aedes aegypti* mosquitoes. He also showed
that mosquitoes once infected remained infective for the entire period of their lives, and that
the bite of a single infected mosquito was sufficient to produce a fatal infection in a monkey.
    Sawyer and colleagues at the Rockerfeller Institute in USA in 1928 showed through cross-
immunity tests of YF virus, (Asibi, French, Brazilian) that all three virus strains produced

protective antibodies in rhesus monkeys. This led to the development of a YF vaccine. Max Theiler, working in Harvard, before joining Sawyer, developed an attenuated YF virus using mouse brains and published these findings in 1930 which became the basis for the attenuated YF vaccine. The vaccine had two parts: a 10% suspension of mouse-brain tissue with YF virus in fresh sterile human serum, and human immune serum from people recently recovered from YF. Dr. D. Bruce Wilson, recently back from Brazil, after volunteering to be vaccinated, showed a positive immune response without any adverse reaction and over the next 4 years, all laboratory staff were immunized protecting against occupationally induced infections.

Theiler and Sawyer from 1931 to 1936 made use of a "mouse protection test" for mapping the disease, mixing serum from people in YF areas, with a laboratory virus and injecting it into mouse brains. If the mouse did not develop encephalitis, it indicated that the serum donor had had YF at some point; the donor's YF antibodies had protected the mouse.

Two live attenuated YF vaccines were developed in the 1930s; the French neurotropic vaccine from human virus passaged in mouse brain and the 17D vaccine (Asibi strain) from human virus passaged in embryonated chicken eggs.

The French neurotropic vaccine was developed in 1932 and between 1939 and 1952 over 38 million doses were administered in French West Africa, in accordance with a departmental order. This caused a marked decline in the incidence of YF in those countries, while during the same period there were major epidemics in the British colonies of Nigeria, (1925–1926), Ghana (1926–1927, 1937), and the Gambia (1934–1935), which had not implemented a policy of preventive immunization. Gambia then instituted mass routine vaccination after its 1979/1980 epidemic and later incorporated YF vaccine into its childhood immunization program with a reported 85% vaccine coverage in 2000. No cases have been reported since 1980, yet the virus remains present in the environment. Due to a high incidence of encephalitic reactions in children, the manufacture of the neurotropic vaccine was discontinued in 1980. Post vaccine encephalitis rates in Nigeria were 3–4/1000 vaccinations, mainly in children, with a case-fatalty rate of 38%.

The 17D vaccine (Asibi strain) human virus was developed in 1936. Fifty nine thousand doses of this vaccine were administered in Brazil in response to an epidemic in 1938. Mild adverse reactions were reported in 10–15% of recipients and more severe reactions in 1–2%. In 1940, human sera was added to the vaccine which led to a major outbreak of hepatitis in US military recruits in 1942.

Serological surveys helped to map the areas in Africa where YF had occurred. Van Campenhout, in 1928, carried out extensive serological testing in the former Belgian Congo and found that most persons testing positive were asymptomatic. Outbreaks were invariably urban or peri-urban and followed the arrival of large numbers of nonimmune immigrants, or other mass population movements.

The largest YF epidemic ever recorded was in Ethiopia in 1960–1962, affecting 10% of the 1 million residents and resulting in 30,000 deaths. *Aedes africanus* and *Aedes simpsoni* mosquitoes were implicated in monkey-to-monkey and low-level monkey-to-human transmission.

In 1965, an epidemic of YF occurred in a dry savannah region of Senegal. Two hundred and forty three cases were officially reported but the true incidence was more likely to be 20,000, and case fatality rate of 10%. Serological surveys suggested that at least 13% of the urban population had been infected.

As a result of an intensive vaccination campaign, there were 248 cases of vaccine associated encephalitis and the manufacture of the French neurotropic vaccine was suspended in 1982. However, in 1988, the Joint WHO/UNICEF Technical Group on Immunization in Africa recommended incorporation of YF vaccine (17D) in routine childhood immunization programs in countries at risk for YF.

Since 1965, approximately eight million doses of 17D-derived vaccine have been administered to US travelers and approximately 300 million doses have been administered to persons in areas where YF is endemic with a very low incidence of adverse reactions.

The Current Vaccine

Yellow fever is preventable by a relatively safe, effective vaccine. Immunization provides immunity within 1 week in 95% of those vaccinated. The live, attenuated 17D-204 and 17DD YF strains are the most commonly used YF vaccines.

Vaccination is highly recommended for travelers to high-risk areas. A vaccination certificate is required for entry to many countries, particularly for travelers arriving in Asia from Africa or South America. Deaths from YF have been reported in unvaccinated tourists. The 17D-204 and 17DD YF vaccines are among the safest and most effective viral vaccines. Since 1965, approximately eight million doses of 17D-derived vaccine have been administered to US travelers and approximately 300 million doses have been administered to persons in areas where YF is endemic. Although 2–5% of persons who receive vaccine report minor adverse reactions, less than 1% report having to change their daily activities.

However, YF vaccine contains live virus, and because of the theoretical risk of vaccine-associated illness, it is contra-indicated for children under 9 months of age, pregnant women and immuno-suppressed individuals, such as those with AIDS or cancer patients receiving immuno-suppressive medications (who should avoid traveling to areas where YF is endemic).

Adverse Reactions

Adverse reactions to the vaccine are usually mild and include headache, myalgia, low-grade fevers or other minor symptoms that may begin within days after vaccination and last 5–10 days after vaccination. Immediate hypersensitivity reactions, characterized by rash, urticaria or difficulty in breathing are uncommon (less than 1 case per 131,000 vaccinees). Egg or chicken allergies or hydrolyzed gelatin used to stabilize the vaccine may be responsible for hypersensitivity reactions.

Most severe YF vaccine-associated adverse events reported following introduction of the vaccine were among infants, and presented as encephalitis. Since 1952, 21 cases of vaccine-associated neurotropic disease have been reported in children or adolescents. Fifteen of these cases occurred prior to 1960, thirteen of which occurred in infants 4 months of age or younger, and two of which occurred in infants 6 and 7 months old. One three-year-old died of encephalitis, and a genetic variant of the vaccine virus was isolated from the brain tissue. This is the only verified fatality due to YF vaccine-associated neurotropic disease. Three other cases of vaccine-associated neurotropic disease since 1960 have occurred in the adults.

A study in Senegal described two fatal cases of encephalitis possibly associated with 17D-204 vaccine following the vaccination of 67,325 children between the ages of 6 months and 2 years.

However, since 1992, five cases of encephalitis and ten cases of autoimmune neurological diseases in adult travelers who received YF vaccine, have been reported to the US Vaccine Adverse Event Reporting System (VAERS). All patients had an onset of illness 4–23 days following vaccination; and they were all first-time vaccine recipients in prior good health. The risk for vaccine-associated neurological disease is estimated to range from 4 to 6 cases per 1,000,000 doses.

Since 1996, nine travelers with YF vaccine-associated viscerotropic disease (YEL-AVD), previously known as febrile multi-organ failure, a disease clinically and pathologically resembling naturally acquired YF, have been reported in the US. An additional 17 cases have been identified worldwide. All the US cases required intensive care after experiencing fever and extremely severe symptoms. Nine of these required dialysis for renal failure and six (67%) cases were fatal. The incidence of vaccine-associated viscerotropic disease is estimated to be from 3 to 5 cases per 1,000,000. Studies are being conducted to clarify the cause and risk factors for these rare adverse events associated with the YF vaccines. The risk for adverse reactions appears to be age-related, being higher in infants and in those over age 60.

Recently, a history of thymus disease has been identified as a contraindication to YF vaccine. Four (15%) of the 26 vaccine recipients with YEL-AVD worldwide have had a history of diseases involving the thymus, all of which are extremely rare, suggesting that compromised thymic function may be another independent risk factor for vaccine-associated visceotropic disease.

In light of the recent reports of severe adverse reactions and vaccine-associated deaths, the risk of disease in the traveler in conditions of negligible risk (e.g. travelers in transit) should be weighed against any potential risks of vaccine-associated reaction.

Conclusion

Although an effective vaccine has been available for 60 years, the number of people infected over the last two decades has increased, and YF is now a serious public health issue again.

International regulations require proof of vaccination for travel to and from certain counties. Travelers should receive a completed International Certificate of Vaccination, signed and validated with the physician's stamp from where the vaccine was given.

Recent studies of adverse events, in travelers receiving the vaccine, revealed severe and fatal events despite the perception of its safety. This should lead to more precise recommendation for vaccine usage and/or to development of a safer vaccine.

References

Agramonte, A. (undated). *The indside of a great medical discovery*. Available at: http://www.worldwideschool.org/library/books/tech/medicine/YellowFever/Chap1.htlm.

Arnebeck, B. (1999). *Destroying angel: Benjamin Rush, yellow fever and the birth of modern medicine.* Available at: http://www.geocities.com/bobarnebeck/fever1793.html.

Cetron, M., et al. (2002). *Yellow fever vaccine recommendations of the Advisory Committee on Immunization Practices (ACIP).* MMWR Nov 8, 2002/51(RR17), pp. 1–10. Available at http://www.cdc.gov/MMWR/preview/mmwrhtml/rr5117a1.htm.

Cox, F. E. (Ed). (1996). *Illustrated History of Tropical Diseases* (pp. 143–147), The Wellcome Trust, London.

The Great Fever-Timeline of Yellow Fever in America. (2006). Available at: http://www.pbs.org/wgbh/amex/fever/timeline/index.html.

Vainio, J., & Cutts F. (1998). Yellow fever. WHO division of emergency and other communicable disease surveillance and control. Global Programme for Vaccines and Immunization. Expanded Programme on Immunization. World Health Organization, Geneva. Available at: http://www.who.int/vaccines-documents/DocsPDF/www9842.pdf.

Chapter 8

Remote Travel Vaccines: The Undulating Fortunes of Typhoid Vaccines

Eyal Meltzer and Eli Schwartz

Preface

About 50 millennia ago, a strain of Salmonella had the misfortune of suffering a severe genetic defect (Kidgell et al., 2002). With a single stroke (technically known as a frameshift), a great many of its genes were inactivated. The organism was left with the ability to infect a single mammalian species — man. However, from this dubious beginning, the bacterium, hand in hand with the exploding human population, forged a great career, becoming one of the great scourges in history, a truly cosmopolitan disease.

A brief overview of this history is presented here, with details on its eradication in some parts of the world, and how the evolution of vaccines influenced the fortunes of travelers — both in war and in peace.

Early Days

For most of its history, typhoid was an anonymous offender. Together with many other conditions and particularly malaria, it was simply noted as "Fever". However, tantalizing details of case descriptions from ancient times suggest that it affected even the most illustrious. For example, a reading of Alexander the Great's last illness, as told in the *Anabasis of Alexander* by Arrian, has led scholars to conclude that he probably died from typhoid (Kidgell, 1998). The list of illustrious probable victims is long, and may include the Emperor Augustus, Saint Louis IX of France, Evangelista Torricelli, Franz Schubert, and many others.

It was in 17th century England that typhoid was first described as a specific entity, differentiating it from other conditions called "typhus" (marked by fever and a cloudy sensorium — the Greek "tuphos" from which the name is derived). Thomas Willis, the great neuroanatomist, in his *De Febribus* in 1659 is credited to have been the first to give a classical description of typhoid, which ravaged the armies fighting the English civil war. During the same era, Jamestown, the first English colony in North America, was decimated where it was thought that 6000 people died of typhoid.

Although the disease had lost its anonymity (in fact it had acquired a great many names including typhus entericus, putrid fever), two centuries were to pass before its mode of transmission was established.

Typhoid in Europe and America up to the End of the 19th Century

During the first part of the 19th century, and largely through the impetus of the recurring cholera epidemics, the Sanitary Idea was promoted. From the 1830s to the 1890s a great revolution took place, convincing the medical profession and then subsequently the population that cleanliness, and especially clean water, was indeed next to godliness.

The contagious nature of typhoid and the special role played by water and food (especially dairy products) were recognized, credited in large part to the work of William Budd MD who was a general practitioner in England (Moorhead, 2002). Working in the Bristol region, he recognized both person-to-person transmission and waterborne disease. Budd urged for more disinfection and water treatment.

Although typhoid was never as notorious as cholera, the disease burden was not insignificant; it was the second most prevalent infectious cause of mortality after tuberculosis. Many of these cases were in children, making the frequent fatalities all the more tragic. Many leaders and luminaries had lost children to typhoid, among them Charles Darwin, Louis Pasteur, Abraham Lincoln, Stonewall Jackson, Robert E. Lee, and others. The most notable cases of typhoid during this period occurred in the British royal family: the Prince Consort, Prince Albert of Saxe-Coburg and Gotha, whose death from typhoid had a major effect on the course of Queen Victoria's reign; and when the Prince of Wales nearly succumbed to the disease a decade after his father, typhoid's notoriety reached new heights.

The Victorian zeal for sanitation, born in response to cholera and typhoid, was to produce rapid results. Typhoid mortality dropped markedly — by 57% from 1875 to 1879. As was commented by the statistician Longstaff in 1884: "the fall in the death rate of (typhoid) fever is without doubt the great triumph of the sanitary reformers" (Longstaff, 1884).

Typhoid Bacillus Identified: First Vaccine Devised

With novel epidemiological tools, and an ongoing improvement in sanitation, incidence rates of typhoid in industrialized countries began to fall. Still, in those pioneering days of bacteriology and vaccinology, the hope was to find a way to eliminate typhoid altogether.

The typhoid bacillus was first isolated in 1880 by Carl J. Eberth and further developments were soon to follow. It was first grown in pure culture by GTA Gaffky in 1884. In 1896, a method of serological diagnosis was described by Georges Vidal, and in the same year the first heat-inactivated typhoid vaccine was launched. It is an open question as to who was the first to devise the vaccine: Richard Pfeiffer, a colleague of Koch who worked in Germany or Almroth Write who worked in the British Army's medical school at Netley. It was Write, however, who aggressively promoted the use of the vaccine — after having first tested it on himself (Groschel & Hornick, 1981). Unfortunately, in his zeal he conducted unofficial trials of the vaccine in India, which, although successful, caused an uproar.

The immediate interest in the new typhoid vaccine came from the military and the colonial authorities in Europe and America; for while great strides in sanitation and infection control were made at home by these nations, in their tropical colonies, typhoid was still prevalent. In India, for example, it was the leading cause of infectious death among Europeans, especially children; its incidence at the turn of the century actually increased, which probably reflected the diminishing exposure at home in Europe, and therefore a decrease in immunity (Guha, 1993).

Typhoid Fever During War

Two wars that occurred at the turn of the century exposed the need for typhoid vaccine. During the Spanish–American War (1898), typhoid accounted for 87% of the total deaths from disease and 82% of all sickness. A year later, the Boer War broke out. The British army was ill equipped and hygienic conditions were bad. As a result, more soldiers suffered from typhoid fever than from battle wounds: 13,000 men lost to typhoid, as compared to 8000 battle deaths. Almroth Wright promoted the universal vaccination of British soldiers. The vaccination was carried out on a voluntary basis, and again, poor recording kept the controversy as to the vaccine's efficacy going. Furthermore, in one of the earliest precursors of meta-analysis, the validity of his results was called into question by Pearson, the leading statistician of the time. Eventually, William Leishman, who succeeded Wright at Netley, in a well-conducted trial, was able to corroborate Wright's results: nearly 10,000 soldiers destined for the tropics were voluntarily vaccinated and followed for at least 2 years, as were nearly 9000 unvaccinated soldiers. The results showed an efficacy of 80–90% for two years (Anonymous, 1914).

Such impressive results led to the adoption of voluntary vaccination in the British army, and universal compulsory vaccination in the German, American, and other armies of the time.

By this time it was apparent that a significant percentage of clinical typhoid was in fact caused by closely related bacteria, *Salmonella paratyphi* A&B, and attempts to provide total protection against enteric fever have resulted in "triple typhoid" or TAB vaccine.

The great test of typhoid vaccination was during World War I. During the bitter trench war that developed in 1915 and the poor sanitary conditions that accompanied it, outbreaks of typhoid were severe. Although typhoid vaccination was voluntary in the British army, it was made compulsory with the moral support of Sir William Osler (whose address to the military "Bacilli and bullets" was circulated as a pamphlet). The French army suffered severely from typhoid during 1915, as most of the troops were not vaccinated. When the typhoid vaccine was adopted, mortality declined, but morbidity from paratyphoid was still significant. When the TAB vaccine was introduced in 1916, this morbid condition was nearly eliminated as well. By the end of the war, the incidence of typhoid among those in the armed forces was significantly lower that in the civilian population.

Thus, by the end of the war, there was a consensus that while the vaccine did not prevent all cases of typhoid it was highly effective, at least for two years after its administration. With the general decline of typhoid in Western countries, the use of typhoid vaccination was now restricted mainly to those civilians and soldiers traveling to the less-developed regions of the world.

Migration and Vaccine: Lessons Learned in Palestine

A little known story that illustrates some of the problems regarding typhoid vaccination at this period relates to the history of typhoid in Palestine. The Jewish immigration to Palestine was one of the largest movements of people from a developed to an underdeveloped region of the world. When the British army conquered Palestine and the British mandate was established, the new authorities had little information about the epidemiology of the country. When large-scale Jewish emigration began in 1922 and many cases of typhoid were reported, the hasty conclusion was that the disease was surely imported, and typhoid vaccination became mandatory for all immigrants. Continued epidemics occurred however despite this measure, although a disproportionate number of the cases indeed occurred among the newly arrived immigrants. A formal commission of enquiry was established in 1926, and its conclusions were clear. The disease was in fact highly endemic in Palestine, and poor sanitation and crowding were the real reasons for explosive epidemics. It was therefore clear that by inoculating only those newly arrived to the country this hyperendemic state could not be remedied. Also, it was clear that in conditions of heavy exposure the vaccine was not very effective.

Within two decades, the much improved sanitary condition among the Jewish population made for a different situation altogether: when typhoid vaccination drives were instituted in the 1940s, with the nearly universal and repeated vaccination of children, the disease incidence decreased markedly. Within the next two decades and despite the absorption of more than half a million new immigrants, typhoid incidence dropped to levels that were similar to those of many European nations. These low rates were maintained ever since, and long after mass typhoid vaccination was discontinued in the mid 1950s.

The problems of typhoid prevention, as seen in Palestine, mirror to a great degree many of the problems still facing travelers today, despite the many changes in vaccine formulation in the last 80 years.

Current Status

Typhoid fever, which is a fecal–oral transmissible disease, occurs in environments where there is overcrowding, poor sanitation, and inadequate water treatment. Humans are the only known reservoir; and transmission occurs through food and water contaminated by the acutely ill or by chronic carriers of the organism. As mentioned above, it had a worldwide distribution that included the Western world (the United States and Europe) until early in the 20th century. In the United States the number of typhoid cases fell from 35,994 in 1920 to an average of 500 cases annually in the 1990s. Changes in sanitation and hygiene have been largely

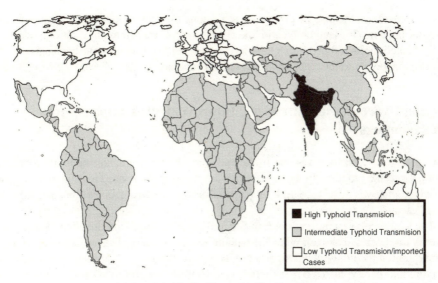

Map 8.1. Typhoid world distribution.

responsible for this dramatic decrease. It is difficult to obtain accurate data on disease burden in developing countries since the diagnosis of typhoid fever is often a clinical one, without blood culture confirmation, and most patients are treated as outpatients.

Annual incidence rates of up to 198 per 100,000 in the Mekong Delta Region in Vietnam and 980 per 100,000 in Delhi, India, have recently been reported. According to the best global estimates, there are at least 16 million new cases of typhoid fever each year with 600,000 deaths. The greatest burden of the disease is in Asia where 13 million cases are assumed with 400,000 deaths annually. There has been a rise in cases since the 1990s.

In developed countries where typhoid fever used to be endemic, there have been two major changes in the pattern of disease. One is a marked decline in incidence in the past half century and the other is that the disease has become predominantly a travel-associated disease in industrialized countries. In the United States, for example, the annual incidence dropped from 7.5 per 10^5 in 1940 to 0.2 per 10^5 in the 1990s, and the proportion of cases related to foreign travel increased from 33% in 1967–1972 to 81% in 1996–1997 (Connor & Schwartz, 2005). In Israel the change was even more marked with an annual incidence of 90 per 100,00 in the early 1950s that had dropped to 0.23 per 100,000 in 2003; from which 57% of cases were acquired abroad. Altogether the range of reported annual incidence in industrialized countries in the last decade is from 0.13–1.2 per 100,000, with an over-whelming majority being imported cases.

The risk for travelers also appears to vary according to the geographic region visited. Reports from several industrialized countries indicate that the risk in travel to the Indian subcontinent is significantly higher than for travel to any other geographic region.

As expected, not adhering to food and water precautions and not receiving pre-travel consultation, as well as a longer duration of travel or travel to rural areas, increases the risk of acquiring the disease. However a recent report analyzing typhoid cases acquired abroad demonstrated that 5% of the cases were travelers who had a short stay of less than a week, and in some cases the disease even occurred among upscale travelers (i.e., businessmen to five-star hotels). This fact, along with the significant increase in multi-antibiotic resistance of the bacterium including to the Quinolones, an excellent drug we have been using for the last decade, points to the necessity of a typhoid vaccine.

Typhoid Vaccines for Travelers: Improvements Coupled with Shortcomings

The current world situation is that in the endemic areas typhoid vaccine is not part of the national vaccine program. In the developed countries there is no need for this vaccine. Thus, a vaccine that was developed and widely used in the Western countries became strictly a travel vaccine.

The whole-cell vaccine was the first one to be used and was introduced in the early 20th century (as described above). When the typhoid vaccine was adopted, mortality declined, but paratyphoid infection was still significant. However, when the TAB vaccine (combination of typhi and paratyphi A+B) was introduced in 1916, the morbidity (studied in military setting) was nearly eliminated. Due to their significant adverse effects, both these vaccines are no longer available.

The complex nature of the pathogenesis of *S. typhi* clinical infection has spurred the development of two primary types of vaccines: parenteral vaccines that take advantage of the protective role of the circulating antibody response and live attenuated oral vaccines that have relied upon vigorous secretory IgA response and cell-mediated immunity to eliminate intracellular bacilli. Both vaccines are safe and relatively well tolerated.

The live oral vaccine is an attenuated *S. typhi* strain, Ty21a, which is a mutant of Ty2. It is avirulent (lacking the Vi antigen) but contains immunogenic cell wall polysaccharides. Primary vaccination consists of one enteric-coated capsule or lyophilized sachet to be taken on alternate days for three to four doses. It causes a vigorous secretory IgA and cell-mediated response. The live attenuated vaccine is theoretically contraindicated in pregnancy and in those with cell-mediated immunosuppression. In addition, the concurrent use of antibiotics or antimalarials may interfere with the antibody response. This vaccine needs to be refrigerated, cannot be given to children under 6 years of age, and relies on the traveler's compliance to complete the three to four required doses. All travel medicine practitioners are familiar with the endless queries as to what to do when travelers forget to keep the vaccine in the refrigerator for several hours (or days) or take it as scheduled every other day. This issue leaves both the traveler and practitioner in a quandary.

The Vi vaccine is the purified capsular polysaccharide antigen. The Vi antigen is the virulence antigen that allows *S. typhi* to survive in blood leading to septicemia. The Vi vaccine contains only the Vi component of *S. typhi* and gives a rapid brisk seroconversion following one dose. However, as a polysaccharide vaccine there is no boosting effect from revaccination, and the duration of protection appears to be between 2 and 3 years. A new *S. typhi* Vi conjugate vaccine has been developed, conjugating Vi to a carrier protein enhancing its immunogenicity; however, this vaccine was never tested in travelers.

A major drawback of vaccine efficacy trials has been that both the oral and the parenteral vaccines have been tested in field trials in endemic countries and among local populations, while the consumers are travelers. The relevance of its efficacy among the local population to its efficacy in travelers is unknown!

The Vi vaccine efficacy field trials in endemic areas such as Nepal showed an overall protective efficacy of 74%, while in South Africa only 55% protective efficacy was noted.

The live oral vaccine, Ty21a, immunogenicity and efficacy studies have also only been performed in typhoid-endemic countries. In a meta-analysis of published studies, the over-all protective efficacy was 71%, ages 5 through 9, and 63%, ages 10 through 14.

However, efficacy data for travelers is sparse, and applying the efficacy results of endemic countries to the traveler population might be inaccurate in several respects. On the one hand, the local population might be better protected due to naturally acquired immunity. On the other hand, the unique phenomenon of typhoid immunity is that it can be overcome by a high inoculum. Those travelers who try to avoid contaminated foods might be better protected. A large-scale study of typhoid vaccine among travelers is not feasible due to the low infection rate.

However, in a retrospective assessment done in Nepal, vaccinated travelers demonstrated a 95% vaccine efficacy. This study was conducted in the CIWEC clinic in Kathmandu (see Chapter 20) in the late 1980s. In this clinic we took care of all foreign travelers, and during a major outbreak in the Kathmandu valley (1987–1988), we diagnosed large number of typhoid cases (proven by culture) among travelers. To our great surprise, the rate of typhoid among Israelis was almost 20 times higher than other Western travelers. A parallel study showed that while among most Westerners the vaccination rate was 90–100%, among the Israelis it was less than 5%.

Thus, calculating the high attack rate of 21 per 10,000 among Israelis, who were not vac-cinated versus the attack rate of 1.2 per 10,000 among the other travelers, most of whom were vaccinated, gave us the result of about 95% efficacy (Schwartz & Shlim, 1990; Schwartz et al., 1990). (However, one should not forget the limitations of a retrospective analysis.)

It was found that at that period the Ministry of Health (MOH) of Israel did not recom-mend the use of typhoid vaccine, and the vaccine was not available in Israel. Thus, in addi-tion to the scientific merit gained by this study, a change of policy was adopted by the Israeli MOH in recommending the vaccine for travelers. In fact, a recent study done by us among Israeli travelers showed that the attack rate, which was 21 per 10,000 travelers to Nepal, dropped to 0.8 per 10,000 (Meltzer et al., 2005). Although a cause and effect relationship cannot be concluded, it is difficult to otherwise explain this decline.

Treating returning travelers with typhoid fever highlights a major disadvantage of both vaccines, which is the lack of protection against *S. paratyphi* infection. In the same study in Nepal it was shown that a switch in pathogens was noted amongst vaccinated travelers. While *S. paratyphi* A accounted for 33% of cases in the non-immunized group (similar to the rate among local population), among the vaccinated patients *S. paratyphi* A was found in the majority of cases, that is to say 67%. Since then several other studies have shown this change in trend of seeing more and more cases of paratyphi A, mainly in the vacci-nated travelers.

Although *S. paratyphi* infection is commonly perceived as being a milder form of typhoid infection, a previous study on travelers in Nepal and our recent study on Israeli travelers demonstrated that there were no clinical differences between *S. typhi* and *S. paratyphi* A infec-tion. In fact, there were more complications among those in the *S. paratyphi* A group.

Due to both the increased antibiotic resistance to *S. typhi* and *S. paratyphi* and the similar clinical course of disease caused by these two pathogens, there is a great need for a combined vaccine. A recent study on Israeli travelers demonstrated that Vi vaccine gave better protection against *S. typhi* amongst travelers to India, while Ty21a gave better protection against *S. paratyphi* A. Thus, until such vaccines become available, sequential vaccination with the available oral and Vi vaccines merits consideration (Meltzer et al., 2005).

Conclusion

Two features characterize the status of typhoid fever in industrialized countries. One is the general decline in the incidence of the disease and the second is the concomitant rise in the percentage of travel-related typhoid fever. The majority of cases in travelers are acquired in the Indian subcontinent where quinolone resistance is increasing. The current vaccines available offer only moderate protection against *S. typhi* and no protection against *S. paratyphi*, which has become a dominant pathogen among travelers. The increase in resistant strains is evident for *S. paratyphi* as well, and therefore an effective vaccine for *S. typhi* and *S. paratyphi* is urgently needed.

References

Anonymous. (1914). Antityphoid vaccination. *Canadian Medical Association of Journals, 4*, 314–321.

Anonymous. (1927). Carl Joseph Eberth (Obituary). *American Journal of Public Health, 17*, 381.

Connor, B. A., & Schwartz, E. (2005). Typhoid and paratyphoid fever in travellers. *The Lancet Infectious Diseases, 5*, 623–628.

Groschel, D. H., & Hornick, R. B. (1981). Who introduced typhoid vaccination: Almroth Write or Richard Pfeiffer? *Revision of the Infectious Disease, 3*, 1251–1254.

Guha, S. (1993). Nutrition, sanitation, hygiene, and the likelihood of death: the British Army in India c. 1870–1920. *Population Studies (Cambridge), 47*, 285–401.

Kidgell, C., Reichard, U., Wain, J., Linz, B., Torpdahl, M., Dougan, G., & Achtman, M. (2002). *Salmonella typhi*, the causative agent of typhoid fever, is approximately 50,000 years old. *Infection, Genetics and Evolution, 2*, 39–45.

Longstaff, G. B. (1884). The recent decline in the English death-rate considered in connection with the causes of death. *Journal of the Statistical Society of London, 47*, 221–258.

Moorhead, R. (2002). William Budd and typhoid fever. *Journal of the Royal Society of Medicine, 95*, 561–564.

Meltzer, E., Sadik, C., & Schwartz, E. (2005). Enteric Fever in Israeli Travelers: a Nation-Wide study. *Journal of Travel Medicine, 12*, 275–281.

Schnorf, H. (1998 Oct 22). A mysterious death. *New England Journal of Medicine, 339*, 1248–1249.

Schwartz, E., & Shlim, D. R. (1990). Enteric fever among Israeli travellers in Nepal: The need for typhoid vaccination. *Israel Journal of Medical Sciences, 26*, 325–327.

Schwartz, E., Shlim, D. R., Eaton, M., Jenks, N., & Houston, R. (1990). The effect of oral and parenteral typhoid vaccination on the rate of infection with *Salmonella typhi* and *Salmonella paratyphi* A among foreigners in Nepal. *Archives of Internal Medicine, 150*, 349–351.

Chapter 9

Dodging the Bullet: Preventing Rabies among International Travelers

Paul M. Arguin and Nicole F. Oechslin

One might find this an unusual pairing for a book chapter about rabies and travel: a medical epidemiologist at the U.S. Centers for Disease Control and Prevention and a college professor and mother living and teaching in rural America. As siblings sharing their work, we have had occasion to discuss the heartbreaking and frustrating stories of travelers who endanger themselves while away from home. The stories are dramatic and compelling and have much to impart to those who travel and those who treat travelers. Consider the following scenarios that are representative of cases that have come up over the years.

While camping in Cambodia, Gilbért befriends a stray dog. He feeds and plays with it, and at some point the dog bites him on the hand. A couple of days later, he finds the dog dead near the campsite and discards the carcass. Gilbért figures that the bite wound, which is already starting to heal, was so small that he did not need to seek medical attention.

A family of missionaries, having lived in India for 5 years, starts to allow Nigel and Myles, their young twins, to play unsupervised with the neighborhood dogs.

Jodi, a nurse practitioner at a student health center is evaluating a group of four students who are leaving in 6 days for a trip to Venezuela, where they will be studying live bats. She realizes that they do not have enough time to complete the vaccination series and is concerned that the vaccine is so expensive. Figuring that a little vaccine is better than nothing, she splits a single dose between the four students.

Upon returning to see his physician in Arizona, Herman, a young man who had been traveling in Chad, reports that he had been attacked and bitten by a crazed dog 9 weeks earlier. He states that the doctors he saw in Africa had no rabies vaccines and suggested that he get rabies shots when he returned home. Herman's American physician tells him that because it happened 9 weeks ago and he is asymptomatic, it is unlikely that he has contracted the disease and, therefore, shots are no longer necessary.

All of the above scenarios should have filled a reader with a sense of dread because they contain critical errors with life-threatening consequences. Unfortunately, mistakes like these

Travel Medicine: Tales Behind the Science
Copyright © 2007 by Elsevier Ltd.
All rights of reproduction in any form reserved.
ISBN: 0-08-045359-7

are made frequently, resulting in unnecessary exposures to rabies, excessive numbers of people receiving post-exposure rabies shots, and sometimes deaths.

Rabies, an encephalitis caused by bullet-shaped viruses in the genus *Lyssavirus*, is transmitted by the bite of an infected mammal. It has the distinction of being virtually 100% fatal once symptoms start, yet is 100% preventable. Rabies prevention includes reducing the number of susceptible animals through vaccination and animal control laws, avoiding animal bites, encouraging pre-exposure prophylaxis of people at higher risk of exposure, and ensuring prompt post-exposure prophylaxis of all rabies exposures. Prophylaxis simply means preventative measures. When applied before an exposure, it consists of three doses of vaccine. When applied after an exposure, there are different regimens depending on the situation. Not all travelers need to get rabies vaccines before they travel. Although rabies can be found in wild mammals all over the world (except Antarctica), the biggest risk worldwide is actually from stray dogs. Travelers going to countries with lots of rabies in their large stray dog populations are prime candidates for rabies vaccinations. A closer look at the cases described above illustrates the many complexities and challenges that face travelers and their health care providers.

The first two examples from our representative cases demonstrate incorrect behavior around dogs in countries with endemic canine rabies. People in countries without endemic canine rabies such as the United States, Canada, and countries in Western Europe are used to having close associations with dogs. According to the U.S. Pet Ownership survey, in 2001 approximately 38 million households (36% of all households in the United States) reported having a dog as a pet. Additionally, many non-dog owners are also dog lovers. Generally speaking, the culture in the United States (and many other developed countries) promotes a high comfort level and appreciation for dogs as companions, athletes, helpers, and all around entertaining characters. Consider the following scenario that we have all probably seen time and again: A man walking with his dog through a city park is approached by some strangers — people with whom he is unacquainted. These strangers will say something like, "Wow, what a great looking dog you have there! What is he?" The owner replies something like, "Oh, Rusty, he is an Alaskan Moose Hound. They were bred to hunt in packs, and so they are known for being very loyal … and friendly." Almost invariably, while dog owners are volunteering information like this or some similarly admirable attribution, one or more of the strangers will extend the back of his or her hand towards the dog's snout, encouraging the dog to sniff it. Once the strangers perceive that they have earned the dog's trust through this action, they drop to their knees and start petting, or hugging the dog. The dog responds in kind usually at least by licking their hands or at worst slobbering all over their faces. The same thoughts always come to mind: How do they know that the dog has been vaccinated for rabies? Do the strangers have any open cuts on their hands? And my gosh, that dog's saliva is getting awfully close to that stranger's mucous membranes!

When these types of interactions occur in the United States, aside from the potential bite issues, usually they are not cause for alarm. Being licked by a dog in a developed country without endemic canine rabies where most dogs are vaccinated is fortunately a very low risk for rabies transmission. Most states or counties require rabies vaccination as a condition of dog ownership. That combined with animal control programs, leash laws, dog licensing, and reduction of stray or free ranging animals eliminated canine rabies in the United States. Perhaps that success has resulted in a maladaptive behavior. People have lost the ability to see dogs as potentially dangerous animals.

Before traveling to another country where canine rabies is still endemic, people need to not just be informed about the risk of rabies, but they actually need to be retrained about how to think about dogs and to alter their fundamental behaviors around dogs. Travelers should be advised to never initiate contact with a dog while traveling in a country where rabies is present. This means no petting, no feeding, no matter what! By attempting to maintain one's distance from dogs that have an unknown rabies vaccination status, the chance of being bitten by a rabid dog decreases substantially. In addition, people need to be taught what to do in the event of a dog bite.

In the first example, the young camper, Gilbért, illustrates two major errors of judgment. First, he was petting and playing with a stray dog in a rabies-endemic country. Second, he did not seek immediate and appropriate medical attention for rabies post-exposure prophylaxis. One might wonder whether he consulted his physician before embarking on his travels, and if so, what kind of information he received about reducing the risk of contracting rabies during this consultation. Rabies prevention strategies for international travelers should include more than just a decision about whether to provide pre-exposure prophylaxis. Travelers should be educated about the need to alter their perceptions about dogs while in rabies-endemic countries and thus alter their behavior around them. In the case of Gilbért and others like him, we wonder if the message about avoiding direct contact with dogs while abroad is sufficiently communicated and understood. By helping travelers reduce unnecessary contact with dogs, the likelihood of rabies exposures will decrease.

Gilbért's case also points to the need to educate travelers about what to do if they might have been exposed to rabies. Travelers should be encouraged to wash a wound thoroughly with at least soap and water; povidone-iodine would be an even better choice if available. Once the wound has been properly cleaned, the person should seek prompt medical attention to receive rabies shots. All travelers should be advised that if high quality medical resources including rabies immune globulin (RIG) and vaccine are not locally available, they need to change their itinerary and travel to a larger metropolitan area (or back home) in order receive the appropriate medical interventions. This would be an inconvenience that could save their lives.

The other rabies prevention intervention that can be useful for travelers like Gilbért and the others is pre-exposure vaccination. Receipt of this three-dose series of vaccines will simplify the post-exposure regimen for the person, should they ever be bitten by a potentially rabid animal. Once travelers have completed their pre-exposure regimen according to the recommended schedule with modern tissue-culture rabies vaccines, there is no need to check serologic titers and no need to provide further pre-exposure booster doses of rabies vaccine. These interventions (titers and boosters) are recommended for persons in higher risk categories such as veterinarians and rabies laboratory workers, but not for international travelers.

Among the groups who specifically should be encouraged to receive rabies pre-exposure prophylaxis are long-term travelers such as missionaries who are at a slightly higher risk of rabies. After living in a higher risk setting for a while and remaining unaffected, some long-term travelers like the family of the twins in the second example tend to let their guard down and begin to take more risks. Over time, immersion in a different new culture in which stray dogs are ubiquitous and are frequently adopted and fed by entire communities may contribute to the erosion of the cautious attitudes, which families like this one embraced upon embarking on a long-term travel adventure. Because young children like

Nigel and Myles are the demographic group with the highest incidence of dog bites, including severe dog bites, they should not be left unsupervised to play with dogs in countries where rabies vaccinations for dogs are the exception instead of the norm. Parents who will be traveling in or moving to a country where canine rabies is endemic should impress upon their children the importance of maintaining caution around dogs. Because long-term travelers and children have a relatively higher chance of sustaining a dog bite, they should consider rabies pre-exposure vaccination a wise investment. Further, travelers living overseas for extended periods who acquire pets such as dogs and cats should also make sure to get them properly vaccinated. This will not only benefit the pets by preventing them from contracting and dying from rabies, it will also reduce the chance of the pets subsequently exposing the owners, other humans, and other animals as well-everybody wins.

The decision to provide rabies pre-exposure prophylaxis is often influenced by cost and timing issues. Rabies vaccines can be very expensive. In the United States, they can cost patients up to $US250 per shot. People traveling to developing countries often need multiple vaccinations (yellow fever, typhoid, hepatitis, etc.). Adding rabies to the list can break the bank. Also, many patients arrive for their pre-travel medical appointments very close to their date of departure, making completion of a three-dose immunization series logistically impossible. Health care providers should be strongly discouraged from deviating from the established and proven-effective vaccination schedules in order to accommodate travel schedules or to reduce costs. Such creative problem solving, as was done by Jodi, the well-intentioned but misguided nurse practitioner in the third example, can result in future difficulties for the patient in the event of a future rabies exposure. For example, if a traveler received only a single dose of rabies vaccine because her doctor thought that one dose is better than nothing, how should she be managed when she receives a bite from a rabid dog one year later? She cannot be regarded as having been pre-vaccinated because she never completed the three-dose series. She would still need to receive RIG and five doses of vaccine, thereby increasing the overall cost as well as the risk of adverse reactions.

Modern rabies immunization no longer consists of "hundreds of shots in the stomach" that most people fear. Today the state-of-the-art rabies biologics are inactivated viruses grown in cell tissue culture which are administered intramuscularly, usually in the arm, as well as RIG, which should be injected mostly at the bite site(s). Rabies pre-exposure prophylaxis consists of a schedule of three shots over a three to four week period. People who have completed this pre-exposure series and are then bitten by a rabid animal only need to get two doses of vaccine afterwards. People who have not been given pre-exposure vaccines and are bitten by a rabid animal need to receive a dose of RIG plus five doses of vaccine administered on a schedule over a month. RIG is expensive and in short supply around the world; thus, people who are traveling need to consider the availability of these products overseas. Some countries still produce older, less safe versions of rabies vaccine including sheep and mouse brain vaccines. These vaccines may be less immunogenic and have higher rates of adverse events and so should be avoided.

Finally, travelers have to realize that there are different national and international guidelines for the administration of rabies shots. Sometimes the economic realities and lack of availability of sufficient quantities of the rabies biologics become incorporated into some of these guidelines and post-exposure management algorithms. For example, in some settings, RIG is rationed, used only for what are perceived to be serious bites and not given for lower risk exposures. Travelers need to ensure that the advice they are being given in some of these local settings is consistent with the standards of medical care they expect in their home countries. Even a small bite from a rabid animal can transmit rabies, and so the previously unvaccinated traveler needs to make sure that he receives both RIG and the appropriate schedule of quality rabies vaccines.

One point that is often confused occurs when post-exposure rabies vaccination is started before the RIG is administered — often because it was not available at the time. The person then travels to another location to complete their post-exposure regimen and the health care provider is unsure whether to administer RIG or not. They think that if a certain amount of time after *the exposure* has elapsed, then RIG should not be given. This is not the case. In fact, RIG can (and should) still be administered up to 7 days after *the first dose of vaccine*. In addition, all persons who sustained rabies exposures should receive post-exposure prophylaxis regardless of the duration of time that has elapsed since the exposure — provided of course that the person has not already started experiencing symptoms of clinical rabies. This is the error that Herman's doctor made in the fourth case. It is incorrect to assume that because he had not started to develop symptoms after an extended period of time since the exposure in Chad, that Herman had in fact dodged the bullet. Although the average incubation period for rabies is 1–2 months, longer intervals certainly do occur, and so no prevention opportunity should be missed. Herman's example also points to the alarming possibility that the message about rabies post-exposure regimens is not always getting through to health care providers, even in the most developed and affluent nations. This in turn suggests the need for greater ongoing professional development and education about rabies for health care providers.

Rabies in international travelers is fortunately very rare. Unfortunately, potential rabies exposures are not. Still, with proper planning, effective communication, and education, this fatal disease is extremely preventable. These elements may sound more like the job description of a teacher rather than an epidemiologist, but really, they have more in common than it might appear on the surface. Both must be concerned with educating people, with encouraging them to examine boundaries and behaviors, and finally with the challenging task of changing habits. Health care providers can learn from the professional educators as to how to provide accurate and consistent information to empower travelers to make better choices. Travelers can most significantly reduce their risk of exposure by changing their behavior around animals while traveling in rabies-endemic countries. By doing this, individuals like all those mentioned in our illustrative cases can obviate the need for rabies pre-exposure prophylaxis. Travelers with a higher probability of rabies exposure should consider pre-exposure prophylaxis. All persons who are exposed to rabies, such as through a bite from a rabid dog, should receive appropriate post-exposure prophylaxis as soon as possible.

SECTION 4:

MALARIA DRUGS AND INFECTIONS OF ADVENTURE

Chapter 10

Barking up the Right Trees? Malaria Drugs from Cinchona to Qing Hao

Patricia Schlagenhauf-Lawlor

In the district of the city of Loja, diocese of Quito, grows a certain kind of large tree, which has a bark like cinnamon, a little more coarse and very bitter: which, ground to a powder is given to those who have a fever, and with only this remedy, it leaves them....

(Bernabe Cabo, 1582–1657)

One of the earliest
illustrations of the Cinchona
tree, published 1662.

The Countess of Chinchon closed her eyes wearily, exhausted from the fevers and rigors racking her body. Why had she insisted on accompanying her husband, the Viceroy, to this God-forsaken land at the end of the world? She had wanted to travel, keen for adventure and excitement, bored with the tedium of court intrigues but now she yearned for the familiar. Would she ever see her beloved Spain again or was she doomed to rest eternally in Lima? In her fevered dreams she had seen a priest holding out the branch of a tree to her, exhorting her to drink an infusion and then, like magic, the fevers had subsided.

Holding her delicate, fevered hand, the Viceroy to Peru was in despair. His beloved Countess was death bound with this incurable ague and the quacks with all their purging, bleeding, mercury and herbal treatments had weakened and worsened her condition. As a last resort he would allow her to drink an infusion of the bark of a native Peruvian tree given to him by a Jesuit priest of Quito and then he too would fall to his knees and pray for a miracle.

The rest is history and the drug became known as the "*pulvis comitissae*" the powder of the Countess; and the good lady who was saved returned to Spain and with the help of the Jesuit priests the magic bark was distributed with great success. Many historians have suggested that this romantic story is inaccurate and that the Countess of Chinchon actually died in Spain before her husband was appointed Viceroy. The story is further complicated by the fact that the Viceroy had two wives, albeit not simultaneously. Others want to preserve the fable and change the name of the genus "*Cinchona*" to "*Chinchona*" to properly honour this wonderful lady.

After its introduction to Europe, the Jesuit cardinal Juan de Lugo propagated the use of the bark; and the Jesuit missionaries imported and used the "Cardinal's powder" or "Jesuit's bark" with remarkable success allegedly even curing Emperor Kang Hsi of China of a stubborn ague in 1692. The bark reached England in 1650. Here, the Cinchona preparation aroused heated emotions, particularly because of the connection to the Jesuits and Oliver Cromwell who may have died prematurely because of his aversion to using the "Popish powder". The bark, however, ensured the fame of another legendary figure, one Richard Talbor, an apprentice apothecary whose secret remedy (a pure formulation of Peruvian bark) made him a famous "feverologist" who cured Charles II of England, was knighted, moved to France and became Louis XIV's physician and then the medical advisor of Louisa Maria the Queen of Spain as well as a host of other noble personages much to the chagrin of the physicians in England. In 1677, the bark became official and appeared as "*Cortex Peruanus*" in the London Pharmacopoeia. The cure was expensive and initially Cinchona was a drug for the royalty and church elite and was, as yet, not available to the masses of malarious Europe. As in every speciality, there were differences of opinion and the value of powdered cinchona bark was supported, disputed or vehemently opposed throughout the continent. The physician of Popes Innocent XI, Innocent XII and Clement XI was an ardent proponent while the famous Danish Professor of Medicine in Copenhagen, Ole Worm, was reluctant to be an advocate. One Guadentius Brunacius virulently described the powder as "a new poison, a diabolical invention to exterminate all non-Catholics". A new era dawned in 1820 when two French pharmacists Pierre Pelletier and Joseph Caventou purified the bark's two active alkaloids, which they named *quinine* and *cinchonine*. It was now possible to quantify and qualify the value of the cinchona barks.

The story of the cultivation of the cinchona tree is full of interesting anecdotes. The Jesuits, demonized in the Da Vinci code, are the unsung heroes of the Cinchona chronicles and they were at the forefront of Cinchona conservation, carefully replacing felled trees with five cuttings in the shape of a cross. The growing demand for the bark led to a mounting threat of shortage and the era of the great botanical expeditions began. Clements Markham successfully brought young trees and seeds from Peru for British plantation in India and Ceylon. Another Briton, Charles Ledger arrived as a clerk in Peru at the tender age of 18

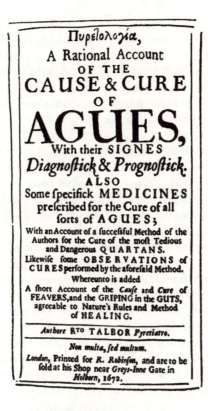

Title page of Robert
Talbor's *Pyretologia-*
published 1672.

and with the help of an Indian named Manuel Incra Mamani, sourced an excellent bark with a high alkaloid content that was to be named *C. ledgeriana* after him. The British government refused to buy his cinchona seeds but through the intercession of the Dutch botanist, Justus Karl Hasskarl, the Dutch government bought the seeds and *C. ledgeriana* flourished in the Dutch East Indies, with a very high quinine yield.

The plantations meant that quinine became cheaper and more widely available and ensured that, while Europe was becoming progressively less malarious, the old powers could use quinine as an instrument of colonialism and a weapon in military campaigns. British and French armies in the 19th century had more losses from fever than from bullets. There was some effort to use quinine prophylaxis in military campaigns and in the colonies, and hence the Victorian fondness for bitters and tonic water (Indian tonic water from the cinchona plantations in India). The gin was just an add-on bonus! During the Second World War, the Japanese took Java and the precious cinchona supplies were in jeopardy and war became the spur to develop new synthetic drugs as a substitute for quinine. German scientists at the I.G. *Farben Industrie* feverishly prepared and are said to have tested more than 12,000 substances for anti-malarial activity.

Chloroquine, originally called resochin (synthesized in 1937), was truly a wonder drug resulting from this effort. It was tested in North Africa by the Germans and although the Allies managed to get hold of some of this potent chemical and put it through their investigative mill, it was quickly put on a back burner as being *"too toxic"* for human use. The synthetic anti-malarials were mainly developed for and by the warring powers, Germany, Great Britain and the United States. The list is impressive; pamaquine, mepacrine, chloroquine, proguanil, pyrimethamine, primaquine and quinocide were first to be rolled out and then the sul-phones and sulphonamides were enlisted. Later came a new generation with mefloquine, tafenoquine, halofantrine, 8-aminoquinolones, naphthoquinone and potent syngeristic com-binations of existing drugs such as atovaquone/proguanil.

No more trees?

Which brings us to another less woody but very green, miracle cure, namely, the wonder-ful Chinese herbal drug *qing hao*, source of Artemisinin — "rediscovered" in the People's Republic of China in the 1970s although the drug was used in traditional Chinese medi-cine over 2000 years ago. The artemisinins (which include artemether, arteether and arte-sunate) constitute today's greatest hope as a component of the combination treatments now at the forefront of the malaria wars and is the WHO-recommended treatment in Africa. Artemisinin, which is poorly soluble in water, can be extracted from three species of the genus *Artemisia*; the most important being *A. annua* with lesser quantities found in *A. apiacea* and *A. lancea*. New research on the historical aspects has shown that according to the famous physician and natural historian Li Shizhen (1518–1593), and in terms of Chinese material medica, *A. annua* is correctly named *"huang hua hao"* and not, as is commonly assumed, *"qing hao"* which is in fact *Artemisia apiacea*, a much poorer source of artemisinin. All very *confusing* — should this piece be read "From Cinchona to huang hua hao?"

Because the cold water, full plant extraction methods used in early Chinese medicine suc-cessfully extracted the pharmacologically active compounds, the potions were effective, even if the plant namely *A apiacea* with the lower artemisinin content, were used. The emi-nent physician Ge Hong, in the 4th century CE, recommended the following cure for inter-mittent fevers:

> take a bunch of qing hao and two sheng (2×0.2 l) of water for soaking it,
> wring it out to obtain the juice and ingest it in it's entirety.
> (*Emergency Prescriptions Kept in One's Sleeve*, Chap. 3.16)

Another method involved soaking the plant in urine rather than water (detailed in a manuscript from a tomb in Hunan province) and this probably enhanced the extraction of the Artemisia sesquiterpenes from the plant. Today, *Artemisia annua* is the plant of choice in the cultivation of this crop as a source of artemisinins. The usual herbal preparation for malaria treatment uses the dried leaves of *A. annua* in a hot water infusion. A recent paper suggests that an extraction, according to the traditional method given above, using the fresh whole plant *A. apiacea* soaked in cold water and wrung out to extract the juice may be a better option to consider.

Looks like we will bark up a few trees yet....

References

Hsu, E. (2006). The history of qing hao in the Chinese material medica. *Transactions of the Royal Society of Tropical Medicine and Hygiene, 100*, 505–508.

Poser, C. M., & Bruyn, G. W. (1999). *An illustrated history of malaria*. London, UK: Parthenon Publishing.

Chapter 11

Infections of Adventure and Leisure

Annelies Wilder-Smith

Travel to exotic places is fascinating, and equally so are infections of exotic travel. The horrors of malaria and other mosquito-borne diseases in travelers have been frequently described elsewhere, and will therefore not be covered here. The consequences of adventurous eating flourish with expanding travel, and our glamorous taste for exotic places leads to exotic cuisine with often even more exotic diseases. Travelers are attracted by water, and beach vacations as well as recreational activities on fresh water abound. This chapter describes infections related to exotic cuisine, beach, seawater and fresh water activities.

Exotic Cuisine

As travel expands, it also expands the range of food-related illnesses. Moreover, one need not be traveling to suffer these maladies; sometimes they travel to you. As the consumption of novel foods and the pleasures of international travel spread and carry the cachet of class and trendiness, the pool of people at risk for these illnesses increases. Many foods, when eaten in their most tasty raw form, such as the seafood or unpasteurized dairy products, can serve as vectors for bacteria, viruses and parasites.

The worms in gourmet delights are plentiful. Humans are not usually the definite hosts. Instead, larvae unable to complete development wander through the unfortunate person's tissues, sometimes for years, causing mayhem and pain as they search for the unobtainable (e.g. a dog's stomach). It is hard to believe that the unfulfilled aspirations of a lost worm can cause such human misery. No food is trendier than sushi. The freshest of seafoods are matched with rice, pickled vegetables, and other condiments, thereby bringing a number of pathogens to the unsuspecting consumer.

Anisakiasis is a potentially catastrophic disease caused by the larval stages of the marine nematodes, sometimes called "herring worms". These parasites are usually found in the stomachs of large sea mammals, and humans are only infected as dead-end hosts. *Anisakis simplex* is a parasite of porpoises and whales. The larvae first develop in small crustaceans and then in fish and squid, which serve as transport (paratenic) hosts. These intermediate-stage

Travel Medicine: Tales Behind the Science
Copyright © 2007 by Elsevier Ltd.
All rights of reproduction in any form reserved.
ISBN: 0-08-045359-7

larvae may be harbored in cod, sole, flounder fluke, salmon, mackerel, herring, yellow corvina, sea eel, octopus and squid. Alas, many of these make delicate sushi and sashimi. The hallmark of acute anisakiasis is sudden abdominal pain, either intermittent or constant, beginning 1–24 hours after the consumption of raw fish.

Another group of horrible parasites transmitted by raw freshwater fish comprises Gnathostoma species. Raw carp, kokanee, ice-fish and loach are savored meals and excellent vectors for Gnathostoma parasites, even loach imported into Korea from China. Thus, the curious and indiscriminating traveler who consumes the odd raw snake, frog, fish, mouse or rat (!) in Southeast Asia risk infection with the apparently equally indiscriminating Gnathostoma. Gnathostomiasis is a major problem in Thailand and other parts in Southeast Asia, where it is considered the most common symptomatic tissue helminth infection. Worms recovered from humans are 2–3 mm long. Most worrisome is their invasions of the central nervous systems and ocular system, which may be fatal. Gnathostomiasis can cause eosinophilic meningitis in association with painful radiculopathy.

Fasciola hepatica is contracted by eating watercress containing infective-stage metacercariae. *Clonorchis* and *Opisthorchis viverrini* occur in Southeast and East Asia and are contracted by eating raw fish containing metacercariae.

Diphyllobothrium latum is a tapeworm acquired by eating the raw or undercooked muscle of fish. It is a big problem, primarily in the sense that it can grow up to 3 m in length. It is written that the "usual" route of acquisition is the ingestion of raw frogs or snakes, or the direct application of raw snake flesh to the skin — but it remains to be wondered what is "usual" about this. Fish species that have been found infected include salmon, white fish, rainbow trout, pike, perch, turbo and ruff.

Apparently, about 10% of people in Scandinavia are infected with *Diphyllobothrium*. Jewish immigrants from Eastern Europe who prepare gefilte fish in the traditional way are at risk of *Diphyllobothrium latum* infection. This ethnic delicacy is made with chopped freshwater fish, and the proper balance of spices can only be achieved as the still uncooked fish dish is being prepared. Indeed, pernicious megalobastic anemia is sometimes caused by the special ability of the tapeworm to take up vitamin B12 in the proximal small intestine.

Raw beef and pork are famous for transmission of the beef and pork tapeworms, *Taenia saginata* and *Taenia solium* respectively. Those of us who favor dishes such as steak tartare are at particular risk. *Taenia saginata* infections are often asymptomatic, with the most common complaint being the passage per anus of motile, muscular proglottids, a rather shocking realization at a personal private moment. In contrast, the pork tapeworm, *Taenia solium*, has a different potential for invasive disease. The larval stages of the parasite can be hematogenously spread from the gut to tissues like the liver, brain, long muscles, subcutaneous tissues and eyes.

Neurocysticercosis remains worldwide the most common cause of adult-onset epilepsy. The larval stages cause neurocysticercosis, but eating raw or uncooked pork is the cause of trichinosis. If planning an adventure holiday to the Arctic regions to experience the traditional food of the Inuit population, such as eating raw walrus and polar bear, be warned that trichinosis may be your newly acquired infection.

An under-appreciated consequence of eating poorly cooked beef may be exposure to bacterial pathogens that cause diarrhea and other intestinal complaints. *Escherichia coli O157:07* is an enteric pathogen that causes a hemorrhagic colitis and is strongly linked with hemolytic-uremic syndrome and thrombotic thrombocytopenic purpura. If we return to the topic of steak tartare, a flavored concoction of raw chopped beef, raw egg, onion, capers and a vinaigrette, things other than *Taenia saginata* may find their way into this delicacy, for example *Toxoplasma gondii*, the etiological agent of toxoplasmosis. Though usually benign and self-limited, and often resembling an infectious mononucleosis-like syndrome, the severe end of the spectrum of clinical manifestations includes myocarditis, pneumonitis and meningoencephalitis. Toxoplasmosis is particularly to be avoided for pregnant travelers because of the congenital disease that can occur. Central nervous system disease due to *Toxoplasma* is of special concern for those travelers with HIV infection.

Unpasteurized milk products have always enjoyed a reputation for a fresher taste and aroma than their pasteurized cousins. In the opinion of many, soft cheeses can only be made with unpasteurized milk. The consequences of unpasteurized milk products could potentially be *Brucella abortus*, *Mycobacterium bovis*, *Listeria monocytogenes*, *Salmonella* species, *Campylobacter jejuni*, *Yersinia enterocolitica* and *Streptococcus zooepidermicus*.

Yoghurt and mayonnaise are wonderful culture media for bacteria like *Staphylococcus aureus* and *Salmonella* species. A buffet-style gourmet meal, waiting to be eaten by hundreds of restaurant visitors, despite being prepared in a five-star hotel, may be a good breeding ground for Staph and Salmonella. In many parts of world, particularly in Asia, leftover rice is stored and eaten the next day. Unfortunately, *Bacillus cereus* and also *Vibrio cholerae* are capable of increasing in number in cooked rice during storage. The traveler who partakes of the leftover rice may be greatly surprised at developing signs and symptoms of bowel disease after ingestion of such organisms.

Giardia lamblia (*intestinalis*) is a single-celled animal, i.e. protozoa, that moves with the aid of five flagella. Ingestion of one or more cysts may cause disease, as contrast to most bacterial illnesses where hundreds to thousands of organisms must be consumed to produce illness. Cool moist conditions favor the survival of the organism. Giardaisis is most frequently associated with the consumption of contaminated water. Unlike many of the above infections that are mostly associated with the tropics and subtropics, this infection can also be caught while remote trekking in the US, Canada, New Zealand etc, in particular if your thirst requires drinking from springs, streams or lakes on the way. Giardiasis usually presents initially with watery diarrhea, followed by chronic malabsorptive diarrhea often associated with weight loss and fatigue. Although not reportedly pathognomic, "egg burping" is frequently reported in relation to infection with giardia. Personally I can attest to this experience, having contracted this infection at least five times during my time in Nepal and India.

Many consider seafood a delicacy. The term "shellfish" includes crustacean (lobsters, shrimp, crabs, scampi and crawfish) and molluscs (oysters, mussles, clams and scallops). Paralytic shellfish poisoning results from the ingestion of marine molluscs containing potent neurotoxins, of which the best known is saxitoxin, named after the Alaskan butter clam, *Saxidomus giganteus*.

Ptychodiscus brevis is the dioflagellate responsible for neurotoxic shellfish poisoning, a syndrome similar to paralytic shellfish poisoning; however, symptomatic are usually milder and paralysis and respiratory failure do not occur. Interestingly, a syndrome called "amnesic shellfish poisoning" also exists. It was only recognized in 1987 when several hundred people ate mussels harvested from river estuaries on Prince Edward Island in Canada. The acute illness was characterized by persistent memory loss! Consumption of puffer fish is a modern way of playing Russian roulette; actually it is a Japanese way of Russian roulette. Known as fugu in Japan, puffer fish is considered a delicacy and is specially prepared by trained individuals who require licenses to serve the popular dish. It therefore costs a fortune. Despite all these precautions, about 50 cases of fugu poisoning still occur annually with these specialty restaurants. The pufferfish poisoning is due to tetraodotoxication.

Ciguatera is a distinct clinical syndrome that follows the ingestion of certain tropical reef fishes. The name was given by Don Antonio Parra in Cuba, in 1787, from the Spanish "cigua", which refers to poisonous turban shellfishes. Ingestion of fish weighing more than 2.3 kg or fish caught during red tides should be avoided by the general public as these are more likely to contain ciguatera toxins.

Scombroid-fish poisoning is an acute clinical syndrome characterized by symptoms of histamine toxicity resulting from the ingestion of spoiled fish. It represents the most common form of ichthyosarcotoxism in the world. The fish that pose a risk are tuna, mackerel, skipjack, bonito and albacore. Histamine is produced during the process of spoilage by certain enzymes. Typically, it takes place when previously refrigerated fish is allowed to lie around for a period of time before it is prepared. Histamine is heat stable and is thus not destroyed by cooking. Symptoms initially appear as flushing and a hot sensation of the skin, dizziness, headache, a burning sensation in the mouth and throat, urticaria and palpitations. Gastrointestinal symptoms follow, as well as sometimes difficulty in swallowing and respiratory diseases with bronchospasm, hypotension, tachycardia and blurred vision.

After all these rare and exotic diseases, the most common has not even been mentioned yet. Montesuma revenge or Turista diarrhea, or simply travelers diarrhea, affects 20–90% of all travelers, depending on the destination of the course, but usually within the first 2 weeks of travel.

In a nutshell: Food is delicious and delightful, and we will all continue to consume it despite the incredible number of gross and unpleasant diseases associated with some of these. Foremost of course, by all means, avoid watercress. The mnemonic to reduce the risk is "not raw, not unpasteurized, not unwashed". And possibly bring along a bag of loperamide and ciprofloxacin or azithromycin, or an even bigger bag with toilet paper....

Infections of Recreational Waters

People love water, and therefore beach vacations and recreational pursuits on freshwater gain increasing popularity. Visiting the beaches and oceans has its attendant risks, in particular if the selected beaches are in the tropics.

Infections of the Beach

The numerous pleasures of recreation at the shore are associated with unintentional exposure to pathogens. While enjoying a bare foot walk on the beach, dog and cat hookworms deposited in sandy soil can penetrate exposed skin and lead to cutaneous larva migrans (creeping eruptions). This leaves migrating pruritic serpiginous tunnels in the epidermis. *Strongyloides stercoralis* can cause a particular form of hive-like cutaneous lesions, usually on the buttocks or thighs. Sand fleas (*Tunga penetrans*) invade the skin (often around the toes) when a person walks barefoot. They are easily removed with fine forceps. Cutaneous myiasis is contracted by travelers to Latin America (*Dermatobia hominis*, the bot fly) and Africa (*Cordylobia anthropophaga*, the tumbu fly). The latter infection occurs from eggs being deposited on clothes that are air dried and un-ironed. Stray dogs frequently roam the beaches; an unexpected bite may ruin your holiday as the hours of sunbathing are now over because finding a clinic that offers post-exposure prophylaxis against rabies can be rather time-consuming.

Uninvited and rather unpleasant travel companions can be ticks, mosquitoes, lice, fleas, mites, bees, wasps, scorpions and spiders; and they are potential carriers of disease. Although potentially serious, the majority of bites from bees, wasps, scorpions and spiders are simply painful. Ticks can transmit infectious diseases such as lyme disease, ehrlichiosis, tularaemia, Colorado tick fever, babesiosis and fievre boutonneuse, but the risks for these diseases increase the more inland you venture from your beach. The hard ticks are of greater concern, since they are more frequently encountered, are difficult to remove and are more likely to transmit diseases to humans. Plans for a good sun tan may be crossed, if avoidance of ticks is a priority: proper wardrobe is essential in preventing tick transmitted diseases, and this means covering the arms, legs and other exposed areas with ankle-high footwear and pant legs that cover the ankles or are worn tucked into the socks. An extremely sexy look that everyone desires! Instead of perfume, it is essential that travelers apply permethrin to clothing to prevent tick attachment. Close and regular inspection of all body parts are however the most essential for the adventurer.

Lice are the main vectors for epidemic typhus. The rat flea transmits murine typhus. Mites transmit scabies, rickettsialpox and scrub typhus.

The most common skin disorders acquired by travelers are cutaneous mycoses. Tinea versicolor is frequently contracted in the tropics. Tinea pedis ("athlete's foot") is particularly common in moist climates, as is tinea cruris ("jock itch").

Infections Related to Seawater

If you have not sustained trauma by marine wildlife, consider the more mundane issue of swimmer's ear. Swimmer's ear is the most common medical problem faced by swimmers. The pathogenesis is multi-factorial, with cerumen playing a major role. Cerumen imparts an acid reaction to the external canal, lowering its pH to 5 and thereby inhibiting bacterial and fungal growth. Excessive moisture in the external canal, which can occur during swimming or bathing, can lead to mechanical disruption of this barrier, with subsequent desquamation and maceration. In addition, the decrease in cerumen results in a rise of the pH, which allows bacterial species to proliferate.

Samples of seawater have been estimated to yield between 5×10^6 and 15×10^6 total viruses per ml. Enteroviruses such as hepatitis A, coxsackievirus, echovirus, poliovirus are detected frequently, even in waters deemed safe for recreational use by fecal coliform standards. Shellfish harvested from contaminated waters are responsible for numerous outbreaks of food-borne illness. Shellfish implicated in cases of hepatitis A include oysters, clams, cockles and mussels. In addition, the illness has been traced to contaminated lettuce, raspberries, strawberries, ice-slush beverages and community water sources. Plankton serves as an important element of the food chain for marine animals. During blooms, these organisms may achieve concentrations high enough to impart a reddish or yellow discoloration of the sea due to the local production of neurotoxins and pigmented proteins; hence, the name "red tide". The association of red tides with human illness has been known since ancient times. Vectors of shellfish poisoning are mainly filter feeders that ingest large quantities of this plankton, many of which are toxigenic.

Vibrios, the "comma-bacilli" (e.g. *Vibrio cholerae*) tend to proliferate in the warmer summer months, and the organisms are frequently associated with plankton and shellfish. Cholera remains very rare in travelers. However, during the cholera outbreak in Peru and surrounding countries in 1991, several cases occurred in travelers as well as in individuals who ingested crabs imported illegally from this part of the world.

Vibrio vulnificus is one of the most invasive and rapidly lethal human pathogens ever described. Two major syndromes can result from infection with this organism. Primary septicemia typically follows the ingestion of raw oysters by individuals with liver disease. This syndrome can have a rapidly fatal course. The other major presentation is that of wound infections, which may occur by either primary inoculation or secondary hematogenous spread in a bacteremia individual. Antibiotics, vigorous debridement and occasionally amputation are necessary to control the massive necrosis and systemic spread that can occur.

Mycobacterium marinum is the most frequently identified mycobacterial species causing skin and subcutaneous infections. It inhabits both fresh- and saltwater environments as a free-living organism. Human infection is usually associated with trauma, such as abrasions, injuries from fish spines or pricks from crustaceans or shellfish, although the injury itself is often trivial. *Mycobacterium marinum* is now a well-recognized cutaneous pathogen with a strong association with an aquatic environment and water-related activities. The organism has been called a "leisure time pathogen", and the disease has been referred to as a "hobby hazard". Manifestations of disease have also been referred to as "fish fancier's finger" and "swimming pool granuloma". The medical description of the disease is of dusky erythematous plaquares, or ferrucoid papules or nodules, usually in the hand and upper extremity.

Fortunately, severe syndromes or infections are relatively rare, and many can be avoided by appropriate precautions, such as lying on clean and ironed towels on the beach, not walking barefoot, avoiding red tides and prompt debridement and therapy of wounds obtained during marine recreation.

Recreational Pursuits of Freshwater

There have been more outbreaks of folliculitis associated with whirlpools or spas than with swimming pools, indicating that the environment of the former is more conductive to the development of folliculitis. In part, this appears to be related to the difficulty in maintaining a stable free-chlorine level in whirlpools compared to swimming pools because of the higher temperature of the water, mechanical agitation and aeration by pressurized jets, and a higher concentration of organic material due to the large number of bathers per volume of water. In addition to the predisposing environmental factors, dilatation of skin pores because of the higher water temperature may facilitate entry of the *Pseudomonas aeruginosa* organisms contained in the water. *Pseudomonas aeruginosa* dermatitis/folliculitis presents after an incubation period of about 48 hours. Showering after exposure to *Pseudomonas aeruginosa*-laden water does not appear to prevent development of the infection, suggesting that the organism rapidly gains access to the deeper regions of the skin pores during water exposure. Acute diffuse otitis externa (swimmer's ear) is also usually caused by *Pseudomonas aeruginosa* and may be similar to *Pseudomonas folliculitis* in its pathogenesis. Swimmer's ear has been seen more frequently in swimming pool users than in whirlpool and spa users, who usually keep their heads out of the water.

Swimming pool conjunctivitis has been associated with a number of adenoviruses. Free-living amoebae of the genus *Acanthamoeba* have been responsible for several hundred reported cases of keratitis. This infection has proven difficult to treat, often resulting in severe impairment or loss of vision. Primary amoebic meningoencephalitis (PAM) is a result of *Naegleria fowleri*. *Naegleria fowleri* is a small amoeba widely distributed in water used for recreation. Although millions of people have been exposed, fortunately only a small number of people have come down with the disease. The organism is thought to enter the central nervous system via the nasal route. Amoeba from contaminated water is deposited on the olfactory mucosal epithelium and penetrates the sub-mucosal nervous plexus and cribiform plate. The progress results in coma, and the infection is often fatal within a week. At some of the spa pools in New Zealand, one will notice signs not to put your head under water.

The two most known diseases in tropical medicine circles that are related to freshwater exposure are leptospirosis and schistosomiasis. Leptospires are motile, spiral microorganisms that contaminate freshwater via rat urine. Leptospires may enter the body through intact mucosal membranes, the conjunctiva or braised skin. Tropical river rafting such as the highly publicised Eco Challenge in Borneo are the most famous stories of exposure to leptospira, but outbreaks have also been reported in the United States and elsewhere. Schistosomes infect particular species of susceptible freshwater snails in endemic areas. The infected snails release cercariae, which are fork-tailed free-swimming larvae approximately 1 mm in length. The cercariae survive in fresh water up to 48 hours, during which time they must attach to human skin or that of another susceptible host mammal or die. Pre-travel advice consists of telling people to be sure not to be one of the hosts wading in the water, a ready target for these cercariae, in particular if you are wading or swimming close to the shore of your fresh-water lake, stream or slow moving river. Cercariae attach to human hosts utilizing oral and ventral suckers. They then migrate through intact skin to dermal veins, and, over the next several days, to the pulmonary vasculature. During this migration, the cercariae metamorphose, shedding tails while developing double-lipid-bilayer teguments that are highly resistant to host immune responses. The organisms, now called schistosomula, then migrate through the pulmonary capillaries to the systemic circulation, which carries them to the portal veins where they mature. Within the portal vasculature, male and female adults pair off. Together they migrate along the endothelium, against portal blood flow, to the mesenteric (*Schistosoma mansoni, Schistosoma japonicum*) or vesicular (*Schistosoma haematobium*) veins where they begin to reproduce eggs. It is the intense granulmatous response to these highly antigenic eggs that produces the illness at the location where they are laid. We have not yet closed the interesting cycle of Schistosoma: the eggs then mature into miracidia. Free-swimming miracidia that are shed into freshwater survive 2–3 weeks, during which time they must infect a snail to complete the life cycle. Within the infected snail, two generations of sporocysts multiply, mature into free-swimming cercariae, exit the snail and search out another human host to begin the cycle all over again.

Disclaimer and Acknowledgements

This chapter certainly does not claim to be comprehensive. The order of presentation does not reflect the order of importance of certain pathogens or organisms, but rather the degree of my fascination. To this end, I acknowledge the book *Infections of Leisure* (David Schlossberg (Ed.), Springer-Verlag, 1999) as the source of most of the above information. I devoured it with morbid fascination and as a result brought forth this chapter.

SECTION 5:

PERSONAL TALES: TRAVEL MEDICINE PRACTITIONERS SHARE THEIR STORIES

Chapter 12

Final Log: Amazonas Adventure

Marc Shaw

Final Log from Marc Shaw, Team Doctor, Sir Peter Blake Expedition to the Amazon

Status: Returned Back Home to New Zealand

January 2002: Home, pleased to be back to with family. Three months of adventure with the Sir Peter Blake Expedition in Brazil and Venezuela, countries in South America that I had often dreamt of though never thought I would venture to.

Rio Negros Expedition

> *'One eye open, from a restless night of dreams;*
> *Then two, to see Rio Negro bathed in deep*
> *Scarlet-turning ochre tinted cotton clouds,*
> *Before turning upon glass-like river to touch Iguana.*
> *Early dark quiet for a moment, until deep*
> *Calling crescendo song of howling monkeys*
> *Drift to touch a stilled early company waking to*
> *Another day of treasured treat in watching beauty*
> *Unfold, moment to next amazing moment as we*
> *Journey through regions dreamed of, urging to be seen.'*

I have time to reflect on what had happened in the last 3 months. I distinctly remember 'the call' to be part of the expedition 4 months earlier, in my comfortable office in Auckland. 'Come and be the expedition doctor', said Blake. A chance like this no one refuses, for that is to fly in the face of the specialty that I love. I was excited!

Did the homework, vaccinated most of the team, studied the diseases and saw the tango in Argentina before meeting the whole crew in Manaus. From then on, the trip was a series

Travel Medicine: Tales Behind the Science
Copyright © 2007 by Elsevier Ltd.
All rights of reproduction in any form reserved.
ISBN: 0-08-045359-7

of images fading in and out of focus as the pain of the death of Blake confused a distraught memory. I learnt so much on this voyage; mostly about myself and my feelings toward others. I also had to fight with the personal demons that occurred with the tragedy that affected the whole expedition deeply; that of the murder of our leader Sir Peter Blake by pirates at the mouth of the Amazon River.

Being in the 'jungle team' at the time of Blake's death left me feeling desperately helpless when I heard of my crewmates and how they had tried to resuscitate their friend and leader from death. It also left me feeling terribly guilty, for the crew had no experience either in saying 'stop the life-support' or in managing their own psychological pain at seeing their mate die wondering if they could have done more. At the time all this was going on, I and the 'jungle team' of the expedition were in our riverboat, bongo, in the middle of Venezuela hundreds of miles away. Didn't hear about any of the trauma until 12 hours later, though fore-warningly we did experience the worst storm of our journey the night that Blake died.

Amazon Storm

> *Amazon rain rushes from far away and beyond*
> *Coloured grey scale timid to harsh, threatening,*
> *Booming sounds with light, with hues of a river's edge*
> *And beauty. Beginning soft to beguile and mesmerise*
> *Only to pound, smash, rumble and angrily rage*
> *Accompanied by smashing thunder booming to*
> *Follow flashing jags and belts of white, orange, yellow*
> *That stamp their mark over an expansive ceiling*
> *Limited by vision and patience to watch, to linger*
> *Until the distance is seen again with clear fresh eye.*

Hearing of his murder brought feelings of gloom and despair — devastation within the crew. I was reading *The Count of Monte Cristo* at the time I heard of the murder. I was feeling quite French at the time. French Franck, the photographer, brought me to my senses by telling me 'something is wrong with Simon and James, the film crew'. I look at them. They are motionless and looking at their satellite phone, actionless upon the floor of the bongo-boat. From that moment the blur of words said about the death of our leader impacts upon us all awe-filled in different ways. None says a word. Silence!

As we traveled up the Casiquiare, the day after Blake's death, I had this amazing image of egrets doing a 'fly-past.' My recollection of the occasion is that there were 21 of them, and they did three passes over our bongo-boat. Stunned, we all quietly thought of the same thing: Peter was watching us.

Blake had mustered this expedition with the express purpose of exploring the interaction between man and the waterways of the world; and I have to say that I was hugely touched by the expedition's tragic outcome, and was left surprisingly exhausted and bewildered. As a doctor, I thought that I would cope well with caring for others' pain at the event. I did not anticipate the nightmares that I got for the next three post-trip months. Like the others, I just wanted to be with my loved-ones, nurtured and cuddled, and have my life mean something to someone. The bubble of excitement and energy for the expedition no longer is there.

Photograph by Franck Socha

Image 12.1. On hearing of the murder of Blake: quiet, painful contemplation.

The initial plan of the expedition was for it to be in two parts; I was in the jungle part (eight people going through the river trails of Venezuela) and the remainder of the group were to stay with the sea master and meet us in the mouth of the Orinoco River, Venezuela.

Plan was, we were then all to go North to the Caribbean for Christmas. Well, events changed all this. In the furore that erupted after Blake died, the team never got to salute and mourn his death. The heart of our journey had gone. I think this has had an ongoing effect on us all, and post-traumatic counseling would have been effective in the early rehabilitation of the crew.

Home, back in my beloved green and blue of New Zealand, I think of the last few days on the bongo in the jungle of the Orinoco River, Venezuela — on route between San Antonio and San Fernando.

Orinoco Travel

Since the shock of Peter's death, we meandered along the Casiquiare River and slightly further up the Orinoco from 'Peter's Spot' to a town called Tamatama. A fascinating place, for it was like visiting a space city right in the heart of the Amazonas Region. You will imagine our surprise at being thrust into a collection of houses with electricity, fridges, motor mowers and an airstrip! Here we are, having just arrived from the depths of adventurer territory, untidy and unshaven, walking into a slice of Americana! Yes, that is right — Americana. Tamatama is a mission town, with origins way back to the 1930s, situated where it can teach schooling and Christian Religious studies to the local Indigenous communities. It is a United States community, primarily, and we met with some of the 15 families that live there. With them, we talked about their works in and around the region. All of us were awed at finding this community in the middle of a jungle. I paused to blink in case I was in the wrong part of the world or the wrong part of my mind!

Another night parked on a sandbank, and then we set forth on our trek down the rivers of Venezuela. Where else in the world can one park a boat on a riverbank, in safety, and set up a camp with about 20 million flies, bugs and moths of all shapes, sizes and bites to accompany you! At 6 pm we were asleep in our hammocks within 30 minutes after it was dark, for to leave a light on meant instant attraction from the local insect community. The next morning all exposed areas on our bongo-boat were covered with small moths. Millions of them; yet brush them into the river and the fish would quickly established their food chain.

Beaches on the river in this part of the Amazonas are different from those where we stopped at down river. More orange-yellow, rather than the white of the Rio Negros. Probably because of the alluvial debris that comes down the river and, also, the fact that the Rio Negro is geologically an older river than the Rio Orinoco.

The recent tragic events have brought our group much closer and given us the resolve to complete our journey. Our health is good and we are eating well, though after 3 weeks on the bongo without any cooling facilities you will imagine that the fresh fruit and meat have long since gone. We are surviving on lentils, pasta and rice. Oh, I almost forgot, also on fish dried on the top of our bongo. I have to say that we could well do with a change in diet; BUT our cook, Augusto, has found 3000 ways to cook the food that I describe, in different dishes, so that we all think that we are eating something different every night. Last night I 'ate' *coq au vin* I am certain!

Augusto is a comic and a really lovely man. He is also one of the very few people in the world that can laugh at his own jokes! I proved this by telling one of my jokes and laughing at it — no one else responded, bland faces looked at me, though crewmember Simon did give a titter but apologized later. Humor has been a sustaining energy for us, and we have found that it helps bind us together at this huge time of tragedy.

Tonight is the last night and the last leg of the 3 months since the mouth of the Amazon. There have been moments of incredible awe and wonder, as we stop to observe a region filled with such natural riches that I would never have dreamt of — forests that spread for ever, flat expanses that seem endless, the low incidence of malaria and other tropical diseases in the region, beaches of the whitest sands that squeak and sparkle underfoot, villages that survive by considering their needs and those of the ecology, waters that alternate black, red or brown, birds that are of the most beautiful colours and a silence at night that makes one hesitant to move for fear of any sounds created.

My final image is one of the storms and the rains that we have seen and been amongst. We have experienced the most severe storms imaginable; in fact we had our worst yet the night that Sir Peter died. These storms display lightening that whooshes across the sky in sheets of white, or snakes to the ground in slices of yellow. The thunder tinkles, crashes, and then booms across the sky in stereophonic sound. The rain follows and completes the triad, storming upon the ground and swinging horizontally to sweep at our campsite from the side. It is as though such storms have a mind, the way that they rocket water to the deepest protected parts of our bongo-boat.

As a team we have all got on very well and enjoyed each other's company. We each have contributed to this most remarkable adventure, traveling from Barcelos in Brazil to Puerto Ayacucho, our intended destination. For my part as the Doc, well I have been Camp Mother to everybody. Loved every bit of it, though I have been fully outside my surgery comfort-zone. The trip, nevertheless, has been unique. Peter Blake's visions for a nature–human alliance have meant something to me and, in my way, I shall do my best to pursue this end.

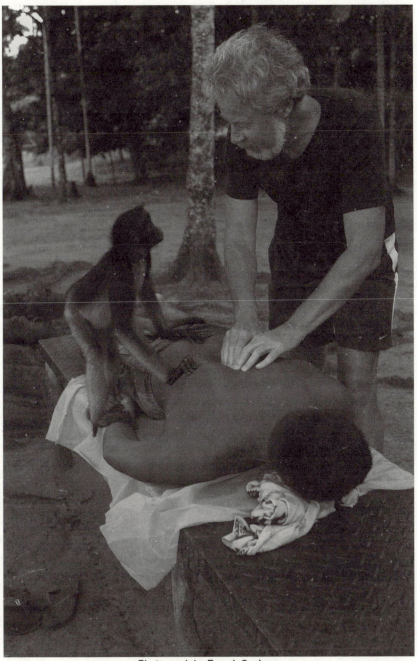

Photograph by Franck Socha

Image 12.2. The monkey and the medicine-man.

Chapter 13

Tales from the Mountains

Ted Lankester

Tom was a medical student and the team leader of a university science expedition. The official objective of this expedition was to study high altitude plants and mammal fleas; the real objective was an excuse for some fun and adventure. Their destination was Nanga Parbat in northern Pakistan. Also known as the Naked Mountain, this dangerous peak, 8126 m high, is the western buttress of the Himalayas.

Tom and his team of three had driven from London to Pakistan by Land Rover. They arrived, hot and very tired, 3 weeks later in Rawalpindi during the monsoon. Just before sunset while the two expedition mechanics checked the equally exhausted vehicle, Tom went off to buy supplies in the local bazaar. Returning home he developed a sudden and troubling pain in his left chest, worse on deep breathing. On bending over he could feel a bubbling sensation in his chest. Feeling otherwise well, he decided it was unlikely to be serious, probably a hiatus hernia that ran in the family. He decided to go for a run in the heat to see if it would settle down. It did not, but he decided to ignore it. Did he feel a bit more short of breath than usual?

The team were troubled by a number of mosquitoes as they went off to sleep that night. Somehow they had assumed that because they were going to the mountains there would be no need to bring mosquito nets with them or to take antimalarials.

The plan was to set off the following morning for the Babusar Pass aiming to get as far as they could in one day. This pass climbs to over 14,000 feet and they were hoping to camp as near the summit as possible. However, they had not borne in mind the risk of altitude sickness, nor considered using Diamox.

The following day dawned wonderfully bright with a break in the monsoon. Largely oblivious of medical dangers and despite the accumulated tiredness of 3 weeks driving, the expedition members were in high spirits. Tom's pain was no worse, the Land Rover was belching less smoke and they headed for the hills.

The road proved difficult. The first day the road was narrowed by lingering snow and they had to transfer to smaller jeeps, crossing snow-covered roads on cedar branches cut from the forest. On the 2nd day the jeeps were too heavy for the bridges and the road too dangerous. They transferred their supplies to a mule train reaching the summit of the pass before nightfall. At least they had spent one night at an intermediate altitude.

Travel Medicine: Tales Behind the Science
Copyright © 2007 by Elsevier Ltd.
All rights of reproduction in any form reserved.
ISBN: 0-08-045359-7

Over the campfire in sub-zero temperatures Tom noticed that one of his colleagues, Adam, had a severe headache, was feeling nauseated and got easily out of breath. Tom, although a medical student, was largely unaware of the dangers of altitude sickness. In any case descending lower at that time of the night with muleteers already asleep was hardly an option. But after an anxious night Adam appeared no worse and the following morning they were able to descend the other side of the pass.

Four days later the team arrived on the eastern flanks of the mountain, camped at 2000 m and was rewarded by breathtaking views of the Karakorum Mountains, and the primeval stillness of the high altitude pine forest. The team eagerly got to work trapping small mammals and collecting high altitude plants. While Tom and his fellow botanist were combing the glacial moraine for what they hoped might be species new to science, the mammal team decided they would work on the donkeys owned by villagers in the high meadowlands. This required a high degree of coordination as donkeys were reversed into huge polythene bags and enough ether, or was it chloroform, was placed in the bags to cause the parasites to jump off in sleepy surprise, without the animal becoming so drowsy it collapsed in a heap. Success was achieved and thousands of specimens, some not previously discovered, were sent off to an enthusiastic professor in California.

Meanwhile Tom, working in the upper forest and glacier, was troubled by recurrent chills, sweating and headaches. At least his chest pain had settled down. One day feeling worse than usual and struggling to reach the moraine, he noticed the fading mosquito bites and it dawned on him what the likely diagnosis might be. Unfortunately there was no chloroquine nor any other malarial treatment in the medicine kit.

Despite these minor health problems the expedition was a success. Later, there was even time for a 2-week trip to Delhi. Unfortunately reckless eating led both Tom and Adam, to sustain severe Shigella dysentery. Adam spent several days in hospital, enough to delay the team, meaning they had to squeeze their overland return to London down to 2 weeks, driving all day and late into the night. Tom arrived just in time for the first pathology lectures of the new university term.

Tom had collected plenty of traveler's tales with which to bore his friends, and an ideal opportunity arose at a college party a couple of weeks later. But it was not to be. On giving the final pull to his double-ended bow tie, the same searing pain in his left chest struck again. Going to A and E the X-ray showed a left-sided pneumothorax. Tom realized that a run in the monsoon heat and heading to 14,000 feet the next day had been an inappropriate form of treatment for his first partially collapsed lung.

Tom's next adventure was one year later in the Nepal Himalayas where he had planned the first of his two overseas electives. By now he was a little older and wiser but still had problems planning ahead. He found the daily grind of having to attend ward rounds and outpatients in the hospital, interesting though it was, less exciting than the thought of putting on climbing boots and hunting out high altitude rhododendrons in the monsoon rain forest. With friend Denise and a tough Tibetan coolie he set off on a 10-day trek.

That year the leech army was out in force after exceptionally heavy rains. The schedule was tight, the plant life fascinating and there was little time to deal with the increasing number of leeches. Also, the ecology was more interesting off-piste than on, and the leech population correspondingly more desperate for a meal. Unfortunately repellents and protective clothing had been overlooked in the hasty preparations.

One evening Tom counted 50 leeches browsing at one sitting from his waist downwards plus a few outliers on his upper body. Each day his boots were squelching water, stained deep red.

Tom although physically fit, got increasingly exhausted and short of breath on the daily ascents of 1000 m or more. It was a great relief when the Tibetan coolie became deeply unconscious for a full 24 hours after an evening's overdose of Chang, the Tibetan rice spirit, giving Tom and Denise an enforced rest.

Shortly after reaching Kathmandu, Tom, seriously exhausted, flew home. The palpitations that had started on the trek worsened, he looked unusually pale to his friends and his GP father registered a career first in diagnosing anaemia from leech bites in a Himalayan trekker.

It is 5 years later. Tom has graduated, worked as a junior hospital doctor and married a fellow traveler. Together they decide it's time for another exposure to the Himalayas. They phone around friends and contacts, and much to their delight find a mission agency that has been praying for someone to drive a new Land Rover to a hospital in Nepal. After 4 weeks Tom had found two other colleagues up for adventure, and they set off on Asia overland trip number 2. But this time Tom, now a responsible doctor, was taking a supply of medicines with him, donated by a number of drug companies. These were not for his needs alone but to help in setting up an informal clinic in a village house in the western Himalayas. Tom had decided this was an ideal opportunity for a career break and was planning to spend 10 months in the Himalayan foothills treating western dropouts and long-term travelers who were unwilling to use conventional clinics and hospitals.

Tom and his wife rented a wooden house towards the end of a long valley in the western Himalayas. They soon got to know the "hippie" population, totalling several hundred, and word got around that anyone sick could come for medicines, advice, prayer or their own chosen combination. The clinic was the veranda, but many travelers were addicted to hard drugs or seriously ill, so Tom made daily visits to village homes scattered in the deodar forest or on slopes facing the mountains.

It was a wonderful summer despite regular letters from home querying the unorthodox career that Tom was following. On first arriving, the high ridges beckoned and it seemed nothing to do a 5000 feet scramble before lunch. But 3 months later things started to change. This came to light one evening when there was a knock on the door after sunset: there was an unusual request.

The British Military attaché holidaying in the area had somehow managed to find Tom's house and now stood on the veranda, explaining that a couple of German missionaries had gone missing. They were last seen heading off early the day before through a steep forested area leading on to high snowfields. Would Tom and his mountaineer friend, staying with him, set out straight away and try to find them. Tom and Matt hastily downed a meal, loaded up a small backpack, took a huge torch and supply of batteries and set off by moonlight. They climbed for several hours, stopping now and then to listen, and to call out. But there were no sounds apart from the barking of dogs and the stillness of the upper forest. High on the path where the forest gave way to meadows they came across shepherd communities, guarded by fierce mastiffs. As dogs approached, thoughts of rabid fangs worried Tom, but not as much as the shepherds' stories that two nights before one sheep had been taken by a leopard, and the night following, an irascible bear had attacked a family member. Tom hoped the missionaries were nimble enough to climb a tree or devise some clever bivouac.

At one in the morning Tom and Matt decided to call off the search. They settled down and slept by a shepherd's fire in sub-zero temperatures, the full moon lighting the snow peaks. Tom was not only concerned by the lack of missionaries, but also perturbed by his lack of stamina. Why was he so exhausted? Three months ago this climb would have seemed nothing. What was the cause? There were no leeches on this path.

The following day after more fruitless searching, they decided to return home. Late that evening two disheveled missionaries limped into port, tired but triumphant that they had found the path, dodged the bears and found an excellent Deodar nook in which to spend the night. But Tom's friends were worried by his appearance.

Over the following few weeks up to nine sick travelers stayed in the 2-bedroom house and on the veranda, all served by one long drop. Three had hepatitis; one weighed only 5 stone. Is this lifestyle sustainable, thought Tom as he noticed his thighs and buttocks thinning daily, and as he drilled a new hole in his belt to keep up his trousers?

Common sense prevailed and after one of the best years of his life, Tom and his wife flew home, a month before schedule. The scales at home showed he had lost 3 stone in as many months, and his wife 2 stone. The hospital diagnosed tropical sprue, nothing that could not be put right by doxycycline, folic acid and a diet of strawberries. The real challenge was psychological; adapting to a year cut short, 3 months of physical exhaustion, an uncertain future and baying relatives.

It is 8 years later and Tom has been a GP for 7 enjoyable years and has 3 daughters under 8. One morning a note drops through the door from a medical colleague working in the Indian Himalayas. "We need some help extending our mountain community health program. Why don't you come and join us?"

Tom feels he has been in this situation before. It's another trip to his parents to explain a crazy scheme, and more advice to be sensible as he resigns from the practice, reduces his income by 80% and buys one-way air tickets for five.

This time it is for the longer haul — 7 years working and walking in the Himalayas, learning how to set up sustainable health programs from more experienced Indian colleagues. The family love it. Home is nearly 2000 metres high up in the Himalayas. The playground is the steep mountain paths and forests. There is no television and often no electricity. The telephone never works, the water is tuned off for hours each day and cooking is by gas or primus stove.

Before dawn one winter morning when gas, electricity and phone were all non-functioning, the semi-wild cat the family had adopted screeches louder than usual. Tom's wife rushes to the rescue, separates it from a marauding male and in so doing sustains a deep scratch on her face and a ragged bite on the earlobe from the visiting feline, which makes off to the forest. Tom agonizes over why the family had not had their rabies immunizations and that HRIG and post-exposure jobs mean a difficult trip to Delhi for the whole family.

Immunizations completed the incident soon fades. The health program goes well, the local schooling is successful and the long trips out to villages by jeep or by foot never lose their fascination.

But the following year dangers and challenges seem to follow in quick succession.

On a day with atrocious weather, the health team decide they would still try to reach a remote health post normally a rough 2-hour drive. Halfway a landslide blocked the road. They knew up to 50 patients would be waiting, many part of the TB program. Tom and Raju, a health worker colleague, set off for the 24 km round trip on foot, stripped to the waste in the torrential rain, with loaded backpacks. They arrived at the clinic, put on dry shirts and saw all the patients within 4 hours, many very grateful that Tom and Raju had braved the elements.

Much to the delight of Tom and Raju the project HQ had guessed their predicament, and sent out a Harley Davidson to bring them home, successfully manhandled by helpful villagers across the landslide. Tom, Raju and the driver set off on the motorbike at dusk, the rain still pounding relentlessly. Fifteen minutes down the road, they sensed a terrifying vibration on the ground below them and the sound of crashing rocks far above. With hardly time to leave the bike and run, huge boulders were started to pulverize the ground around them. Raju yelled to Tom to jump to the right as a boulder the size of a jeep missed squashing Tom by feet. Dodging rocks for what seemed an age, the team managed to sprint backwards to safety.

On arrival home many hours later, Tom was moved to hear that the family had sensed he was in danger at exactly the time of the rock fall, had stopped their evening meal and prayed for his safety.

Tom decided to add writing "Travel Guidelines for Bad Weather" to his to-do list, but not before the next incident. Ali, the daughter of Tom's vicar from England, was coming to visit and Tom knew she would want to gain front-line experience of what the health team was doing.

The day after her arrival Tom and Ali set off for another distant clinic. The day could not have been different; warm, sunny, with 20,000 feet high mountain peaks gleaming to the north, as they headed out along the ridge road.

Two hours later and about 5 km before reaching the clinic, Tom was surprised when the owner of a teashop where they sometimes stopped for "chai" rushed out and handed him a note written in broken English: "Turn around immediately, there is crowd on the road waiting to burn your car." Tom decided to continue all the same.

Everything seemed normal until they rounded the final bend before the clinic. There indeed was a menacing crowd throwing stones and threatening to burn the vehicle. They surrounded the jeep saying they would kidnap Tom and his friend. At that moment Raju bravely stepped forwards and made an impassioned plea in the village dialect for the crowd to disperse so the clinic could continue. Slowly the crowd backed away but not before locking three of the team into the clinic. Their plan for a full kidnap had failed, hatched days before in the hope that by capturing foreigners, pressure would be put on the government to address their grievances.

On arriving home Tom added "Guidelines on Team Security" to his to-do list.

That evening the family sat down and enjoyed an evening meal with relish. But Tom felt uneasy — not just because of the day's event, but also because of the richness of the food. Since employing a new part-time cook, the meals had become soaked ever more in saturated fat. Images of practical pathology and atheromatous arteries flashed across his mind. But the cook had many times been told about this, so surely she must have changed to healthier cooking oils.

It is 12 years later, and the new millennium. After 7 years in the Himalayas, Tom has been back in England for several years enjoying medical practice. He has just celebrated his half-century, glad he is still able to enjoy cross-country running in the heathlands of central Sussex.

He is puzzled however that almost always when reaching a certain tree on his common running route, he develops an ache in his left shoulder. He is sure it is muscular, but having learnt a few painful medical lessons in the past, he now takes his health seriously. The next week he checks in with a cardiologist. A resting ECG is normal but there are some worrying signs on the treadmill. Three weeks later he has an angiogram and a blocked left lower descending coronary artery is diagnosed. Tom is one of the unlucky ones that week and suffers a cardiac arrest. But he is also one of the lucky ones. His expert consultant bounces him back to life, restents him and 2 days later Tom returns home.

As his health revives Tom dreams of future squash matches and cross-country runs and is glad when after a few weeks he can return to have his treadmill repeated along with a thorough check from his cardiologist. He feels great and is pleased he can comfortably reach Bruce Protocol 4. Walking away from the hospital, Tom is wondering when he will next put on his running shoes, when an ominous pain starts in the left shoulder, worsening rapidly. Can he get back to cardiology outpatients? What should he do? He walks back as quickly as the pain, now reaching a crescendo, allows him. He reaches the out-patient desk, and collapses in severe pain on the floor. The rest is hazy. The following day recovering in ITU from an acute coronary syndrome, the specialist registrar says it's not everyday that patients are lucky enough to arrange their heart attacks outside the consulting room of the President of the British Cardiac Society.

It is now 5 years later and with common sense, statins, careful follow up and a family keen to monitor Tom's well being, he is able to return to gentle running up to 12 km at a steady pace, free from chest pain. He often talks with gratitude about the wonders of modern plumbing.

Tom now works in travel medicine. Some of his colleagues wonder why he has a particular interest in specific health topics: control of cholesterol, the value of treadmill, ECGs, safety and security for development teams, acute mountain sickness, malaria, undiagnosed chest pain, dysentery and rabies.

Tom is especially interested in how to engage with travelers, development workers and others whose job or inclination is to be risk takers. How can reasonable risk and sensible precaution be packaged, owned and followed by the present day traveler and aid worker? Tom is still learning. And he is dreaming of another Himalayan trek.

Chapter 14

Confessions of a 'Reality TV' Doc

Marc Shaw

I am bulked into the middle seat on the right side of the plane while coming back to New Zealand from Namibia. On my left is a fat man with body odor 'big-time' and on my right is a lovely French woman who has a lilt to her voice that makes your heart sing. I am cramped — again. My long legs. For a moment I wonder whom to ask if I can rest my head on their shoulder, but a puff of fetid breath makes my mind up for me. I snooze and reflect on a successful journey to Southern Africa, as a doctor for 25 folk on a reality TV program. I don't get to go on TV, damn it, but I do get to care for the group's medical needs.

Reality TV — this sort of work is increasing now. Globally, the standard was set by the 'survivor'-type programs, and now the trend has permeated through to programs being made in other countries such as New Zealand. My role on this one was to oversee two Australian (Aussies) and two New Zealand (Kiwi) families going to Namibia and South Africa to have a 'reality TV adventure', and also to look after the crew of 15 as well.

Quite a task, I can say. Adventure and expedition medicine is an exciting new field of travel derived from the idea that people wish to place themselves into risky situations and talk of how they survived them. OK, so I am a cynic about this reality TV stuff. Nevertheless, the medical side of the task is involved and quite detailed. Practically, the task involved: pre- and intra-travel health perspectives and finally, on completion of the journey, post-travel surveillance.

First thing I had to do was to scrutinize the crew and the intending families, codeword: talent! The usual: full medical check-up, lab data and country-specific vaccinations. Had to deny a couple of families the trip actually, as there were significant health risks with them: diabetes, allergies and the like. Couldn't take the risk, being so remote. Pressure from the company to bear but I stand firm on the health of the team that is to go. This is the whole point of my role.

Interesting thing medico-legally was brought up. How do you give advice to folk going to an area that they don't know about? What do you do about giving medication for malaria and how do you manage giving appropriate vaccinations? The film company handled this validly with a variety of caveats, for part of the TV deal was to make sure that the talent

Travel Medicine: Tales Behind the Science
Copyright © 2007 by Elsevier Ltd.
All rights of reproduction in any form reserved.
ISBN: 0-08-045359-7

was not told where they were going. The film crew had to 'shoot' the shock of 'the revealing' at the airport as they were being told.

Next to do was to build an adequate medical kit for the 2 months we were going to be away. Heaps of thought on this, and I have written elsewhere on what needs to be contained in the kit. Our kit in two huge bags was absolutely fantastic, all the right stuff!

Two locations, in South Africa and in Namibia, and my day-to-day role was to look after the crew and the families. The Aussies were a pleasant family: just SO 'the Osbournes'! Initially they hated the whole thing and told the film crew so, to the latter's joy and delight. This is the food for reality TV because the whole point is to stress the families and see how they respond. Makes for good TV apparently. The doctor becomes the intermediary in this situation. I was the good guy, because I was not TV. This prompted many minor illness assessments by me for the family, though these tended to decrease exponentially over time as the families' enjoyment of experience increased. The Kiwis were good wholesome families from heartland New Zealand, though not as histrionic as the Aussies. I liked them, though I soon learnt that it was not me but the camera that had to do the real censuring.

On this section of the trip, I saw 150 different medical illnesses amongst my charges within the crew and talent. Principally, three different types of complaints: gut problems, respiratory problems and minor trauma. All went as expected with easy and quick management in the main, except for one day where I got the 'bot' and found myself abed being cared for by the crew.

Namibia is a lovely country with a wonderful 'feel' to it. I can see why Branjolina had their baby there. Amazing colors and contrasts, from bright to pastel, and the capital Windhoek is absolutely delightful and way more established than ever I would have thought. Only 1.4 million people in a country, two-thirds the size of South Africa but without the big deal on security.

North from the capital, we then go to the border of Angola to live amongst the Himba people for 2 weeks to film the program. An amazing group of women — they have a matriarchal society. My mouth drops in amazement at the way that the women and girls are dressed up in their unique manner with ochre paste and cows fat applied all over the whole body every 1–2 days. They have no need to wash, though I have no concept of this. As I watch the members of this wealthy tribe, I can view the lovely and unusual images that they present: the redness and the fineness of their skin, hair that is plaided in thick plaits with mud and ochre dye, huge bands of jewellery around their necks, wrists, ankles and waists; faces that are proud and backs that are straight. When these women walk they do so with innate pride and upright presence, and their bodies seem to glide amongst the terrain within which they live … their apparent tallness made more so by the leather thongs denoting their marriage on their heads.

Part of the exchange in the village is that I need to do a medical clinic for the Himba folk. They never get to see a doctor. Sounds good, I think, and I plan for and look forward to this. I am ambivalent about developing country medicine as I know little about it and fear that I cannot do much in 10 days for anyone, particularly if they have some sort of chronic disease process. Checked out the authorities in Windhoek and they are OK with me doing my clinical work. After previous expeditions, I now always call local authorities for permission to practice. Too many do-gooders in health care stuff up local resources with their 'well meaning' patronization.

I resolve to do two clinics a day: 9–10 and 4–5. From day one it is good that I have made this decision, as there are large numbers of folk that come to 'the doctor' for cure and care. First clinic was 10 men in an hour and a half, all with backaches and chest pains and all of which have been with them for years and years. Just the sort of problems that such clinics are made for. I acknowledge this and try to do my best. Women getting shunted out by the men at this clinic, so I resolve to have a women and children's clinic in the afternoon. Seems to work well, and the women love it when men turn up at their clinic time expecting to 'walk right on in' and get told 'come back another day' — how the women laugh! Over the next 10 days I see around 200 folk for mainly chronic illnesses such as:

1. 'Backache' and 'total body aches' from years of hard toil.
2. 'Eye pain' from years of eyes straining against the sun — pterygium and pingueculae abound.
3. Fat tummies in the children from malaria and malnutrition.
4. Rashes from the ever-present scabies.
5. Osteoarthritis (OA) of aged joints. There is no cure for OA. How do you tell this to a 70 year old woman who can walk and believes that YOU can make her do so?

The drugs that I have are really very limited and I am basically working with analgesics, vitamins, eye ointments, antibiotics and anti-helminthics. I did my homework in assessing what I perceived to be the medical issues in the region, but nothing really prepares you for the 'real thing' — the hands-on communication, the interaction and the managements of conditions read about but rarely seen.

It is hard to write down exactly what routine 'the doc' follows for managing the crew and 'talent'. For me, while the role is primarily medical, I remain available to talk on any issue — or to at least listen and add valid comment. On any expedition, the 'doc' is always seen in a different light to how they see themselves. They are carers, 'mothers and fathers', academics, friends and the morale indicator for the trip.

Practically I make sure that I have always with me a variety of medications and dressings for the common medical conditions in gut, respiratory and minor traumatic illnesses. Other things I carry as a routine are: toilet paper, sunscreen and mossie repellent. In a chest pocket I have a pen and some paper to make notes, and will also carry my 'leatherman' knife. I thus try to have all the common things available so that when the crew say 'Have you got X, Y or Z?' I can say, 'Here it is'. So far I have done OK, and have not missed anything. Even I am surprised, but then one look at me, and you will see a portable supermarket!

The doc's role is a supportive one and he/she is there mainly for the team and in particular the crew. The crew are hardy, having traveled extensively, and they know a lot about their own bodies. They are an intelligent team, with unusually quick minds and strong assessment abilities. They are foul mouthed and do not mind who hears their ribald jokes and their coarse language, but I love being with them and enjoy each and every one of them. I still have much to do to reach the heights to which I aspire in this form of medicine, but I am growing into it and I am loving my learning.

Chapter 15

Tomb Raider's Crew Doctor

Laragh Gollogly

In the dusty market in Siem Reap, where women butchered chickens with cleavers on tree stumps, hunched squatting in the shade thrown by tarpaulins strung between bamboo poles, and stallholders loitered besides piles of plastic shoes, a white man in a black shirt was trying to buy silk. He was saying to the interpreter "What do you mean she only wants ten dollars for it? Tell her I can pay a hundred." This is what is known in the development sector as lack of absorptive capacity. The Paramount crew was in town for 6 weeks to shoot some footage for Tomb Raider at Angkor Wat, and they had 20 million dollars to spend. It is not easy to spend this amount of money in a country of 11 million people with an annual per capita income of 250 dollars, but they were determined to have a good time trying. The location manager had scouted the country from north to south, working through all the logistics that accompany a big-budget film. He checked the Thai border at Poipet, the seaport at Kompong Cham, and the sights in Phnom Penh. He booked out two hotels in Siem Reap, recruited hundreds of drivers, interpreters, guards and extras, and after a narrow miss in a motorbike accident, advised the producers that — contrary to usual practice — the next lot of crew would need to bring a doctor with them.

I didn't need to be asked twice to take 6 weeks off from treating sprained ankles in the emergency room in Oxford, and got on the next flight out of London. On the flight, I had a chance to learn something about both the film and the crew. They outlined the whole plot to me very patiently, several times, as I had never played the video game, or seen any of the director's previous films. Nor could I recognize any of the cast. Although I have since endured weeks of filming, watched the rushes every night, and have had the chance to clarify this plot line with everyone that determined it, the details are still fuzzy. The carpenters, set painters, and costume designers took it in turn explaining that the Lara Croft character, played by Angelina Jolie, collects artifacts from ancient ruins, in order (on this occasion) to thwart a secret society called the Illuminati in their quest to control the passage of time. The Illuminati need to find the "All-Seeing Eye" to help them find the "Triangle of Light" and they have to find it this week or wait for another 5000 years when the planets are lined up again. Lara Croft just happens to find this "All-Seeing Eye" in her house. The Illuminati steal it; she receives some posthumous mail from her father, Sir Richard (played by Angelina's

Travel Medicine: Tales Behind the Science
Copyright © 2007 by Elsevier Ltd.
All rights of reproduction in any form reserved.
ISBN: 0-08-045359-7

actual father, Jon Voigt), instructing her to recover the Eye and destroy the Triangle before the Illuminati can get their hands on it. Her character was supposed to be a female cross between James Bond and Indiana Jones. Even I understood this meant interminable car chases, hand-to-hand combat, and silly accents. Although I never got a clear answer as to why they chose Cambodia, the special effects' man summed up what we were supposed to be filming at Angkor: "there will be fog and atmosphere, and some bullet hits, and a giant statue will fall over."

The chief carpenter obviously thought I was a bit slow, and I had to explain that I knew nothing about movies, but I did know something about snakes, malaria, and landmines, which were pre-occupying the production managers when I had met them in London. While these risks were indeed a feature of life in Siem Reap, and made medical work in Cambodia particularly grim and compelling, this highly protected crew was much more likely to be troubled with minor gastrointestinal and sexually transmitted infections. The set designer was particularly interested in the local snakes, which were preventing the rest of his crew from getting the styrofoam imitation of Angor Wat's east gate built to schedule. His men had seen a snake the previous week, and downed tools. They were holding a work stoppage in Siem Reap and refusing to go back to the site until I appeared with some antivenom, which we had to bring over from the snake farm in Bangkok. In exchange for the film synopsis I gave them tidbits from the chapter on venomous snakes of medical importance in David Warrell's book *The Clinical Management of Snake Bites in the South East Asian Region*, and we had a nice chat about the fangs of cobras, kraits, coral snakes, and sea snakes. When I had been to see David Warrell in Oxford before leaving, he advised me to be quick with the adrenaline for anaphylaxis, and asked that we photograph any snakes that were captured. The crewmembers were really interested in the details and design of fangs: How the venom is injected through channels in the tooth, just like the channel of a intramuscular needle, into the snakes' usual prey, and how spitting cobras can spray venom into the eyes of an attacker. However, trying to explain that, even if one is bitten, one is not necessarily envenomed was entirely fruitless. They were also totally uninterested in the details of malaria transmission or any bugs for that matter, but landmines fascinated them.

I explained that Cambodia was littered with both anti-personnel mines, which look like a tin of shoe polish and are designed to blow off an arm or a leg, and anti-tank mines, about the size and the shape of a bedpan. De-mining activities in Cambodia were run by various organizations, including the Mine Action Group, HALO Trust, and Cambodian Mine Action Center (CMAC). These groups were using a variety of ways to de-mine — the Swedish army brought over mine-sniffing dogs, the Finnish army supplied an armored flail that beats the ground with steel chains to a depth of 6 inches, in an effort to detonate all the surrounding mines, and the Cambodians mostly do manual de-mining (a man probes the ground with a stick until he locates a mine, and then blows it up on site).

Although the incidence of mine injuries is finally decreasing, Cambodia has the highest prevalence of amputations in the world. There is one amputee for every 250 people, and the Ministry of Planning estimates that 4–6 million landmines remain in the ground. Part of the formal brief that I gave to the crew emphasized the interest of staying to well-traveled paths, and not wandering off into the jungle around the set. While the fledgling tourist industry had ensured that Angkor Wat had been an early focus of the government's de-mining efforts, much of the countryside was still being cleared, an arm and a leg at a time, and farmers used mines as primitive fences, digging them up during the day and replacing them at night.

As Angelina prided herself on doing her own stunts, Paramount was wary of letting her go to Siem Reap without some medical assistance on set. The crew confirmed that they usually got by with a couple of nurses at the studios in Slough, but there had been a fatal accident on a shoot in South America earlier in the year, and the industry was changing its mind about relying on local medical personnel in dubious locations. I had met their nurse before leaving, and she had given me a list of all their personal preferences in terms of vitamins, mosquito repellents, sunscreens, anti-inflammatories, antacids, cortisone ointments, and nonsedating antihistamines. I had dutifully stocked up and prescribed malaria prophylaxis to everyone, but I did wonder how this trip would go.

No one had shot a film in Cambodia since Peter O'Toole played Lord Jim in 1964. Even "The Killing Fields" had been filmed in Thailand in 1984. I had found on previous trips that people always gave you a count of things before and after Pol Pot: 13,000 doctors before, 341 after; 23 cinemas in Phonm Penh, not one left. What was it going to be like to make a film in a country where it could never be screened? Refrigerated trucks were not the only things missing, and I would have imagined that these were very low priority, but a film crew of this size brings its own caterers, and they need the refrigerated trucks to produce bacon and eggs, and chicken and chips at regular intervals. The Khmer crew had local cooks and ingredients, and I went straight to their tent at mealtimes.

I spent a lot of time planning for the worst case scenario: a crew member stepping on a mine, getting malaria, falling off the scaffolding, or being smashed in a car accident. With the help of a very practical nurse from the Yukon, we prepared supply lists, transport, and medivac arrangements accordingly. I hadn't anticipated that we would actually be most effectively employed in mixing 200 liters of oral rehydration solution each morning, transporting huge chests of the stuff onsite each day, and trying to keep up with the demand (both from the expatriate crew who were convinced it was a killer cure for their hangovers, and for the Khmers who were happy for extra calories — even if the liquid was a little salty.) The Paramount crew had hundreds of plastic bottles, and we did try to wash and recycle them, but the Khmers served themselves from a ladle dipped in the bucket — probably one of the more effective ways of ensuring fecal–oral transmission of any viruses that were circulating. In case you are ever in the same situation, the recipe is: 7 litres of water to 1 and a half cups of sugar, 7 teaspoons of salt, and 3 litres of orange juice.

In the early 1990s, it was hard to find a Cambodian living outside of Siem Reap who had actually seen Angkor, but it remained a resonant symbol of their ancestry. Present-day Khmers see themselves as direct descendants of the Angkor Empire that built this elaborate capital city, from which the god-kings ruled over much of Southeast Asia during its zenith between the 10th and 13th centuries. The Angkor Empire transitioned between Hinduism and Buddhism and declined slowly, progressively weakened by attacks from the west (Thailand) and the east (now Vietnam). The King of Cambodia placed the country under French protection in 1863, and it became part of French Indochina in 1887. Following Japanese occupation in World War II, Cambodia gained full independence from France in 1953. In 1975, Communist Khmer Rouge forces captured Phnom Penh and evacuated all the urban areas, forcing the population to an illiterate agrarian uniformity, consistent with Pol

Pot's notion of year zero. Between 1.5 and 3 million Cambodians are estimated to have died during Khmer Rouge regime. The 1978 Vietnamese invasion drove the Khmer Rouge into the countryside, began a 10-year Vietnamese occupation, and started a civil war that lasted for 13 years. Democratic elections and a ceasefire were mandated by the Paris Peace Accords, signed in 1991. Although the Khmer Rouge did not maintain this ceasefire, and a dry-season offensive continued all through the United Nations Transitional Authority (UNTAC) years, a coalition government was formed after the country's first democratic election, supervised by the UN in 1993. The first coalition government dissolved in 1997, but a second election in 1998 formed another, and the country has enjoyed relative political stability since. There have been efforts to bring the surviving Khmer Rouge leaders to trial, most of whom surrendered in early 1999.

Cambodia's biggest economic struggle is coping with its skewed demography — a result of the Khmer Rouge killings. More than 50% of the population is 20 years of age or younger, and it is difficult to counter the lack of infrastructure, education, and training, to create enough jobs to handle this imbalance. Tourism is an obvious place to start, and the government was easily persuaded that giving up censorship rights on this film was a fair trade-off for such a potential boost to the industry. Still, it was a violent film staged in a Buddhist country, and run-of-the-mill Hollywood artifice in a country that had seen more bloody and arbitrary changes of plot than anything a scriptwriter could have conceived. The entire budget was 94 million dollars, 20 million of which the producers planned to spend in Cambodia. This was approximately double the total amount that the government spent on health care for the entire population in a year. I wanted to get the most use out of this money in terms of medical supplies that could be left behind after the shooting was over.

When we arrived, I put the precious antivenom into a little beer cooler and hung it on a tree on site at the start of each day. The carpenters were perfectly satisfied with this symbolic gesture, and went back to work on their admittedly superb models of the east gate. Angelina kept fit, the stunt work went without a hitch, and I was so bored with the endless takes that I started a lump-and-bump clinic in my room at the Sofitel. I removed a Guinea worm (a souvenir from travels in Africa; dracunculiasis is not endemic in Cambodia) from the diver's foot, and an infected sebaceous cyst off the neck of one of the publicity agents. The boom operator had a small verruca on the back of his hand. He was impressed that the local anesthetic effectively divorced the image (a scalpel drawing blood) from the expected sensation — "just like an effect."

In the end, no-one was bitten by a snake, and I left the antivenom with a local NGO, who gave it to Chhouk Rin's army surgeon in the south of Cambodia. He put it to good use, reportedly saving the life, two months later, of someone bitten by a cobra. Chhouk Rin is a former Khmer Rouge general now serving a life imprisonment for having murdered three foreign backpackers in 1994 in Anlong Seng.

The silver Land Rover that Lara Croft drives to the temple in the film was imported at great expense and hassle from England, and was stuck for over a month in the customs office at Kompong Som while bribes were negotiated. No wonder they did not want to let it go. The Khmers love four-wheel drives: faster than a bicycle and smoother than a tank.

At the end of every day's shooting the rushes were hand-carried on a commercial flight to Bangkok, where they were developed and flown back, so that the director could screen them in one of the rooms of the hotel.

Most of the actual work on site went into building sets that did not make the final cut. There was a very elaborate scene that involved the construction of a temporary floating village on the lake at the Bayon, and a road that needed to be rebuilt to the top of Phnom Bahkeng — the highest point at Angkor. The floating village was dismantled, but the roadworks stayed, and with rather unrealistic expectations in the market, remains the only lasting indication of the crew's presence in Siem Reap. We donated all the drugs, instruments, defibrillator, and mobile phones to a local clinic, and Angelina adopted a Cambodian baby.

Chapter 16

The Woman Atop the Crocodile: Newton's Law in Africa

Stephen Toovey

Which interfering and ill-informed medic said obesity is bad for you? Obviously, one who has neither sojourned nor journeyed in African climes tropical. And for the traveler specifically, weight is a more important issue than generally realized: the economy class traveler packing with an eye to airline excess baggage charges may, quite unknowingly, be taking unnecessary risks with his health. Contrary to what most believe, excess baggage might just be good for your health.

The Zambezi river, rising in Zambia, flows through Angola, forming part of the international frontiers of Namibia, Botswana, Zimbabwe, and Zambia; after traversing Mozambique, it empties into the Indian Ocean, having completed a total course of 2574 km (1600 miles). The Zambezi has its own place in travel medicine history, the first European to describe the river was the famous missionary and explorer Dr David Livingstone.

Many travelers have followed Livingstone, and today the Zambezi river and its breathtaking Victoria falls are renowned tourist attractions. A good number of tour operators offer the visitor a good number of different ways of enjoying the natural beauty and splendor of the river: these include white water rafting, hot air ballooning, hang gliding, canoeing, and many others. White water rafting, undertaken in the gorge below the Victoria falls, offers an exhilirating day's adventure. Canoeing, on the other hand, offers a more leisurely way of enjoying the river. Canoe safaris last a number of days, the occupants passing many a pleasant hour drifting languorously along the river, occasionally being required to provide some direction and motive force by paddling. Canoeing lacks the adrenalin rushes, at least it usually does, that white water rafting provides, but it does allow a close and unrushed view of Africa's magnificent fauna and flora. Sometimes, however, the view can be uncomfortably close.

But first, it is important to understand how a canoe safari on the Zambezi proceeds. Participants in the safari are assigned two to a canoe, and each given a paddle. A local guide, familiar with the river and local conditions, takes up a seat at the rear of the canoe. Thus set, the canoes wend their way slowly downstream, a small flotilla of *Homo sapiens* in its

Travel Medicine: Tales Behind the Science
Copyright © 2007 by Elsevier Ltd.
ISBN: 0-08-045359-7

ancestral home, pulling in to the bank for the occasional beverage break, and for overnight rest. *H. sapiens*, however, is not the only creature to claim Africa as home.

Those who have traveled in small boats before will understand the importance of mass and balance. Weight should be distributed, especially in very small boats, as evenly as possible, with the maximum load being placed over the boat's center of gravity, i.e., in the center of the boat. Smaller, lighter individuals may be placed further from the center of gravity, i.e., at the bow and the stern (the front and the rear for non-nautical types). And so it was when my 55 kg (121 lb) friend Joanna and her very large companion named 'Bonny' were assigned places in their canoe; although Bonny's exact weight remains unknown to this day, enthusiastic, and perhaps unkind, estimates looked at multiples of Joanna's weight; at the rear end of their canoe sat Joshua their guide, a man of approximately 60 kg.

All went well for the safari party, including Joanna and Bonny, on the first day. A good number of hippos, elephants, fish eagles, and other wildlife were sighted, all obligingly providing photo opportunities for the safari group as it drifted slowly towards Mozambique. The first day also gave the party a chance to become acquainted with the ancient art of paddling, a skill lost by most modern city dwellers. The first night, encamped on the bank, was spent under a cloudless and moonlit sky, with talk of the day's events around the campfire. All awoke refreshed and invigorated on day 2, ready for more adventure.

As on the first day, Joanna, Bonny, and Joshua were seated in their allocated canoe positions, with the second day passing much as the first, the little band becoming more relaxed the further it proceeded, with only the occasional bout of paddling being needed to aid progress and maintain direction. It was during one of these short paddling spells that what might be termed a most unfriendly incident occurred. As Joanna, gazing lazily ahead, dipped the left side of her paddle into the water, she suddenly experienced a burning sensation in her hand. Next thing, she was ripped out of her canoe, finding herself in a welter of thrashing water. She had been taken by a crocodile. *Crocodylus niloticus*, the Nile crocodile, once on the brink of extinction, was intent on placing Joanna in the same category. Although the exact size of the brute that had grasped Joanna by the hand and pulled her out of the canoe remains the subject of continuing speculation (nobody had the courage to dive in with a tape measure and take an accurate reading from teeth to tail): witnesses in the accompanying canoes however placed it at between 4 and 5 m in length (approximately 13–19 feet).

You might at this stage be wondering what my opening discourse on weight and travel has to do with poor Joanna's lot as the prey of a Nile crocodile. The reason will shortly become clear. As suddenly as Joanna was removed from the canoe, so equally and suddenly did its carefully calculated mass and balance became mass with no balance. With no occupant in the front, the rear dug itself into the river, elevating Bonny to a point of maximum spatial instability, at which point she succumbed to Newton's law of universal gravitation, plummeting out of the canoe. Bonny, being of not insubstantial mass, impacted the water with considerable momentum.

At this point, a word on the Nile crocodile's preferred method of killing its prey is in order. Contrary to what is imagined by many people, crocodiles do not kill their victims by ripping them savagely apart in the water; rather, the crocodile drowns its victims, holding them between its jaws, and rolling with them underwater, until they expire. The lifeless victim is then stashed away in the crocodile's lair, usually under the riverbank, where it putrefies. Once sufficiently decomposed, to the point where the crocodile's palate is tempted, the victim is consumed.

So, back to Bonny and her involuntary plunge into the Zambezi, and Joanna, who is at this point in a bit of a spin, under water with the crocodile. Bonny's trajectory thrust her directly onto the crocodile, preoccupied with trying to drown Joanna. We may only conjecture what went through the crocodile's mind when Bonny's mass crashed against it, but images involving angry hippopotami may well have flashed through its brain. Whatever the image was, it was sufficient to persuade the crocodile that reptilian life and limb were in danger, and that instant evacuation was required. The crocodile released Joanna and disappeared. Joanna bobbed to the surface with a very confused look on her face, to see an equally perturbed Bonny floating past.

Both Bonny and Joanna were gathered in by the rest of the party, and both were largely unharmed, at least physically. Joanna bore a number of small incisions on her left hand, where the crocodile had held her fast: simple cleansing and wound care was all that was required, and within 10 days Joanna had nothing more to show for her ordeal than a few very fine scars, resembling those from razor incisions, on her hand.

And so to the point of the story. Had Joanna's companion, Bonny, not been a woman of considerable substance, it is unlikely that the crocodile would have bitten off more than it could chew, and Joanna would have ended up as croc fodder. There are clearly instances where size not only counts, but can also be life-saving.

SECTION 6:

TALES BEHIND THE RESEARCH IN TRAVEL MEDICINE

Chapter 17

The Borneo Eco-Challenge: GeoSentinel and Rapid Global Sharing of Disease Outbreak Information

David O. Freedman

Today, GeoSentinel (www.geosentinel.org) is a well-known and respected worldwide communications and data collection network operated by the International Society of Travel Medicine (ISTM) in partnership with the US Centers for Disease Control and Prevention (CDC). Thirty-three travel/tropical medicine ISTM clinics, called GeoSentinel sites, participate in full sentinel surveillance and are located on all six continents. An additional 145 ISTM clinics have joined the GeoSentinel Network Members program from around the world; they communicate unusual cases to GeoSentinel and as well participate in enhanced surveillance or response activities. GeoSentinel tracks emerging infectious diseases at their point of entry into domestic populations, monitors global trends in disease occurrence among travelers, and responds to urgent public health queries. GeoSentinel aids in rapid response by electronically disseminating alerts to surveillance sites, to the 2000 ISTM members in 55 countries, and to partner organizations globally.

Like most enterprises, GeoSentinel had a modest beginning in 1995, as will be described. By September 11, 2000, we were pleased that some data were beginning to accumulate that would allow us to begin examine disease trends in ill travelers. However, it was not until that day when a rapid series of events surrounding a sporting event on the other side of the world occurred, that we realized the speed with which the network we had set up could detect disease and respond in a way that would have immediate impact on the health of people who fell ill anywhere in the world.

The Beginning of GeoSentinel

In the summer of 1995, I drove for 2 hours from my office at the University of Alabama at Birmingham to a meeting in the office of Phyllis Kozarsky at Emory University in Atlanta, GA, where we were joined by Martin Cetron from the CDC. We had previously informally discussed the need for a rapid and efficient way to track travel-related diseases in an increasingly globalized world. The Internet was emerging and I had a good deal of experience in organizing online communities of medical providers. Marty was at the beginning of a fast-track career that would soon result in his current appointment as Director of Quarantine at CDC. He brought extraordinary epidemiologic and surveillance skills from several years in the Division of Parasitic Diseases at CDC. Phyllis was a travel medicine pioneer and one of the founders of the ISTM. By the end of that 1-day meeting, among beautifully collected artifacts from Phyllis' world travels, we decided to recruit a working group of eight US-based ISTM member travel clinics run by trusted and eminent colleagues to establish the network. Among others, these original members also included Jay Keystone in Toronto, Elaine Jong at the University of Washington, Murray Wittner and Brad Connor in New York, and Gordon Frierson at the University of California, San Francisco.

The vision of the then ISTM President Jay Keystone led to the ISTM providing the generous sum of $50,000 seed money to develop the network until independent funding could be secured. Fortunately, through a newly formed initiative at the time, by May 1996 GeoSentinel was awarded competitive funding through the Division of Quarantine, CDC under an initiative to strengthen surveillance and response to emerging pathogens. Other US-based initiatives had been funded to do domestic surveillance and we were to focus on global disease issues. Over the next year, pilot studies, which resulted in a refined surveillance instrument usable by practicing clinicians, were run. International surveillance sites began to join the network. By the end of 1997, GeoSentinel went "live" at participating surveillance sites using a set of data fields that linked destination, date of travel, and disease diagnosis in returning travelers. Data from all sites were aggregated at an Atlanta data center operated by GeoSentinel. By September of 2000, we had 14 sites in North America and had added 10 other leading clinical centers globally. These included Louis Loutan in Geneva, Frank Sonnenburg in Munich, Eli Schwartz in Jerusalem, Prativa Pandey in Kathmandu, Jane Zuckerman and Charles Easmon in London, Graham Brown and Joe Torresi in Melbourne, and Marc Shaw in Auckland.

We had started to have regular annual Site Directors meetings that brought together the combined expertise and intellect of many of the key leaders in the field of travel medicine. By then, the database contained records on 10,000 ill travelers, migrants, and refugees, and we were lucky to have recruited a talented bio-statistician, Leisa Weld, who happened to be a world traveler herself. She very quickly tamed the intricacies of the dataset in order to allow us to differentiate the usual from the unusual on an ongoing basis.

September 11, 2000: Travelers in Trouble

0745: I arrived for work in my office at the University of Alabama at Birmingham and, as every morning, began to check each of the multiple e-mail boxes I maintain for overseeing different discussion groups, projects, and functions. When I got to the GeoSentinel e-mail box I found a message from Charlie Easmon, site director at the Hospital for Tropical Diseases (HTD), London noting four travelers who were all ill after competing in an adventure race called the Borneo EcoChallenge. Could I query other GeoS sites?

"Dear David,
These are the details: Cases 1–3 have now been sent home. Case 1 renal impairment and conjunctival injection. Case 2 muscle aches and loose stools. Case 3 abnormal renal function which resolved. Case 4 is still in HTD. She was admitted to another hospital September 9 and transferred to HTD September 11 with pains in lower back, headache, fever 39C and haemoptysis. She had WBC 8.9, ALP 152 AST 120 gamma GT 80. She returned directly from Borneo. Leptospirosis serology is awaited.
Yrs, Charlie"

A quick surf to the Eco-Challenge website disclosed that this annual made for TV event was in 2000 a 12-day round-the-clock race in the jungles and off the coast of Borneo, where participants sailed on open ocean, mountain biked, kayaked, scuba dived, caved, and slogged through torrential jungle rain and mud while being assaulted by voracious leeches. After that, they swam and canoed in a storm-swollen river on August 25, and then waded through caves filled with bat guano. In all, 76 four-person teams from 26 countries were selected from hundreds of applicants and paid $12,500 to enter the Eco-Challenge, plus thousands more on equipment and travel. The first team finished the race on August 26 after 6 days but some other teams did not cross the finish line until as late as September 2.

Leptospirosis is caused by coming into contact with or swallowing water contaminated with animal urine. It is especially easy to get when someone has open cuts. The incubation period (time from exposure to the bacteria until first illness onset) can be as much as 3 weeks. Thus scheduling the event in Borneo during monsoon season may have been an unhealthy choice. The bacteria responsible for this disease normally live in rats and mice, and are excreted in their urine, so when there is a lot of excrement their urine gets mixed in with the water supply. Symptoms include fever, chills, headache, nausea and vomiting, jaundice (yellowing of the skin and whites of the eyes), muscle aches, and rash. Doctors generally treat the disease with antibiotics.

0800: Using the pre-programmed GeoSentinel e-mail distribution, a query was forwarded to all 26 GeoS sites worldwide with a request to immediately notify GeoS of any suspected cases.

1000: Brad Connor, NYC site director, e-mailed to describe what was later determined to be the first case. The 40-year-old racer was a managing director at Salomon Smith Barney who participated as part of Team RacingThePlanet.com. He had been ill since August 29, had been treated in Borneo for a fever of 104 degrees with fluid and antibiotics but was still feeling poorly when he returned to New York and consulted Brad, his travel medicine physician. He still had abnormal liver function tests and Brad's clinical impression was also leptospirosis.

1430: Brad had contacted his patient again who was then able to provide to GeoSentinel e-mail correspondence from a participant discussion forum indicating at least 15 other ill participants worldwide. GeoSentinel also obtained copies of records from the hospital in Borneo and ascertained that race organizers were aware of illness among participants beginning September 8.

1600: Jay Keystone, Toronto site director, telephoned to describe four additional cases from Toronto and surrounding areas with classical clinical findings of leptospirosis and expert clinician concurrence that this was typical leptospirosis.

1700: After discussions with fellow GeoSentinel directors Phyllis and Marty, a decision was made to utilize all the broader resources available to GeoSentinel and ISTM to put out a worldwide alert together with our partners. Because the diagnosis was certain in the hands of our expert clinicians, but laboratory confirmation was still pending, the alert would properly go out from GeoSentinel and ISTM and not wait for signoff by public health authorities. The urgency was dictated as leptospirosis is a treatable disease and many individuals at risk were still potentially in the incubation period.

2000–2200: After a break for family obligations, I was back in the office to generate and send the advisories/alerts that went out by e-mail to all GeoSentinel sites (26), ProMedmail (20,000 public health and press subscribers in 130 countries), TravelMed (ISTM listserv 400 subscribers), TropMed (American Society of Tropical Medicine listerv 200 subscribers), the entire ISTM membership of 1500 travel medicine specialists in 55 countries, and a request to the Infectious Diseases Society of America network to post to their 800 US-based infectious disease specialists. A copy was forwarded to race organizers.

At the end of the day, the elapsed time from the first indication of a problem to the worldwide dissemination of an alert after consultation and verification of the problem within our network of experts was 14 hours.

Tracking and Notifying Potentially Infected Travelers

Tuesday, September 12, 2000
0800: ProMedmail posts the GeoSentinel alert.

> Archive Number 20000912.1553
> Published Date 12-SEP-2000
> LEPTOSPIROSIS – UK, USA, CANADA EX MALAYSIA (BORNEO)
>
> Date: 11 Sep 2000 22:09:55-0500
> From: David Freedman <dfreedman@geomed.dom.uab.edu>
> Source: GeoSentinel
>
> Since some EcoChallenge participants may still be in the incubation phase and clinical outcomes can be improved with early treatment, we hope you can help us get the word out as soon as possible.
>
> D. Freedman
> for GeoSentinel
>
> GeoSentinel-Outbreak of Leptospirosis in Ecochallenge 2000 Participants
>
> Within the past 24 hours 3 GeoSentinel sites in London (Hospital for Tropical Diseases; C. Easmon), New York (Travelers Health Services; B. Connor), and

Toronto (Toronto Hospital Tropical Disease Unit; J. Keystone) have independently reported clusters totalling 9 participants from the 20 Aug 2000 to 1 Sep 2000 Ecochallenge Adventure race in Borneo ....
.... All ill, febrile patients with a history of Ecochallenge participation should be treated empirically for leptospirosis with penicillin or doxycycline unless another diagnosis is obvious. Because the incubation period can be as long as 2 weeks some participants may still present with new onset illness.

David O. Freedman &
Phyllis E. Kozarsky
For GeoSentinel
The Global Surveillance Network of the
International Society of Travel Medicine

Because the race organizers were US-based, the US CDC was by this time able to request a list of all race participants with contact information. GeoSentinel sites were present in all countries with the bulk of known race participants, but international public health channels have inherent delays. GeoSentinel agreed to provide the participant lists to our sites in each affected country to allow our site directors, who are uniformly well connected within their own national communities, to link with relevant public health authorities domestically.

Wednesday, September 13, 2000
0800: CDC supplies lists and contacts of all Australian, Canadian, and UK participants to GeoSentinel. GeoS forwards to those sites with a request to contact those participants or to contact relevant national public health authorities. In each case, public health authorities in those countries are contacted in less than 24 hours and begin immediate case finding and investigations.
1000: *The Associated Press* and *New York Times*, which had noted the ProMed piece, contact GeoSentinel. The story runs on the AP Wire and *New York Times* service the same day and then in hundreds of newspaper and media outlets worldwide further enhancing awareness of potentially infected people.

Next Days of September 2000
A South African ISTM member at large informs of two cases in S. Africa and forwards complete clinical details on September 21.
An ISTM member at large in Ft Collins, Co. reports two cases to GeoS by e-mail.
An ISTM member at large in Hamel Minnesota e-mails with a case.
An ISTM member at large e-mails report of patient in Houston hospitalized on 9/15 there after being hospitalized in Borneo. Lepto titer of 12,800.

E-mail from Graham Brown, Chairman of Medicine, University of Melbourne Australia

Subject: Eco Challenge Race outbreak — Australia
To: David Freedman <dfreedman@geomed.dom.uab.edu>, mzc4@cdc.gov
CC: BROWN_G@wehi.EDU.AU

Dear David and Marty,
Great work with the ECO challenge outbreak.
GEOSENTINEL also helped last week when our networks allowed us to
quickly link Marty and CDC team preparing website for Olympic travel to
Australia with key officials here.
Keep up your great work. It is a privilege to be part of this important inter-
national network!

Regards
Graham

What was Learned about Leptospirosis

Prior to the Borneo Eco-challenge, leptospirosis had long been recognized as a risk to those spending with significant outdoors exposure in moist rural or remote environments. The risk to soldiers on jungle maneuvers was recognized many decades ago. Sporadic clusters of cases of leptospirosis were reported in the 1990s in river rafters in Costa Rica and in triathletes in Illinois and Texas. However, the 2000 Borneo Eco-Challenge most dramatically illustrated the consequences when significant numbers of travelers end up in the wrong place at the wrong time. In the end, 80 of the 189 race participants who were contacted later by investigators met the clinical case definition for leptospirosis. A small number of race participants had been aware of decades old data from the US military demonstrating that pre-exposure therapy with a tetracycline antibiotic could prevent leptospirosis, and those that took this antibiotic before the race were not affected in this outbreak. The use of prophylactic doxycycline has now become standard among adventure racers and is now more often recommended by travel medicine doctors for individual adventure travelers.

What was Learned about the Potential of GeoSentinel

Presently, in 2007, instantaneous global sharing of information around disease outbreaks is taken for granted. This has been well demonstrated during severe acute respiratory syndrome (SARS) and avian influenza outbreaks that have occurred in recent years. However, in September 2000 GeoSentinel provided one of the first demonstrations of the beginning of the exciting adventure in the way global surveillance data can rapidly be turned into information for action. Oubreak detection and management now run on a 24-hour clock because someone is always awake somewhere. The Eco-Challenge outbreak demonstrated that the growth of partnerships between ISTM, CDC, and other medical societies, governments, and private organizations had become one of the surveillance network's greatest assets. This outbreak also demonstrated the value of front-line clinical observation by expert physicians and the ability of the doctor–patient relationship to rapidly gather information. The information and documentation gathered by Brad Connor in New York in less than 3 hours because of a physician's rapport with his patient could not have been accomplished otherwise.

GeoSentinel Since and Today

Continued public health response and collaboration of this sort serve to effectively contain infectious diseases and minimize disease-related morbidity. In 2003, the GeoSentinel site in Toronto saw some of the first cases of SARS outside Asia and quickly notified the network that SARS was not just an Asian problem, as per the World Health Organization alerts, but was now a global problem.

Today GeoSentinel has 33 sites in all the six continents (see the map at the end). A strategic expansion starting in 2004 after SARS has added sites in Beijing, Tokyo, Singapore, Ho Chi Minh City, and Bangkok. The GeoSentinel dataset now contains over 60,000 patient records that cover traveler exposures in over 237 countries and territories. Of these 516 diagnoses are monitored by region, by precise location, by time of exposure, and by risk group. Ongoing trends are tracked on a month-to-month basis for 60 key diagnoses.

In response to the pandemic influenza threat, GeoSentinel has developed a response plan to allow focused enhanced surveillance for respiratory diagnoses immediately upon indications of the onset of human-to-human transmission. The plan includes daily visual review of the geographic exposures of every suspected respiratory illness submitted to GeoSentinel, and weekly examination of monthly trends in suspected pneumonias, atypical pneumonia, influenza, lower respiratory illness, and presenting respiratory complaints, a strategy that was validated during the SARS outbreak.

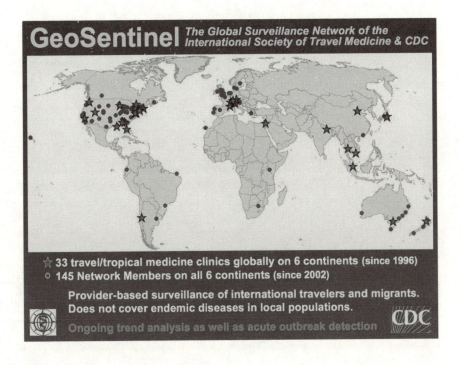

GeoSentinel — The Global Surveillance Network of the International Society of Travel Medicine & CDC

☆ 33 travel/tropical medicine clinics globally on 6 continents (since 1996)
○ 145 Network Members on all 6 continents (since 2002)

Provider-based surveillance of international travelers and migrants. Does not cover endemic diseases in local populations.

Ongoing trend analysis as well as acute outbreak detection

Chapter 18

Understanding Malaria Prophylaxis: Lessons Learnt on the Omo River, Ethiopia

Eli Schwartz

One morning in mid-January 1996, the physician who was on night shift mentioned that a returning traveler had been admitted the night before with probable malaria. I went to see the patient to get more information about his medical history and travel itinerary. The patient was a tour guide who had started to conduct rafting trips in Ethiopia. His last trip had been 3 months earlier for about 2 weeks in Southern Ethiopia. Since I had been in this country, I wanted to find out the exact place of the rafting trip, and was told that it took place on the Omo River, the second largest river in Ethiopia that flows from the central highlands

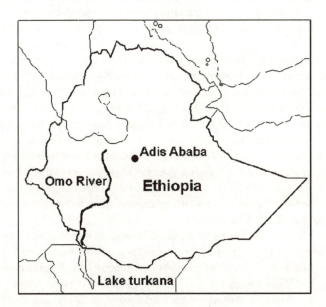

Map 18.1. Map of Ethiopia and the Omo river.

Travel Medicine: Tales Behind the Science
Copyright © 2007 by Elsevier Ltd.
All rights of reproduction in any form reserved.
ISBN: 0-08-045359-7

of south Ethiopia, ending in Turkana Lake in Kenya. An important point was that since the patient's last trip 3 months previously, he had not visited any other tropical countries.

The patient stated very definitely that he had taken mefloquine (Lariam) as malaria prophylaxis, starting 1 week prior to his departure and continuing for 4 weeks after return, as recommended. He insisted that he had not missed any doses and that he was compliant with treatment for the 4 weeks after return. It was an unusual case, that of contracting malaria despite taking the recommended new drug (at that time Lariam was quite new in the market). The malaria species in question was identified as malaria vivax.

The next day the patient told me that, interestingly enough, his friend on the same trip had just called to tell him that he had spiking fever as well. I asked him to be brought to the hospital, and sure enough, he had vivax malaria as well. He was also very definite about having been compliant in taking Lariam as malaria prophylaxis.

Two cases of malaria at the same time were quite unusual. To make it more unusual, a day later, another member of the group called to report that he had fever, and after that, almost daily, other members of the group presented with fever that was found to be vivax malaria. Altogether 6 people out of the 12 in the rafting group were affected.

It was extremely unusual to have a group of people coming back from Africa with malaria, especially when they all had taken malaria prophylaxis. A few months later, when another group went on a rafting trip to the Omo River with the same tour guide, I asked him to inform me if any of the rafters were to get fever after their return.

The people in this group also took Lariam, the recommended drug for malaria prophylaxis, and the same pattern repeated itself: exactly 3 months after coming back from the rafting trip, like a Swiss clock, the first case of malaria fever presented to my department with spiking fever that was diagnosed as vivax malaria. Following the previous experience, a survey was conducted of the group to find out if anyone else had fever. Again, almost every day, another member contracted fever, and out of the 14 people, 7 became ill with malaria. Again, further investigation revealed that they all claimed to have taken the prophylaxis without missing any doses. The drug had been bought in Israel, had not expired, and in spite of this, they contracted malaria.

The managers of the rafting tour company asked me what could be done for the next trip, and intuitively I answered that if mefloquine does not work they should switch to doxycycline.

A year later, the next rafting trip took place, and this time the group took doxycycline as prophylaxis. However, there was no difference, and about half of the group came down with a vivax malaria attack after 3 months.

At this point I became fascinated by the malaria enigma of Omo River. The first unusual manifestation was the very high attack rate, which was consistently about 50%, more than 10 times higher than the attack rate of travelers to Africa. In fact, the attack rate of travelers to Africa, who do not use prophylaxis, is usually less than 5% per month of stay whereas rafting on the Omo River for only two weeks resulted in an attack rate of at least 50%.

The second unusual point was that malaria occurred among people taking the best-known malaria prophylaxis (mefloquine and doxycyline). Resistance has been known to occur in falciparum malaria; however, the species that was diagnosed for all these rafters was vivax malaria in which resistance is very uncommon, especially with the new drugs such as mefloquine.

In vivax malaria, sporozoites enter the liver after the bite of an infected mosquito. Some sporozoites will go into a hypnotic state called hypnozoites, to become dormant in the liver.

What probably occurred was that the routine anti-malaria drug that was taken did not prevent this process. Only those parasites that emerged from the liver shortly after the bite (within two weeks after infection) would be eradicated by the anti-malaria drug. The hypnozoites, dormant in the liver, wake up and invade the erythrocytes only after a few months of the initial infection when there is no more chemoprophylaxis in the blood, thus causing late infection.

So the explanation must be that the current drug used for malaria prophylaxis eradicated only the blood stage of malaria, and not the hypnozoites that remained dormant in the liver, and therefore all the late emergence of malaria would not be targeted by anti-malaria drug in the blood.

The startling conclusion at this point was that the anti-malaria drug that we routinely recommend may be good for preventing falciparum malaria, but in the case of vivax malaria only prevents the primary infection, and only delays the onset of the first clinical manifestation by a few months, thus confounding the diagnosis.

Understanding this did not, however, help solve the problem. People still wanted to go on rafting trips and, knowing that the chance of getting malaria was very high, demanded a different medical recommendation. It came to my mind to try to go back to the very old drug primaquine. This drug that had been developed in the late 1940s for malaria prophylaxis, was for some reason not indicated for this purpose, and continued to serve only as radical treatment for vivax malaria patients. Patients who present with vivax malaria are to take 2 weeks of primaquine at the end of chloroquine therapy in order to kill the hypnozoites in the liver. Primaquine has been the only drug in the past 60 years known to kill hypnozoites of vivax malaria in the liver.

I hypothesized that if primaquine is effective in eradicating vivax malaria in the liver, it might be good as a preventive. It is also important to remember that falciparum malaria is endemic in Africa, and travelers should not be sent without protection from falciparum as well.

I started to investigate the old literature, "old" meaning the early 1950s. Literature that cannot be found today on Medline, thus inaccessible, is usually ignored. Nonetheless, there are treasures to be found there. In our case, the many studies performed by Alving in the 1950s showed that falciparum malaria is very sensitive to primaquine. I therefore thought that primaquine might be a suitable weapon as a single agent of malaria prophylaxis for travelers to the Omo River region, as it can prevent falciparum malaria and has the capacity to kill the hypnozoites of the vivax as well. The other advantage of using primaquine could be that since it works on the liver (liver stage prophylaxis), there is no need to continue it for a month after return from the endemic country, a point that significantly may increase compliance among travelers.

As was mentioned before, the other puzzling point in these incidents was the very high attack rate, and I was curious to know whether in this remote area of the world there might be unique kinds of anophiline mosquitoes that are much more efficient in transmitting malaria. I decided to go myself on the rafting trip, to try to catch mosquitoes along the way, and to try taking primaquine to check whether it would be effective as a prophylaxis against both vivax and falciparum malaria. The guides on the trip, having had already been in the area and experienced malaria while taking the routinely recommended prophylaxis, decided they wanted to take primaquine as well.

I had previously been to Ethiopia while working with the refugees, but mainly in Addis Ababa, and in other high places of the country that are areas free from malaria. I had never been to the southern part of Ethiopia, which is more African in character.

After a night in Addis Ababa, we drove the 4 × 4 vehicles loaded with three rubber rafts and gear, and after a day-long trip, we reached the riverbank. The Omo River flows in a deep gorge, and is inaccessible from land in most places. There are only a few points at which the river can be accessed. On one of the bridges, we left our jeeps and carried the boats down to the river, pumped them up, and loaded them with supplies for a 2-week trip. Our course went south with the flow of the river for 300 km. As was mentioned, the river is in a deep gorge, and once you start the trip, you cannot leave the river for 2 weeks until reaching another bridge where a vehicle can wait.

We were five people and a guide on each of the boats. At first, the flow was gentle and no strenuous paddling was necessary. We knew that during the rafting trip we could expect to meet some rapids, some up to grade 5, and in fact we navigated many of them. Sometimes we managed the rapids, keeping all the people in the boat and sometimes a few were thrown out into the whirlpools and turbulence formed by the rapids.

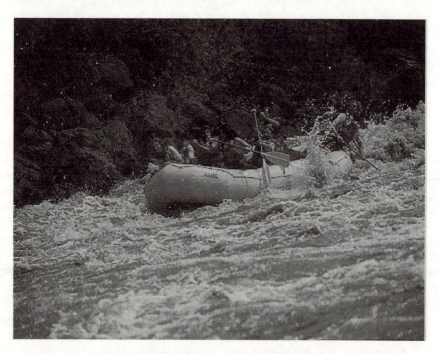

Image 18.1. Rafting on the Omo river.

In the absence of motors, we could enjoy the sounds of the jungle. Along the banks we could hear baboons screaming and the sounds of many birds, including raptors. We were told there were many animals around, and that we had to watch out for crocodiles and hippopotami in the river. In fact, the most frightening animals on the trip were the hippos that although vegetarian, are very territorial, and therefore very aggressive. While invading their territory in the river (marked by their excretion), the dominant male would swim rapidly towards us and try to attack the boat. When this would happen, we had to row energetically to escape their fangs. Indeed, I found out later on that the hippos are the number one hazard to both travelers and the local population.

Image 18.2. A surprise meeting with hippos on the Omo.

Every afternoon, we would look around for a camping ground. We had to be sure that it would not be the territory of hippos or other animals. We would disembark, unload the gear, and start to set up camp. The tents were well screened to keep out mosquitoes. However, there were many hours of activity from sundown to when people actually entered the tents to sleep under their nets. During this time camp was set up, dinner was made, and people socialized, and entertained themselves. Only 4–5 hours after sundown, did the people enter the tents into the protection of the mosquito nets. It was during those evening hours that the anopheline mosquitoes took their blood meal. We tried to keep ourselves covered with long sleeves and trousers and to use mosquito repellent in order to prevent bites, but those measures were not always effective.

Image 18.3. Camping on the bank of the Omo.

The trip continued in that fashion day after day, for 12 strenuous days. On most days we did not see any local people. Only during the last few days of the trip did we start to come across the local inhabitants. These were the many tribes that could only be reached by river rafting, tribes that did not speak the language of the country, and mostly individuals who had never come across white people.

Many of the men were dressed in loin clothes that during the day were placed on the head serving as a hat, and in the evening were put around the hips to cover up. The women's upper bodies were exposed, and leather skirts covered their hips. Their breasts were bare, and when meeting us, some tried to peak under the clothes of the women in our group to see what secrets their bras were hiding. In any case, the African garments in that environment left a lot of exposed skin for the anopheline mosquitoes, and it did not seem that they had any problem in obtaining infected blood. This might partly explain the high rate of infection.

Image 18.4. Local rafters.

After 12 intensive days on the river, we reached the bridge at the end of our adventure, the end point from which we returned a distance of a 2-day journey with the 4 × 4 vehicles to Addis Ababa.

Back in Israel, I handed in the anopheline mosquito larva that I had collected for identification. They were identified as *Anopheles gambiensis*, the common vector of malaria in Africa. This mosquito is a more efficient malaria vector than the *Anopheles* species prevalent in the Far East and in South America, which partially may explain the high prevalence of malaria in Africa. However, it is the same species that exists in the rest of Sub-Saharan Africa. The species of vector could therefore not explain the high rate of attack. The high attack rate may be explained by the nature of the trip, and the many hours of exposure at the camping sites along the river.

The second point of interest was how many of the people would come down with malaria, and what would happen in the primaquine group. Not surprisingly, the people in the non-primaquine group started presenting with fever 3 months after the trip, while none of the people in the primaquine group became ill with malaria.

This gave us encouragement that we were on the right track in finding a good malaria prophylaxis for that area. Indeed on the next trips, people heard of the success of the primaquine group, and more and more people wanted to obtain this drug as an effective prophylaxis. After 3 years of rafting trips, we could summarize that in the primaquine group 5% contracted malaria compared to 50% with the other drugs.

It should be noted that the reputation of primaquine at that time was that it was a very toxic drug, and therefore we did not dare prescribe more than one tablet a day (15 mg). However, when using it, we noticed very few side effects. We thought that 15 mg per day for an average-sized Western traveler, who is heavier than local people, was probably not a high enough dose, and that might be the reason for the failed cases. After increasing the dose to two tablets a day (the dose recommended by the CDC currently) we hardly had any failures.

It is important to emphasize that people who want to take primaquine should be screened for the level of G6PD enzyme. People with G6PD deficiency are at risk for significant hemolysis. However, when excluding this group of susceptible people, there were hardly any significant adverse events in our experience with hundreds of people.

As of now, it seems that primaquine is the suitable drug for prophylaxis against both vivax and falciparum malaria.

The fact that people returned from that area of the world, and 3 months after exposure contracted malaria, demonstrated to me that the routinely prescribed drugs do not work in places where vivax malaria exists. If there is no resistance, the drugs will prevent falciparum. But in any region where vivax malaria exists, they will not prevent malaria, but only delay the clinical onset. The Omo River rafters were my great teachers, clearly showing me that when we travel medicine practitioners prescribed malaria prophylaxis for travelers, we are not really providing them with malaria prophylaxis but rather with falciparum prophylaxis. Vivax malaria is not covered.

My intuition told me that if this phenomenon was so obvious among the Omo River rafters because they served as a cohort, the same situation could exist among the entire population of travelers in Israel.

Maybe other vivax malaria cases occurred in Israel not because of non-compliance with prophylactic drugs, but rather among those who took prophylaxis and had a late onset of infection. I therefore reviewed the patient files in my clinic, and the files of cases registered in the Ministry of Health for the previous 5 years; and sure enough, I found that, indeed, 80% of vivax cases in Israeli patients occurred in patients who took the recommended prophylaxis treatment. Furthermore, all those cases occurred as late infection, more than 2 months after returning from the trip. This confirmed that most cases of vivax malaria occurred as delayed infection to persons who were compliant with prophylactic treatment.

Just as I was not satisfied to limit my sample to the Omo River rafting trips, I did not want to limit the sample to Israeli travelers, and the next step was to see what occurred in other traveler groups. Through my connections with the CDC in Atlanta, Georgia, I was able to review the data of American travelers for the last 5 years, a sample which is 10 times larger than the Israeli cohort. Indeed, the observation on Israeli travelers was repeated in American travelers. This proved that the drugs we have for malaria prophylaxis could prevent falciparum malaria, which is very important, as falciparum malaria is a major cause of mortality; however, they do not prevent vivax malaria, which is a major cause of morbidity.

Moreover, travelers who were told that they were taking malaria prophylaxis and then returned with vivax malaria, not aware of the type of malaria they had contracted, reported that the malaria prophylaxis they received was not effective. Therefore, on their next trip, or when advising friends, they would be apt to recommend not taking malaria prophylaxis.

It is important for the medical practitioners, who deal with travelers, to know that our drug inventory does not fulfill the needs of all travelers. Until today, the only drug that is the prototype of effective treatment against all types of malaria is, after all, primaquine. Its main drawback is that it is contraindicated for people with G6PD deficiency.

The world of medicine is conservative, and does not accept changes readily, especially if instead of recommending a new drug, a very old drug is recommended. However, awareness is growing, and a number of international organizations such as the American CDC are listing primaquine in their arsenal of recommended drugs for malaria prophylaxis in travelers, albeit hesitantly.

My adventure on the Omo River was not only an adventure in wild life and rafting, but it also turned out to be a voyage in understanding malaria far beyond the Omo region.

References

Schwartz, E., & Sidi, Y. (1998). New aspects of malaria imported from Ethiopia. *Clinical Infectious Disease, 26*, 1089–1091.

Schwartz, E., & Regev-Yochay, G. (1999). Primaquine as prophylaxis for malaria for non-immune travelers; comparison to mefloquine or doxycycline. *Clinical Infectious Disease, 29*, 1502–1506.

Schwartz, E. (2001). Primaquine for malaria prophylaxis. In: P. Schlagenhauf (Ed.), *Travelers' Malaria*. Canada: BC Decker Inc.

Schwartz, E., Parise, M., Kozarsky, P., & Cetron, M. (2003). Delayed onset of malaria: Implications for chemoprophylaxis in travelers. *New England Journal of Medicine, 349*, 1510–1516.

Chapter 19

Travelers' Diarrhea: Tales from Mexico

Charles D. Ericsson

Our group has been studying travelers' diarrhea in Mexico for nearly 30 years. Our study population is college students studying in Mexico during the summer. We take along fourth-year medical students to help us with the field research. It has been hard for any of us not to develop a scatological sense of humor. Needless to say, I have encountered several interesting situations over the years, some of which are more humorous with the passage of time.

The lab has been an easy target for silly humor. We clinicians giggled for hours wondering how loud the screeches would be when the sealed stool cup was opened to reveal the largest beetle I had ever seen. It filled a pint container that we used to collect stool samples. It had huge pincers that clacked together menacingly. No one in the lab owned up to actually yelling, and to this day I have no idea what happened to the poor beetle.

In the same vein, imagine a crushed Baby Ruth bar mixed with a little water to make thick slurry. Then take a paper towel and tear off very thin strips about one inch long. Apply red Magic Marker to the strips and mix with the slurry. The red color actually diffuses very realistically into the mess and the nut chunks and caramel strands lend a quite believable appearance. We were impressed when the lab reported back "occult ink positive" and isolation of *Escherichia candiensis*.

Before enrolling patients in treatment studies, we needed to confirm that the subject was really passing unformed stools. I recall vividly one patient who had had cramps and alleged that he had passed 10 stools within the last few hours. His stool sample, however, had a positive "marble test". (A shaken stool cup creates the sound of a marble rolling around in it.) When confronted with this obviously scybalous stool, the patient became indignant when it was suggested he had not really passed 10 stools in such a short period of time. He most definitely *had* passed 10; when he was finished with his bowel movement, he had turned around and counted them!

We became adept at recognizing likely shigellosis by the bloody, mucoid appearance of the stool and the characteristic smell. Once I was diligently examining a stool sample submitted by a sick student. Our clinic was on the second floor of a building with a lovely courtyard below. I was standing at the railing holding the open sample out over the railing so as to dissipate the smell as much as possible. Across the courtyard a colleague happened to snap a picture of my intent inspection with my nose wrinkled from the pungent odor. It was not until we had the film developed that we realized that below me in the courtyard, scores of students were sitting around tables of a makeshift school cafeteria eating lunch! Thankfully, enteric pathogens are not airborne, but I doubt the students below me would have been pleased had they realized what was happening.

Toward the end of the summer school session, some of our student population gets low on beer money. We needed to be careful that patients really had diarrhea before enrolling them, since our protocols do pay them a modest amount for their time and trouble. We confronted one fellow and refused to pay when the results of analysis of his appropriately watery stool sample returned from the lab: "normal dog parasites"!

One of the hardest things we ever did with our student population was to collect "normal" stool samples. We were comparing the isolation of enteroaggregative *E. coli* from the ill and the well students. You realize how high the taboo over stools is in our society when you ask for normal stool even when you are willing to pay a small amount for each sample. Fortunately, my wife (a nonmedical grade school teacher) had the right idea. We toned down the joking about the process and placed discreet signs in all the bathrooms rationalizing the reasons for our request and supplied stool cups with instructions in each stall. Cooperation improved considerably. We did need to "cut off" two young children of one of the professors, who wanted to give daily samples! And there was the fellow who was very proud of himself as he handed in a pint container filled to the brim and neatly leveled off. I nearly dropped the container as it was so heavy. I did need to document that the sample was formed, but there was so much stool that getting the top back on the container was a challenge. The fellow seemed satisfied with my amazement, smiled enigmatically, and walked out of the clinic without getting paid for his sample.

Enrolling ourselves in protocols was a common practice. One medical student who was working with us became ill and enrolled himself in a 5-day protocol comparing furazolidone and ampicillin. Furazolidone has a disulfiram-like effect if you drink alcohol with it. At the end of day one, the student declared that he knew which drug he was on since his urine did not smell like penicillin. At dinner he was determined to "study" the disulfiram effect and ordered a rum and coke, his favorite alcoholic beverage. He drank about half of it before he developed a bright red flushed face. We all laughed and cautioned him not to drink any more. The next evening he did it again and flushed after only about a quarter of his drink. The third evening when he ordered a rum and coke again, I threatened to flunk him, but he took a swig anyway. I think he finally learned his lesson when he flushed intensely and became dizzy. We had to stretch him out in a booth and put his legs up in the air to overcome his hypotension. I do give him credit for curiosity, and all's well that ends well: he is now a very successful ID physician!

I suppose you cannot count yourself a seasoned researcher in travelers' diarrhea without having experienced the syndrome first hand. If that is an indicator for seniority, then I am an old hand! I have long been the culinary hedonist in our group and I have paid the price, but I have also had some superb meals.

My next to worse experience followed eating key lime pie in Manzanillo. It was wonderful. The "limons" in Mexico are the equivalent of key limes; they make an excellent pie. However, the next morning I got sick just as my wife, two kids, and I needed to check out of our hotel. We had planned to visit the nearby town and shop until our flight returned us to Guadalajara later that afternoon. I spent the 6 hours before the flight camped outside the hotel lobby bathroom anticipating my next movement. Needless to say I was not my family's favorite person, especially since I had so obviously not practiced what I preached.

My worst experience followed the time I broke down and added diced onions to my pazole (a sort of hominy stew). I "met criteria" 3 hours after passing the first loose stool. No one was in the clinic at the time when I decided to enroll myself in a treatment study. All went well until I had to draw my own blood. I now have a lot of respect for the skill of IV drug abusers. Once you get the tourniquet into place and finish drawing the blood, how do you release the tourniquet with the needle still in place? My teeth were not long enough. Fortunately a colleague came into the clinic just in time. (For the record I subsequently learned how to draw blood from myself without using a tourniquet; when it is time to remove the needle just raise your arm and the vein collapses and does not bleed.) That night I was so weak I literally crawled to the john (multiple times). At one point I think I had perioral paresthesias and was probably a little delirious. But 12 hours into therapy (around 6 AM), an elephant got off my chest and I felt somewhat better. I managed to make it to work at the school clinic where I was the only physician on call. A language professor came by to chat and commented that I looked like s—t. But as a testimony to the benefits of antibiotic therapy, I was jogging the next morning! My sample came back positive for enterotoxigenic *E. coli* plus *Shigella*. This experience convinced me that I needed to be more cautious about eating dangerous foods.

By now you can probably guess that my approach was not to give up on good eating. By this time we had shown that single-dose antibiotic therapy worked very well in the treatment of travelers' diarrhea, and I reasoned that if a single dose of an antibiotic was good enough to cure the disease, then a single dose would work very well as post-exposure prophylaxis. Our medical students marveled at my intestinal fortitude as I enjoyed items like fresh raw green mango dipped in lemon juice and cayenne pepper. Those who followed my example often "contributed" to the cause of science. Eventually, I would break down and tell them that I popped a dose of antibiotic after any obviously dangerous meal. They took the news graciously and chided me good naturedly, but I also noticed that they had not told the next year's batch of medical students.

Finally, my approach caught up with me and I got my just desserts (so to speak). That summer the medical students were especially adventuresome. They found some wonderful ethnic, small, and cheap restaurants. Many featured special sauces that I sampled liberally. I was probably popping a dose of antibiotic 3 or 4 days out of each week and enjoying the cuisine immensely. All went well until I returned to the States, and eventually realized I was having intermittent, remittent mild diarrhea and cramps. My wife eventually threatened to kick me out of the house because of the foul-smelling flatus. Sure enough I had giardiasis, which of course had not been prevented by taking antibiotic prophylaxis. I responded well to metronidazole but not being able to drink margaritas for the better part of 2 weeks (owing to the disulfiram-like effect of the metronidazole) was punishment enough to make me revise my approach to eating in Mexico.

I am now much more circumspect about what I eat; and I can report that now I only rarely take post-exposure prophylaxis. I am, however, actively considering what to do with the ceramic dog turd that I bought during my last visit to wonderful Mexico. It fits perfectly into the bottom of one of our stool cups...

I attest that each tale conforms loosely to the truth.

Chapter 20

The History of the CIWEC Clinic in Kathmandu, Nepal

Prativa Pandey and David R. Shlim

The CIWEC Clinic Travel Medicine Centre is one of the best-known travel medicine clinics in the world. However, not that many people are familiar with the actual history of the clinic, as that story has not been written down before. It was the world's first destination travel clinic — the first Western clinic to focus on the care of travelers in a destination country. The clinic has produced over 40 original articles on travel medicine issues, helped discover a novel intestinal pathogen, *Cyclospora*, and become an important contributor to the GeoSentinel Project of the International Society of Travel Medicine (ISTM). The current president of the ISTM is the Medical Director of the CIWEC Clinic, Dr. Prativa Pandey.

The clinic was started in 1982 in Kathmandu, Nepal, with much more humble ambitions. The CIWEC project in Nepal was a Canadian aid project that was mapping and advising on hydroelectric resources. CIWEC stood for Canadian International Water and Energy Consultants, and was a consortium of three commercial Canadian engineering firms, joined together to work on aid projects. There was no medical component to their work. However, medical care in Kathmandu in the early 1980s was extremely poor and difficult for Westerners to obtain. Emergency rooms barely functioned, and the hospital clinics were busy, dirty, and indifferently staffed. Nepali doctors, who were required to work for the government, often had a private practice for 2 hours in the evening. These practices were hasty affairs, conducted behind a thin curtain. Patients waited in one room, then entered the exam room for a 2–5 minute visit, without much privacy. Records were not kept of the visits.

The CIWEC project had grown to 15 families by early 1982. They began to look for a way to obtain ongoing medical care that would be more accessible and more reliable. The project turned to David Petersen, an American physician who was living in Nepal because his wife, Kathi, was working for UNICEF. Dr. Petersen was an accomplished Himalayan mountaineer. He had run the student health clinic at the Evergreen State College in Olympia, Washington before coming to Nepal. The CIWEC project asked him to set up a clinic that would be used mainly by the aid project families.

Dr. Petersen set up shop in a one-story, two-bedroom house located directly behind where he was living in Maharajganj, which in those days was on the edge of Kathmandu surrounded by rice paddies. The clinic rapidly became popular with most of the expatriate community. As the volume grew, Dr. Petersen hired expatriate receptionists and two American nurse practitioners to help him.

The clinic became known as the CIWEC Clinic, and had authorization from the Nepalese government to operate, although the mandate limited its scope of operation to the people in the CIWEC project. As a result of this limited mandate, the clinic did not promote itself to the tourist population. However, word of mouth, a powerful tool among world travelers, led tourists to seek out the clinic despite its out of the way location.

After the clinic had been operating for a year, Dr. Petersen received a visit from David R. Shlim, M.D., who had just come down to Kathmandu after completing his third volunteer season at the Himalayan Rescue Association Aid Post in Pheriche, near the base of Mt. Everest. Dr. Shlim had heard about the CIWEC Clinic while he was up in the mountains, and decided to see if he could work there in the future.

Dr. Shlim joined the clinic in August of 1983. Now the clinic consisted of two doctors, two nurse practitioners, Western nurses, and a phenomenally reliable lab technician named Ramachandran Rajah, a Malaysian who had moved to Nepal. Word of mouth continued to grow, and the clinic made its way into the guidebooks to Nepal. The clinic offered care 24 hours a day, 7 days a week. With only two doctors, this meant being on call every other night, and every day when the other doctor was away.

The clinic grew by accident. If a foreign doctor had applied for permission to open and operate such a clinic for the benefit of everyone in Nepal, it would have been denied, as there were no provisions among Nepali health laws for such a clinic. However, the clinic was allowed as an adjunct to an existing aid project. As the diplomatic and aid communities began to use the clinic, the Nepali authorities must have been aware. They condoned the clinic as a support to diplomatic relations, aid projects, and eventually, support of the tourist sector.

The clinic business grew. However, after 2 years the clinic was still not paying for itself. The CIWEC project continued to subsidize the cost of running the clinic, even though their own employees had become less than 5% of the patients. They wanted the situation to change. At a series of meetings with the community, it became clear that there were no agencies or embassies willing and/or able to subsidize the clinic to keep it open. The only solution was to somehow make it self-supporting. At this critical juncture, Dr. Petersen left to go back to the U.S.A., and David Shlim became the Medical Director whose job was to make the clinic self-supporting, and to pay back half the start-up costs of the CIWEC project. As far as anyone knew, a self-supporting clinic for foreigners had never been accomplished in any developing country.

There were some features unique to Nepal, which may have contributed to the clinic's eventual success. Nepal had a very weak medical infrastructure at the time, which created an instant demand for a foreign-run clinic. In other countries, there might be more competition from local services. Kathmandu, the capital city, was the entry and exit point for over 90% of the tourists. This allowed us to see people at the beginning or end of their trips, or when they had to come back to Kathmandu because of illness or injury. At the same time, Nepal was an immensely appealing destination that drew people from all over the world to see the Himalayas, the culture, and the wildlife.

One thing that continued to work against the financial success of the clinic was how inexpensive everything else was in Nepal. In the early 1980s, a traveler could spend less than $5 to $10 a night for a room, and eat for less than that. Our charges looked to some travelers as if we were trying to take advantage of the limited competition, when in fact we were just trying to survive. Back then, we charged $25 for a consultation, and $8 for a stool exam.

By finding doctors who were willing to work for less than an international wage in order to be able to live in Nepal, we kept our major expenses down. Because our permission to see patients was constrained, we made it a conscious point not to advertise or try to draw attention to the clinic. This made it harder to grow the business, but kept us from attracting unwanted attention.

In 1986, Dr. Shlim was introduced to Dr. David Taylor, a diarrhea researcher at the U.S. Armed Forces Research Institute of Medical Science (AFRIMS), based in Bangkok. The U.S. army in those days had a mandate to study diseases around the world in order to be prepared in case U.S. forces had to deploy there. There had been no studies of the etiology of diarrhea in Nepal. We decided to do one. Dr. Shlim had never done any medical research prior to this.

In order to do a comprehensive survey, we would need to ship the stool to Bangkok in regular shipments, on ice. We would do the parasitologic exam in Kathmandu. There were too many patients coming with diarrhea to be able to enroll everyone in our study. We needed a random selection. A novel entry criterion was chosen: the first two stool samples submitted each day that were soft enough to conform to the stool cup would be entered in our study. What was different is that the stool was the entrance criteria, and not the patient. The history of their diarrheal illness would be obtained after they had been entered into the study.

The study ended up consisting of 180 people. The etiology was mainly bacterial, with enterotoxigenic *E. coli* (ETEC) the most common, followed by *Shigella* and *Campylobacter*.

Viruses were present is less than 10% of the samples. This turned out to be the first study of the etiology of diarrhea that had ever been done in Nepal, on locals or tourists. The study enabled Dr. Shlim to help create empiric treatment recommendations for trekkers headed into the mountains away from medical care. With bacteria as the main cause of diarrhea, and bacterial diarrhea having a distinct abrupt onset, we could recommend an antibiotic for the "abrupt onset of relatively uncomfortable diarrhea." These recommendations eventually became part of standard advice for tourists to all developing countries.

The diarrhea study inspired Dr. Shlim to do a study to find out the main causes of deaths and accidents among trekkers in Nepal. This was also the first such study ever done. Until this study was done, virtually everyone assumed that altitude illness was the main risk of dying while trekking. We were able to define the risk of dying while trekking in Nepal — 15 per 100,000 trekkers. It turned out that trauma was the main cause of death, rather than altitude illness.

In 1987, a young and enthusiastic Israeli doctor named Eli Schwartz came to visit the clinic. His wife was in Nepal pursuing her musicology research. Eli started working at the clinic. At that same time, an American nurse practitioner named Nancy Piper Jenks was also working at the clinic. Both have gone on to have long and successful careers in travel medicine.

One of the main causes of prolonged fever in our practice was enteric fever — infection with either *Salmonella typhi* or *Salmonella paratyphi* A. We decided to try to document our experience with enteric fever. We had an overall rough denominator in the number of tourists who entered Nepal. We performed a survey in our clinic to try to determine the immunization rate for typhoid fever among tourists. We then recorded all cases of culture proven enteric fever. Limiting our numbers to only culture-proven cases probably underestimated the actual cases by half, as blood culture is negative in at least half the cases of enteric fever. Nonetheless, we found an extraordinarily high rate of disease among unimmunized travelers.

We found out, at that time, that the Israeli government had not approved the use of the whole cell killed typhoid vaccine, fearing that its side effects were worse than the disease. Therefore, the Israeli travelers inadvertently represented a control group that we could not otherwise have ethically created — unvaccinated tourists.

Unsurprisingly, the Israeli travelers had a rate of infection that was seven times higher than among other Western travelers (who had a 91% immunization rate for typhoid vaccine). The Israelis were getting typhoid fever at the same rate as the local Nepali people. Only 6% of Israeli travelers had typhoid vaccine, and those people had obtained it from Thailand. Dr. Schwartz and Dr. Shlim wrote up their findings especially for the main Israeli medical journal. The publication of the article made it into Israeli newspapers at the time, but the Israeli government continued to insist that the dangers of the typhoid vaccine outweighed the benefits. Israel eventually licensed the oral typhoid vaccine for travelers.

We found that the whole cell killed typhoid vaccine not only had excellent protective efficacy against *S. typhi* but appeared to show protection against *S. paratyphi* as well. The question of whether typhoid vaccines protect against *S. paratyphi* remains unresolved. Oral typhoid vaccine appeared to offer less protection against *S. typhi*. It was concluded that typhoid vaccination ought to be recommended strongly for all travelers to the region. The whole cell killed vaccine that we had studied is no longer available.

Overall, the typhoid vaccines seemed to offer more protection to travelers than they did among the local people on whom the vaccines were originally tested. Dr. Shlim hypothesized that the efforts that travelers make to avoid eating contaminated food and water may greatly decrease the inoculum of *S. typhi* and *S. paratyphi* that is ingested, thus increasing the apparent efficacy of the vaccines.

When we started work in Nepal, there was a general impression from other doctors and from textbooks that paratyphoid fever was a much less severe illness than typhoid fever. Our experience seemed to indicate that the two illnesses were clinically indistinguishable in travelers. We looked at this more formally in a study, and found that the severity of the illnesses was identical.

We also noticed that Israeli patients presented more often with hepatitis A than other travelers. Dr. Shlim contacted the Ministry of Health in Israel about this even before Dr. Schwartz joined the CIWEC Clinic. The Israeli authorities had assumed that Israelis became immune to hepatitis A while growing up in Israel, something that had once been true. However, with improvements in local sanitation, this new generation was mainly nonimmune to hepatitis A. They did not receive immune globulin prior to travel, and the high number of cases suggested that they should have. This was proved later on by studying the level of hepatitis A antibodies in prospective Israeli travelers. In this case, the Israeli authorities began to offer immune globulin, and later hepatitis A vaccine to Israeli travelers.

During this time we came across two patients who had concomitant typhoid fever and hepatitis A. Both these patients had presented as febrile illnesses confirmed to be typhoid and during the course of illness developed jaundice and marked liver function abnormalities. Subsequent tests confirmed acute hepatitis A infection. The existence of these cases challenged the syndrome of so-called "typhoid hepatitis." In a highly endemic environment, it may be more likely that enteric fever with severe liver involvement may be due to a second infection.

Eli Schwartz left the CIWEC Clinic after 2 years, and went on to become one of the foremost travel medicine and infectious disease experts in Israel and the world. If asked where one can learn about travel medicine, Eli still states that the CIWEC Clinic is the best training ground in the entire world.

In travel medicine we are often forced to repeat conventional wisdom, in the absence of any actual case reports or research. This was the case in relation to women taking oral contraceptives and going to altitude. Because of the slightly increased risk of thrombo-embolism from oral contraceptives at sea level, it was assumed that the risk would be greater at high altitude. A 33-year-old woman arrived in Kathmandu in a jeep from Mt. Everest base camp in Tibet. She had been evacuated from the mountain for what seemed like high-altitude pulmonary edema. However, persistent dyspnea on exertion at base camp (6000 feet lower than the altitude at which she became ill) led them to further evacuate her to Kathmandu.

She arrived during a "bandh" (a strike called by protestors that keeps anyone from traveling around by car or motorcycle). Dr. Shlim was not able to see her until the next day. She was concerned about what seemed to be a strained calf muscle and wondered when she could run again. Examination revealed what looked like thrombophlebitis, and a subsequent venogram was positive. Her chest x-ray showed a wedge shaped infiltrate, and subsequent lung scan was positive for pulmonary embolism. This was the first — and to our knowledge remains the only — documented pulmonary embolism case in a woman at high altitude on birth control pills.

Although we published a number of case reports, we actually saw a lot more interesting cases than we had time to report. Sometimes we lacked follow-up, or a definitive diagnosis. The biggest regret that Dr. Shlim has in relation to his record of publications is that he did not capture sufficient data on the 11 cases of rhinoceros versus tourist trauma that we treated. The great Indian one-horned rhinoceros does not use its horn as a weapon. Instead, they curl back their lips and slash with a sharpened incisor tooth. The results are long and deep, machete-like wounds, mostly on the backs and legs of the unfortunate tourists. The rhinoceros would run them down, and then as the tourist lay face down on the ground, slash them three to five times, then run off.

In order to know what cases to report, one needs to understand how the case in question might contribute to our knowledge of either disease processes or unusual presentations of known diseases. Dr. Shlim ran across an elderly Swedish woman in the Holiday Inn Hotel in Lhasa, Tibet, who had developed right hemiparesis within 12 hours of arriving in Lhasa. Subsequent CAT scan revealed a large previously completely asymptomatic meningioma in the left tempero-frontal lobe of the woman. While discussing this case at a mountain medicine conference in Davos, Switzerland, Dr. Shlim met a Dutch doctor who had encountered two similar cases in much younger people. These three cases were published under the title, "Suddenly symptomatic brain tumors at altitude," and remain the only such case reports in the literature. However, one such case has subsequently been seen at the CIWEC Clinic in a traveler and one by Dr. Shlim in a 5-year-old boy near Jackson Hole, Wyoming.

Operating the CIWEC Clinic in Nepal has always taken an immense, behind-the-scenes effort. Importing medications, vaccines, and supplies that are not available in Nepal is challenging and frustrating. Staffing the clinic, training new people, and dealing with insurance companies all have their special considerations. Having made the commitment to run a Western-style clinic in Nepal, we wanted to be sure to have crucial supplies when we really needed them. One of the most critical of these supplies is human rabies immune globulin (HRIG).

The CIWEC Clinic for many years was the only source of HRIG in Nepal. Later on, other clinics would occasionally have some, but the supply was not guaranteed. One time we did run out of HRIG, and scrambled for a month to re-supply ourselves. Our usual supplier in Bangkok could not get any. A supplier in the USA referred us to their supplier in Europe. They wanted us to deal with a supplier in India, but we did not trust that supply route at the time. After 10 days of trying to get them to sell him some HRIG, Dr. Shlim finally said, "You make the HRIG in order to sell it. I want to buy it. What is the problem?" It still took 2 more weeks.

How often is post-exposure rabies immunoprophylaxis required by tourists and expatriates? This issue had not been well studied. Occasionally, airport surveys that asked departing travelers whether they had been bitten or licked by an animal while in that particular country (not Nepal) would reveal extremely high rates of potential exposure (1–2%). However, none of these people had been concerned enough to seek post-exposure rabies treatment, and, as far as we know, none of them developed rabies. Since the CIWEC Clinic was the only complete source of post-exposure rabies prophylaxis in Nepal, it made sense to try to do a study to see how often people sought treatment, and to better understand the risk factors for getting bitten.

We found that only 1 in 6000 foreign travelers to Nepal received an animal bite that resulted in seeking medical care to prevent a possible rabies exposure. We published a paper in 1991 that showed that even in a high-risk country like Nepal, the risk of requiring rabies post-exposure prophylaxis was low, and if a traveler was willing to put up with the cost and inconvenience of full post-exposure prophylaxis, which includes HRIG and five doses of rabies vaccine, pre-exposure immunization was probably not necessary for travel to Nepal. We repeated the study 10 years later. Dr. Pandey headed the study and found that the risk of being bitten while trekking was actually lower than in visitors who stayed in Kathmandu. In fact, over 50% of tourist bite exposures occurred at one cultural site in Kathmandu — the monkey temple at Swayambunath. The temple harbors hundreds of monkeys and street dogs. Knowledge about this potential risk apparently can prevent a bite, as no foreign residents were bitten at the monkey temple during the study. Expatriates, however, had a higher risk of being bitten by dogs in general, due to perhaps keeping pets, taking walks in their neighborhoods, and taking in stray dogs. Women were more likely than men to be bitten in both studies.

One-third of our patients at the clinic are seen for diarrhea. This has not changed since the clinic started operating in 1982. Our laboratory technician, Ramachandran Rajah, whom we call Rama, has excelled in stool examinations and his help has been invaluable in conducting all of the diarrhea research at the clinic. Dr. Carl Mason, a collaborator in our research from AFRIMS, once called Rama "better than PCR" for *Cyclospora* identification. With the help of researchers in AFRIMS, including David N. Taylor, Charles Hoge, Carl Mason, and Ladaporn Bodhidatta, we have been able to look at the etiology, risk factors, symptoms, and immunity among travelers and expatriates in Nepal.

We became aware of *Blastocystis hominis* in 1984 when a couple of new articles suggested that this organism was a neglected cause of diarrhea in humans. We initially thought that *B. hominis* could be the cause of diarrhea, but later we found that it was present in more than 34% of our patients, whether they had diarrhea or not. If we treated people for *B. hominis*, one of the three outcomes occurred: the patient got better, but the organism was still present; the patient did not get better, but the organism was gone; or the patient got better and the organism was gone.

B. hominis was first noted in 1911, but uncertainty as to whether it was pathogenic persists to this day. To try to determine whether *B. hominis* was a pathogen in our patient population, we conducted a case control study by comparing the prevalence of *B. hominis* among patients with diarrhea to that among a control group without diarrhea. We looked for the presence of the parasite, its concentration, clinical symptoms associated with it, and the presence of other enteric pathogens in persons with diarrhea and asymptomatic controls. *B. hominis* was no more likely to be found in the stools of patients with diarrhea than in those of asymptomatic controls. Patients with diarrhea who had *B. hominis* in their stools were just as likely to have another pathogen in their stools, as were patients from whom the organism was not recovered. There were no specific symptoms associated with *B. hominis* infection. These data suggested that *B. hominis* is not a cause of travelers' diarrhea.

From 1989 onwards, much attention was focused on the newly discovered organism that was responsible for causing prolonged diarrhea in the summer months. The fascinating story of the discovery of *Cyclospora* in Nepal is the subject of another chapter in this book. When Dr. Prativa Pandey joined the clinic in 1993, *Cyclospora* infection still had no available treatment. People who got the disease were destined to have 2–12 weeks of intermittent diarrhea, nausea, and profound fatigue and anorexia. She started working at the clinic in July 1993, a peak *Cyclospora* month. *Cyclospora* had become the major cause of diarrhea in the summer months, surpassing ETEC. The disease caused so much fatigue that the doctors in the clinic could pick out *Cyclospora* patients while they sat in the waiting room.

Dr. Pandey participated in the trial that established that sulfamethoxazole and trimethoprim was an extremely effective treatment for *Cyclospora*. However, since many people are allergic to sulfa drugs, the search has continued through a long list of drugs to find an alternative treatment for *Cyclospora*. So far, no other drug has proven effective.

The clinic did an unprecedented year-long prospective study of the risk of diarrhea in foreign residents. We called all the patients every 2 weeks, and asked them to submit a stool sample for every episode of diarrhea. We found that foreign residents, in their first year of residence in Nepal, had an average of 3.3 episodes of diarrhea per person per year. While this figure actually surprised us as being lower than we had anticipated, it proved to be almost identical to the risk of a Nepali child living in a village. In other words, all the efforts that foreigners make to avoid diarrhea are no better than if they lived in a village and ate and drank like a Nepali! We do not, however, recommend that foreigners take up this particular life style.

During the late 1980s and 1990s, quinolones worked wonderfully in treating bacterial-caused travelers' diarrhea. One or two doses would cure any bacteria travelers' diarrhea. In the late 1990s, we started to see occasional quinolone failures. A few trekkers had to be evacuated from the mountains by helicopter due to severe bacterial diarrhea that did not respond to ciprofloxacin. We got back in touch with AFRIMS and decided to do another 2-year study of the etiology of TD and — in particular — antibiotic resistance of diarrheal pathogens in Nepal. This second study, which has yet to be published, found that *Campylobacter* had surpassed ETEC as the number one pathogen for travelers' diarrhea in Nepal. In vitro resistance of *Campylobacter* to quinolones had reached 70%.

Dr. Pandey was the first Nepali physician to work at the CIWEC Clinic. She went to medical school in Delhi, India, as there were no medical schools in Nepal at that time. She did an internal medicine residency in the USA and became board certified in internal medicine. She worked 11 years in Boston, seven of which were in a community practice in East Boston where she was also a clinical instructor at Harvard Medical School and admitted patients to Beth Israel Hospital. She moved back to Nepal to help and care for her aging parents. Both Dr. Pandey and Dr. Shlim have found that running the clinic can be almost overwhelming at times. The clinic serves as a family practice for 2500 expatriates. We do well-baby exams, prenatal care, and treat hypertension, heart disease, diabetes, and all the normal diseases of aging. On top of that, the clinic serves as an urgency care center for up to 300,000 foreign tourists per year. In the peak of each tourist season, in the spring and fall, the doctors can face day and night patient care, phone calls, and evacuations that make one wonder if we can keep going. These concerns are often played out against the difficulties of the recent political difficulties, strikes, and demonstrations that would cut transportation or impose curfews. At times, pinned in their homes by strict, shoot-on-sight curfews, the doctors could only provide medical advice over the phone. Fortunately, Nepal appears headed into a more peaceful time, which means that only the normal bureaucratic and logistical difficulties will have to be faced.

Over the years the clinic went through ups and downs in terms of its survival. In the year 1996, the Canadian Embassy based in Kathmandu finally advised that the clinic could no longer operate under their name. The clinic could have closed down at that time except that so many patients now depended on it. We desperately looked for ways to survive and many alternatives were explored. It was deemed possible for the clinic to survive as a foreign joint venture investment. This was pursued and license was obtained from the government to run a small private hospital as a Nepali enterprise to promote travel medicine.

In late 1997 the clinic was visited by Marty Cetron, one of the project directors at the time for the GeoSentinel project of the International Society of Travel Medicine. He felt that CIWEC Clinic would be an ideal destination clinic to participate in the global surveillance network of clinics to monitor emerging illnesses and disease trends in travelers. Challenges were enormous in 1998 when CIWEC joined the project and it took almost a year to work out a way to send data regularly to the central database in Atlanta. An additional employee had to be hired just to do the GeoSentinel data entries. The clinic is now one of the 32 clinics worldwide that contribute to the GeoSentinel system, and is the largest single contributor of patient records.

After 15 years at the CIWEC Clinic, Dr. Shlim made the decision to move back to the USA He had moved to Nepal as a single, 34-year-old doctor, and was now leaving with a Canadian wife and two children. Dr. Prativa Pandey took over as the medical director. The transition from Dr. Shlim to Dr. Pandey was looked upon nervously by some since Dr. Shlim had been responsible for giving the clinic an international reputation as a place for clinical excellence and research. However, it was the perfect time for a Nepali doctor to take over the clinic, and Dr. Pandey has not only continued the clinic's high level of medical care, but has also overseen the design and building of an entirely new CIWEC Clinic facility. The most challenging aspect remains recruiting a well-trained medical staff with a commitment to the kinds of medical challenges and stresses that can come from living and practicing in Nepal. Dr. Pandey continues to recruit both Western and Nepali doctors to work at the clinic. Finding the appropriate doctor, whether Western or Nepali, has been challenging. Western doctors fresh out of training may lack the experience to make difficult decisions without someone to back them up. They may also face a substantial financial burden from loans. More established doctors might find it difficult to leave a practice to come to Nepal. The most qualified young Nepali doctors tend to leave for Western countries, mainly the USA and UK. Older Nepali doctors are already established in a hospital position or private practice.

During the last 10 years, Nepal has suffered from a conflict with Maoist rebels. Although the expatriates in Nepal have been safe throughout all this unfortunate fighting, there has been a lot of uncertainty. The uncertainty made it more difficult to recruit Western doctors to come, and harder to keep Nepali doctors in Nepal.

William Cave is a good example of the type of doctor who was attracted to work in Nepal. He joined the clinic, and only later we found out that he and his wife had sailed a 32-foot sailboat around the world over a 3-year period. His modesty, coupled with the kind of self-confidence that comes from dealing with all the hardships that such a sailing venture entails, made him a worthy associate. He worked enthusiastically at the clinic for 5 years and helped contribute to our research, particularly by studying the confusing array of malaria prophylaxis advice (and the actual risk of malaria) among travelers to Nepal.

Will and his family left Nepal in 2003 to try to live closer to the sea in Sri Lanka, and to see if he could replicate a destination travel clinic similar to the CIWEC Clinic. However, local medical politics made it nearly impossible to run the clinic successfully, and he moved home to England.

Many travel medicine enthusiasts from around the world have worked at CIWEC at various times. At the ISTM meeting every 2 years, we may see as many as 20–30 people who have spent time at the CIWEC Clinic and have maintained their enthusiasm for travel medicine. In a given year the CIWEC Clinic will have seen patients from 75 different countries and we will have dealt with all aspects of travel medicine from pre-travel, during travel, and post-travel.

People often ask, "What is the most difficult problem that you face while working at the clinic?" Without a doubt, the most difficult situation involves trying to care for acutely psychotic tourists or expatriates. We have seen young schizophrenic patients who think they are now Vishnu. We have dealt with severe and prolonged psychosis induced by local mushrooms, or *ditura* (loco weed). Sometimes people are simply overwhelmed by their environment and experience an acute situational psychosis. Others have the accelerating onset of the manic phase of bipolar disease and start showing up at embassies for secret "spy" meetings in the middle of the night. One chronically schizophrenic young man spent 2 years in a hotel in Thamel without ever leaving his room. His family sent money to support him there. He was only forced to leave eventually because he had overstayed his legal visa by 21 months.

Psychiatric emergencies not only make the lives of doctors difficult but also cause extreme distress to the embassy officials of the country that this person belongs to as well as their family members back home. These emergencies are handled by clinic doctors who have not specifically been trained in psychiatry. As overall medical care gets better in Nepal, psychiatric services for Nepali and foreign patients continues to be ignored, perhaps because it is a low priority on public health agendas.

Doctors are judged not by their easy patients, but by the difficult situations that they are forced to manage. The mother of a particularly difficult psychiatric patient whom we had to keep at the clinic for 3 nights later wrote to us to say: "Throughout our stay at CIWEC, we experienced time and time again the same blend of wonderful professionalism and simple human warmth and compassion. This is truly what the best medicine is about — healing bodies and hearts — and you did this beautifully, all of you."

The CIWEC Clinic has put Nepal in a prominent place in the world of travel medicine. It is gratifying to sit back at international meetings and see how often research from Nepal is cited by speakers from around the world. In addition, Dr. Pandey became president of the ISTM in 2005. However, even though we are best known around the world for our contribution to travel medicine research, in the end the CIWEC Clinic exists to offer a resource for those who are sick and in need in a foreign environment. Personally, we are most proud of the compassionate care that we have always strived to offer. Dr. Shlim, who volunteered his time to take care of the Tibetan monastic community and newly arrived Tibetan refugees, subsequently helped create a book in conjunction with Chokyi Nyima Rinpoche, a Tibetan lama who is the head of a large monastery near Kathmandu. The book is called *Medicine and Compassion: A Tibetan Lama's Guidance for Caregivers*. This book is a reminder of the value of compassion and wisdom, and how it might be possible to train more directly in these two qualities. After all, scientifically based, compassionate medical care is the goal that we all strive to attain in medicine.

References

Freedman, D. O., Weld, L. H., Kozarsky, P. E., Fisk, T., Robins, R., von Sonnenburg, F., Keystone, J. S., Pandey, P., & Cetron, M. S. (2006). GeoSentinel Surveillance Network. Spectrum of disease and relation to place of exposure among ill returned travelers. *New England Journal of Medicine, 354*(2), 119–130 (Jan. 12).

Hoge, C. W., Shlim, D. R., Echeverria, P., Rajah, R., Hermann, J. E., & Cross, J. H. (1996). Epidemiology of diarrhea among expatriate residents living in a highly endemic environment. *Journal of American Medical Association, 275*, 533–538.

Hoge, C. W., Shlim, D. R., Ghimire, M., Rabold, J. G., Pandey, P., Walsh, A., Rajah, R., Gaudio, P., & Echeverria, P. (1995). Placebo-controlled trial of co-trimoxazole for the treatment of Cyclospora infections among travelers and foreign residents in Nepal. *Lancet, 345*, 691–693.

Hoge, C. W., Shlim, D. R., Rajah, R., Triplett, J., Shear, M., Rabold, J. G., & Echeverria, P. (1993). The epidemiology of diarrheal illness associated with a coccidian-like organism among travelers and foreign residents in Nepal. *Lancet, 341*, 1175–1179.

Pandey, P., Cave, W., & Shlim, D. R. (2000). Hepatitis A post hepatitis A vaccination? *J Travel Med., 7*, 213–214. [*Awarded "Best Short Article" in the Journal of Travel Medicine for the years 1999–2001.*]

Pandey, P., Shlim, D. R., Cave, W., & Springer, M. (2002). Risk of possible exposure to rabies among tourists and foreign residents in Nepal. *Journal of Travel Medicine, 9*, 127–131.

Schwartz, E., Shlim, D. R., Eaton, M., Jenks, N., & Houston, R. (1990). The effect of oral and parenteral typhoid vaccination on the rate of infection with *Salmonella typhi* and *Salmonella paratyphi* A among foreigners in Nepal. *Archives of Internal Medicine, 150*, 349–351.

Shlim, D. R., Cohen, M. T., Eaton, M., Rajah, R., Long, E. G., & Ungar, B. L. P. (1991). An alga-like organism associated with an outbreak of prolonged diarrhea among foreigners in Nepal. *The American Journal of Tropical Medicine and Hygiene, 45*, 383–389.

Shlim, D. R., & Gallie, J. (1992). The causes of death among trekkers in Nepal. *International Journal of Sports Medicine, 13*, S74–S76.

Taylor, D. N., Houston, R., Shlim, D. R., Bhaibulaya, M., Ungar, B. L. P., & Echeverria, P. (1988). Etiology of diarrhea among travelers and foreign residents in Nepal. *Journal of American Medical Association, 260*, 1245–1248.

Chapter 21

History of Cyclospora at the CIWEC Clinic, Nepal

David R. Shlim*

On June 19, 1989, the laboratory technician at the CIWEC Clinic Travel Medicine Centre in Kathmandu asked me to look at something that he had noticed in a stool exam. The object in question was round and appeared to have some internal structures that suggested the spokes of a wheel. It resembled *Cryptosporidium*, but was larger. Cryptosporidia are 4–6 μm in diameter, and this particle was 8–10 μm. Our laboratory technician, Ramachandran Rajah, whom we called "Rama," had proven to be as good as any parasitologist we had ever met, so when he pointed out something, I listened. He had picked the object out from the clutter of vegetable matter, cells, and legitimate pathogens and non-pathogens that form the background of all stool examinations.

However, Rama was hesitant. He had been seeing this particle since he began work at the clinic in 1982. It was not in any textbooks, so he had been ignoring it. A few years before, he had noted a similar, but much larger, particle that he could not identify. After some major sleuthing, he had proven that *those* objects were actually undigested pollen particles from cauliflower. He had taken some cauliflower and made a smear from the flower and proved his point. The current particle had a faint resemblance to a pollen particle. The summer before I had met Dr. Beth Ungar, a *Cryptosporidium* expert at the Uniformed Services University of the Health Sciences in Washington, D.C. She had shown me two ways to test for *Cryptosporidium* under the microscope. Because the new object resembled *Cryptosporidium*, we decided to apply these two tests.

Cryptosporidium floats to the top of a drop of Sheather's sucrose solution placed on the slide. Other stool pathogens do not float. This object floated to the surface. In addition, *Cryptosporidium* stains with a modified acid-fast stain. This object stained as well, although the results were variable. Could this be a new coccidian of some sort?

---

*David R. Shlim, M.D. was the Medical Director of the CIWEC Clinic Travel Medicine Centre in Kathmandu, Nepal, from 1983 to 1998. He currently directs Jackson Hole Travel and Tropical Medicine in Jackson Hole, Wyoming.

From the moment Rama pointed out this particle, I was open to the possibility that this could be a real finding. For the last 2 months we had been seeing patients with a persistent gastrointestinal illness that had no clear cause, and did not respond to any of our empiric treatments. The patients had an abrupt onset of cramps and diarrhea and nausea. After a few days, the acute symptoms got better, but the patients continued to experience profound anorexia and fatigue, out of proportion to any of the symptoms caused by the other stool pathogens that we saw regularly, such as *Giardia lamblia, Entamoeba histolytica*, or *Dientamoeba fragilis*. The anorexia and fatigue were consistently present, even though diarrhea and nausea became intermittent after a while. We tried treating patients with ciprofloxacin, tinidazole, or quinacrine, but the symptoms did not change. We even tried tetracycline and folic acid (the treatment for tropical sprue), but that was also ineffective. The illness would last 1–2 months, and then the patients would recover. Weight loss averaged 6 lbs per patient.

I thought back to the spring of 1985, when I had seen a similar cluster of patients. At that time, we had just read a couple of articles about *Blastocystis hominis*. I had asked Rama to start reporting *B. hominis* on the stool examination reports. *B. hominis* proved to be so common in our population that it was, indeed, present in a number of people who presented with symptoms of prolonged diarrhea, fatigue, and anorexia. However, like many subsequent authors who reported on *B. hominis*, we ignored the fact that it was also present in many people who did not have similar symptoms. Nonetheless, feeling that we had made a new observation about *B. hominis*, we wrote a letter that was published in the *New England Journal of Medicine*.

I had not noticed patients with prolonged fatigue and anorexia in the intervening years from 1986 to 1988. We had subsequently determined that *B. hominis* was not a pathogen in our patient population. In 1986, we began a collaboration with the Armed Forces Research Institute of Medical Science (AFRIMS), in Bangkok, working with David N. Taylor, M.D. Dr. Taylor was a former Centers for Disease Control epidemiologist and infectious disease specialist. He helped us perform the first survey of the etiology of diarrhea in Nepal. The unknown particle had not been noted during this study.

Now, in 1989, we were confronted with patients with symptoms similar to that of 1985, but this time with an unidentified particle in several stool examinations. If there was a connection between these two observations, how would we prove it?

I asked Rama to record on the lab slip whenever he spotted the new particle. He initially wrote "? pollen," since we did not know what else to call it. Right away we saw that this "pollen" was present in every patient who had the syndrome of prolonged fatigue and anorexia. Perhaps more significantly, the particle was not present in *any* asymptomatic people. We followed the patients for weeks, repeating their stool examinations frequently. As long as they had symptoms, the particle would be there. As soon as they became well, the particle would disappear.

Part way through the summer, I left Nepal to go on home leave in the United States. I carried a sample of stool and mailed it to Beth Ungar, whom I had been introduced to the summer before by David Taylor. Dr. Ungar was excited about the sample. She agreed that it looked like a large *Cryptosporidium*. She took the sample across the street to show to Willadene Zierdt, the head parasitologist at the National Institutes of Health. Dr. Zierdt agreed with Dr. Ungar, and volunteered that she had seen a similar specimen once, from a patient who had been in Haiti.

Coccidia are much more common pathogens in animals than in humans, so Dr. Ungar sent the specimen to a veterinary coccidia expert in Washington, D.C. He told her, "I don't know what it is, but it's not a coccidia."

Since all we could do is look at the particle — or organism — under the microscope, the decision as to what it might be came down to a matter of opinion. Not knowing what kind of organism it might be, no one knew how it could be cultivated in the lab. Without an adequate number of particles, it would not be possible to try to infect any animals. At that point, Beth Ungar was shown a draft of a paper describing an identical organism. Earl Long, a parasitologist at the Centers for Disease Control, had received 8 specimens containing this organism. He had decided that it might be a cyanobacteria, based on electron micrograph studies. He looked at our specimen and agreed that it was identical to the specimens he had already seen.

By November of 1989, the organism no longer appeared in stool examinations at the CIWEC Clinic. The new syndrome associated with profound fatigue and anorexia also disappeared. We decided to report what we had learned so far. We suspected that we had found a new cause of diarrhea in humans, but just what that cause was remained undetermined.

We documented a total of 55 cases. We devised a graph that showed that each patient was ill while the organism was present, and recovered only after the organism was gone. The symptoms were remarkably consistent, as described above. The duration of illness ranged from 2 to 12 weeks, with an average of 6 weeks. In late June, when we started recording the infections, the rate of new cases per week was at a high point. It gradually dropped off each week until they disappeared. The curve looked like the second half of a typical epidemic curve. This further reinforced our idea that this was a genuine observation, and not just a random occurrence in the stool examinations.

I was bothered by the fact that the organism had been called a cyanobacteria. That would not necessarily explain the fact that it floated in Sheather's sucrose solution, or stained with modified acid-fast stain. There were no examples in the literature of cyanobacteria that could infect the intestine. I wondered how a bacterium that processes sunlight could survive in the human intestine, a place where light never shines. However, certain cyanobacteria were known to produce toxins that could cause vomiting and diarrhea when people drank from algae-infested ponds, suggesting a possible mechanism of disease.

Our paper from the summer of 1989 was rejected by the *New England Journal of Medicine*. It was finally published in 1991 in the *American Journal of Tropical Medicine and Hygiene*. Still unsure of what we were dealing with, we referred to the particle as "an alga-like organism."

During the time it took to get our paper published, the organism had returned in the spring of 1990. This time we traced a complete epidemic curve. Just as we had suspected, the epidemic started off slowly with a few cases in early May, increased steadily until it reached a peak during the last week of June and the first week of July, then diminished throughout the rest of the monsoon, until the last case occurred in November (see Figure 21.1). This distribution was not the same as that of the other enteric pathogens that we found at the clinic. The risk of the other diarrheal pathogens doubled in April, May, and June, and then dropped off abruptly to their baseline rate when the monsoon arrived.

One of the criticisms of our first paper was that we had not proven that the organism was associated with diarrhea. We had considered recruiting an asymptomatic control

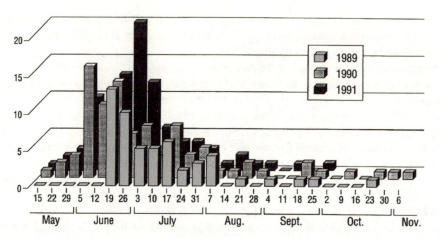

Figure 21.1. The number of cases of *Cyclospora* per week during the years 1989–1991, showing the distinct seasonality. The organism was not seen during those years from December through April. In 1989, we only started recording the organism on June 19th.

group, but I had rejected it since we had so many other stool examinations that did not have this organism in it, and those people had completely different symptoms. This represented inexperience on my part. We planned another study, this time a case-control study to prove that this organism was associated with diarrhea, and to try to detect any risk factors.

David Taylor had left Bangkok and moved back to work at the Walter Reed Army Institute of Research in Washington, D.C. Charles Hoge was David Taylor's replacement at AFRIMS. Charles was also a CDC-trained epidemiologist who was enthusiastic about solving the riddle of this new organism (and spending time in Nepal). We enrolled cases with the organism, and recruited an equal number of controls without diarrhea. Both groups completed questionnaires. The study allowed us to further characterize the illness. It also convincingly showed that the organism was associated with diarrhea. One hundred percent of the 108 cases infected with the unknown organism had gastrointestinal symptoms, while only one person among the 96 asymptomatic controls had the organism detected in the stool. That one person became ill with a typical illness 3 days later.

Drinking untreated water or milk emerged as the only risk factors for the disease. But we had proven that the organism was associated with diarrhea, and further characterized the symptoms of the illness and its natural history.

In May of 1991, I presented our experience with the organism at the 1st conference of the International Society of Travel Medicine in Atlanta. The organism's name had gone through a few iterations. After "alga-like organism," it became "Cyanobacteria-like body," or CLB. Momentum for the cyanobacteria hypothesis began to wane, boosting the concept that this was, in fact, a coccidia. CLB came to stand for "coccidia-like body."

Bradley Connor was in the audience in Atlanta. A gastroenterologist who was destined to be a future president of the ISTM, he was intrigued. Because of the profound anorexia, fatigue, and nausea associated with the illness, he suspected that the infection must be in the upper intestine. It should be within reach of an upper endoscope. He introduced himself to me after my talk, and suggested that we could do upper endoscopy on the patients and obtain biopsies of the duodenum.

I told him that we had no funding, but if he wanted to come to Nepal, we would certainly have patients with CLB in June. He thought about it for a few days, and then called me at my parents' house in Portland, Oregon just before I flew back to Nepal. A month later he showed up with all the equipment he would need.

Brad endoscoped nine patients with the unknown organism, and seven normal controls. We recruited the controls in order to be able to prove that whatever findings were present on biopsy were not just the result of repeated insults from living in a high-risk developing country. Although I had hoped to go my whole life without undergoing upper endoscopy, I had to volunteer to be one of the controls after having talked my wife Jane — who was infected with CLB — into being in the study.

Jane and I had married in 1990. She had spent her first year living in Nepal pregnant with our son. She had avoided eating in restaurants while she was pregnant, and had stayed free of diarrheal disease. Our son was born in March of 1991, and Jane had begun to eat more freely. She became ill with CLB in mid-May. She was nursing our son, and going without a lot of sleep. The additional fatigue and lack of appetite were a tremendous strain. I had been living in Nepal for 9 years at that point. Was I immune to this organism? I thought back to my first year in Nepal. I remembered having a prolonged episode of profound fatigue and anorexia that lasted over a month in late spring of 1984.

All of the patients with CLB had distinctly abnormal duodenal biopsies. The organism itself was found in two of the aspirates from the duodenum, but we did not identify the organism within the intestinal mucosa. One of the controls had the same pathologic findings as the CLB group. She developed symptoms a few days later.

As we were reviewing our specimens with a pathologist, a British group of researchers reported on their experience with CLB in some returned travelers. Their duodenal biopsy specimens showed the same pathologic findings, but unlike our biopsies, they demonstrated intracellular parasites.

In 1993, Ynes Ortega and Charles Sterling published their definitive account of documenting sporulation in preserved specimens of CLB obtained from Peruvian patients. The sporulation confirmed that the organism was a coccidia, and the fact that it formed two sporocysts and four sporozoites steered them toward a previously rarely encountered coccidian called "*Cyclospora*." This species, which was identical to the one that we were seeing morphologically, appeared to be new. The Peruvian researchers named it *Cyclospora cayetanensis*, after the university in Lima where the research was done (the Universidad Peruana Cayetano Heredia).

Four years later, I had dinner with Ynes Ortega after we met at a conference in Washington, D.C., on *Cyclospora*. I wanted to know how they had solved the mystery. Coccidia usually sporulate after just 2–3 days in potassium dichromate, but *Cyclospora* takes 7 days or more to do so. How did they think to observe it for so much longer? The answer was: serendipity. Dr. Ortega was reviewing a number of stored specimens to catalog what organisms were in them. Some of the specimens were CLB. She noted that they had sporulated. When I showed the photos from their article to Rama, he said that he had seen this in some of his stored specimens, but had not realized the significance of it.

The organism now had a name, but there were still a number of unsolved problems. There was no known treatment. No one had any idea what the reservoir in the environment might be, if any. A researcher from the London School of Tropical Medicine had come to Kathmandu during the monsoon of 1993 and collected as many different animal stool specimens as he could obtain. He did not find any *Cyclospora*. How could the organism disappear for 4 months each year, and then predictably reappear?

During this time, I came up with a likely hypothesis that appeared to explain most of what we observed. The organism appeared like clockwork each season, and departed just as regularly. It slowly built up until the monsoon rains reached their peak, and then began to disappear. There was epidemiologic evidence that it was waterborne. I decided that it must be carried by waterfowl that migrated regularly to Nepal. The birds returned each spring. They would make their nests along the water, and begin to infect the water supply slowly. Then the monsoon rains would hit and wash in all the duck feces from along the banks of the river, and the epidemic would peak. Gradually it would wash out of the environment, resulting in fewer infections. We had shown that untreated water was a proven risk factor for the diseases. When the feces had washed out, the ducks would depart in the fall, taking the organism with them. It was an elegant explanation. There proved to be only one flaw in my thinking.

When I contacted an expert on birds in Nepal, I found out that there were no ducks or other waterfowl that nested seasonally upstream from Kathmandu. The waterfowl overflew the valley and nested in the streams in the Terai, the semi-tropical lowland area of Nepal. My elegant hypothesis was wrong. A decade later, a famous epidemiologist from Minnesota would propose the same explanation for *Cyclospora* infections, with equal lack of proof.

Even if we could not find the source of *Cyclospora* infections, we still urgently needed to find a cure. Diagnosing *Cyclospora* in a patient was like passing a sentence — usually 4–6 weeks of misery. In August of 1993, I was spending the summer in Grand Teton National Park, where my wife worked for the main mountain guide service. I was perusing my copy of *Lancet* when I came across a letter from a *Cyclospora* researcher in Peru. A lab technician had treated himself empirically for diarrhea with trimethoprim-sulfamethoxazole for a presumed bacterial infection. He recovered rapidly. Later he processed his own stool specimen and was surprised to find *Cyclospora*. Trimethoprim-sulfamethoxazole was tried in several other patients with *Cyclospora*, and it appeared to work in each case. Standing in a meadow in the shadow of the Grand Tetons, I phoned Prativa Pandey, my partner in Kathmandu. She tried the cotrimoxazole on the remaining *Cyclospora* cases that summer, and they all got better rapidly.

Charles Hoge, along with Prativa and myself, designed a double-blind, placebo-controlled trial for the following 1994 *Cyclospora* season. We enrolled 40 patients who were infected with *Cyclospora*, 21 of whom received trimethoprim-sulfamethoxazole and 19 who received placebo. Only 1 of 16 patients who completed the study had *Cyclospora* after 7 days in the treatment group, whereas 88 percent of 17 patients in the placebo group were still infected. The paper was published in *Lancet* in 1995.

There still had been no studies that looked for *Cyclospora* in Nepalis. In 1994, we joined forces with a group studying homeopathic treatment of diarrhea in Nepalese children under 5 years of age. *Cyclospora* was not found in 74 children under the age of 18 months, but was found in 6 of 50 children who were over that age.

We continued to search for an alternative to cotrimoxazole to treat *Cyclospora* infection. Too many people had a history of sulfa allergy, and could not be offered definitive treatment. We had already eliminated a number of contenders: nalidixic acid, norfloxacin, ciprofloxacin, tinidazole, quinacrine, albendazole, paromomycin, tetracycline, and azithromycin. I decided to try trimethoprim alone. If people were allergic to sulfa drugs, it should be safe for them to take trimethoprim alone, and there was reason to think that it could be effective by itself. We offered the drug to people who had been allergic to sulfa in the past. Not only did it not treat *Cyclospora*, but to our profound surprise, two people had allergic reactions to trimethoprim.

By 1994, there had been an editorial in the *Journal of Medical Microbiology* that said that "the identification of a newly recognized cyclosporan parasite of man is exciting even if the infection is shown to be of restricted importance in developed countries." Then *Cyclospora* burst onto the North American stage.

There had been less than 20 cases of *Cyclospora* reported in the U.S. from 1989 to 1995. Other than an outbreak of seven cases among the housestaff at Cook County Hospital in Chicago in 1990, each case was isolated. Then, in 1996, a number of cases occurred in rapid succession associated with weddings, or other large catered events. A state epidemiologist in Texas thought that her investigation of the vehicle for these cases implicated California strawberries. Although I was later told that some of her colleagues had asked her not to implicate the strawberries because the causal link was weak, she felt she had a duty to inform the public. Her announcement cost the California strawberry growers $23,000,000 dollars that year. That would have been okay if she had been right. But it was not the strawberries.

Further investigation implicated raspberries grown in Guatemala. Since these were often served in desserts at function mixed in with strawberries, it was easy to see how the Texas Department of Health was misled. The fact that raspberries proved to be the vehicle for *Cyclospora* into the USA was a disaster for the growers in Guatemala. Taking advantage of a high plateau with a temperate climate near Antigua, the growers had planted their first raspberry bushes in 1987. They hoped to capture a market for fresh fruit that would be out of season in North America and Europe. It had taken years to get the raspberry bushes to a sufficient yield to be profitable. *Cyclospora* was previously unknown in Guatemala. That it should first show up on exported fruit from that country was extremely bad luck.

Cyclospora was subsequently found in stool examinations from Guatemalans. But how was it getting onto the raspberries? The growers supplied outhouses in the fields, and water for handwashing. The raspberry plants were only watered at their roots — the berries themselves were never sprayed with irrigation water.

Raspberries themselves are incredibly delicate. They rot easily in transit. To help preserve the fragile berries as they traveled in refrigerated vehicles to the U.S., they were sprayed with a fungicide. The fungicide was mixed with untreated local water. All of this was discovered by CDC investigators. Their recommendation: treat the water used to mix the fungicide with chlorine before mixing the solution.

In 1997, the outbreaks of *Cyclospora* associated with Guatemalan raspberries continued. By the spring of 1998, Guatemalan raspberries were banned in the U.S. The outbreaks stopped. Canada chose not to ban the importation of Guatemalan raspberries, and had more outbreaks in 1998.

Why didn't the CDC suggestion to chlorinate the fungicide water prevent further cases of *Cyclospora*? One possible answer may be that *Cyclospora* oocysts are resistant to disinfection with chlorine. We investigated a *Cyclospora* outbreak in a British Gurkha camp near Pokhara in Nepal. A number of people became ill, and *Cyclospora* oocysts were discovered in the chlorinated water tanks. *Cyclospora* was apparently resistant to purification with chlorine. We had been suspicious because *Cryptosporidium* was notoriously resistant to decontamination with either iodine or chlorine. Probably the chlorination of the fungicide solution had not solved the problem. We had published our observation in a letter in *Lancet* in 1994, but it had probably not been noticed at the CDC, for whom *Cyclospora* was off their radar at that point.

In the end, it turned out that we did not actually "discover" *Cyclospora*. The organism that would prove to be *Cyclospora* was actually discovered independently at least five different times from 1979 to 1993. The first acknowledged recognition of the organism was published in 1979, when Ashford reported on three cases of diarrhea associated with a previously unrecognized organism in Papua New Guinea, which he postulated to be a coccidian. The article included photomicrographs that later confirmed the identity of *Cyclospora* in retrospect. The report received little attention, and only came to light when *Cyclospora* was re-discovered a decade later. The next known report of the organism was in an abstract published in 1986 by Rosemary Soave in which she described what she thought was a new, pathogenic coccidian in four patients from Haiti and Mexico.

Earl Long "discovered" the organism again in 1989, just as we became aware of it in Nepal. Similarly, the group in Peru "discovered" *Cyclospora* on its own. I realized that there is no way to search the literature for an organism that does not have a name. In each case, the organism was first noted not by doctors, but by an alert lab technician.

The CIWEC Clinic contributed significantly to the understanding of *Cyclospora*. We learned how to recognize it in stool examinations without staining. We discovered that it concentrates well after formalin-ether centrifugation, which greatly increases the chances of making a diagnosis. We published the first description of the clinical illness, and the natural history of the disease. We did the first epidemiologic study, and the first double-blind treatment study. The group in Peru contributed significantly by confirming that the organism was a coccidia.

We thought we were mainly solving the problems of travelers and expatriates in Nepal. But due to our efforts in Nepal — and the contributions of the researchers in Peru — the outbreaks of *Cyclospora* arrived in North America already gift-wrapped. Without our contributions, the disease would have arrived with no syndrome, no sure way of diagnosis, and no treatment. The *Cyclospora* story is one of the triumphs of travel medicine. By studying travelers, we were able to detect a disease risk before it inevitably appeared in the travelers' home countries. It is not only people who travel, but the diseases themselves.

Is *Cyclospora cayetanensis* a pathogen only of humans? There is reason to think so. The other *Cyclosporas* are very host specific. Efforts to infect animal models have all failed. The organism has not been found in any stool samples from any animals, birds, or insects living in areas where *Cyclospora* infection in humans has been documented. The life cycle of the organism, and the reservoir or vector for the organism outside of humans remains unknown. Researchers have postulated that the organism has to undergo sporulation outside of the human host before it can become infective. This would mean that direct person-to-person transmission would be unlikely, which is compatible with our observations among expatriates in Nepal. I have heard of efforts to infect human volunteers with oocysts of *Cyclospora* purified directly from stool. None of the volunteers became ill. Using sporulated oocysts still did not result in infection. The life cycle of *Cyclospora* in relation to humans remains to be written.

Was *Cyclospora* always present in Nepal, or did it get introduced in the 1980's? We do not know. Rama recalled seeing it from his early days at the CIWEC Clinic. However, from 1982 to 1986 we used cotrimoxazole as our main empiric treatment for bacterial-caused diarrhea. As cotrimoxazole became less effective, due to bacterial resistance, we switched to fluoroquinolones. It was shortly after that that we noted the *Cyclospora* cases. Perhaps the empiric use of cotrimoxazole had obscured the presentation of *Cyclospora* until we stopped using it.

There were other reasons why it took some time to "discover" *Cyclospora* in our own practice. The fact that the particle was not in any textbooks was the biggest obstacle. It was difficult to imagine that an undetected protozoal pathogen had never been noticed in the stool — and that *we* would be the ones to finally notice it! Rama initially assumed that it must be some type of innocent object that simply resembled a protozoan. There were examples of this in the literature: morrell mushroom spores closely resemble *Hymenolepsis nana* eggs.

In addition, we were practicing in a sea of gastrointestinal symptoms. It took us a number of years to get accustomed to the exact syndromes that were associated with the various existing pathogens. After 6 years, I was more able to discern that the fatigue and anorexia that were so prominent in *Cyclospora* infections, were not as prominent in other conditions.

Cyclospora was the first new intestinal protozoal pathogen discovered in 70 years. A few years ago, I wrote an article in the *ISTM NewShare*, comparing the practice of travel medicine to bird watching. Like bird watchers, travel medicine practitioners are passionate. They travel to experience new diseases and environments. They collect diseases that they have diagnosed like bird watchers collect life lists of sightings. *Cyclospora*, for those of us at the CIWEC Clinic, was like discovering a new bird species. It is rare enough among bird watchers, and even more rare among travel medicine practitioners. And it was only possible because of our lab technician, Rama.

When I shared that dinner with Ynes Ortega, one of the things she wanted to know about the CIWEC Clinic was how big our parasitology department was. I realized that she had no idea that we operated out of a tiny, rented house in Kathmandu. I replied, "We don't have a parasitology department — we just have Rama."

References

Ashford R. W. (1979). Occurrence of an undescribed coccidian in man in Papua New Guinea. *Annals of Tropical Medicine and Parasitology, 73*, 497–500.

Connor, B. A., & Shlim, D. R. (1995). Foodborne transmission of Cyclospora. *Lancet, 346*, 1634.

Connor, B. A., Shlim, D. R., Scholes, J. V., Rayburn, J. L., Reidy, J., & Rajah, R. (1993). Pathologic changes in the small bowel in nine patients with diarrhea associated with a coccidia-like body. *Annals of Internal Medicine, 119*, 377–382.

Eberhard, M. L., Ortega, Y. R., Hanes, D. E., et al. (2000). Attempts to establish experimental *Cyclospora cayetanensis* infection in laboratory animals. *Journal of Parasitololgy, 86*, 577–582.

Herwaldt, B. L. (2000). *Cyclospora cayetanensis*: A review, focusing on the outbreaks of Cyclosporiasis in the 1990s. *Clinical Infectious Diseases, 31*, 1040–1057.

Herwaldt, B. L., Beach, M. J., & Cyclospora Working Group. (1999). The return of *Cyclospora* in 1997: Another outbreak of cyclosporiasis in North America associated with imported raspberries. *Annals of Internal Medicine, 130*, 210–220.

Hoge, C. W., Echeverria, P., Rajah, R., Jacobs, J., Malthouse, S., Chapman, E., Jimenez, L. M., & Shlim, D. R. (1995). Prevalence of Cyclospora species and other enteric pathogens among children less than 5 years of age in Nepal. *Journal of Clinical Microbiology, 33*, 3058–3060.

Hoge, C. W., Shlim, D. R., Ghimire, M., et al. (1995). Placebo-controlled trial of cotrimoxazole for Cyclospora infections among travellers and foreign residents in Nepal. *Lancet, 345*, 691–693.

Hoge, C. W., Shlim, D. R., Rajah, R., et al. (1993). Epidemiology of diarrhoeal illness associated with coccidian-like organism among travellers and foreign residents in Nepal. *Lancet, 341*, 1175–1179.

Long, E. G., Ebrahimzadeh, A., White, E. H., Swisher, B., & Callaway, C. S. (1990). Alga associated with diarrhea in patients with acquired immunodeficiency syndrome and in travelers. *Journal of Clinical Microbiology, 28*, 1101–1104.

Ortega, Y. R., Sterling, C. R., Gilman, R. H., et al. (1993). Cyclospora species — A new protozoan pathogen of humans. *New England Journal of Medicine, 328*, 1308–1312.

Rabold, J. G., Hoge, C. W., Shlim, D. R., Kefford, C., Rajah, R., & Echeverria, P. (1994). Cyclospora outbreak associated with chlorinated drinking water. *Lancet, 344*, 1360–1361.

Shlim, D. R., Cohen, M. T., Eaton, M., Rajah, R., Long, E. G., & Ungar, B. L. P. (1991). An alga-like organism associated with an outbreak of prolonged diarrhea among foreigners in Nepal. *American Journal of Tropical Medicine and Hygiene, 45*, 383–389.

Shlim, D. R., Pandey, P., Rabold, J. G., Walch, A., & Rajah, R. (1997). An open trial of trimethoprim versus Cyclospora infections. *Journal of Travel Medicine, 4*, 44–45.

Soave, R., Dubey, J. P., Ramos, L. J., & Tummings, M. (1986). A new intestinal pathogen? [abstract]. *Clinical Research, 34*, 533A.

Chapter 22

Meningococcal Disease and the Hajj Pilgrimage

Annelies Wilder-Smith

Every piece of research has a story behind it that goes far beyond that what ends up getting published in the scientific literature. There is also a story behind my research on W135 meningococcal disease and the Hajj pilgrimage.

I had just started my position as Head of the Travellers Health & Vaccination Centre in Singapore in March 2000, when a week later, reports emerged about a new problem in Singapore. In the recent weeks, several cases of W135 meningococcal disease had occurred in Singaporean pilgrims who had just returned from the Hajj, and some of them had fatal outcomes. The Ministry of Health, Singapore, contacted the experts at my hospital for our opinion. The request somehow landed on my desk. So within a week of commencing my new position, I found myself investigating a problem that I knew not much about.

The Hajj pilgrimage attracts some two million pilgrims from all over the world. As conditions of overcrowding during this pilgrimage facilitate person-to-person transmission of meningococci, the Hajj has been associated with outbreaks of meningococcal disease in the past, notably the outbreak due to serogroup A in 1987. In response, the introduction of vaccination against serogroup A as a Hajj visa requirement led to the control of outbreaks with this serogroup. The emergence of W135 — obviously not covered with the current serogroup A vaccine — attracted lots of media attention, as it was a serogroup which previously had not been associated with sporadic disease, thus making the current Hajj-related outbreak the largest ever reported due to W135. More than 400 pilgrims were affected during the Hajj. And what was of even greater concern was the observation in Singapore and elsewhere that contacts of returning pilgrims also came down with the disease. After researching the literature on the Hajj and various WHO and CDC reports on the recent outbreak of W135 meningococcal disease during the Hajj, I finally wrote my recommendation. From my studies of the facts, I came to the conclusion that the Ministry should implement an immediate change in their recommendation from the bivalent meningococcal vaccine to the tetravalent meningococcal vaccine, which also offered protection against W135. I am not sure whether it was my recommendation, but indeed the change to the tetravalent vaccine was

Travel Medicine: Tales Behind the Science
Copyright © 2007 by Elsevier Ltd.
All rights of reproduction in any form reserved.
ISBN: 0-08-045359-7

immediately officially implemented by the Ministry of Health in Singapore. It was the correct public health response. And in my mind, this was the end of the story.

However, within weeks of this notification to the Moslem authorities, I saw my clinic being swamped by literally hundreds of Moslem pilgrims who were about to embark for the Umrah — the all year round pilgrimage. In preparation for the Umrah, they had already received the bivalent vaccine before the tetravalent vaccine became available (and known to be a necessity). I searched the literature for possible adverse events or contraindications to a repeat vaccination, but I could not find any data. Crossover vaccination with the tetravalent vaccine was justified in light of the serious outbreak of meningococcal disease with W135, even if there were no data published about the safety of vaccination with the tetravalent vaccine after recent administration of the bivalent vaccine. So we went ahead, but I quickly obtained the ethics committee approval to conduct a study to assess the safety and side effect profile. Fortunately, in my study group of 323 pilgrims that I recruited within a period of only 2 weeks, no increase in adverse events were detected in comparison to the control group that did not receive preceding vaccination with the bivalent vaccine. However, given the urgency of the situation, I was not able to assess whether there could have been a reduced seroconversion response to serogroup C — a phenomenon that has been reported for this serogroup after repeated vaccinations.

Several months passed. The deadline for grant applications was rapidly approaching. My head of department urged me to submit a grant. I was indeed keen to be involved in more research, and kept trying to think of research ideas related to travel medicine. The Hajj pilgrimage for the year 2001 was coming up. The idea came suddenly; in fact, the idea came while I was reading a fairy tale to my children. All of a sudden it hit me that the epidemiology of the 2000 Hajj-associated W135 meningococcal disease was hampered by the lack of knowledge on carriage rates. Meningococcal disease is primarily transmitted by tonsillopharyngeal carriers of *Neisseria meningitidis*. While polysaccharide meningococcal vaccines protect against disease, they do not protect against carriage. The pilgrims now protected with the tetravalent meningococcal vaccine for the Hajj 2001 may now be protected but what about their close unvaccinated contacts? Within seconds, I formulated the study design for a prospective cohort study that would involve studying transmission from pilgrims to household contacts. I was so excited about the idea that — to the surprise of my children — I jumped up from my seat, put down the book of fairy tales, and phoned two colleagues to share my idea. Both of them were excited, too. That night I stayed up to do an intense literature search. I found out that indeed carriage studies had been conducted in the past amongst pilgrims. But no studies had ever been conducted that quantified the risk of transmission from carriers to contacts, neither in the context of the Hajj nor in the context of other groups or the general population. In the ensuing week, I frenetically wrote the grant application and literally in the last minute before closure, I personally dropped the application at the application office. The study design was a prospective cohort study, taking throat swabs from pilgrims before the Hajj, and from pilgrims and their household contacts within 2 weeks after the pilgrims' return from the Hajj.

The Hajj pilgrimage was to take place in February 2001. So I recruited the subjects during the month of January. Recruitment of study subjects proved to be a rather difficult process. In order to avoid any potential problems, I had obtained permission not only from the ethics committee but also from the main Moslem organization in Singapore. Visiting the Moslem authorities was a unique experience. I was treated with great respect, served delicious Malay food, and enjoyed engaging in conversations about the origin of the world, the Creator God and the Islamic belief system. We found some common ground when I shared with them the work of my father-in-law who had dedicated his life to the credibility of God as Creator of the universe. After all these meetings, I had the official go-ahead for the study. With this trail of paper work in my hand, I hired a study team and visited the Mosque at the time of a mass vaccination for pilgrims going for the Hajj 2001. However, when I entered the mosque, the imam immediately approached me and said that as an "alien" (yes, this is the term he used), I should immediately leave the premises. I should have known the cultural sensitivities: I am a woman and rather foreign looking (I am blond and tall). However, it was a big blow to me, as I had used a big chunk of my study budget for the weekend pay for my study team that was now lost. I changed my recruitment strategy and kept in the background when we recruited subjects. In the following weeks, we managed to recruit 204 pilgrims prior to their departure to the Hajj. Upon return, 171 of these returned for their post-Hajj throat swab, and we also took swabs from 233 of their close household contacts.

The results of the pre-Hajj swabs showed that 0.5% were carriers, but there was no carrier for W135. Then results from the post-Hajj swabs came back, and there were numerous carriers. We were excited. The results were far more astonishing than my hypothesis. Fifteen percent of the returning pilgrims had acquired meningococcal carriage, of which 90% was W135. On pulsed field gel electrophoresis, these were all a single clone. Such a uniform carriage was unique. The acquisition rate of this clone in the household contacts of returning carriers with the same clone was 13%. All but one of the contacts now carrying the W135 clone were contacts of returning pilgrims. With these results, we had proven that there was a high acquisition rate of a single clone of W135 during the 2001 pilgrimage, and that this was associated with a high risk of transmission to household contacts, thereby providing an explanation for the cases of W135 disease seen in contacts around the world who had not been on the Hajj themselves, but were at risk because of their relatives who had returned from the Hajj. Several cases of W135 meningococcal disease occurred again in Singapore following the 2001 Hajj, but that year the burden of disease was mainly with the contacts, not with the pilgrims as the latter had all received the tetravalent meningococcal vaccine. With the help of my colleagues in microbiology, we were able to get some isolates of these patients and showed that the isolates were identical to those that we isolated from the throat swabs.

We published these findings in the British Medical Journal (BMJ). In the week the article was supposed to come out, I received an e-mail from the BMJ asking me to be available for press interviews. This came at a rather inopportune moment, as I was traveling with my children from Brazil via Germany to Singapore. A phone interview with the BBC was arranged for the day of my stopover in Germany. It was the first time in my life that I would be on a live interview with the BBC, so I was understandably nervous and excited. I had five interviews that day. It was a challenge to make sure that my children did not pick up the phone, and an even greater challenge to make sure that they did not interrupt me during the interview. At one stage, my little daughter burst in on the middle of the interview and her voice was heard on the BBC. I struggled to give intelligent answers to the BBC interviewer while at the same time trying to coax my girl into another room.

Our study findings would support a policy of administering antibiotics to pilgrims prior to their return to their countries of origin to eradicate carriage and thereby protect household contacts. However, this was a major policy decision that needed to be reflected upon carefully. More research questions remained: how long would carriage last, and, therefore, how much returning pilgrims would continue to be a reservoir for ongoing transmission to contacts or even the community at large? Feverishly, I scrambled together another application for the ethics committee that would allow me to increase my sample size and do a follow-up study over the next months. It was granted exceptionally expediently; I recruited a total of 373 pilgrims, and also I followed up contacts of positive carriers. Interestingly, this study showed that 55% were still carriers 6 months later. Transmission to their unvaccinated household contacts occurred only within the first few weeks, and there was no late transmission. The absence of late transmission in this cohort was also consistent with the national epidemiological data, which showed that all the cases of invasive W135 meningococcal disease in contacts of Hajj returnees occurred within 2 months of the end of the Hajj with no further cases afterwards. I then tried to obtain further information from the Ministry and the Singapore Islamic Religious Council: based on transmission rates of W135 carriage and national epidemiological data, the risk of an unvaccinated household contact (who had acquired W135 carriage) developing invasive meningococcal disease was estimated to be 1:70.

It was an exciting time indeed, and we had intense discussions with the Ministry of Health, Singapore, about the public health implications of our findings. I was eventually also invited to share our results at CDC Atlanta, a very special occasion. I was so excited about being at the CDC and took so many pictures that I almost arrived too late to deliver my lecture! Another highlight was certainly the invitation by the Kingdom of Saudi Arabia for a conference in Riyadh. My cultural adaptation to having to wear a black *abaya* at all times was rather slow, I must admit. However, riding on a camel in the middle of the desert, and eating delicious Arabian food sitting on thick carpets made up for the inconveniences of the *abaya*.

Back to the studies again: Based on the findings, we concluded that vaccination of all household contacts would be justifiable. However, this would be expensive, and uptake may be low — after all, we are talking of 2 million pilgrims with possibly at least 5 to 10 million contacts. Another approach that we discussed would be a policy of administering antibiotics to pilgrims before their return to their countries of origin to eradicate carriage and thereby protect household contacts. However, administering antibiotics to 2 million returning pilgrims raise issues of safety, development of resistance, as well as costs, not to mention political and cultural issues. These were public health policies of grand proportions that needed to be thought through carefully. Therefore, before such a large-scale program would be implemented, we felt that we should wait for the next Hajj. The Kingdom of Saudi Arabia had announced that the tetravalent meningococcal vaccine would be a Hajj visa requirement for the year 2002. We felt we would need to study the impact of improved coverage with tetravalent meningococcal vaccine of all pilgrims on carriage in pilgrims and incidence of the disease in household contacts.

So in the year 2002, after gaining another grant and ethics approval, I embarked on yet another study on W135 carriage in pilgrims. As the task of recruiting is such a major effort, I decided to take the opportunity to simultaneously study some other problems — and combined this study with investigations on the risk of pertussis and latent tuberculosis infection during the Hajj. I will leave out the details about the other study results, but remain focused on the primary question: would better vaccine coverage reduce carriage rates and, thereby, reduce the risk of transmission to contacts of Hajj returnees? We were eager to find out, and were relieved when the results came back: we documented an absence of carriage of W135 of the sequence type 11 for the Hajj 2002! This absence was also reflected by the absence of Hajj-associated clinical cases of W135 disease in Singapore in 2002. There was also no outbreak of W135 in pilgrims during the Hajj itself. It appeared that the epidemiology of carriage had changed or was controlled by vaccination. It is always difficult to predict when an outbreak will start but equally difficult to predict when an outbreak ends. Moreover, the Saudi Arabia authorities had intensified their efforts of administering antibiotics to incoming pilgrims from Africa and the Indian subcontinent, and they also had introduced a policy of antibiotic administration to their local returning Saudi Hajjis. It is impossible to tease out which factor contributed most to the significant reduction of W135 carriage for the Hajj 2002, but we were all pleased that the outbreak had now been controlled. Our conclusion, therefore, was that administration of antibiotics to all returning pilgrims is not necessary at the present time, but that ongoing surveillance continues to be necessary.

The high carriage rates, persistence and substantial transmissibility in combination with a high attack rate and case fatality rate of the Hajj-associated W135 outbreak clone certainly raise considerable concern about the public health consequences of widespread dissemination of this organism and the potential for future epidemics. And indeed, while the problem of W135 disease has now been controlled in relation to the Hajj, the problem has gone far beyond the Hajj: a major outbreak of W135 meningococcal disease occurred in predominantly Muslim countries in Africa affecting far larger numbers than the Hajj-associated outbreak. W135 disease is now an emerging problem worldwide.

Acknowledgements

All my thanks go to Associate Professor Nicholas Paton, Head of the Department of Infectious Diseases, Tan Tock Seng Hospital, Singapore. He created a research environment in the department, which provided the freedom and support to develop my own research ideas. He was my mentor, and rigorous critique of all my writings. Many thanks also to the other co-authors on most papers presented here: Dr Timothy Barkham, microbiologist, and Arul Earnest, the quickest statistician I have ever met. My sincerest thanks also to Fatimah Karim and Anushia Panchalingam, research coordinators, who within a time period of several months took literally hundreds and thousands of throat swabs. I would like to thank Dr Martin Cetron, Director of Quarantine at CDC Atlanta, for inviting me to speak about the results of above studies at CDC Atlanta. It was such an honor to me to be at the famous CDC. It also was a great educational experience to talk with so many US specialists on meningococcal disease. I would like to acknowledge Dr Ziad Memish who provided me with a lot of insights and pictures on the Hajj pilgrimage, and who was instrumental in inviting me to present these studies at a conference in Riyadh, Saudi Arabia. I am indebted to all the Malay participants. Without them, these studies would not have been possible. Special thanks to the support given by Majlis Ugama Islam Singapura. Last not least, my heartfelt thanks to my husband who remained a pillar of support throughout these studies and many weekends and nights spent at writing them up, and to my parents who put up the most spectacular celebration for my PhD on meningococcal disease.

References

Wilder-Smith, A., Barkham, T. M. S., Chew, S. K., & Paton, N. I. (2003). Absence of *N. meningitidis* W135 of the electrophoretic type 37 in pilgrims returning from the year 2002 Hajj. *Emerging Infectious Diseases, 9*(6), 734–737.

Wilder-Smith, A., Barkham, T. M. S., Earnest, A., & Paton, N. I. (2002). Acquisition of meningococcal carriage in Hajj pilgrims and transmission to household contacts: A prospective study. *British Medical Journal, 325*(7360), 365–366.

Wilder-Smith, A., Barkham, T. M. S., & Paton, N. I. (2002). Sustained outbreak of W135 meningococcal disease in east London, UK. *Lancet, 360*(9333), 644–645.

Wilder-Smith, A., Barkham, T. M. S, Ravindran, S., & Paton, N. I. (2003). Persistence of W135 *N. meningitidis* carriage in returning Hajj pilgrims: Risk of early and late transmission to household contacts. *Emerging Infectious Diseases, 9*(1), 123–126.

Wilder-Smith, A., Goh, K. T., Barkham, T. M. S., & Paton, N. I. (2003). Virulence of the Hajj associated W135 outbreak strain: Estimates of attack rate in a defined population and the risk of developing invasive disease in carriers. *Clinical Infectious Disease, 36*, 679–683.

Wilder-Smith A., & Paton, N. I. (2002). Crossover vaccination with quadrivalent meningococcal vaccine (against A/C/Y/W-135) following recent application of bivalent meningococcal vaccine (against A/C): Assessment of safety and side effect profile. *Journal of Travel Medicine, 9*(1), 20–23.

Chapter 23

Too High Too Fast: Experiences at High Altitude

Ken Zafren

We were nine friends from mountain rescue who craved a bit of adventure. Our goal was the summit of Chimborazo (6270 meters) in Ecuador. We all lived in Boulder County, Colorado, so we had exaggerated ideas of our own pre-acclimatization from living at 1700 meters. I was an emergency medical technician — the only current one on the expedition and, therefore, the most highly medically trained. Medical school was still in my future. I had climbed above 5000 meters three times, 2 years before, summiting the Mexican volcanoes, Iztaccihuatl, Popocatepetl, and Citlaltepetl (Pico de Orizaba) and above 6000 meters, the year before, to the top of Denali (Mt. McKinley) in Alaska, so I was also the most accomplished high-altitude climber in the group. Still, nobody really took me seriously when I suggested another acclimatization day at the "hut" at 4700 meters, which we had reached by road and a few hours hike after two nights spent in Quito. Water was scarce in the vicinity of the hut, so we would ascend.

We easily ascended to our next camp at 5700 meters, except for one of our group who dragged into the high camp somewhat behind the rest of us. On the way, we had passed a much more comfortable camping spot — the Campo Japones (Japanese Camp) at about 5300 meters, but I do not think we really noticed it. In the morning, the climber who had been unexpectedly slow the day before woke up complaining of a headache, and then promptly became unconscious. The diagnosis was clear — high-altitude cerebral edema (HACE) — but what should we do?

There were six of us who were old expedition and rescue hands and two who were less experienced, in addition to our patient who was unconscious. The six most experienced climbers put our patient in a sleeping bag inside a bivouac sack and slid him down the snow until we were far below the high camp. Fortunately, he woke up at this point and was able to walk downhill with assistance. I went back up to the high camp to rejoin the two least experienced members of the expedition who had stayed there during the rescue.

After a horrible, mostly sleepless night, I knew — dimly — that it would not be healthy to spend another night at 5700 meters. I was barely able to motivate myself to pack up and descend and even more barely able to motivate my companions. One of them concluded that I was overbearing and continued all the way down to the hut, while the other two of us established our new camp at the level site of the Campo Japones where there was plenty of snow to melt for water.

A few days later, the rest of the group — minus our recovering climber — re-ascended. They passed us in the fog on their way up, but did not come close to the summit. After that, we all returned to Quito. This was my introduction to the dangers of going too high too fast. This was a lot more serious than the bit of acute mountain sickness (AMS) I had had on Denali.

Fast forward a few years from 1978 to 1989. I had finished medical school and was practicing medicine, but I still lived for adventure. I had taken care of a climber with high-altitude pulmonary edema (HAPE) and HACE in Nepal, and I was a volunteer doctor for the Himalayan Rescue Association (HRA) at Pheriche. I received indoctrination in the Golden Rules of Altitude by David Shlim. These rules are: 1) If you are ill at altitude, it is because of the altitude until proven otherwise; 2) If you have symptoms due to altitude, do not ascend further until the symptoms resolve; and 3) If you are very ill or getting worse, descend. These rules have served me well over subsequent years, along with the advice my teammates on Chimborazo should have heeded: do not go too high too fast. Since that time, I have learned that there are some other Golden Rules. Golden Rule number 4 is not to leave anyone with altitude illness alone and Golden Rule number 5, taught to me by Buddha Basnyat, is that even doctors can get altitude illness.

I volunteered at the HRA after I visited the clinics in Manang and Pheriche. Shortly after my visit to the clinic at Pheriche, I took care of a climber on Island Peak, (6189 meters) near Mt. Everest. He had climbed to high camp (about 5400 meters), the day I climbed the mountain, and had awakened the following day with a cough and some gurgling in his chest. He did not tell his climbing partners, but started the ascent. As he ascended, he became weaker and weaker. A well-meaning Sherpa took his pack from him and they continued up. At the base of the headwall (about 5800 meters), he finally realized that he could ascend no further. He was helped back to base camp (about 5100 meters), where I was having a pleasant rest day. This was during the days before pulse oximetry was widely available, but the descent seemed to have done him good. His lungs were no longer gurgling. He seemed tired but not short of breath. It is a long way on level ground before one can lose much altitude on the way down from Island Peak Base Camp. It was late November and it was dark. We decided to stay put until morning. I kept an eye on the ill climber in my tent through the night.

In the morning, I helped my patient pack his pack and suggested he start off. He went a step or two before collapsing. It seemed I had overlooked the fact that he had HACE in addition to HAPE. With two Sherpas first helping him walk, then a succession of Sherpas carrying him, we made rapid progress down valley. We sent word to Pheriche and a doctor met us with a horse. I tried a CPAP mask I had brought along. It seemed to help, but after a while, was just too hot and confining. We spent the night in Dingboche (about 4350 m) with oxygen kindly provided by the HRA doctor. The next day, our ill climber continued down valley by horseback.

Two years later, I was an HRA doctor and had the privilege of staying up at night treating patients with altitude illness. There was a Korean climber, whose leader was delayed in Kathmandu due to radio permit problems. He told the others not to go too high too fast.

Whether this had an effect, I will never know, but they ascended quite rapidly with the result that one of them developed a rather bad case of HAPE. This was one of the last times I used furosemide in the treatment of HAPE. Shortly after that, we learned that nifedipine was safer and more effective. We put our ill climber in the Gamow bag with a pee bottle. After 45 minutes, he held up the full pee bottle so we would know that we had to let him out to urinate. He may have had some problems with acclimatization, but he must have been very experienced with a pee bottle. He had filled it almost to the brim without spilling a drop! He recovered and went down to Phunki Tenga (3250 m), the lowest point in the Khumbu (Everest region) to recover. He eventually re-ascended and took part in the Everest expedition. I never found out if he reached the summit.

That same season, three Japanese trekkers died in the Gokyo Valley. At least one of them was being carried up Gokyo Ri when he became too ill to ascend. The others were left in the open in a village farther down. A helicopter came for them, but one was already dead and the other died en route to Kathmandu. Their itinerary was a common one for Japanese trekkers at the time: two weeks from Tokyo to Nepal including Gokyo Ri and Kala Patar and return to Tokyo. An American climber tried to persuade the ill trekker, who was being carried up, to descend instead, but the ill climber told him that he had paid for the trek and deserved to have the view. Ultimately, he paid for the trek with his life. Altitude illness is serious business.

Although it is rewarding to save lives of patients with HAPE and HACE using portable hyperbaric chambers, usually in the middle of the night, the most important work of the HRA is preventive medicine. We have succeeded in popularizing a reasonable ascent plan of gradual ascent for trekkers, especially in the Everest region, and we give daily altitude lectures at our aid posts as well as regular altitude lectures in the village of Dingboche, near Pheriche. We teach the Golden Rules and also try to instill a sense of responsibility toward employees of the trekking groups and toward fellow trekkers. One of my sickest patients from my first season at Pheriche was a lowland Sherpa employee of a trekking group.

It was on one of my visits to Dingboche to give the altitude lecture that I found an Italian woman in the lodge where I gave the lectures. She was complaining of a headache, nausea, and blurred vision. We spoke in French, in which neither of us was particularly fluent. Her problems had begun in earnest while taking a shower. Now, several hours later, she was waiting for me to arrive at the lodge for the altitude lecture. I examined her and was alarmed to find that one of her pupils was dilated and fixed. Could she have had a stroke? Otherwise, she seemed to have a case of AMS. She was not ataxic. A few volunteer trekkers and I walked her over the ridge to Pheriche, where we put her in the Gamow bag. A group of Italians who did not know her helped me communicate with her. No, she was not taking any medicines, and had not had any weakness or slurred speech. About 30 minutes into her Gamow-bag treatment, she remembered something, however. Her doctor in Italy had given her a transdermal scopalomine patch to use in case of nausea. I worked out that she had inadvertently touched it in the shower and then touched her eye, causing the dilated pupil. I felt foolish, but relieved.

Another incident that year also had a happy ending, but it could have been otherwise. A man and his teenage son ascended Kala Patar. The man was an avid photographer, who was intent on taking a 360° panorama from the summit (about 5700 meters, at the higher of two summits) with a special tripod head he had constructed. The son started vomiting partway up. The man sent his son down to a lodge at Gorak Shep (5180 meters) to wait for him. The son continued to vomit. At the lodge, some trekkers who had attended our lecture at Pheriche felt (correctly) that it would be best for the son to descend further, so they helped him down to a lodge at Lobuje (4930 meters). Eventually, the father found the son at Lobuje. Many people to whom I have talked thought that the father might have been angry at his son for not waiting at Gorak Shep as instructed. As far as I know, this was not the case. The father's first words to his son were: "I got the panorama."

Many changes have taken place at Pheriche (and Manang) in the years since I was a volunteer. Now, I recruit the volunteers, but I cannot resist visiting and doing a bit of work now and again. I brought pulse oximeters for both aid posts in Fall 1989. The one at Pheriche eventually broke and I suppose the one at Manang did also, but by that time, portable pulse oximeters were commonplace. In 1989, getting a helicopter for an evacuation was a difficult and sometimes impossible proposition. With the advent of private helicopter companies and satellite phones, there is usually little difficulty, as long as the patient has a credit card. Until sometime in the 1990s, most people who survived altitude illness at Pheriche or Manang eventually walked to the nearest airport, often a several day proposition. In the last several years, the volunteers at Pheriche and Manng usually just have to arrest the course of HAPE or HACE until the helicopter can arrive.

In Fall 2001, I was visiting the HRA aid post at Pheriche and had told the doctors there to take a well-deserved break together while I would be on duty. They had not yet left for their two-day trek when one of them went out to the trail with me to admire a particularly nice view. Looking up the trail we could see our next patient, visibly cyanotic even from a distance and being supported by two Sherpas. We put the patient on the oxygen concentrator, but could not maintain acceptable oxygen saturation. I suggested that we put the patient in a portable hyperbaric chamber with supplemental oxygen. It turned out that they had not used a chamber at all that season. Most of the patients did just fine on the concentrator until the helicopter arrived! The patient did well in the chamber with extra oxygen via a cylinder. A few hours later, the helicopter did arrive. It all seemed so much easier than the old days.

There is an old Afghan proverb: The sight of a horse makes the strong man lame. I have coined a new one: The sight of a helicopter makes the strong rescuer lame. Who knows what changes are in store for the prevention and treatment of altitude illness in the next decade or two? Recent work has shown that dexamethasone, our old standby for HACE, may be useful in the prophylaxis of HAPE, and we are currently studying acetazolamide, our favorite drug for preventing AMS, for HAPE prevention. One thing seems certain, however, the Golden Rules will always be the best key to prevention.

Image 23.1. Ken Zafren, MD and his guru, Mi Tsering, at the Mani Rimdu festival, Thyangboche Monastery, Nepal in 1992.

Chapter 24

The Pleasures and Perils of Traveling with Young Children

Karl Neumann

The ease, speed, and comforts of modern travel are enabling parents to take ever younger children to ever more exotic destinations, occasionally to destinations that lie well beyond the boundaries of good sense.

Family travel is growing rapidly. Club Med, once a haven for adult singles, has family resorts. Disney Cruises caters solely to families. Emirates Airlines wants business travelers to bring their children, offering those between 2 and 16 years of age membership in the Airline's new children's Frequent Flyers Club called Skysurfers. Benefits include free flights, Fun Tray Meals, a cake and portrait (Polaroid) if flying on ones' birthday, and special interactive games. China Southern Airlines and Northwest/KLM have "adoption packages" for parents adopting children from overseas, expediting the return trip with an additional passenger. In the USA alone, there are about 25,000 overseas adoptions each year.

For the most part, family travel is a positive experience for the entire family and, in general, parents use good judgment in formulating plans. And most children make great travelers. They are inquisitive, fun loving, and when they are motivated, adaptable and inexhaustible. Overseas travel, whether a week in Paris or several years in a developing country, provides children with knowledge and experiences that enrich their education, build their self-confidence, promote family cohesiveness, and create memories for tomorrow.

But some parents opt for travels that, by most standards, are beyond the boundaries of good sense. Parents contemplating taking their children for adventurous trips or to live for extended periods in a developing country should look at their plans through the eyes of their children and ask themselves:

> "Are my parents unreasonably risking my health and welfare to further their careers, practice their religious and political convictions, fulfill their sense of adventure, or to show me to my grandparents? Am I just another backpack?"

Below are scenarios that we have encountered in recent years in our family travel medicine clinic or have been consulted on by other health care professionals. While these trips may, indeed, have some merit, are they in the best interest of the children? And, should travel health advisors interject themselves in the decision making of the parents?

- Spending 2 weeks at the house of a grandmother, who lives in a small town in Nigeria. The grandmother is "very sick" and "coughing up blood" and this may be her last chance to see the children, aged 1 and 3 years.
- Two graduate students in Eastern religions taking their 7-month-old baby traveling across India by local transportation or hitching rides and staying at small guesthouses and shrines.
- Taking two preverbal children to Machu Picchu, Peru, to see the ruins.
- An 11-year-old child with a probably terminal illness and slightly immunosuppressed, whose wish is to see the game parks in East Africa.
- Children of missionaries to live in extremely poor and remote region of a developing country where their parents' religious teachings are unpopular with most of the local population.

How many vaccines and prophylactic medications do you administer to infants and young children and how many hazards to you expose them to that would not be necessary if the family stayed at home, or chose a more benign destination? In many developed countries, health care professionals, especially pediatricians, are increasingly considered to be advocates of children, charged with protecting them from unwise whims of parents and other adults. If parents visited a clinic and said that they plan to expose their children to health and safety hazards of the magnitude depicted in the scenarios presented — but did not mention that the hazards were travel-related — the parents might be reported to the local child welfare agency.

Basics of Traveling with Children

Even "routine" travel with children is never all fun and games. Parents should understand what overseas travel/living entails. Arduous trips are best avoided by parents and children who are finicky and who prefer adhering to strict schedules. Overseas living generally requires a good deal of flexibility and improvisation. Parents should be familiar with the area; ideally one parent should have spent some time there. Items that are taken for granted in the home country — over-the-counter medications, disposable diapers, and infant's formula, for example — may not be readily available, have unfamiliar names, and contain different ingredients. Reading labels carefully and checking expiration dates of products, often in a foreign language, are part of the excitement — or the hassle — of being overseas. How parents consider such chores is an important determination of their adaptability.

Many parents do have feelings of apprehension and ambivalence about taking children overseas. (Likely, these are the parents who consult travel health professionals; probably many more parents do not, and subject their children to even greater risks.) Professionals who have had overseas experience themselves can generally give the necessary guidance. If they cannot, parents should be referred to people who can. Virtually every large medical center has people knowledgeable about the health aspects of overseas travel and living.

Such people can generally be found in travelers' clinics and in departments of tropical diseases and international health.

Parents should be encouraged to read books, browse the Internet, and speak to parents who have "been there and done that." There are many books in the library and in bookstores about family travel and living overseas. And parents should become not only knowledgeable about the country that they plan to visit but familiar with the specific area in that country where they intend to spend much of their time. Standards of living and medical facilities in a capital city, for example, may not reflect conditions in rural areas. Capital cities may be close in miles but distant in time due to unreliable transportation and communications.

Some parents have perceptions of travel and overseas living that are poorly thought out and inappropriate. In most such cases, parents will listen to criticism, especially if they are advised not to abandon their plans, but rather to alter or postpone them to a later date, based on a child's age or medical problem or conditions at the destination. A more delicate situation arises when travel plans are inappropriate or based on the parents' lack of sophistication or stability. Some mentally unstable individuals believe erroneously that travel is a way for them to get away from their problems, "to flee their demons," so to speak. In fact, travel often does the opposite, removing such people from the few stabilizing influences in their lives, and exposing them to changes and stresses that they are specifically unable to cope with. Such parents may listen if they are told that their plans are not in the best interest of their children. Sometimes a referral to a mental health counselor can be helpful.

Psychological Aspects of Traveling with Children

Including children in the planning process of travel helps alleviate children's apprehension of the unknown. Older children can be shown maps and brochures of hotels, airlines, and national parks, for example. When possible, children should be allowed to choose from several reasonable alternatives. Younger children can participate in the seat selection on airplanes, choose the floor at a hotel, or select the color of a rental car, for example. Most reservation clerks are happy to cooperate, if the process does not take too much time. Children who will be living overseas can be shown books and videotapes of the country that will be their temporary home. Smaller children can be involved by allowing them to mail letters concerning the trip and opening the replies when they arrive, or press buttons on the computer. Participation gives children a sense of inclusion and accomplishment, which helps motivation and peace of mind.

In general, taking children out of school for leisure travel sends children the wrong message. But there are occasional situations where such trips may be justified on the basis of exposure to new experiences and for promoting family cohesiveness. Taking the family along on an occasional trip may be important in families where one parent is frequently away on business. Frequent absence from home of one parent appears to cause stress-related symptoms in the business traveler parent as well as psychosocial symptoms in their spouses and their children. Teachers should approve of such trips and the child should miss minimal school. For living overseas, firm plans for uninterrupted education should be in place before leaving home. Again there are many books and websites about educating children under such circumstances.

Homesickness is common in children and teenagers who are away from home alone — on teen tours, visiting relatives, on cultural exchange/educational programs, and attending summer camps, for example — but also occurs in older children traveling with their families. Often homesickness involves somatic symptoms — gastrointestinal, sleep disturbances, loss of appetite, headaches, absent-mindedness, and fatigue — all of which are symptoms associated with depression. Distance from home is less important than the length of stays and absence of acquaintances. Staying in touch — by telephone, regular mail, and e-mail often helps minimize symptoms. Symptoms tend to lessen and disappear with time.

Successful trips with children must be oriented toward children. For example, children often find many hours in the car and long dinners "boring" and "a drag." Parents should plan trips with a reasonable ratio between recreation and education, swimming versus museums, for example, and not become upset if the children seem to prefer the swimming pool to the art gallery. Visiting cultural sites does seem to have a lasting impression on children, as can be heard when they later tell (or boast to) their friends and their teachers where they have been and what they have seen. Some children take to travel situations better than others. Unreasonable parental expectations result in children becoming obstinate, and spoil the trip for the entire family.

Preparing Children for Overseas Travel

Children going overseas for an extended period should have thorough health assessments. All positive findings in the history and physical should be flagged and evaluated in the context of the travel/overseas living scenario contemplated.

For parent of children with ongoing medical issues, the availability of competent and readily available medical facilities at the destination is of prime importance.

Routine immunizations should be updated and travel-related immunizations may be indicated. For long stays overseas, parents must be advised about the timing of future immunizations and the advisability and availability of receiving them overseas. Sometimes immunizations can await the children's return home. Parents should carry each child's immunization record, and entries should be legible and state the name of each vaccine, not the trade name of multiple vaccine preparations.

Some positive findings in the health assessment will need further evaluation and, rarely, limit travel. For example, air travel and destinations at higher altitudes are risky for children with sickle cell disease. Parents with children having diabetes must know how to cope with changes in insulin requirements brought about by travel through many time zones, gastrointestinal illnesses, and motion sickness. Children with asthma do well at higher altitudes but may experience symptoms in chemically polluted urban areas or where pollen counts are high.

Parents can consult allergists about travel plans involving allergy-prone children. Most allergists have charts depicting the geographical and seasonal distribution of various allergens around the world. Air quality is especially poor in some parts of Eastern Europe and in many large cities in the developing world. (Some years ago, the air was so bad in Mexico City that diplomats from Western Europe were advised not to take their children for long stays there.) Indoor air pollution, from burning wood and poor-grade coal for cooking and heating, is an important cause of respiratory problems in developing countries. The problem is acute in Eastern Europe, especially during wintertime.

Questions remain whether children with seizure disorders are more prone to having seizures at higher elevations and whether such children should receive mefloquine for malaria chemoprophylaxis; melfoquine may lower the threshold of seizure activity. And experts differ on continuing medications for attention deficit disease when children are not in school. Some believe that such medications are important as a safety issue in new situations, such as travel.

A child's ongoing health issues must be considered when giving children travel-related immunizations or prescribing medications. Severe egg allergy may negate yellow fever vaccine, and a history of urticaria tends to worsen reactions to Japanese encephalitis vaccine. Previous adverse reactions to sulfonamides rules out using acetazolamide, a medication often given to prevent and treat acute mountain sickness.

Preparing Parents to Travel Overseas with Children

Parents should update their own vaccinations against childhood diseases. Adults taking children overseas may be at a somewhat greater risk of contracting childhood diseases themselves because their children may have contacts with local children. Some adults are not immune to measles, mumps, rubella, and varicella, for example.

Adults traveling overseas to adopt children should update their immunizations, especially against hepatitis B. Most such adoptions take place in Latin America, Eastern Europe, and Southeast Asia where the incidence of the disease is high, especially in children in orphanages. Inevitably, caring for small children brings adults into close contact with the body fluids of children. Other adult caretakers of the child and siblings-to-be should also be vaccinated. Parents should start hepatitis B vaccinations as soon as they begin the adoption process in order to receive the three injections necessary for immunity.

Preparing Parents to Handle Illnesses Overseas

When children become ill overseas, parents will probably be far more on their own than back home: no family support system and an unfamiliar health care system. Competent care may be difficult to find, and personnel may be less approachable and may spend little time answering questions. Language may be a problem. Treatments may seem at odds with those that the parents are accustomed to at home. Problems with medications overseas have already been mentioned.

As a general rule, health care in developing countries is poor. Health care workers frequently give unnecessarily potent medications and use injections for minor illnesses, and may use needles and syringes that are suspect. Medications may be of poor quality and outdated. Diagnostic techniques and equipment, taken for granted at home, are often absent. Parents should be made aware that injections are rarely indicted for minor illnesses. In non-emergency situations, when treatment recommendations seem to be out of the ordinary, parents may want to check with their health care providers back home.

Medical Kit

A telephone, the telephone numbers of all the children's health care providers, and, perhaps, a digital camera are integral parts of a modern first aid kit. Whenever possible, parents should contact their health care providers back home when their children are ill. This gives parents peace of mind and often solves the problem at hand.

Small medical kits specifically prepared for each child are very helpful. A three-prong approach helps in assembling such kits:

- Medications for illnesses that the child experiences at home. Even in the tropics, a child is far more likely to have the illnesses that the child is susceptible to at home, earaches and stomachaches, for example, than exotic diseases.
- First aid-type items — thermometers and bandages, for example.
- Trip-specific items — rehydrating powder and antimalarials, for example.

Finding Competent Medical Help Overseas

It is very reassuring for parents to go overseas and have the name and address of a qualified health care provider at the families' destination(s). In the USA, all board-certified specialists have directories of all members of that specialty, including overseas members. Names can also be obtained from the specialties' national offices. Most physicians involved with travel medicine have contacts overseas. International Association for Medical Assistance to Travelers (IAMAT) (716-754-4883) has a directory, which supplies lists of English-speaking physicians in all parts of the world. These physicians meet standards set by IAMAT, and agree to charge the fees published in the directory.

Nearly every illness — cardiopulmonary conditions, food allergies, diabetes, and physical handicaps, to mention just a few — has national associations, and most of these have travel-related information. The information is usually posted on the association's website. Some associations have affiliate groups overseas.

Health and Accident Insurance

Having — and understanding — comprehensive health and accident insurance coverage is extremely important when traveling with children. Most families do have such insurance at home, and the policies generally have provisions to reimburse for events occurring overseas. However, often such reimbursement is vague and takes place months after the bills are submitted. Some insurance companies reimburse only for "emergencies" with the company defining the emergency. (In one dispute, an insurance company claimed that a visit to an emergency room on a Caribbean island for a young child with a high fever and severe earache did not constitute an emergency.) Other companies want to be notified before a policy holder receives medical assistance or the company will not pay the costs. Very few overseas physicians and hospitals accept foreign insurance plans in lieu of payment.

Parents should consider carrying travelers' assistance insurance. The companies maintain world-wide, 24-hour telephone "hotlines." These are manned by experts who can direct the caller to competent English-speaking physicians and hospitals, and guarantee the costs of treatments and hospitalizations at the time of the incidence. In addition, if the patient requires medical care that is not available at the location of the incidence, the company will arrange and pay for evacuation to a medical facility that can provide such treatment. In cases of severe illness or accident, the patient will be transported home, by ambulance airplane, if necessary. These policies will also pay the costs for changing airline tickets due to illness, bring other family members to the site of a serious medical problem, and, in case of death, arrange for and pay the costs of returning the remains back home. Policies should be read carefully and, perhaps, shown to an expert. Disputes arise because the company, not the client, decides when an evacuation is necessary, and where to the patient should be evacuated, for example.

Families may have access to travelers' assistance insurance if a parent is employed by a major corporation, large university, or religious organization, for example. Holders of major credit cards may find that the issuing company may provide such insurance, sometimes for a small additional fee. Companies providing travelers' assistance insurance include Medex and AEA International.

When a child receives medical care overseas, it is important to ask for the diagnosis, the results of tests performed, and the treatment given. This becomes helpful in ongoing illnesses. Also, parents should ask for documentation of all fees paid, for later reimbursement.

Many countries have national health insurance systems that may provide health care for visitors and long-time residents at no or low cost. The information is generally available from that country's embassy or consulate, sometimes on the Internet. In most cases, the coverage is only for emergency care, and only at government-run clinics and hospitals, where care may not be up to the Western standards. Overseas, private care, if available, is often very expensive.

In cases of medical emergency, when possible, parents should take their children to the largest medical facility in the area, rather than wait for medical help to reach them. Physicians can do little in a hotel room, for example, and may take a long time to get there. Many countries have no or poor ambulance services. Large medical facilities are more likely to have pediatric units and trauma services.

Safety Concerns

While travel health education stresses illness prevention, accidents prevention may even be more important. Parents must teach themselves that safety cannot be taken for granted, especially in new situations, and even in developed countries. A study in the U.S. found at least one safety problem with cribs, playgrounds, or pools in 82% of the hotels and motels randomly selected for inspection. And the houses of friends and relatives may not be "childproofed"; there may be medications on nightstands, no gates on stairs, no locks on kitchen cabinets, and lamps at the edges of tables, for example.

The outdoors/wilderness presents many potential hazards. In U.S. National Parks, the most common sources of injuries are automobile-related, falls, knives and axes, and fires for cooking. All Parks have visitors' centers, which have brochures and bulletin boards for interesting and safe activities and information about inclement weather, hazardous animals, polluted water, and emergency telephone numbers. Such information may also be available at information centers in theme parks, in resorts, and on cruise ships. Parents should be in the habit of writing down emergency numbers posted along highways and carrying a cellular telephone.

Children should be taught to stay away from animals and to report even minor animal bites and licks to their parents. Rabies continues to be a problem, especially in developing countries. In India, there are about 30,000 rabies-related deaths per year. In many areas where the disease exists, 40% of cases occur in children. Children tend to be fascinated with animals and may use poor judgment around them. They may not report minor incidences, and, because of their height, are more likely to suffer bites around the head and neck, bites that may be more likely to cause rabies. Stray dogs are common in developing countries. Monkeys congregate around temples and other shrines in India and parts of Southeast Asia, and some are rabid. Food should not be eaten where there are monkeys nearby, lest the monkey jumps for the food and bites the person in the process.

Overseas, safety concepts are different, and in most developing countries standards are poorly enforced; leading causes of accidents are motor vehicle-related, waterfront, and falls. Parents must consciously evaluate each new situation: check balcony railings for proper heights and for spaces young children can crawl through. Bathroom faucets can be confusing with different letters used for hot and cold, and water may be scalding hot. Toys bought locally are not necessarily safe. Amusement park rides may be poorly maintained and rarely inspected.

In summary, while this chapter enumerates the many perils of overseas and adventure travel for children — and may give casual readers the impression that its purpose is to dissuade family travel — in fact, the opposite is the intent. The key words for parents are: look at proposed trips through the eyes of your children, and plan appropriately. With few exceptions, travel itineraries can be adjusted for children, with adjustments depending on the ages and personalities of the children. True, travel is never an absolutely safe activity. Neither are at-home activities. But travel is more fun than staying home.

Chapter 25

Mongolian Expedition

Marc Shaw

Expedition medicine is becoming a lot more popular with travelers now, so 'tis important to have some idea about it when advising on issues of remote travel. I was approached to give medical expertise on an expedition to Outer Mongolia whose role was to find out how many snow leopards are there in the region. The task sounded quite exciting actually, and apart from my role as Expedition Doctor (ED), I figured that I would have an equally hard task of keeping beloved Lynne, also known as 'the Memsahib', actively enthusiastic about the journey. When I mentioned the idea to her, she was bland faced and not too much excited; so I declined to tell her about the camping we would be doing at altitude in the snowline. OK, so it was a mistake, more so because the region just happens to be 'quite' windy and she hates wind. Had to be careful, else I fear that morale could dip a little on our journey. Figured that I would take lots of happy-juice and family photos along with me.

The modern practice of expedition medicine is to encourage adventure but to attempt to minimize the risk of trauma and diseases by proper planning involving risk assessment, preventive measures such as vaccinations, prophylactic drugs and medical equipment, knowledge of first aid, emergency and primary healthcare skills, communication skills, and an attitude of caring for both the anticipated team and the anticipated cultures of the expedition. So, the usual 'medical stuff' but with expedition planning needs to cover all contingencies: from mild illnesses and disease to group health insurances, through to unforeseen events such as evacuating a seriously-ill, injured or dead person. Important also in the pre-trip planning is local knowledge of the area to be traveled. To this end, the ED needs to investigate local knowledge in the country. This was hard to do in Mongolia, mainly because very few people speak English and there are very few adequate medical facilities outside the main city of Ulaanbaatar.

Many groups of expeditioners travel without a doctor, nurse or suitably qualified paramedic. Notwithstanding this, an experienced doctor is a valuable member of any team and has the role of looking after such medically related issues as managing pre-existing health problems, advising on suitable immunizations and anti-malarials, assessing any travel-related health risks, and finally making preparations for the trip that include the assembly of a suitable medical kit. Good stuff, but hard work. Medical problems may arise during or after

Travel Medicine: Tales Behind the Science
Copyright © 2007 by Elsevier Ltd.
All rights of reproduction in any form reserved.
ISBN: 0-08-045359-7

the expedition and the ED needs confidence in dealing with the varying demands of an expedition team, which will vary enormously depending on the individuals, the task of the expedition and the location.

Preparing for Expeditionary Life

The most successful EDs contribute to the many aspects of an expedition in a number of valued ways.

First and foremost, the MO needs to be able to deal with the medical problems that are most likely to occur. This is obvious stuff, but there needs to be a confidence in the management of care from minor ailments through to, in a worst case scenario, multiple casualties with major trauma. For this expedition, I checked out issues of desert travel, temperature-dependent injuries, including environmental problems such as hot and cold extremes, and escape routes for the Memsahib if things got really tough.

Being a useful expedition 'doc' is much more than just doing the medicine alone. An ED needs to ensure that they don't become a liability during the trip, and so depend on other team members to ensure their own or a casualty's safety. Essentially this means that the ED should feel entirely comfortable in the expedition environments, be it on mountains, underwater, in the jungle or in a desert. Additional skills such as navigation abilities, photography, multi-vehicle driving licenses are always going to be a bonus for any expedition, but hell, no one is perfect.

Having said that, the more prepared one is for a particular climate, the more likely one can survive. Things are never equal however, and luck and personal physical conditioning are probably the most important, albeit, the most uncontrollable factor. Nevertheless, there are several controllable factors and that is the 'jump-start' that one needs to get a little sanity on the expedition — stuff like physical conditioning, clothing, survival kit, and survival skills that will prevent needless deaths in the desert. Yep, I suppose that this is useful but it just sounds so clinical! As does the need for physical conditioning and acclimatization, a couple of days acclimatizing before starting out on hikes more than 5 kilometers, the large temperature variations between hot and cold, and altitude and zero-level. Mustn't forget sunscreen, chapstick, and sunglasses are to protect the eyes from corneal abrasions from the blowing sand, leather gloves to protect the hands, and (most importantly) footwear that will make your days seem like breathing, if you get them a bit right. If you don't, it's gonna be a long trip!

Done the preparation, and now for the travel. Hard work, 'cos all travel usually is, but finally Mongolia, I couldn't believe that I was there. Memsahib and I had totally done it. We had arrived into Ulaanbaatar (UB), a city still living on the dubious laurels of Genghis Khan. Compared to Beijing, the city was rugged and dirty and unkempt but it was honest; Beijing isn't. The clear bright skies overlording the city and the surrounding hills augured for our upcoming sojourn, the aims of which were by now becoming clearer: to assist a local palaeontologist in digging fossils, to collect rare plant specimens for a University botanist, and to track the route of the snow leopard in southern Mongolia.

It was at this stage of the briefing that Memsahib casually asked how high we were traveling to. '3500 meters' came the reply from Simon our leader. 'Going to be bloody cold, about minus 10, and we won't have any water to shower or wash in for 4 weeks'. Memsahib looked at me, daggers in her eyes and with a knowing 'I told you I didn't need to be here' look. 'But', said I to Simon 'we can use body-wipes can't we?' nodding to she-with-closed-eyes. I got the strangest look from the rest of the 15-person party.

Simon had just finishing addressing the group as to the risks and hazards of our anticipated travel south into the Gobi. Now, I have always wanted to go there, ever since W.E. Johns wrote a fine book called 'Biggles in the Gobi'. For me then this was a voyage of discovery and revelation, built upon childhood images. When I told this to the group, they stared at me. Memsahib told me to 'settle down and check the medical kit'. I obediently complied; she still has that influence over me! Yep, the kit was a big call and on any expedition it needs to cover a wide variety of possible emergencies. But which ones? The lot really, save for those where there is no hope or no chance. This is a much harder call that it would seem for it is easy to include all that one 'might need', much more difficult to be objective about an expedition's actual requirements. Obviously this latter is very dependent on itinerary and also on the health of the expeditioners. Our kit was compact, pretty inclusive, and very practical and, like most expedition medical kits, wasn't actually needed very much at all!

Over the last couple of years, there have been more and more folk going to Mongolia, and the reality is that the level of medical services provided is not up to Western standards. In the countryside, outside of UB, medical care is very difficult to access. All Mongolian hospitals are very short of most medical supplies, including basic care items, drugs, and spare parts for medical equipment, though having said that I visited a local hospital in Dalandzadgad, south of the country and in the Gobi, where I was amazed at how well it was equipped. Only problem was that while the gear was good, no one knew how to use it. So it needs be said that if a traveler needs care in UB, and this generally goes for all developing countries, then several things should be kept in mind when dealing with local healthcare providers:

1. Assume that there are generally no English-speaking physicians or staff at any of the local hospitals or clinics. In Mongolia, many local doctors had trained in the former Soviet Union, and therefore spoke only Russian.
2. Most Mongolian hospitals have not established fixed fees for foreign patients. To avoid being charged exorbitant fees for even routine care, patients should inquire about fees before services are rendered.
3. One should always telephone the hospital or clinic before visiting to be sure that it is open, that the proper staff is on duty, and that the hospital has the supplies and equipment to perform the desired service. Once again, no English-speaking staff will generally be available to answer your call.

Recently an international clinic opened in the city, but apart from this facility there are limited medical choices. Often the way in developing countries, that's why it's good to rely on your own resources. Checked out the pharmacy services in the city, equally fraught with bureaucracy and thus the brief is 'take your own medication, in fact double the amount just in case some gets lost'.

Finally, in this strange eventful history, there's a need to check the food and its adequacy for the trip. In UB, the fresh fruit and vegetables, which used to be subject to seasonal changes, are now available throughout the year. In the countryside, however, it is very difficult to find fresh fruit and vegetables, and it's meat, meat and MEAT — in all its variety of forms. No 'special cuts' just a 'cut a hunk' policy.

So, get the food, have the health, and with morale high we depart the city. It's easy to do now, for we have been here a week sussing things out. The journey is south and into the remote regions for which we were ready. Day one: an hour later, we had the first breakdown of our trucks, an overheated engine. This was to be the harbinger of about ten breakdowns every day, at least gave the team to mix and mingle, talk about the 'trip so far' and walk around the oroos, or stupor, in prayer of good luck for the rest of the journey. We arrive at camp, late, to put up the tents in the dark. Away in the distance the sounds of dogs, jackals and the occasionally distressed child add music to the grunts and groans of a bunch of Europeans who were adjusting to their first night on the harshness of rugged ground. The Memsahib was not looking pleased. I brought out some chocolate that had melted through the day, but which had re-formed. 'No thanks'; the reply. Morale was low, I could tell. Jokes, dance routines, me smiling just did not work. I could see it was on to 'level 2' euphoriants: vodka and fermented mare's milk.

'I can't breathe', Memsahib announced to me just as we finished the reviled taste. I was trying to drown its revolting tang with vodka-for-medicinal-purposes-only. 'Just take big breathes, Sweetheart', said I. 'No, I seriously cannot {gasp}...' she wheezed. I looked to her and saw this red and swollen frog face appearing before my eyes. 'Anaphylaxis' I yelled to no one in particular. 'Don't Panic, Don't Panic' — I thought as I maintained normality in finishing my dinner with a peculiar sort of calm before rushing off to our tent to get appropriate medication. A nurse, the Memsahib refused me to inject adrenaline preferring instead to go with a variety of anti-histamines, rescue remedies, herbs and steams, and some huge curses thrown in my direction. I fussed around giving comfort to only myself, while the poor old Memsahib struggled for air, not the slightest bit reassured. Over the next few hours she settled and by morning she could swallow her saliva, though she was still looking a little blue. Overall, a good indication, I felt, that the acute reaction was resolving. Phew, and we were only into day 2 of our month-long journey, but fortunately I had got a good night's sleep!

Van 'sort of' repaired, we were traveling, the countryside was rolling and had a slight hue of green. No fences and all stock cared for in nomad style, a horseman or a child watching over grazing animals. Over to the right of the road, a family surrounds their 'ger'; a circular felt-made traveling home. The men on horses and the women watching, as the round-up of mares occurs — the collection of the milk was beginning. Although this was the source of the angst for Memsahib, it was a scene so attractive, so different to anything that she and I had ever viewed; such visions are the source of memories of travel. The milk collected, the drinking of it tactfully declined, we mount our trucks and travel south.

Thusly was the mode for 4 days; arise 0700 hours, decamp, travel, lunch, travel, 2100, pitch tents overnight. It got dark at around 2245, so the evenings were rather beguiling, making us think it was earlier than it was. The consequence was that by the time we had reached our 3000 meter camp high in Gurvansaikhan National Park, we were exhausted. Here, however, we got to restore our energies by hunting the tracks of the snow leopard for the next week. This was one of the attractions of this expedition, for we had with us three eminent scientists from UB.

Here also was the stimulus to find out about the Mongolians, proud folk with a history allied to that of Russia more than China. Such folk with very Polynesian features made me think of the association with the Pacific. Travelers talk of the generosity of the indigenous folk of the regions where they travel. This was no different and is surely a reflection of social communication, the sort of thing that prevents tensions and wars and promotes 'understandings'. The smile that cracks a solemn face, the humor or salutation that promotes it, and the joy that results from a gnarled laugh are indeed harmony to the mind. The journey was a hard one: limited water, hard hot days without shade, snow in a tent at altitude, windy days where sand blew in your face relentlessly, and always the same people some of whom you liked and some that you didn't. Memsahib and I had each other, one helping the other. Apart from this personal bonus, there were other aspects of this journey that made it memorable for me: (i) the country that beguiled and bewitched, (ii) the people that were entrancing and (iii) such amazing images of life and living that travel to Mongolia gave to me and the Memsahib.

I think as a team doctor, people perceive one in a light different to that one shines with. There were a few aspects that I had to resolve before I could feel comfortable with my contribution to this journey. The knowledge I had of the fellow travelers' health was essential, the equipping of a medical kit of the journey was 'a given', the taking care of the folk on the journey, and my own personal psychology to help me cope with the (at times) tense moments that occurred within the group.

Hmmm. My own psychology: the doc needs to be a rational and approachable person, non-biased, and non-judgmental on such journeys. It is easy to dislike the folk that others dislike, it is harder often to mask this in a way that gives equality to all travelers in one's care. But, hey, that's what primary care is all about. It's what we are good at!

Overall, I saw around 50 different medical conditions from within the group, on the journey. The usual stuff: skin abrasions, cuts and allergies, accidents like falling from a horse or knife cuts, and headaches and motion sickness. Commonly there were three sorts of infections that our expeditioners were most likely to get: respiratory tract, gastro germs, and skin blemishes. If I went again, I would concentrate on these issues. Forget the shower, it's so easy to enjoy one at the end of the trip and who cares about smell when it pervades the whole group. Bottoms and toilets never really seem to be a problem on trips like this — what with sand and shovels to do the job of the flushing.

The medical support required, to make an expedition successful, is challenging and requires essential and complex pre-planning on both a personal and a professional level. Expedition medicine is a reflection of many dipoles: personal and interpersonal, social and intimate, security and insecurity, and finally ecological and materialistic. The expedition doc may be asked to opine on any of them, and will need to communicate at many levels on them all.

The journey over a magical month was everything that I had imagined it would be. A journey of mainly good memories and vastly different images to my days in a medical surgery. Such journeys, for me, are always personally revealing. I try hard to interact with all on the trip; that's my job. I never talk about other people on the trip unless it is to the expedition leader, and finally I try hard to be honest: to myself and about myself. After all, I get to look in the mirror when I come home! And yes, the Memsahib has finally forgiven me and we laugh, with warmth and love, at all the photos — together.

Image 25.1. The memsahib – "What am I doing here?"

Chapter 26

Evacuation of Travelers: Personal Anecdotes, Pearls and Conclusions

Yoel Donchin and Steven Marc Friedman

The first time I transferred a patient as a young doctor, I learned a lesson that I shall never be able to forget. It illustrates the wide range of possibilities and challenges of doing medical work at 20,000 feet, at airport terminals and on board of a running ambulance in an unfamiliar city.

It was during my second year of residency (YD) in anesthesia. A young patient in our ICU was diagnosed as suffering from multiple sclerosis (MS) or maybe some other debilitating neurological disease. She underwent tracheotomy, and after a few weeks, without improvement in the medical ICU, she was transferred to the department of neurology with very poor prognosis. A few days later, a physician who was not familiar with the patient verdict did a physical examination and based on his clinical impression, he guessed that the patient had a brain tumor or brain aneurysm. As CT scan was taking its first steps in the world, we suggested an angiography and the patient's family agreed.

To our surprise the X-ray revealed a huge aneurysm at the base of the skull. The X-ray was sent to famous neurosurgeons all over the world and most of them were reluctant to operate. However, a Canadian neurosurgeon from London, Ontario sent a positive response, mentioning that if the patient could be transferred to his hospital, he thought he could do it. At this point I got a call from the ICU and since I was rotating in internal medicine I could escort the patient without affecting the daily routine of the ICU. The patient was dependent on a ventilator during the night, could not move her legs and had a nasogastric tube for feeding. I had less than 12 hours to prepare myself. I started to collect equipment from anesthesia tables and old storage places, laryngoscopes, IV fluids, food and drugs. I had packed them all in a small doctor bag and was ready to travel. I did not know how difficult it was to load a stretcher on the aircraft, nor did I have the slightest idea as how to supply oxygen and how to do simple nursing work on a stretcher.

Finally, we arrived at the airport: the patient's husband, her mother and the inexperienced physician who was full of confidence in himself and in his power as an anesthesiologist to cope with every unexpected event.

Once we were on board the aircraft, the patient did not show any signs of distress, her family supported her and I was just observing. I measured blood pressure from time to time (with a sphygmomanometer), exchanged the urine bag and did not even notice that the tracheostomy cannula was moving with each heart beat. (I paid attention to this dangerous phenomenon only after a passenger told me that he is an ENT physician and was worried regarding the possibility of the cannula penetrating into the blood vessels).

At midnight, we landed at the empty Montréal airport, the patient on a stretcher. I assisted her in ventilation by hand as she was tired, and we waited for the ambulance that was to transfer us to another airport where a private air ambulance would take us to London, Ontario. Suddenly, a nurse dressed in red uniform approached us, gave me her card and said that she was from the ambulance that was waiting outside the terminal. At this moment, the patient's mother told the nurse something that caused my blood to freeze. She said, 'I know you! You were a Kapo in the concentration camp in Hungry!'

The nurse became pale and, without a word, left the place immediately.

I sent the husband to look for the ambulance and finally we convinced the driver not to wait for the nurse. We drove to a nearby terminal where an 'air ambulance' was parked ready for us, but they did not realize that we had a patient on a stretcher and we would not be able to take her through the door. At this point I wrapped the patient in a blanket and weboarded her through the window. An hour later we landed in Ontario and, exhausted, I handed over the patient to the local physician that came with the ambulance.

I slept for 20 hours after leaving the hospital, I lost most of my equipment, but I brought the patient alive. She was operated within 24 hours and was kept in the ICU for 6 months.

She came back to Israel without any medical escort.

I did the anesthesia for her ceasarian section a few years later, — as except for a slight limp she had a full recovery.

When I look at this event 20 years later, with more experience, it is hard to believe that transfer like this can also take place.

A patient who is paralyzed and needs assist ventilation should never fly transatlantic or for more than 14 hours without two doctors on board. The equipment must be checked and ready. Before flying, it is necessary to have the phone numbers of the contact persons in the admitting hospital. It is also necessary to prepare a detailed plan like in a military operation in which the commander has to create scenarios for situations that may occur — What if there is a delay of a few hours? What if the ambulance is late or the roads are closed due to snow? and so on.

The transfer starts by creating a mental model of the journey after getting the documents from the hospital. (Ahh! they open only at 8 and we have to depart from the floor at 06:30).

In foreign countries one may encounter a different culture — a different attitude.

In China, it is necessary to report if one is carrying human blood, for this is a biological item and needs a special license that can be purchased at the gate in the airport for a nominal fee, but it may take 2 hours to go through all the procedures.

When I try to get permission of one German airline's physician to transfer an almost perfectly healthy patient, I realize that I shall need to bribe him, or may be this is the official way to get things going. In Thailand, we have been facing problems like medical equipment not released from customs — What to do? — How to cope with the need for bribery? How to get an insight of 'unexpected' expenses?

Sometimes things do not go as planned.

After a road traffic accident, four Israelis were brought to a local hospital in Nairobi; we did not have accurate medical information, but we came to know that at least one would need a stretcher. The only flight from Israel was a charter flight that was about to depart within the next few hours. A trained physician took his equipment and an international mobile phone and rushed to the airport to be the last passenger to arrive and the plane immediately took off, only to realize after 3 hours that Nairobi had refused to allow the flight to land for unknown reasons. The physician found himself back at his home airport after 6 hours and we knew that now the patients would need evacuation. The patients were already at the Nairobi terminal waiting for their physician to arrive. I spoke with the head of the station who explained to me that without an escort doctor the patient would not be able to fly but then he realized that the patients cannot be left at the terminal. I asked him to check if there was a doctor among the other passengers and if he found one, I would instruct him what to do. Fortunately, there were two physicians — a dermatologist and an oncologist, who checked the patient and gave full medical information that showed that the patients could be transferred. The oncologist agreed to be the escort; the flight captain was cooperative as well and told us that we could have phone contact during the flight. The ambulances were waiting at the home airport and everyone was happy in the end.

To transfer a single patient may be a logistic procedure but to transfer 14 can be a real challenge. A truck carrying a heavy load of sugar beet collided with a small tourist bus in a remote area of Turkey. All the passengers, including three children, were injured — few with minor abrasions while three suffered from fracture of the femur. The first thing that the injured did after the accident was to call their health insurance companies and after a first evaluation with the aide over the blessed mobile phone, we decided to send two air ambulances each with a team of nurses and physicians. It took us less than 4 hours to be ready and after another 2 hours of flight we landed in Marmaris, where all the wounded were waiting for us on the tarmac with medical supervision by the local emergency medicine staff. Two more hours and everyone was in bed at the trauma center in Tel Aviv. This was an effort of several insurance companies that knew that this is the only way to overcome the local problems.

Repatriation of a patient from Europe back home may be a problem; there are some places that prefer to leave the patient in their domain for a long time (some for medical reasons and the others for other causes). Very little medical information is volunteered by local doctors, and getting a good summary or a discharge letter may be mission impossible. The information is not disclosed considering the patient's privacy, which is not relevant, as all insured patients agree to share information with their insurance companies or their escort doctor. In Germany, a patient after myocardial infarction is requested to stay in bed for a long period, while we prefer to mobilize the patient as soon as possible. In such cases, we advise the patient to sign out and leave the hospital and a medical escort is waiting for him at the gate.

However, there is a different attitude, e.g. in Sweden.

A road traffic accident at the northern part of Sweden killed a woman, injured her two children and the driver, the father, who was airlifted to a trauma center with a GCS of 6 and multiple limb fractures, pneumothorax and abdominal injury.

The head of the ICU gave full information from the very first minute, but this time we knew from a distance for every hour what is the medical situation, as in this unit the chart was not a handwritten but a computerized digital information flowchart that was transferred to us via the Internet. Moreover, the team took a short video recording of the patient himself in his bed, and the decision when to transfer him was a mutual one as the escort team and the local physicians worked as a team and not as enemies. In due time, proper equipment and the team arrived at the hospital and the meeting was like between friends who knew each other. Based on the information from the video, we came to know that the patient was restless and needed sedation; therefore, we took a huge supply of propofol, which was used until the last bottle, a team of two and a special scoop stretcher to ease the transfer.

The experience of an emergency physician from the other side of the world who worked hand in hand with me (YD), is also very similar. Dr. Friedman tells his story:

I finished my emergency medicine fellowship training in Canada in 1995, followed by a Masters in Public Health at Harvard in 1996. Like many of my colleagues, I was eager for a variety of challenges. A patient who was walked into the emergency department still breathing and complaining of something as mundane as an early heart attack or a hemorrhaging limb was not nearly as exciting as a patient who required paralysis and ventilatory support at 35,000 feet above the North Sea.

My cumulative experience in medical evacuation and transportation taught me this: knowledge and competence are essential, but not sufficient. It is communication that will keep your patient alive, preserve your sanity and career longevity, and might even prevent you from freezing to death in a tiny little raft in the middle of the North Sea. Allow me to explain.

Before this, a primer on the aeromedical transportation business: Suppose you use your credit card to purchase a two dollar or five dollar per day health insurance package that will cover you for a week or two for illnesses and injuries you may sustain while traveling abroad. The benefits include a host of services that could become very expensive if you had to pay for them yourself. One included benefit is repatriation to a medical facility at home.

The repatriation component of traveler's insurance has spawned a medical evacuation business. This is for several reasons. First, the medically rational and humane reason: Western hospitals or even a well-equipped and staffed medical evacuation jet often can provide a far higher standard of care than that which is available in a third world country. To that end the insurance company has a moral and contractual obligation to repatriate the patient as soon as it is medically reasonable, so that definitive treatment can be provided at a western standard of care. They might be sued if they left you to languish in an environment where you were sure to have substandard surgery, or to receive a blood transfusion that had a high likelihood of infecting you with HIV or Hepatitis C.

The other reason is about saving the insurer money. In many cases, the city where you have your massive myocardial infarction or hip injury may in fact provide high-tech, boutique-level quality of care that might even outstrip the quality or price of what is available at home. For that reason, the insurer has a more practical reason to bring you home, and fast. I practice in Canada, where all patients are provided by a federally funded, one payer, socialized health care system. If you have a heart attack in Toronto, you only need to present to the emergency department with your health card and you will be provided with a host of expensive investigations and treatments including thrombolysis, ultrasound, stress testing, nuclear imaging, angiography, angioplasty, coronary bypass surgery, cardiac rehabilitation and transportation home where a visiting nurse will attend to you daily. No charge to you or to the private insurer, as long as you are a tax-paying Canadian citizen. However, if you're vacationing in Miami

Beach and present to the hospital with chest pain, the emergency physician or cardiologist may order the same buffet of investigations and treatments, ultimately culminating with an ICU care stay and multiple coronary artery stents or bypasses, the cost of which can quickly exceed $100,000. In the past, if the treating physician declared that the patient was unsafe to travel home, then the insurance company would be compelled to allow the treatment and swallow the enormous bill.

Private medical evacuation companies targeted this interface of healthcare and business. These companies now operate small executive jets — such as Lear jets — that can be converted into mobile intensive care units. At prices ranging from $25,000 to $50,000 (depending on complexity and distance), the use of such a jet is often a cost-effective option for an insurer. The companies can transport patients who are too sick to travel by any other means in a rapid and generally safe manner.

A corporate jet may sound like a luxurious way to travel — a preferred mode of transport for heads of state and rock stars — but the reality is completely opposite when used for medical transport. The jet cabin is typically completely stripped of most seating, and is converted to hold two pilots in the front, a patient on a stretcher, a physician seated on a bench across from him (for 3, 6 or 10 hours), and a nurse or respiratory therapist manning a ventilator at the patient's head. No flight attendant. No meal service. No movie. No bathroom.

The medical repatriation companies run an increasingly competitive business that operates on thin margins. Corporate jets are extremely expensive to own, run and insure. There is great pressure on the company to not have the jet set idle, and so as soon as an opportunity for patient transport becomes available, the company will seek for the opportunity to transport him or her. The medical director of the medical evacuation company is under great pressure to approve any potential patient as soon as they are reasonably safe to transfer, and to have carrying a paying customer on all legs of the journey.

The neophyte emergency physician doing part-time medical transport quickly learns that communication with all parties — no matter how tangentially related to the care of the patient, if at all — is essential for preservation of both the patient's well-being and the treating physician's sanity.

The first step is communication with the company nurse. The company nurse will relate to you a patient history. However, with regard to information that comes your way, *caveat emptor*: Let the buyer beware. Or, to quote an old saying favored by Russian leaders, *Trust but Verify*. The nurse who communicates with you has likely received her information from a string of people before her. You may now be the fifth in line. Each person relaying the history in channel has a different set of skills (nursing, administration, medicine), as well as a different set of competing priorities (save the patient, save the company, save my job, etc.). You have to know and trust the nursing staff in the company, but also recognize their limitations.

But that is not sufficient. If at all possible, one must communicate as well with the medical director (physician-in-charge) of the company. The medical director vets all the fundamental issues at play. I always ask him whether he has actually seen the documentation and communicated with the treating doctor, and try to gauge his confidence with the appropriateness of the transport. How thorough, up-to-date and reliable is his information? Ultimately, the medevac physician has the duty of assessing the patient upon arrival, and the prerogative of declaring the patient unfit to fly. However, the physician who frequently takes a staffed executive jet across the ocean and returns with it lacking cargo (a paying customer) will not have a long career in the air.

Frank communication with the company dispatcher who books the flights will save your job, your patient and your marriage. Medical evacuation companies want to run a two-way business: '*We pick up, and we deliver*'. It's a sure bet that if you are asked to pick up a patient in New York and repatriate the patient to London, somewhere along the line, a dispatcher will inform you that you have been requested to make one small side trip with the jet over to Belfast to pick up a patient and bring her to Montréal. Or Texas. Voila… your one-day trip has turned into a several-day odyssey. (But what about those theater tickets with your new girl-friend, you ask?) While this can initially be exciting and make for a multicity adventure in your private jet, it can quickly turn into a sleep-deprived odyssey wherein the physician and medical staff cross half a dozen time zones in 72 hours, build up an enormous sleep debt and sustain themselves on little more than a pizza, which the pilot has ordered ahead 30 minutes before landing at a small commercial airstrip. (You will eat this pizza on the tarmac, happily breathing fresh cold air from the open door as the jet is refueled, the soft whir and whoosh of the ventilator by your head reminding you that this is not a pleasure cruise on The Love Boat.) This problem is mitigated when the physician and dispatcher have established a solid working relationship and an open stream of communication, and understand each other's needs and limitations. If you meet eye to eye (or they really need your eyes on the patient), they will show sympathy on you and fly you home in a commercial carrier. (But you will still probably miss the opera, or ballet, or simply sleep through it.)

Communicating with the medical team that treated the patient is imperative. My first priority on landing is to make a preliminary visit to the hospital, assess the patient and liaise with nursing team. This is done immediately, even if our team is not flying out until later the following morning. Frequently things are very different from how they were presented to you when you agreed (on your cell phone, or half asleep at home in bed) to fly across the ocean. This is for several reasons.

First, as stated, information that has passed from hand to hand invariably becomes inaccurate. Second, standards of care and practice vary from country to country and what may have been presented to you as a stable patient by the standards of the host country acts will frequently be regarded as not fit to travel by North American standards. Third, disease is a dynamic process. The information regarding the patient may have been accurate a day or week ago, but may no longer be remotely representative of the patient before you. (Two days ago his congestive heat failure was under control, but today he may be swollen to his knees and gasping for air. And will you be able to auscultate his lungs above the roar of the jets?) Fourth, there are specific attributes to transporting a patient by the air, which may elude the knowledge of a medical team that generally does not transport patient further from the emergency department to a medical floor. What peripheral lines are likely to become dislodged on transport? Will an arterial line be a more practical way of assessing blood pressure in the air? Is there a likelihood of seizures, or hypertensive emergency, or airway emergency, and should these eventualities be managed in a proactive and prophylactic manner on the ground? In such a scenario, the physician must act in concert with his or her flight nurse or respiratory therapist; typically, they are skilled professionals who see the patient from a different perspective and identify hazards that may elude the MD. Consider yourself as an infantry officer trying to safely map out and crawl through a minefield: all information must be scruntinized. Laboratory reports, ECGs and X-rays may provide critical (and sometimes critically worrisome) information that was not conveyed to you earlier. Family members involved in the patient's care will provide essential collateral information — they have known the patient for years, and as well, may have spent more time at the patient's bedside than the treating doctors or nurses. And the patient must be reassessed, and again.

Communicating with the treating physician at the patient's bedside is indispensable. Medical 'rounds' at bedside have been central to medical practice since the days of Hippocrates, and while current technology — telephone, email, videoconference — are all helpful, there is still no substitute. The bedside meeting allows you to directly assess both the patient and physician who has treated him. You see the patient through another person's eyes and gain personal knowledge of the medical case and challenges that lie before you.

Moreover, this is a wonderful experience from an educational and cultural perspective. Doctors are blessed with having a common language — medicine — and camaraderie is virtually always established at the patient's bedside, even if communication has been incomplete up to this point. The receiving physician will often look upon the medevac physician as an angel, who has alighted from the heavens only to relieve him of an often problematic patient who typically speaks a 'foreign' language. Out of gratitude, he will frequently become your tour guide and restaurateur. My first exposure to the Algarve was with the physician of a stroke victim that I would be repatriating to Toronto the next morning. He showed me his hospital with pride, drove me around his town and introduced me to Portuguese cuisine and wine.

Communication with taxi drivers will help you get fresh air and fresh perspective. The benefit of a multicity air trip by a personal jet is that what modicum of free time you do have can be thoroughly enjoyed for a few dollars. On prolonged trips, pilots have a maximum duty time of approximately 12–14 hours (this varies from country to country). The result is that after a sustained amount of time on duty, pilots are required to stand down and the crew gets a well-needed (though far too short) period to check into a hotel, shower and sleep. This is when the occupied medevac physician can remove his mind from the jet, his patient and the medical model, and come alive.

Taxi drivers will be thrilled to serve as a tour guide for 2–3 hours. After a quickly negotiated price, the driver will act as your personal chauffeur, in a style that is far more enjoyable than the personal jet you have been flying in. Taxi drivers happily lack the pretense and practiced showmanship of some professional guides, and will take you not only to the major spots of a local city, but also to the small, warm and inviting (or perhaps rough around the edges) spots that are only familiar to someone who has lived in the city for a decade or more. I found this to be a very efficient way to see and stroll the major sites in Geneva — a city that likely only take several hours to quickly review. On a return weekend medical repatriation trip to Europe, a more obscure tour through Belfast, Ireland via cabbie ended up with a tour of IRA bombing sites, an explanation of the conflict and some tea at the local Sinn Fein headquarters.

Finally, communication with the pilot is essential, as his responsibility for the jet and crew acts in tandem with your responsibility for the patient. Sometimes, though, frank communication can be more than you bargained for. On one occasion, returning from Belfast to Toronto, we had to divert as fuel was recognized to be potentially inadequate for the trip, and the weather was becoming increasingly rough. The jet was being buffeted as we passed through storm clouds. I mentioned to the pilot that I was curious that the life raft/survival kit was not stored next to the door, as it had been on other flights I had worked on. Our raft and survival gear was stowed at the back of the jet, under all our medical packs and jackets, and would be totally inaccessible in an emergency. The pilot was a veteran of the Canadian military, smart, cynical and blunt. He looked back at me and replied wryly that he had no intention of drifting in a life raft in the North Sea for 24–48 hours until we froze to death. He stated that if the plane suffered an irretrievable, catastrophic failure, his plan of action would be to steer high speed, nose first, into the water. Hence, no need for a life raft.

Fortunately for me, we had been traveling for about 36 hours, we were returning to base without a patient, and I was sleep deprived and thoroughly spent. I closed my eyes and dreamt of sandy beaches.

Overall, critical-care transport is an exciting field of medicine. However, it is not for the unskilled. An evolving subspecialty, those who are most equipped for it are emergency physicians, anesthesiologists, and critical-care physicians. The discipline requires a distinct body of knowledge, a resilience in the face of mishap (how you will respond when a ventilator fails at 30,000 feet?), the ability to work closely in a team and the psychological makeup for irregular hours in often physically and mentally demanding conditions. However, for the right sort, it's intellectually rewarding, medically challenging and a unique way to see the world.

Take Home Messages to be Learned

- Medical transportation requires anticipation of all logistical factors that may impact on your medical management and evacuation of the patient. These include cultural, political and bureaucratic matters particular to each country, and meteorology (the weather).
- Know the limitations of your equipment. If you do not have a practical back up plan for the failure of a specific piece of equipment, then you are unsafe to travel.
- Disease is a dynamic process. Therefore, you will seldom arrive to find the patient in the state he was described to you before you left.
- The more parties involved in relaying information, the more inaccurate the information will be. As such, direct communication with the treating doctor and nurse is essential.
- The sooner you assess your patient before transport, the easier your trip will be.
- Exploit your free hours to converse with local people, find new horizons and gain fresh perspectives. Otherwise, you could have just stayed at home.
- The Israeli ministry of transportation divides the patients that need transfer into five categories, which can serve every one who needs to choose a medical escort. We highly recommend using it on a board basis.

A1 — A patient who suffers from a disease that does not endanger him or passengers.

A — A patient who needs help (nursing) but flight will not endanger him or other passengers.

B — A patient who may need a life-saving procedure on the flight (ventilation, chest tube).

B1 — A patient who needs faculties equal to ICU.

C — A patient who endangers the passengers with a contagious disease.

D — A psychiatric patient.

P — A sick child.

P1 — A sick infant.

Based on the above, patients in category B and B1 should be escorted only with a physician with at least 3 years of experience in ICU.

Category D should be escorted by a psychiatrist.

Children who need PICU should be escorted by a PICU doctor.

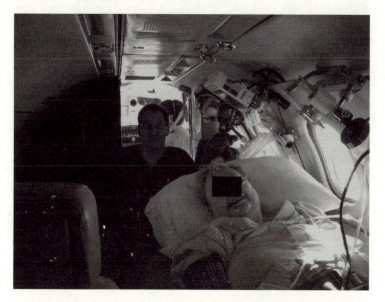

Image 26.1. Dr. Friedman, transporting a patient via Lear Jet.

Image 26.2. Copilot has nutrition break during brief stop to refuel.

Image 26.3.   Belfast shipyards, after dusk. We await a ground ambulance to complete transfer
of our patient to hospital.

SECTION 7:

TRAVELING FOR A CAUSE

Chapter 27

Globalization, Migration and Health: The History of Disease and Disparity in the Global Village*

Brian Gushulak

The influences of what has traditionally been called migration on human health and the practice of medicine have been and remain extensive. As communities and populations have moved across the globe, their health and the health of those they encounter have been affected. The health outcomes that may follow or accompany migrants were major reasons behind the development of quarantine legislation and practices. At the global level, health issues associated with migration have influenced the need for international health legislation, represented by the International Health Regulations, the central legal framework representing disease control. Currently, several of the public health principles developed to manage the health of migrants provide part of the rationale behind the massive global public health efforts to mitigate the potential development of Pandemic Influenza, which is probably one of the largest international public health undertakings since the origin of the HIV/AIDS pandemic. Additionally, and importantly for this book, migration has increasing and significant impact on the practice of travel medicine.

The recognition of the impact and influences of migration in the field of health has not been widespread. Awareness of this issue tends to wax and wane in response to real or perceived threats associated with population movement. We are currently in a period of time with the perception of threat elevated, and there is generalized interest and concern about the consequences of disease importation and introduction. As explained in more detail below, this period of elevated interest in the risks of imported disease began to gather steam in the 1980s. As this interest has developed and evolved, it has begun to exert increasing influence on the nature and practice of public health and infectious disease control. Some of the concern, as noted above, is focused on the potential role played by migration. Additionally, as population

---

*This is not intended to be a detailed scientific dissertation on the subject. For brevity, the context is limited to European and North American examples. This is not intended to minimize or reduce the importance of migration and population mobility in other areas of the world.

---

movements increase in volume and change in diversity, there is a growing recognition that some populations of migrants are at increased risk of certain diseases compared to domestic or host populations. Much of the increased incidence of disease in migrants is observed in regard to infectious diseases. This creates an obvious link to the efforts directed at national and international disease control.

At the same time, migration itself is rapidly evolving. Emerging and re-emerging patterns of population flow differ from those of only 30 years ago and now involve many new destinations and origins. Migration is now front-page news and comment in several nations that, as recently as two decades ago, were considered to have no migration profile. Traditional, historical patterns of emigration and immigration do not apply in a modern integrated globalized world. For that reason, the term "migration," which often has administrative and legal connotations, is less contextually relevant in terms of health. It is now progressively being replaced by "population mobility," a term that more clearly reflects modern processes of people movement. Focusing on the process rather than the administrative status of the migrant provides a more useful way of comparing information and outcomes. It also removes much of the confusion associated with common terms that are used in different context to describe different migrants such as immigrant, refugee, asylum seeker, and illegal migrant, for example.

While much of this interest and activity appear to be new and in some cases novel, in reality the world has been down many of these paths before. The collective responses to disease threats posed by strangers represent some of the oldest recorded public health measures. The fear and anxiety associated with the real or potential risks of imported diseases have sociological links, which go back many centuries. Together they make up a narrative through which it is possible to trace common historical threads that have and continue to influence policies and practices focused on health and migration.

The Medieval Origins of Migration Health

Considering health and migration from a sociological perspective, it is the desire to protect oneself and one's families that have always been behind the attempts to manage or mitigate the external health risks posed by strangers or travelers. This is particularly true when the health threat is a transmissible disease. In this situation, public fear has been often transferred from the disease itself to the arrival of a new person who is believed to carry or spread the infection. This sociological interface between the desire to protect the health of the public while at the same time preserving the rights of migrants and travelers can still be observed in the purpose of the International Health Regulations, which are intended to:

> prevent, protect against, control and provide a public health response to the international spread of disease in ways that are commensurate with and restricted to public health risks, and which avoid unnecessary interference with international traffic and trade. WHO (2005)

This response to infections imported by new arrivals and mobile populations continues to exert effect today. Many screening processes and practices directed at immigrants and refugees are based on principles designed to reduce the risk of imported infectious diseases. Some of the principles upon which those processes are based originated more than one thousand years ago.

In Europe, some of the earliest recorded attempts to manage human disease in an organized, systematic manner involved an infection that created a great deal of fear in the local population: leprosy. While records of isolating individuals with leprosy date back to the Babylonian Empire, organized approaches on a broad scale developed in the Middle Ages. At that time leprosy manifested two characteristics that continue to be present in diseases that provoke extensive public anxiety and fear. Firstly, the disease produced scarring and disfiguring outcomes, and secondly, society at the time was unable to provide either preventive or curative interventions. Similar situations occur today, and excessive public fear and concerns that exceed scientific or epidemiological risk are observed for maladies that either cause disfiguring or ghastly complications and/or for which there is no simple treatment or prevention. Modern examples have included pneumonic plague in India in 1994, viral hemorrhagic fevers such as Ebola in Africa in 1995, necrotizing fasciitis (Flesh Eating Disease), the initial response to West Nile infection in North America and more recently Avian Influenza.

The approach to leprosy was also influenced by a religious association that placed the authority of the church in the process. Aside from providing an example about the origins of migration health, the biblical associations of leprosy are interesting because they may not be based on disease itself. Scholars suggest that when the Hebrew bible was translated into Greek, the Hebrew word *tsaraath (zaraath)* was translated as *lepra*. *Lepra* at that time was not a word that referred to the same disease that we know as leprosy, today. It is believed that both words were general terms for skin diseases with flaking or scaly lesions and could have referred to seborrhea, psoriasis, or other skin conditions. The error in translation had important consequences however, as it provided the basis for the application of the proscribed purification and exclusion activities defined in the Book of Leviticus. This biblical association of historic religious proscriptions and the spread of leprosy resulted in some of the approaches to those afflicted with the disease in Europe. These associations continued for centuries. In 1880, a retired American Civil War general, Lew Wallace, who was governor of New Mexico Territory wrote a historical novel, *Ben Hur, A Tale of the Christ*. The loathing and banishment associated with leprosy in the novel and in its transfer to the movie screen are well known.

As a final historical footnote, it is unclear if real leprosy was an affliction of the Hebrew populations. The term *tsaraath* is believed to have referred to several skin conditions, some of which might have improved during the isolation proscribed in Leviticus (Hastings & Opromolla, 1994).

Given the degree of public anxiety, lack of any medical capacity to manage the disease, and the religious environment of the time, society managed leprosy by isolating and limiting the movement of those believed to be infected. While classical quarantine would be developed some three hundred years later, the principle of isolating the inflicted was commonly applied to leprosy in Europe much earlier. In addition to isolation, other methods to reduce the likelihood of community members contacting lepers were introduced. Some cities required the mandatory medical inspection of certain individuals and groups of arriving travelers. This process was called *Lepraschau*. Once diagnosed, the infected were separated and prevented from entering public areas, a practice not all that different in context from modern infectious disease isolation. Finally, in some locations, those determined to be affected were required to sound a bell or rattle to alert others to their presence. Again, because of the religious association to leprosy, this was known as the Lazarus Bell, but it can be seen in retrospect as an early public health warning system.

Quarantine

Driven by the religious requirements to provide charity to the less advantaged, care and support to pilgrims, the sick, and feeble were often provided by religious orders in medieval Europe. As they provided "hospitality" in the form of shelter, accommodation, food, and in some cases clothing, they provided the origin of the modern words, hospital and hospice. Some of these institutions, known as Lazarettos or Leprosaria, specifically took care of those with leprosy. By the 1300s, there were many of these institutions in Europe and in some cities and city states, municipal authorities had become involved in their management in addition to or replacing religious organizations.

In a manner that was similar, in context, to modern aspects of globalization. Europeans were involved in a period of great economic growth and expanded international trade and commerce. Merchants and maritime traders had begun to regularly visit more distant regions as trade routes expanded. This expanded commercial activity and associated travel took place while the second pandemic of plague extended from Central Asia. In the mid 1300s, ports of call in the Crimea, visited by traders from Italian cities began to report plague, and the disease had reached Constantinople by 1347 (Gottfried, 1983).

At that time, Venice was one of the wealthiest and most important cities in Europe. The management of the city was organized, developed, and relatively integrated. There were civic officials responsible for city sanitation and general aspects of community health. Venice also had municipal physicians and hospitals and LAZARETTOS administered by the city both of which provided historical context against which health threats were addressed (Garrison, 1929). When disease and pestilence, manifest by cases of plague in trading vessels arriving from the Crimean and other ports, appeared in Venice, the subsequent response was not surprising. Even though the germ theory of disease would not be developed for centuries, there was clear knowledge that illness and death followed the arrival of travelers and goods from areas already affected by disease. As noted in an early history of the World Health Organization, *"The fact, though not the mechanism, of the importation of infection was early recognized"* (Goodman, 1952).

As a consequence, new arrivals were isolated and examined by officials. Ships, cargo, crew, and some passengers were held in defined areas or zones before being allowed to proceed. Initially these isolation periods were in the region of a month or 30 days. These were extended to 40 days (the author has been unable to determine if there is any biblical association with this time period or if it was developed totally as a result of observation), the Italian translation providing the origin to the term *quarantine*. In spite of the fact that quarantine was unsuccessful in controlling the spread of plague, throughout Europe it was adopted in many locations and became the traditional response to the threat of imported epidemics. Many of the practices and undertakings related to maritime quarantine, such as the yellow flag flown by ships before clearance, the concept of *free practique*, and holding of vessels, their cargo and travelers in defined quarantine areas continue today and many have been extended to air travel and airports.

While John Snow and story of the Broad Street pump are often presented as the initial origin of modern public health, there is a case to be made that Snow's approach to cholera in 19th Century London represents the birth of applied epidemiology. Aspects and practices of public health that continue to have application and relevance today can be traced much further back in history and have direct linkages to human travel and migration.

Immigration and Quarantine

The process of isolating and holding off ships from epidemic-affected areas accompanied European colonial expansion. In New France (the future Canadian province of Quebec), ships from Marseilles were quarantined because of plague as early as 1720. Quarantine and inspection stations were established by colonies and cities in North America in the 18th century as the flow of immigrants to that continent increased. By the early 19th century, the threat of plague had diminished, but it was quickly replaced by a new disease, perhaps even more related to migration. Cholera, arriving in Europe with vessels and travelers from Asia was a major health challenge for many European locations from the 1830s and continued to a threat until the 1880s.

Cholera is important in the history of migration health for two major reasons. Firstly, it affected large numbers of migrants destined to North America and was primarily responsible for the development of the routine medical examination of new immigrants. Large numbers of immigrants leaving Europe either left cholera-infected ports or acquired the disease on crowded sailing vessels with limited sanitation and poor water quality. Epidemics of the disease followed the arrival of what became commonly know as "*coffin ships,*" many from Ireland where the concurrent potato famine stimulated immigration at the same time as cholera spread in Europe. Preventing cholera arriving in migrants from spreading to the new cities of North America became a major public health undertaking. This undertaking was responsible for the development of civic boards of health in the 1840s and was instrumental in the construction of large quarantine stations where all ships were routinely inspected. Up until this time, only vessels arriving from certain "affected" areas or those which had declared the presence of infection were subject to inspection.

Cholera control methods developed in the mid-1800s and defined in legislation and regulation required the routine inspection of arriving vessels and passengers whether the vessel had declared illness on board or not. That process would in the next century be expanded and further standardized into the familiar Ellis Island model of immigrant medical screening. In today's world of multiple international ports of entry, primarily reached by air, managing disease control at borders is a complex and difficult task. It is often forgotten that in the age of sea travel, when the initial screening procedures were developed, cost and time at sea favored the use of only a limited number of access points to North America. As most migration to Canada and the USA when immigration screening was implemented originated in Europe, the most commonly used ports were located in the Northeast. In the USA, 70% of migrants arrived via New York around the turn of the 20th Century while Montreal admitted 75% of migrants to Canada.

The second historical importance of cholera relates to its role as the stimulus for the uniform application of control efforts. Cholera and the proposed methods of control for this disease were the impetus behind international attempts at standardized infectious disease control practices at ports. Beginning in 1851, national representatives met in a series of Sanitary Conferences designed to codify and harmonize methods of controlling the importation of cholera and later other infections. These meetings, interrupted by conflicts, and influenced by advances in the medical and transportation sector continued for a hundred years, and in 1951 produced the International Sanitary Regulations, which later became the International Health Regulations of the WHO.

Keeping Out the Undesirables — Medical Screening of Migrants in the Early 20th Century

Beginning in the late 1800s and continuing until the 1920s, issues of public and social health were areas of great interest and activity in North America. Issues of welfare provision, the rights of workers and employers, the health effects of poor working and living conditions, and the rights of women and children began to be considered in terms of both social policy and legislation. In retrospect it can be easily seen that these activities were taking place at the same time as three other important processes were underway.

One of those processes, which generated great concern and not inconsiderable fear at the time, was development, beginning primarily in Europe, of international socialist labor organizations. The First International, known at the time as the International Workingmen's Association, was founded in 1864. The first volume of *Das Kapital* was published by Karl Marx in 1867; Engels edited and published volumes two and three in 1884 and 1894, respectively. While often relegated to the ranks of obscure events today, the creation and bloody end of the Paris Commune that followed the Franco-Prussian war of 1870–1871 and subsequent creation of the Second International in 1889 had great impact in industry and politics in Europe and North America.

The second concomitant process underway at the same time was the great expansion in immigration, now from regions of Central and Eastern Europe, to North America. These movements were, in the social context, often different than preceding waves of immigration. Language, religion, and cultural aspects were noticeably different and many of the families arriving from the villages, shtetls, and farms of Eastern Europe were very poor and often lacked education. Those differences began to generate concerns about how well and how effectively such migrants would fit into the new industrial framework of North America. Comment and extrapolation of the effects resulting from the arrival of "undesirable" migrants became more common, in both public and bureaucratic venues. Slums, widespread poverty, mental disorders, and debauchery, clearly the predicable consequences of the large-scale migration into metropolitan areas, were often considered as *old world problems* brought to North America by immigrants.

The final of the three factors at play at that time was the new and still incompletely understood science of genetics and heredity. Sir Francis Galton, an accomplished scientist known to statisticians and epidemiologists as the originator of the concepts of regression and correlation, was the cousin of Charles Darwin and appreciated many of the concepts of evolution. Beginning in the 1860s, he considered the implications of society's role in influencing the processes of natural selection and survival of the fittest in the human context. He coined the term *eugenics* to apply to the principles of improving the genetic or inborn characteristics of the population. In simple terms, eugenics principles supported the reproduction of those with what were considered advantages while trying to discourage the reproduction of negative biological outcomes.

Limits in the understanding of medicine, genetics, and biology present at the time suggested that the application of these principles could produce positive social benefit. Alexander Graham Bell, for example, through his work with the deaf, believed that much of the disorder was genetic in origin. He noted that by discouraging the deaf to marry and have children and preventing the immigration of deaf migrants, the future need for services for the deaf could be mitigated. The center of the "scientific" approach to eugenics in North America was the Eugenics Record Office, located at the Cold Spring Harbor Laboratory in New York. Its founder, the noted biologist Charles Davenport, and its director, Harry Laughton, a supporter of the prevention of reproduction in less fit populations, both became involved in immigration issues.

These three factors, occurring during a period of great social and welfare development and investment, produced what in today's terms would be called a perfect storm in terms of immigration health. What better way to reduce some of the major social burdens, mitigate the impact of imported labor unrest, and ensure the genetic potential of the future than to reduce the immigration of the less fit? As a consequence, immigration legislation in Canada and the United States began to be concerned with non-infectious disease issues such as mental and psychiatric conditions, chronic disabilities, seizure disorders, and limits to vision and hearing. Grouped into categories that suggested such migrants would become public charges or be unable to support themselves, examination for these conditions became a part of the existing infectious disease screening systems at place in major ports of entry.

An interesting anecdote in this regard was the great concern posed by trachoma. Eye diseases such as trachoma were believed to be related to the customs and habits of immigrants primarily from Eastern Europe, the Middle East, and Asia. A 1911 encyclopedia definition is indicative:

> TRACHOMA, the name given to a chronic destructive form of inflammation of the conjunctiva of the eye (see EYE: Diseases), or "granular conjunctivitis" (See also: Egyptian ophthalmia). It is a contagious disease, associated with dirty conditions, and common in Egypt, Arabia and parts of Europe, especially among the lower class of Jews. Hence it has become important, in connexion with the alien immigration into the United Kingdom and America, and the rejection of those who are afflicted with it. It is important that all cases should be isolated, and that the spread of the infection should be prevented. (Vol. 27, p. 116 of the 1911 Encyclopedia Britannica)

Trachoma provided a link between social conditions, infection, and the concerns about employability and need for future public services. In addition, it was relatively easy to screen for, and many of the surviving photos of the medical examination of migrants in North America from the early part of the 20th century show officials examining the eyes of new arrivals. It was a common reason for denial of admission and the return of migrants to Europe. Those afflicted could either be detained or returned. The belief that trachoma reflected deeper social and moral risks is evident. In Canada, detention for the assessment of trachoma allowed the authorities a period of closer observation, which allowed the officials to determine "as *to whether the immigrant is not only readily curable of his disease, but also whether he is in other respects desirable*" (Sears, 1990).

Moving the Barrier — Extending Immigration Screening to the Point of Origin

The extension of routine immigration medical screening beyond infectious diseases of quarantine relevance and the rendering of chronic non-infectious conditions as reasons for inadmissibility had implications for both the travel and immigration sectors. Detaining individuals to rule out incubating infections or referring them to medical institutions was a short-term and a relatively low cost measure. Returning those inadmissible to Europe was a different matter. Shipping and railway companies, while often required by law to pay, complained about having to absorb these costs. Sometimes the vessels did not return directly to original ports of embarkation, depositing "undesirable" or "rejected" immigrants in other nations. This actually affected immigration policy discussion in Britain in terms of Eastern Europeans returned because of trachoma (Maglen, 2005).

As a consequence, beginning in 1925, the U.S. Public Health Service began to station officers abroad to undertake pre-departure screening. Canada followed suit in 1927, and by 1931 the Canadian Medical Association, still reflecting principles from the eugenics lobby, observed that:

> We conclude that the medical service overseas is now the established proce-
> dure for the examination of immigrants. No system of medical examination
> can be perfect because of the limits to medical knowledge and to the capabil-
> ities of physicians, who after all, are only human. However, it seems obvious
> that the medical examination overseas of prospective emigrants offers a much
> better opportunity for protecting Canada from undesirables and for selection
> of the type of man we want in Canada than does the previous system of exam-
> ination at the port of arrival. (Anonymous. (1931). The Immigration Medical
> Services for Canada. Canadian Medical Association Journal, 24, 435.)

Interrupted by the Second World War pre-departure, medical screening continues to provide the basis of immigration health for nations with organized immigration programs such as Australia, Canada, and the United States. Approaching the issue in a different manner, Israel, a country of large immigration dynamics and several European nations deal with all migration-related health issues through on-arrival processes. The demise of the eugenics movement removed a considerable amount of the social pressure behind the process, although the concepts of becoming a public charge and the demands associated with the presence of chronic diseases and disabilities continued to remain in legislation. At the same time, advances in medical science and the treatment of infectious diseases that followed the discovery of antibiotics allowed the focus of health and migration to become relatively static. Until recently much of that interest was limited primarily to those working directly with immigrants and refugees.

This phenomenon was not limited to the area of migration and health. Many other areas of medicine, particularly the area of infectious disease control, experienced similar situations in response to the perception of decreased threats and consequently decreased need. The unappreciated migration-related issues, which only became apparent following the recognition of the HIV/AIDS pandemic, were deficiencies in focusing on health and disease from a national, domestic perspective. Approaching health issues from a national viewpoint isolated from global forces and influences had progressively limited effectiveness in an ever more mobile world.

Tuberculosis control in North America is a salient example of not recognizing that national success in disease control however laudable would be ineffective over the longer term. The closing of sanatoria and the attrition of laboratory and clinical capacity in the 1980s may have had logical consistency from a domestic point of view. However, in a world where 30% of the global population was infected with the disease and migration and travel were increasing, it can be seen in retrospect to have been short sighted. The full impact of those decisions would not become apparent until the 1990s.

The Modern Era — Migration Becomes Population Mobility

During the last four decades the world has experienced many changes that affect migration. The volume of movement of people has increased and air travel replaced sea travel, increasing the speed with which they travel. At the same time the nature of migration evolved in response to a combination of factors, known as globalization. Globalization, which is both a process and an influence, is now recognized as having many effects on social, economic, political, and health outcomes. Those changes have affected not only migration but other broader aspects of health as well.

The driving forces that have changed migration in recent times have affected the demography of those moving, regions of origin, and places of destination. They have included:

(1)   Post-Colonial Population Flows, Following European Decolonialization,
(2)   Vietnam War Related Refugee Movements,
(3)   Global Population Growth,
(4)   Expanding Low Cost International Travel,
(5)   The Collapse of the Former Soviet Union, and
(6)   The Process of Globalization.

Together they have combined to change both the nature and characteristics of migrants. Those changes in their own way affect the health of those who are moving as well as the health systems and practices of receiving locations.

Changes in the nature and speed of travel have had many effects on the practicality and utility of many of the historical principles of migration health. Once the speed of travel increased to a point where the migratory journey was less than the incubation period of an infectious disease, many of the principles associated with the quarantine inspection were invalidated. Individuals infected with diseases of public health importance, could be clinically well after a short journey from the place of infection. In the absence of rapid screening tests, on-arrival examination would be unrewarding. When faced with a new threat which provokes fear in the receiving society, such as that observed with SARS in 2003, a return to on-arrival screening and discussions of the applicability of quarantine can occur. However, it is clear to most that the effectiveness of the border or frontier as a defense against the importation or admission of disease is marginal or severely limited at best.

The demise of the role of the border and the limits of migration screening and quarantine and the changes in the dynamics of migration have effectively moved the impact of migration and travel related health issues into the sphere of primary care. Since the 1970s individuals with illnesses acquired abroad or during travel are less likely to present on arrival than their predecessors who arrived by sea. Clearing customs and immigration with their disease undetected they are more likely to present with illness in the community. These events were first observed by practitioners in traditional immigration receiving nations in the 1980s and 1990s and are now commonly seen in Europe and other locations. Initially noted in infectious diseases such as tuberculosis, migration-related influences are now well recognized in the epidemiology of many illnesses and infections.

As the demography of migration has evolved as a consequence of the six factors noted above, many of the principles of immigration and migration health have changed as well. The prevalence and incidence of some illness and disease have been observed to be more functionally related to risk and travel history than to the administrative immigration classification of the individual. Where you come from, where you travel, what you have been exposed to and how and where you live are often more important factors in relation to health than whether you are an official immigrant or a foreign worker. Additionally, the availability and accessibility of international travel, combined with social and political changes that allow situations of dual citizenship and frequent return visits have dramatically influenced the travel behavior of millions of migrants.

As demonstrated by the health outcomes of travelers who visit friends and relatives, citizenship and immigration status may not be as effective discriminators of health risk as they once were. The implications for the practice of travel medicine are obvious and can be expected to increase as global surveillance activities continue to define populations at increased risk of travel associated disease. Finally, the ongoing process of globalization and its' associated relationships to the global labor force and integration is further blurring the concepts and previous limits of residence and geographic influences on health.

Together these factors and processes have produced what the Canadian communications theorist and educator Marshall McLuhan, noted in the context of the media, a global village. The mobility of people, which while including immigration in the traditional sense, extends to temporary and semi-permanent residence and recurrent travel, is in effect globalizing health risks. This has current and will have greater impact on the practice of medicine as population mobility affects national demographic characteristics. For example, migrants of all kinds currently make up more than 20% of the total population of more than 40 nations.

The global medical village that is a consequence of population mobility has significant implications for the "hoof beats and zebras" analogy regarding previously rare or uncommon diseases. In a growing number of locations it is now necessary for the practitioner to consider the origin and travel history of the rider in addition to the sound of the hooves. The global medical village also has had considerable consequences in the field of public health. The weakness of national approaches and the impacts of globalization have both stimulated and supported integrated and collective international strategies to manage many public health risks. Beginning with the eradication of smallpox, stimulated by HIV and extending to malaria, tuberculosis, SARS and more recently avian and pandemic influenza, multinational, global approaches to managing public health are now recognized as necessary to successfully meet many disease challenges.

Several of the tools considered and used in these endeavors such as quarantine and immigration health screening are old. Attempts to use them in a collective and integrated manner that extends beyond national boundaries reflect more modern approaches. Behind them all however, and extending across centuries, are the principles resulting from population mobility. It is this ancient relationship between health and movement that provides an interesting window through which to observe the factors that link today's news stories about dealing with the threats of imported disease with distant but similar concerns in across the centuries.

References

Garrison, F. H. (1929). *An introduction to the history of medicine* (4th ed., pp. 178–180). Philadelphia, PA: W.B. Saunders Company.

Goodman, N. M. (1952). *International health organizations and their work*. Philadelphia, PA: Blakison.

Gottfried, R. S. (1983). The Black Death. *Natural and human disaster in medieval Europe*. New York: The Free Press.

Hastings, R. C., Opromolla, D. V. A. (1994). *Leprosy* (2nd ed.). Edinburgh: Churchill Livingstone; Rogers, L., Muir, E. (1946). *Leprosy* (3rd ed.). Bristol: John Wright & Sons.

Maglen, K. (2005). Importing trachoma: The introduction into Britain of American ideas of an 'Immigrant Disease', 1892–1906. *Immigrants and minorities, 23*, 80–99.

Sears, A. (1990). Immigration controls as social policy: The case of Canadian medical inspection 1900–1920. *Studies in Political Economy, 33*, 91–111.

WHO. The International Health Regulations 2005. The Organization, Geneva 2005. Available from URL: http://www.who.int/csr/ihr/IHRWHA58_3-en.pdf (Last accessed December 28, 2006).

Chapter 28

Stories of Undocumented Migrants to the USA

Nancy Piper Jenks

Migration is not a new story. Searching for greener pastures, the hope of improving the quality of life for oneself or one's children is an age-old quest. Migration is traveling for a cause, with a one-way ticket. In the 21st century, the numbers are staggering and the stories seemingly endless. Having an opportunity to hear even one migration story, a person can begin to appreciate the physical and psychological hardship inherent in the journey. The struggle, of course, does not end at the destination.

The river town of Peekskill is tucked along the Hudson River with a beautiful view of the Hudson Highlands. The Kitchawank, a Native American tribe, greeted a migrant Dutchman named Jan Peek when he traveled up the river in the mid-1600s to establish a trading post (hence, Peekskill — "kill" is Dutch for "stream.") The land was eventually bought and taken over by this migrant Dutch population after Chief Sirham accepted one thousand fishing hooks, among other items, for the land.

There are approximately 24,000 inhabitants in Peekskill today and it is one of the fastest growing cities in the state of New York. In the 1980s, Central and South Americans began to settle in the city and in 2005 there were an estimated 8,000 new immigrants living in Peekskill. New York State has the second largest number of immigrants in the USA, after California. The flow of immigrants to Peekskill (which is 30 miles north of New York City) is in part due to affordable housing and a greater opportunity for employment because of certain industries, particularly construction. The majority of these new arrivals are from villages near the city of Cuenca in the highlands of Ecuador. Many have come overland or "*andando por la pampa*" (literally, walking across the plains) and virtually all are undocumented. Under the weight of Ecuador's political and economic turmoil, these men and women have made this expensive and dangerous journey, to meet their uncles, their cousins, their friends, and their husbands, with the hope of finding a better life. The influx of migrants into Peekskill is apparent as one walks through the streets and recognizes the faces of the indigenous people of the Andean highlands. Everyday but Sunday, on one particular street corner in the city, there are over one hundred laborers anxiously watching for cars and trucks to slow down and pick

Travel Medicine: Tales Behind the Science
Copyright © 2007 by Elsevier Ltd.
All rights of reproduction in any form reserved.
ISBN: 0-08-045359-7

them up for a day's work. There are Ecuadorian restaurants cropping up on different blocks of the city and on any given Sunday afternoon along the river, football games are being played and guinea pigs are being roasted. In the suburbs around Peekskill, there are Ecuadorian men mowing lawns and building stonewalls. Ecuadorian women are cleaning houses.

The immigrant population in the USA reached a new high of more than 35 million in 2005, accounting for 12.1% of the total population, the highest percentage in eight decades. Approximately one-third (9.8 million) of the immigrants are undocumented. Data indicate that the first half of this decade has been the highest five-year period of immigration in American history. Between January 2000 and March 2005, 7.9 new immigrants came into the USA and nearly half (3.7 million) were undocumented (Camarota, 2005). In the New York region, historical migration patterns have changed and immigrants often bypass the city, heading directly to the suburbs in search of jobs and affordable housing. Scattered pockets around the country, such as Peekskill, are swelling with immigrants in unprecedented numbers. New data from the Census Bureau's American Community Survey show that the population of New York's suburbs is now 21.3% foreign born, up from 14.1% in 1990 (American Community Survey: U.S. Census Bureau, 2005).

The health status of new migrants is variable. They can suffer from infections such as tuberculosis (TB) and intestinal parasites that originate in their countries of origin or that are picked up during their travel. Physical injuries during the often-dangerous crossing can have an impact on their health. Their mental health may be affected by the trauma of the journey or the adjustment to their new environment. Although these migrants move to a country with seemingly more opportunities, the financial barriers, lack of documentation, and the lack of access to health care take their toll.

Childless Mothers: Laura's Story

Laura is 35 years old and has lived in Peekskill for two years. We sit at an outside table of a café in town as she recounts her story. She glances around every time someone walks by and lowers her voice. Her 11-month-old son is nestled contentedly at her breast as she describes her life in Ecuador, her journey here, and her new life. Laura is the fourth of seven children and grew up in Giron, 30 miles south of Cuenca. Her childhood home was a three-room adobe house, with a dirt floor and no running water. Over the years, her parents were able to add two more rooms and they now have indoor plumbing. She attended school until she was 14 years old before going to work in a factory.

She married at the age of 18 and had two children. Her husband drove taxis in Cuenca and they lived with her parents. They had very little money and were partly dependent on her brother-in-law who had moved to Peekskill 10 years earlier and would send money to them sporadically. Laura's husband decided to migrate to Peekskill seven years ago, leaving her two small children with no father. She emphatically states that every family in her town has a relative who has migrated to the States. She describes new social problems among families whose children grow up without fathers. There is a lack of discipline, she explains. She also describes the many new homes being built in her town, financed by those who have left.

Two years ago, Laura's husband arranged for her passage. It cost $12,000. They made a down payment of $5000 and are now trying to repay the loan and accruing interest. Laura remembers that her move happened very quickly. She was told that upon being contacted by the "guide," she would have to be ready to go. Migrating to the States was such a norm, that she admits never really thinking through the issue of leaving her children. Laura's eyes well up with tears as she describes the despair that began the very first minute that she was swept up into the movement of migration. She got the call one night and left the next day. She was numb when she left, traveling to La Paz, Bolivia. She stayed for three weeks in a small room with seven other Ecuadorians. There was no electricity and she sat quietly much of the time in the dark. There was not enough food. She knew no one. But there was no possibility of turning back. She felt then and she feels now, two years later, that leaving her children was the biggest mistake of her life. She longs to turn the clock back.

From La Paz she flew to Mexico and then started the overland journey. She hid in houses and in the shadows of trees, she walked for miles and she squatted in the back of a truck for hours, in a small space behind a partition. She waded across the Rio Grande crossing the border from Mexico into the USA. She doesn't swim and the water was up to her neck. She was petrified. As the group reached the other side with their two "coyotes" (guides), she could see hundreds of snakes on the embankment. She shudders as she recalls the sight.

Laura's reunion with her husband and brother-in-law brought some comfort but she could not escape the pain of separation from her children. The pain has not lessened over the past two years. She sometimes thinks that she will "go crazy" from grief. She calls her children weekly. They are living with her parents and youngest sister. They often cry and beg her to come home (to ease the pain of leaving, she had told them when she left that she would return in two years — they remind her that the two years are up). Laura and her husband have had another child who will turn one next week. They live in a tiny one-bedroom apartment with four other men from Cuenca. Laura thinks that her children in Ecuador believe that they will be forgotten.

Laura's story has been told time and time again. Mothers migrating to Peekskill come without their children and because they have no legal status, there is no hope of bringing their children here. Their mental anguish manifests itself sometimes in somatic complaints and often in anxiety and depression. Medication and therapy cannot alleviate the emotional suffering. Even time doesn't seem to heal their sorrow. At Hudson River Community Health Center some of these women attend a weekly support group and according to Laura, that group is very important to her. These women have made a choice to sacrifice their peace of mind and separate from their children in the hopes of giving them a better future.

Access to Health Care: Looking for a Leg

Health insurance is not an entitlement in the United States. There are 45 million Americans without health insurance and medical costs make comprehensive health care unattainable for many. One-third of all immigrants in the USA lack health insurance (Camarota, 2005). Among the undocumented migrants, virtually all are uninsured (exceptions in New York State include pregnant women, those infected with HIV, and those under the age of 18). Financial barriers limit access to health care for the migrant population, as do linguistic barriers and cultural differences. Without legal documentation, some migrants fear deportation when accessing care.

In Peekskill, Hudson River Health Care, a community health center, runs a weekly clinic called, *Casa de Salud,* which targets the migrant population. There are many patients who come in during this popular evening clinic seeking help for medical and psychosocial problems. The clinic offers bilingual primary-care clinicians and some basic lab services. Thousands of visits have been documented since the inception of this clinic in 2001. The majority of visits fall into the categories of infectious diseases, chronic diseases, and injuries.

Treatment for infectious diseases is often empirical since lab tests are too costly for individuals to afford. Migrants may come in with infections that were contracted in their countries or with infections picked up along the one- to two-month journey here. Migrants, who come in with, for example, symptoms of intestinal parasites, are often treated without stool tests to identify pathogens. Dermatological infections are rarely cultured due to the cost.

Undocumented migrants who enter the USA are not screened for TB and active TB is not uncommon. In 2005, foreign-born persons in the USA had a TB rate that was 8.7 times that of the U.S.-born persons (MMWR, 2006). Many migrants in Peekskill live in crowded housing conditions and there have been delays in treatment due to health care access issues and fear of deportation. Cases of both pulmonary and extra-pulmonary TB have been diagnosed during our evening clinic.

Diabetics come in symptomatic with abnormally high blood glucose. We dig into our sample cabinet for medication. We help with applications for free medication. We try to convince them that they need to take medication daily, not just when they have symptoms.

Day laborers often present to the Center with injuries. Falls, lacerations, eye injuries are all common. One late evening during our weekly clinic, I met a young man looking for a leg. Manuel was from Ecuador and had just arrived the week before. During the arduous journey overland from his village near Cuenca, he lost his right leg. He left Cuenca for the coast of Ecuador and traveled by boat to Guatemala. He then went by van, bus, and on foot to Mexico. He finally crossed into the USA and headed north on a freight train. He fell from the train and his leg was severed. The amputation took place at a hospital in Texas and he was given a very basic prosthetic leg that did not fit. He had met up with his brother in Peekskill and was living in an apartment with six other men. Manuel was stuck. He couldn't walk, he couldn't work, he couldn't pay back his loan, and he couldn't send money home. He hobbled into our Health Center at 9:00 p.m. and was the last patient to be seen. It was close to the Christmas holidays and the clinic had been busy. That particular evening we had seen a patient with neurocysticercosis who was having seizures. We had struggled to put together a plan for her care. We had seen a patient with what looked like leishmaniasis and wondered how to make a definitive diagnosis. A young girl had come in with a possible wrist fracture and we managed to arrange for a reduced rate for an X-ray at the local hospital.

It had been a long evening and I thought the challenges of the day had ended until I met my last patient, Manuel. He looked younger than his twenty years. He recounted his story with sadness in his eyes. He had risked a lot for this passage and had lost his leg. But, how could he ask me to conjure up a leg? His stump was raw and appeared infected. After treating the skin infection, I could only stall for time and ask him to return the following week. Maybe I could figure out something...

The following morning, back at the Health Center, my first patient was a 40-year-old American man who had come in for a routine work physical. I got his history: medicines, allergies, family history … past surgery? The answer to the last question caught my attention — he had had his right leg amputated twenty years ago. Two amputees in the same examination room within twelve hours of each other? The patient was a member of a well-known New York amputee basketball team and one of his teammates owns a company where they make prostheses. A phone call was made and a plan was hatched. Manuel was fitted for a state-of-the-art prosthesis. That was two years ago. I see him in town occasionally. He works in construction. He and his brother want to support his cousin's journey here. He is hopeful. He was lucky.

The Day Laborers with Bull's Eye Rings

In the summer of 2002, during a weekly evening clinic for the migrant population at our community health center in Peekskill, three patients who were relatively new arrivals from Ecuador, presented with erythema migrans (EM) rashes. No fever, no body aches, just this telltale bull's eye. None of them knew what this odd-looking rash meant yet all three were curious enough to pay the $15 for a visit with a clinician for a diagnosis.

Lyme disease is the most common vector-borne disease in the United States, with more than 80% of reported cases occurring in the Northeast. New York State has the highest number of reported cases. Lyme disease is hyperendemic in this county (Westchester) with an incidence rate of 79.6 per 100,000 residents. Peekskill is located in the north of the county and borders on the counties of Putnam, Duchess, and Columbia, where the incidence rates of Lyme are 308.4, 445.9, and 1,422.9 per 100,000, respectively (Communicable disease in New York State, 2006).

Many new migrant workers are employed as day laborers and work outside during the spring and summer months doing landscaping or construction. This places them at an even higher risk for Lyme disease than the general population in this community. During the summer of 2002, clinicians who worked with the migrant population at our Center were interested in learning if these new migrants knew anything about Lyme disease. We conducted interviews with 80 migrants, who had been in the area less than 4 years, to find out if they could recognize the EM rash or if they knew how the infection was transmitted. From those we interviewed, not one patient was familiar with this tick-borne infection (Jenks & Trapasso, 2005). We have diagnosed dozens of cases of Lyme disease among our migrant population and there are undoubtedly many cases contracted that go undiagnosed due to the lack of awareness.

The story of Lyme disease among the migrant population is an ironic twist on the story of travel medicine. One typically thinks of travel medicine in the context of Westerns traveling to infected endemic areas. Who would imagine that migrants, who sacrifice everything to reach the haven of North America, would be at high risk for and sometimes contract an infectious disease such as Lyme, which can lead in some cases to chronic and debilitating disease? Among the migrant population at our Center, a simple educational intervention raised awareness of Lyme identification, prevention, and treatment (Jenks and Trapasso, 2005).

Thousands of migrants have come to Peekskill. They have come here because they have circles of family and friends who have come before them. They use a very elaborate financial,

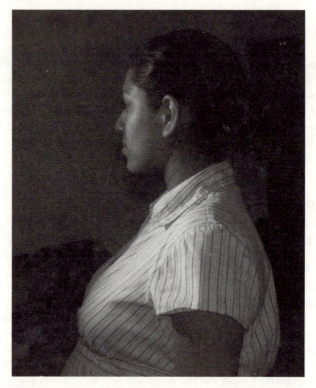

Image 28.1. Laura migrated to the States without her children.

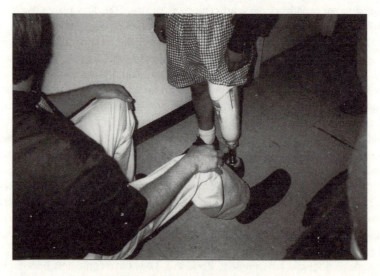

Image 28.2. Manuel tries on his new leg.

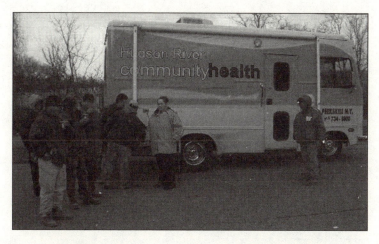

Image 28.3. Migrant day laborers wait for work near community outreach van.

familial, and underground network to negotiate their passage. The journey is never easy. The story of these migrants is really three stories: their decision to leave, their journey here, and their adaptation to their new environment. What unites these three stories is the extraordinary hardship that confronts the migrant at every step.

References

American Community Survey: U.S. Census Bureau. (2005). Available at: http://www.census.gove/acs/www/(Accessed 2006, Sep. 12).

Camarota, S. (2005) *Immigrants at mid-decade: A snapshot of American's foreign-born population in 2005*. Washington DC: Center for Immigration Studies.

Communicable disease in New York State: Rate per 100,000 (2002). Available at: http//www.health.state.ny.us/nysdoh/cdc/2001/rates2htm (Accessed 2006, Sep. 12).

MMWR. (March 24, 2006). Trends in Tuberculosis-United States. *Morbidity and Mortality Weekly Report. 55*(11), 305–308.

Piper Jenks, N., & Trapasso, J. (2005). Lyme risk for immigrants to the United States: The role of an educational tool. *Journal of Travel Medicine, 12*, 157–160.

Chapter 29

Between Crossing Boundaries and Respecting Norms: The Story of African Women Labor-Migrants in Israel

Galia Sabar

> *"I'm back from Zambia. I'm home. I made it...I'm so happy. They gave me*
> *a job as a nurse at the Ghana Refineries...If I'm good, they'll take me as a*
> *permanent worker at the clinic...Thank God I had my savings...otherwise I*
> *would not have been able to do it...You can tell all my friends in Israel that*
> *I'm a nurse, they will be proud...they will be happy for me...they are the*
> *ones who told me I can do it...In Israel I saw that women can do anything*
> *they want. You trusted me, you people always knew I will make it".*

Charity, a 35-year-old Ghanaian woman, said this to me over the phone at the beginning of September 2006. Her call came after many months of silence when I didn't know what had happened to her. Charity came to Israel on her own in 1999 as a pilgrim to the Holy Land and stayed as an undocumented migrant laborer. For 5 years she cleaned houses during the day and studied to be a priest in the evenings. She was deported to Ghana in 2004. In Ghana she tried for months to establish her own church and failed. Then she decided to enroll as a student in a local Nursing College. Using her savings and with some assistance from Israeli friends she managed to pay for her tuition and graduated as a practical nurse in 2005. However, finding a job was once again difficult and over the phone she sounded desperate. She had to move to Zambia to work as a nanny for a rich local family. Finally, in 2006, she moved back to Ghana after her job application had been accepted. This can be considered a success story: A young woman who migrated on her own to Israel, worked, saved and was able to return home to learn a new profession.

This study, based mainly on qualitative research methodology,[1] will analyze the life stories of African women labor-migrants who started coming to Israel in the 1990s. Emphasis will be on the ways migration has become a dominant factor in the complex process of the women migrants' identity structuring. I shall analyze the ways in which migration compelled women to take initiative and act independently, making autonomous decisions. Yet, on the other hand, survival in Israel and the existential need to belong to the African immigrant community led them to adhere to norms in the sphere of gender relations and the division of labor within the family, considered traditional. This complexity and ambiguity will be the focus of this chapter.

Through the interviews and observations I carried out in the years 1999–2005, I became acquainted with an active and lively African community in the heart of the white Jewish city of Tel Aviv. I spent weekends and festivals in African churches and at other social gatherings all over Tel Aviv. I spent various evenings with groups of women, at prayer meetings, conferences and local economic committee meetings. I joined labor-migrants on their trips in the Holy Land and was invited to visit their families, their home-based businesses, and participated in family and community events. Thus I gradually came to know an ever-growing group of African women and men, who had come to Israel to change their lives for the better.

In order to widen my perspective, I interviewed African migrants living in Holland, Germany, Turkey, Ireland and USA. I also carried out research in the African countries from which migrants had come to Israel, among them Kenya, Ghana, Senegal and Cameroon. I explored research literature about labor-migrants in Israel, African communities in western countries and women migrants in our times.

Introduction: Labor-Migration to Israel

Unlike most western countries, international migrant workers, including thousands of Africans, began to arrive in Israel only in the late 1980s, following a government decision to facilitate a greater influx of international migrant laborers.[2] At the time, no clear policy concerning international laborers existed, since the government considered them as temporary workers and not migrants and prospective citizens. Once the borders were opened, Africans without working permits came, first in a trickle and then in a flood.

Most of them came from Ghana and Nigeria, entering Israel on a pilgrim or tourist visa. It was easy to enter the country; hourly wages for cleaning work, which they did, were relatively high; and those who followed had a good support system to help them find employment, housing and friends. These advantages helped overcome the obstacles, namely the exclusiveness of the Law of Return[3] (entitling Jews to immigrate to Israel and receive automatic citizenship); the danger of Palestinian terrorist attacks, and, beginning in the late 1990s, the government's policy of deporting undocumented migrant laborers.

Since most Africans came without work permits, there are no official figures as to how many African labor-migrants were in Israel at the time. Yet, by the end of the 1990s, it was estimated that 14,000 African men and women were living in Israel (out of a total of 250,000 international migrant laborers).[4] However, due to massive deportation in 2002–2003, the total number of Africans was reduced to somewhere between 4000 and 8000. By the beginning of 2006, it was estimated that only 1000–2000 Africans remained, mostly single mothers with children.

Feminization of Migration

Until recently, research literature about African labor-migrants presumed men were leading the migration and women usually arrived only in the wake of their fathers, husbands or other male relatives.[5] Recently it has become evident that women were opening up new migration routes and destinations, and playing a central role in building up immigrant communities.[6] The numbers of women migrants, African and others, are so significant that certain researchers speak of "feminization of migration".[7] This has substantial implications, both for the societies absorbing them and for their countries of origin: Barbara Ehrenreich maintains that migration of women from Third World countries to the West has caused, among other things, the transformation of women's traditional work patterns on a global scale, thus throwing a new light on globalization as a whole.[8] Researchers dealing with the implications of globalization have recently examined how globalization — which includes women's migration from the Third World to the salaried labor market — provides women with new avenues of struggle against suppressing and marginalizing aspect's of society. The question arises — Is salaried work within the capitalist labor market a potentially liberating and empowering feature, or is it yet another means of oppression and exploitation?[9]

The story of Sub-Saharan migration to Israel has recently been dealt with in various research studies.[10] However, the women's role in the process of migration, in the building up of the local community and its survival has rarely been considered.

Even superficial knowledge of Sub-Saharan cultures makes it plain that most of the societies are build on social constructs that limit, subdue and marginalize women in many and varied ways, especially in the public domain. Recent research has emphasized various strategies implemented by women desiring to increase their autonomy and expand their influence (Kandiyoti, 1988). And yet most women are still rarely able to make autonomous decisions, even when their relative power within the domestic domain has grown.

Taking into account the differences between the values and norms of behavior that the women migrants brought with them and those they acquired in Israel, I shall examine their role within the community of African labor-migrants between 1990 and 2006. An analysis of their discourse enables us to enter the women's world and raises important questions about processes related to their empowerment, gender relations within the Israeli context and also within their families, and to ascertain as to what extent migration has precipitated changes in their worldview and way of life.[11]

"I Wanted Something Else" — Between the African Rock and the Israeli Hard Place

> *"I'm just like my sister and my cousin...there are so many women back home that want change...they all want something else. They want to work, save and get away...What kind of future do we have? The best that can happen to us is that we marry a rich man (laughs), have children, and then he will lock us up at home so we stay with them...If you are really lucky, you get your own shop...maybe a fish stand or a hairdressing salon...But then if you get married, you have to take care of the shop, the kids and your husband...I know that many women want a different life, but only a few really do something about it...It is hard as a woman with no man to protect you to get up and go...only a few do it. For me it was clear. What I had at home was not for me. I wanted a different life".* (Charity, Tel Aviv, March 1999)

I got to know Charity in 1999 during the first stages of my research. Her life story and that of other African women throw a vivid personal light on transnational migration. These people are not merely uprooted individuals, trying to make good in their new homes, but part of a huge and constant flow of people crossing national, cultural and economic borders (Appadurai, 1991). Hence challenging us to view them not as passive displaced persons, but rather social agents, preserving a complex network of relations with their original homes and cultures and developing various new identities and diverse links both with the world they left behind and the one they have entered (Basch, Schiller, & Blanc, 1994).

One of the most important insights derived from the women's stories is the realization that they, as well as the other family members, experience a constant conflict between different and sometimes incompatible value-laden arenas. While in reality the arenas are not really dichotomous, they may be identified in the following way: the African family system, emphasizing the needs of the community and the individual's obligations to the extended family; the western Israeli system, lending legitimacy to the individual's desires and perceiving the fulfillment of personal aspirations as a central value; and the African-Israeli arena, merging values and patterns of both the above arenas.[12]

Survival Strategies

African women who migrated on their own confronted the difficulties of migration together with the stigmas adhering to women unprotected by men. Migrating alone compelled them to build and use supportive networks other than those they had left behind:

> *"When I came I stayed with my sister and her husband...I was there for two months...they introduced me to many friends...Then I found a room and moved. It was expensive, but I already had a few houses that I cleaned, so I managed...If you know English, it's easy. The most important thing is that your friends will help you find jobs...Here most of my life is around the church [African Independent Church]...women's committees, evening prayers, social gatherings with others who came from my area...If there is a national holiday in Ghana, our union organizes a party and everybody comes, even Nigerians and Congolese...The truth is that almost every week we have special events in our community or in the church...women's meetings, social committees, Bible school...it takes a lot of time and money (laughs)...I learn a lot in the church: how to organize things, raise funds...I have very little time for anything else, but for me being with other Africans is important. I think it is like this for most [African] women I know here...It's like home for me...maybe even like my family. I know they will always be there if I need them".* (Charity, March 1999)

African migrants in Israel, similarly to labor-migrants in other countries,[13] have set up organizations based on family ties, ethnic identity, shared occupations, religious identity and similar problems and objectives. Joining up in this way was a basic survival strategy. Being part of an organization helped new migrants cope with loneliness, alienation and confusion, stemming from their lack of knowledge of the new society's culture and norms, and affected their behavior within the African arena in Israel.

Recent research on immigrants, and in particular labor-migrants worldwide, has revealed that women are particularly active in these organizations, investing both time and money in their functions and in the community they create (Sabar Ben Yoshua, 1998, pp. 101–105; Pessar, 1999). They are rewarded not only with friendship and support but also with the acquisition of organizational, fund raising and other skills they consider useful. Such an existential need and subsequent commitment were not reflected equally in the interviews with the men.

It is noteworthy that in the case of African migrants in Israel, the prevalence of associational organizations and their active support has strong African roots. Their membership in various religious, occupational and women's organizations is a widespread phenomenon, the basis for an active civil society.[14] These associational organizations have also created channels towards mobility for marginal sectors in society, such as women, meeting needs not met through any other frameworks. Thus activity in organizations pertaining to civil society became the main source of empowerment for millions of women in Africa; to name but two — Winnie Mandela, who headed youth and sports organizations (somewhat problematic ones) under the Apartheid regime, and on a totally different plane, Professor Wangari Maathai, Nobel Prize for Peace awardee in 2004 who established the Green Belt Movement, empowering millions of women in Africa by means of agricultural projects. Similarly, our data show that the African community in Israel, with its various organizations, has served as an anchor for its members, in particular to women, providing concrete assistance on a daily basis, as well as a warm family atmosphere and a source of empowerment and change.

"Here, I Can Do It" — Vocational Training as an Avenue for Change

Realizing that economic independence is the main means to obtain power, many women mentioned that they wished to acquire a new profession in Israel, potentially better paid. When asked whether she learned a new profession in Israel, Charity replied:

> *"I've just graduated from a computer course...I know visual basic, windows and more...but just now I started a course in our church...I have a long way to go, but after I finish many courses I want to be a minister. Many people told me it is not a good job for a woman, that I should do something else...my family is not happy with this, but I hope they will accept my choice when they see I'm happy and making money...even some of my friends and Pastors in our community in Israel said this is not for me, not for a woman...But I decided to do it, so I am learning at the Pentecostal Church in Jerusalem. We are 15 students from Ghana, Philippines and other places. I'm not the only woman...we are three...we meet once a week in the evening...It will take me about one year and then I will get my diploma. After that I want to open my own church. I can do it like all those who open churches here and everywhere around the world. Here I can do it like those men who did it. I want to be a leader in our community. I don't want to make people angry...I will do it in my own, pleasant way. No fights. In Israel I saw women do such things. I can also do it"*. (Charity, Tel Aviv, May 2002)

Charity's dilemma was not whether to acquire a profession, but what type of profession. In many African countries there are wealthy professional women, so this was actually not a new idea for Charity. And yet almost all women mentioned that in Israel there are more professional women than at home, and their power within the family and the society is greater. Thus her choice of computer studies and learning to be a priest came from her awareness of the importance of professional training, enabling her to work and advance wherever she chooses to live, whether in Ghana, Israel or any other country.

However, her dilemma highlights the conflict between Western and African values: Her choices were not detached from her African cultural arena, and she was well aware of the difficulties she may encounter. She believed she was able to serve as a spiritual leader and did not accept the women's apprehension at serving in high priestly positions; she also resisted attempts to silence her voice or downplay her opinions. She said that in Israel she was able to choose to some extent with whom to work, with whom to spend her spare time, with whom to share a room and her life and, above all, to decide about her future. In the end, when she was unable to establish a church in Ghana, Charity chose to acquire a different profession, to become a practical nurse.

On the other hand Juliet, a labor-migrant from Liberia, living in Israel with her husband and two children, said she wanted to learn a profession she could do from home.

> *"This way I can be with my kids...I can look after my land...I want to have a job that will give me money for what I need...my dream is to open a salon, like in Israel".* (Juliet, Tel Aviv, June 2000)

Even though Juliet's aspirations were confined to the domestic domain, she also wanted to be economically independent. Moreover, she dreamed of establishing a business on a high level, as in Israel. Both women represent a desire for change, and each in a different way reveals the dialectical aspect of their lives as migrants coming from a traditional society to a modern one. Their attitude reflects their desire to become integrated in the modern way of life, while simultaneously preserving certain features of their pervious life. For Charity, her desire to be a woman priest with computer skills reflects a perfect combination, obliterating conventional dichotomies between traditional and modern life, the African as opposed to the western world, between feminine and masculine professions, emotional and rational features and so on.

Moreover, in Israel women migrants were exposed to the local tendency to perceive long-term planning and saving not only as means of survival but also as important values.

> *"Almost all my bosses ask me what I plan to do with all my money. They say — How will you secure your future...what will you do when you have no strength to clean, when you are older?...In the beginning I did not really understand what they were asking...Quickly I learned...you Israelis always think about the future. You have insurance; you have savings to keep you when you are old. We Africans have our land and our family...we have it now and we will have it in the future".* (Charity, Ghana 2005)

Her realization that acquiring a profession to ensure her economic independence in the long term is a precondition for self-empowerment, is also reflected in other studies examining African migrants in Europe on the verge of returning to Africa.[15] The findings show that

professional training acquired before returning home is perceived as an important investment to further a smooth reintegration at home.

In *A Room of One's Own*, Virginia Woolf estimated the cost of women's independence
at $100 and was one of the first to consider economic independence as the basis for a
change in women's status in society. Subsequently, many studies followed, stressing that
economic independence led to a change in the way women perceived themselves and their
relative power in society.[16] African women migrants behaved according to this concept,
whether they wished to become hairdressers, nursery school teachers, nurses, priests or
computer specialists.

"They Push Me…But in the End I'm the One that Decides" — Gender Relations, Family Ties, Marriage and the 'Self'

The life stories of the women migrants provide additional insights regarding their self-
perception, their status, family relationships and marital relations. While in the past the
assumption was that migration cuts women migrants off from their previous ways of life,
norms and modes of existence and forges their identity according to that of women in the
absorbing society, current research presents a more complex view: In some cases the process
of migration reinforces tendencies towards greater individualism, in others it strengthens
commitment to the family left behind, and willingness to forego personal aspirations.
Sometimes these tendencies appear simultaneously and a new identity develops.

In answer to the questions: How do you live with the fact of not being married? Doesn't
the family at home put pressure on you? Charity replied:

> *"They push and push me…but I'm here and they are there…so in the end I'm
> the one that decides (laughs). Look at Amy, she has a husband, so she can't
> do what she wants…even if she is dead after work, she comes home and
> cooks for both of them…But still I think that Amy and others who are mar-
> ried are different here than at home. Here they have their own money…they
> don't tell their husband, so they are free to do some things, like buying
> clothes or doing their hair or giving donations in the church…Most of the
> fights between men and women in Israel are about money…How much to
> send home? To which side of the family? When you are living abroad, your
> family depends on you and they say to you: give me…give me all the
> time…This makes problems, they think we must give them money, especially
> if they helped you travel or if they look after your kids and your land… I
> don't have a husband, I don't have kids, so I decide what to do with my time,
> with my money. I save some, I send some to my mom and sisters. They built
> me a house. When I go back I will stay there. I have no other home. When I
> get old and have kids I will go back there"*. (Charity, Tel Aviv 2000)

Charity and many other women saw themselves as independent, strong women, with
fairly good life and work skills, living without male protection. Yet, they also perceived
themselves as Ghanaian women, linked to their extensive family, with specific obligations
and responsibilities. Although many of them were critical of the marriage system back

home, they did not object to getting married and having children, even though they did not want to play the customary inferior role. Their relations with their extended family back home were also portrayed in a dual way: on the one hand they were important and vital, and on the other hand as burdensome and vexatious. Every woman mentioned that she would not have been able to leave Africa and improve her lot without her family's support, so she is beholden to them. However, all of them added that their obligations are burdensome to them, making it harder for them to fulfill their dreams; they deepen the cultural gap and bind them to the home they left behind. The conflict between their personal aspirations and those connected to family and community life is clearly evident.

Conflicting values were also apparent in their attitude to couple relationships, marriage and the woman's place within it. In this respect the findings are particularly interesting, since some of the women arrived in Israel already married, others got married in Israel, while some returned home to marry. Gina, a 26-year-old labor-migrant from Nigeria, highlighted the dilemma related to marriage and couple relationships, while explaining how she got to know her husband:

> "I met Marc about three years ago. He is from Nigeria, but not from my home town. I thought he is a good man. He worked. We got married...not like at home, but he did send gifts to my parents...They preferred I get married, though this was not the man they wanted for me...For them it was less bad than if I stay here alone...They said that a woman with no man in Israel means trouble, that people say bad things about her...Even in our community here people said to me I better get married...They said that a woman alone is no good...I had no choice. My family back home did not want me to go back home to get married, because they needed the money I was sending from here". (Gina, June 2000)

Clearly she had no choice in the matter of marriage, even though she did choose her partner. She did not mention love. However, she did say that although they were married in Israel, her husband still behaved in a rather traditional way. In other words, in spite of being both physically and culturally away from home, both partners considered it important to adhere to some of the traditional dictates.

Gina's remarks about marriage enable us to include in our discourse considerations underlying migration not directly connected to the economic situation: While economic reasons undoubtedly figured in the decision to migrate and in the family's support, the family's dilemma reveals that status and prestige were also involved. These findings resemble those of Pessar's study of Dominican women and their extended families, and Wolf's study of Indonesian women (Pessar, 1995/1999; Woolf, 1992). Gina and her family had to confront conflicting considerations, because she migrated on her own, which was a stain on the family's reputation. Gina's family insisted that she should marry, while Gina demanded her right to partial autonomy within their rigid value system. Her physical distance from home and control of her financial resources enabled her to achieve such autonomy. Her marriage shows the solution they found, accepted on all sides, which included economic, value-laden as well as personal considerations. Such solutions bridge the gaps between the migrant's aspirations, the new society and the family tradition.

In a Bible class about love and marriage, the Ghanaian priest Ampadu explained the situation his community faced:

> *"Back home most of us don't get married because they are in love — as they say...Our families choose for us...they don't force us like in the old days. But here, in Israel, because of how we live and because we can't travel, there are so many changes...Some of the things we do like back home and some we do like we think we should do here. We want to look after you, after your sacred bond of marriage, but in Israel things change so much. It is not easy for us"*. (Pastor Y. Ampadu, May 1999)

Here we can discern the complexity of the lives of transnational migrants, trying to preserve their traditions and yet adapting them to changes, due also to their inability to travel since they arrived undocumented. His comments, as well as the story behind Gina's marriage, reveal the dilemmas faced by migrants in their physical and spiritual relocation from one home to another. Their move expands the conceptual boundaries of 'home', 'dispersion', and 'country of immigration', as well as of concepts such as: 'couple relationship', 'marriage' and 'love', and makes them somewhat flexible and fluid. This enables the migrants to avoid complete disengagement from their original home, and at the same time does not compel them to adopt wholeheartedly the values of their new home. Furthermore, our data shows that their perception of the values prevalent in their new home appears to include not only western values and in particular those of Israeli society, but also those underlying the life of the African community in Israel. Thus the migrants' world draws upon several sources of values and identities, which they examine carefully and critically.

The Price of Belonging: The Watchful Eye of "The Community"

Both Charity and Gina were closely connected to African migrants in Israel and their opinions were important to them, even if not always to their liking. They realized that the price they had to pay for their membership in that community was also — or maybe mainly — the acceptance of clear boundaries of what is permitted, what is considered morally acceptable or unacceptable. Like others, they were painfully aware of the community's power in this respect, and of its impact on their behavior. Following Benedict Anderson we may say that the African community in Israel functioned not only as an active framework with fees and regular activities, but also, and maybe mainly, as a representational system, bestowing on its members a sense of belonging and identity, and thereby dictating specific modes of behavior. Thus, although Gina was a migrant in a strange city, far from her family and free to choose her own way of life, she acted according to the unwritten laws of a somewhat loose community. In spite of the distance from home and the precepts of traditional African society, the fear of not belonging to any community caused her to feel trapped under the watchful eye of "the community". Its power and the sense of being trapped is evident in Gina's description of her difficult marriage:

> *"After we got married Marc started to beat me...he came from work, went to drink and then came home and asked me — Where is your money?...What*

did you do all day?...Why are you spending all the money? — He was beating and screaming...He thought I was his slave. I was working all day too. He made money and I made money. But at the end of the day he would go to drink and wanted me to go home and cook for him...and clean...Even when I was pregnant he beat me. I did not tell my friends but some knew...one of them told me that she will speak with her pastor and he will talk with my husband...but I refused. One of them told me she will ask her Israeli friends what to do...I did not want to go to the police because I have no visa and I did not want them to deport me...I did not want the police to come home. If I go to the police, then all those in our community will not talk with me. They don't want us to go to the police...but I told Marc I will go to the police...After my daughter was born, I had to go back to work...now I need money also for babysitting and for all those things...he does not give much...Three months ago he was arrested and sent home. Now he always calls and wants me to send him money. I don't want to".
(Gina, June 2000)

Her story reflects a painful sense of stifling loneliness, of helplessness in the face of violence. When asked why she did not approach Israeli authorities to stop the violence, she spoke about her existential dilemma: stopping the violence by involving the police — as opposed to the fear (justified or unfounded) that she would be ostracized by the local African community. She preferred to suffer from his violent behavior rather than be rejected by her own community. This would mean that besides being a battered migrant, without a visa and in danger of being deported, she would be isolated and expelled from the only social framework she belonged to.

Gina's refusal to turn to the law enforcement authorities for help is in line with the behavior of battered women worldwide and not merely typical of migrant or African women. However, it is noteworthy that Gina mentioned people from her community who urged her to insist on her right to be treated fairly, and considered this to be desirable in the eyes of the community, and also turning to the Israeli authorities as legitimate. These African women had a less stringent view of the repressive nature of their society than Gina. Yet Gina perceived their advice as subversive and too costly for her. Paradoxically, her husband's deportation was for her a saving grace.

Her desire for independence together with her fear of radical changes is clearly evident also in the way she describes her future life. In answer to the question how she would like to be as a person, she said:

"I don't know...I really don't know how to say it. I think I want to be stronger than my mother. But I don't want to be like you, Israeli women, who boss everyone in the house, give orders, scream at their husband. No. I don't want that...Your men divorce you because you are like that...It is hard for me to say how to be".

Within the wide range of possibilities open to her, including the African way of life as she experiences it and life in the western world, she no longer accepted the former but did not wish to undermine it. Nor did she totally accept the way of life in the new country. Gina described her home as a place where women are considered the property of men, and they had little possibility to live on their own or to negotiate regarding issues such as married life, the gender division of labor, responsibility and financial matters. Her perception of Israeli women stems from that what she has observed in Israel. She had left her family in order to improve her life economically and personally, so as not to follow in her mother's footsteps. While insisting on choosing her husband, she did not leave him in spite of his violent behavior; and yet she does not wish to resemble Israeli women who pay the high price of divorce for their autonomy.

"He...Wants Me to Send Him Money. I Don't Want to" — Does Money Mean Power?

Gina is committed to her home and family, while insisting on her right to make decisions contrary to her parents' and husband's wishes. In being able to decide to whom and how much money to send, she actually redefines the boundaries of the patriarchal nature of the relationships. She creates a new framework of rules for the institution of marriage, combining her own views with those of her extended family.

Control of financial resources was a focal point in the discourse of many African women. In Israel they were exposed to a system where the responsibility for the family's capital and for the household and the children appeared to them as shared, even though equality in this respect is far from complete in reality. They perceived the African couple relationship as oppressive and discriminatory. In Israel, in trying to change that situation, married African women chose to conceal their real earnings from their husbands to enable them to make some autonomous decisions. However, this procedure, like in many other migrant communities world wide, did not change the power relations within their married life in any substantial way.[17]

In recent years, in the wake of the feminization of migration, many researchers maintain that women have become social agents, making autonomous choices. While crossing national borders in the global world, they have redefined the institution of marriage and the gender division of labor.[18] Gina's words and reports by others reveal a more complex situation; the crossing of physical borders is *insufficient* for the redefinition of basic institutions and for radical changes in value-laden attitudes. In her article "Maid or Madam", Pei-Chia Lan asserts that women labor-migrants who sell their work on the global market acquire economic power within the family structure. However, this power does not effect a substantial change in their status, since they continue to bear the heavy burden in their family, fulfilling traditional female functions (Pei-Chia Lan, 2003).

Similarly to Philippino women migrants, many African migrants are trapped. In the eyes of her parents and her husband, Gina appears to challenge the institution of marriage, as she knows it, by demanding more freedom of choice regarding her body (her feminity), her work and her earnings. She does so by refusing to send money to her husband. According to Spitzer,[19] the issues raised by Gina as to her rights as a married woman can be defined as renegotiating the gender division of roles and the process of decision-making within the family. While relating to Puerto Rican women migrants in the USA, Toro-Morn Maura (1995) maintains that even in developed western societies marriages hamper changes.

Judging by Gina's case and Charity's perception of marriage, it appears that *women's migration-related achievements are curtailed owing to marriages*. The achievements of migration as a strategy for survival and advancement in the sphere of gender relations in the social and domestic domains have thus been limited owing to the rigid norms of the African institution of marriage.

My study reveals that simultaneously with the rise in the status of African women migrants in Israel, there has been a drop in their partners' status. African men in Israel have been compelled not only to do cleaning work, considered feminine in Africa, but also to receive instructions from Israeli women (and sometimes young girls). In interviews I conducted with African men who had lived in Israel and returned home, many of them mentioned that fact as one of their hardest and most humiliating experiences as labor-migrants.[20] One evening, displaying unusual frankness, a Ghanaian said to me:

> *"I will never marry an Israeli woman...you don't know how to take care of your man...You think that you are smart like God who created the world...you think you have much power and much brain...If I was married to an Israeli, I would stop being a man...When I go to work and my boss is a woman and she tells me what to do, I feel bad...but she has the money, she pays me....I always look at her husband and he says nothing...I don't understand it. Sorry".* (Jonathan, Tema Ghana Ja, 2005)

Conclusion

Kamir (2004), relating to women's struggle worldwide, maintained that it was impossible to erase thousands of years of oppression in one day, merely by passing a law...She perceived it as an ongoing process. And indeed, in examining the situation among African women labor migrants in Israel, we cannot point to any rapid change, headed in one specific direction. The findings of my study are congruent with research about women migrants in other parts of the world.[21] There is no clear progression from submissive women arriving from Africa, obeying the rules of a male dominant society, to women equal in status to men, with a high self-concept, able to act at will. These women, probably like million others around the world, live in a hybrid reality — both traditional and western, progressive and conservative, empowering and debilitating, liberating as well as oppressive. The forging of an identity in such a complex situation calls for awareness of ongoing changes in the environment and for flexibility and ability to adapt to them.

The women's life stories enabled us to identify survival strategies they adopted to cope with the situations, and we focused on the ways they objected, compromised, adapted and argued regarding resources, rights and obligations. Our analysis of these processes reinforces the perception that migration per se shakes up some of the basic values of the migrating group and leads to a reexamination, both by women and men, of the interplay of power in such areas as marriage, divorce, family structure and the gender-related division of labor. The findings of this study show that identities and modes of consciousness do not grow on the ruins of the old, but rather develop through long processes of complex individual and political, sometimes dialectical, struggles.

The women's migration from Africa to Israel, in particular when they are on their own, points to a growing awareness of their ability to cope with the difficulties of daily life, even in a place physically and culturally far removed from their homes. In the course of the years they have maneuvered between their personal needs and the demands of their families, their own desires and the unwritten laws of the immigrant community. Many women are well aware of the price they have to pay for each choice they make, and those who choose greater autonomy and freedom appear well aware of the cost. Nevertheless, the women's discourse shows that in reality there is no unambiguous dichotomy between their several worlds, and they have been able to fashion a life where the community, the family, mutual responsibility and a sense of belonging exist side by side with independence and autonomy, within the heart of their experience as African women migrants in Israel.

We may say that our analysis of the reality of these women's lives, as they have chosen to describe it, negates the accepted dichotomous perception, postulating tradition versus modernity, African versus Western, feminine versus male occupations, emotional versus rational and so on. It appears that every woman finds her own way and place within the wide range of possibilities along the continuum between autonomy and bondage, between freedom to act and acceptance of conventions, between the need to break through boundaries and the existential need to safeguard her family heritage as a source of strength in times of crisis.

Notes

1. This study is based on 24 open-ended in-depth interviews, conducted in Israel and in Africa, and many hundreds of hours of participant observations of different activities of African migrants in Israel. Interviewees were located through snowballing, beginning with an African friend of mine who introduced me to many other members of the African community. The interviewees consisted of an almost equal number of men and women, aged 20–40, from various African countries, mainly Ghana and Nigeria. Once the interviews were under way, the interviewees were encouraged to talk freely about their daily lives in Israel, with minimal interference other than requests for examples and clarifications. Participant observations began shortly after the first interview and were carried out throughout the interviewing process. The interviews were transcribed, verbatim insofar as possible, in the course of the conversation or immediately afterwards. The transcripts and notes from the interviews and observations were analyzed using the constant comparative method (Strauss, A. L., & Corbin, J. M. (1998). *Basics of qualitative research: Techniques and procedures for developing grounded theory* (2nd ed.). London: Sage Publication.

   For further discussion on Qualitative research methodologies, see: Dayan, I. (1999). The methodology of qualitative research — A case study. In: A. Shai, & Bar-Shalom (Eds), *Qualitative research in education*. Tel Aviv: Hemmed, 73–90 (in Hebrew); Sabar Ben Yehoshua, N. (1998). *Kibutz LA*. New York: Sunny Press; Sabar Ben Yehoshua, N. (Ed.). (2001). *Genres and traditions in qualitative research*. Tel Aviv: Dvir (in Hebrew).
2. On the reasons for opening Israel to international-migrant laborers, mainly the Palestinian uprising, see: Sabar, G. (2004). African Christianity in the Jewish state: Adaptation,

accommodation and legitimization of migrant workers' churches 1990–2003. *Journal of Religion in Africa, 34*(4), 407–437.

3. *The Law of Return* (1950) entitles Jews from anywhere in the world to immigrate to Israel and grants them automatic citizenship upon their arrival in the country. Non-Jews, by contrast, have almost no legal avenues to citizenship. Israel does not allow residence without a work permit, does not recognize right of family reunification, and does not guarantee access to housing, social benefits or medical care. It does, however, allow for the arrest and expulsion of undocumented migrants at any time by simple administrative decree. One of the main outcomes of this self-definition as a Jewish state is the prevalent perception in Israel that labor migrants are temporary workers and not prospective citizens; they are outsiders culturally, socially and politically.

4. The African Workers Union, the General Federation of Trade in Israel, African Church leaders and other NGOs.

5. Margaret, P. (1995). Ghanaians abroad. *African affairs*, 94, 345–367; Attah Poku, A. (1996). *The socio-cultural adjustment question — The role of Ghanaian immigrant ethnic association in America.* Aldershot: Avebury; Adepoju, A. (1998). Emigration dynamics in Sub-Saharan Africa. In: R. Appleyard (Ed.), *Emigration dynamics in developing countries* (Vol. I: Sub-Saharan Africa). Abingdon: Bookpoint.

6. Adepoju, A. (2004). Trends in international migration in and from Africa. In: D. S. Massey, & J. E. Taylor (Eds). *International migration prospects and policies in a global market*. Oxford: Oxford University Press; Adepoju, A. (2004). Review of research and data on human trafficking in Sub-Saharan Africa. Paper presented at the IOM International Expert Meeting on Improving Data and Research on Human Trafficking, Rome, 27–28 May; Adepoju, A. (2003). Continuity and changing configurations of migration to and from the Republic of South Africa. *International Migration, 41*(1); (2002). Women in the brain drain: Gender and skilled migration from South Africa, Migration Policy Series No. 23; Belinda, D. (2002). Discrimination by default? Gender concerns in South African migration policy. *Africa Today, 48*(3), 73–89; Ulicki, T., & Crush, J. (Eds.) (2000). Poverty and women's migrancy: Lesotho farmworkers in the eastern free state". In: *Borderline farming: Foreign migrants in South African commercial agriculture*, Migration Policy Series No. 16; Ulicki, T., & Crush, J. (2002). Gender, farmwork, and women's migration from Lesotho to the New South Africa. In: J. Crush, & D. A. McDonald (Eds), *Transnationalism and New African immigration to South Africa.* Toronto: Southern Publishers.

7. Ehrenreich, B., & Hochschild, A. R. (Eds). (2003). *Global women nannies, maids and sex workers in the new economy*. New York: Henry Hold Books; Hondagneu-Sotelo, P. (1992). Overcoming patriarchal constraints: The reconstitution of gender among Mexican immigrant women and men. *Gender and Society*, 6, 393–415; Hondagneu-Sotelo, P. (1994). *Gendered transitions: Mexican experiences of immigration.* Berkeley, CA: University of California Press; Hondagneu-Sotelo, P. (2001). *Domestica, immigrant workers cleaning and caring in the shadows of affluence.* Berkeley, CA: University of California Press; Morokvasic, M. (1984). Birds of passage are also women. *International Migration Review, 18*, 886–907; Pedraza, S. A. (1991), Pessar, P. (1999). Engendering migration studies, *American Behavioral Scientist, 42*, 577–600; Phizacklea, A. (1983). *One way ticket: Migration and female labor.* Boston: Routledge Kegam Paul;

Salazar Parrenas, R. (2000). Migrant Filipina domestic workers and the international division of reproductive labor. *Gender and Society, 14*(4), 560–581; Salazar Parrenas, R. (2001). *Servants of globalization: Women, migration and domestic work.* Stanford, CA: Stanford University Press; Wong, D. (1996). Foreign domestic workers in Singapore. *Asian and Pacific Migration Journal, 5,* 117–138.

8. Hochschild, A. R. (2000). The nanny chain. *American Prospect, 4,* 32–36; Hondagneu-Sotelo, P. (2001). Hondagneu-Sotelo, P., & Avila, E. (1997). I'm here, but I'm there. The meanings of Latina transnational motherhood. *Gender and Society, 11,* 548–571.

9. On the debate regarding globalization and women's labor, see: Berkowitz, N. (2002). Apocalypse now? — On globalization and other problems. *Israeli Sociology, 4*(2), 471–472.

10. The only published work that deals specifically with the African migrant laborers in Israel is Sabar, G. (2004). I'm a Black Christian illegal worker in Jewish Israel. In: A. Kleinberg (Ed.), *Hard to believe — A different perspective on religiosity* (pp. 15–95). Tel Aviv: Tel Aviv University Press. Several MA theses have been published on different aspects of the African community, all in Hebrew. On migrant workers in Israel, including the Africans, see: Bar Zuri, R. (1996). Ovdim Zarim in Israel; Nathanzon, R. (Ed.), *The new labor market* (pp. 13–34). Jerusalem Ministry of Economics (in Hebrew); Schnell, I., & Graicer, I. (1994). Rejuvenation of population in Tel-Aviv inner city. *The Geographical Journal, 160*(2), 185–197; Rosenhek, Z. (1999). The politics of claims-making by labour migrants in Israel. *Journal of Ethnic and Migration Studies, 25*(4), 575–595; Kemp, A., Raijman, R., Resnik, J., & Schammah Gesser, S. (2000). Contesting the limits of political participation: Latinos and black African migrant workers in Israel. *Ethnic and Racial Studies, 23*(1), 94–119; Kemp, A., & Raijman, R. (2003). Christian Zionists in the holy land: Evangelical churches, labor migrants and the Jewish state. *Identities: Global Studies in Culture and Power, 10,* 295–318. See: Kandiyoti, D. (1988). Bargaining with patriarchy. *Gender and Society, 2*(3), 274–290.

11. I am aware of the problem regarding the concepts 'African women' or 'African women migrants'. Africa is a large continent with a tremendous variety of societies and cultures, and any generalizations, in particular about women, arouse doubts about the validity of research pronouncements. Such questions arise regarding countries such as Nigeria and Ghana, owing to their ethnic and religious diversity. I am aware of these differences, and the qualitative method I have chosen (explained in detail later) enables me to confront this problem; I move from the individual to the general, reducing the problems inherent in terms such as African or Ghanaian women. See: Appadurai, A. (1991). Global ethnoscopes: Notes and queries for a transnational anthropology. In: R. G. Fox (Ed.), *Recapturing anthropology* (pp. 191–210). Santa Fe NM: School of American Research Press and Basch, L. G., Schiller, N. G., & Blanc, C. S. (1994). *Nations unbound: Transnational projects, postcolonial predicaments and deterritorialized nation states.* London: Routledge.

12. On similar conflicts see for example: Spitzer, D., Neufeld, A., Harrison, M., & Hughes, K. (2003). Caregiving in transnational context, "My wings have been cut" where can I fly? *Gender and Society, 17*(2), 267.

13. Pérez-Herranz, C. A. (1996). Our two full-time jobs: Women garment workers balance factory and domestic demands in Puerto Rico. In: A. Ortiz (Ed.), *Puerto Rican women*

and work: Bridges in transnational labor. Philadelphia: Temple University Press; Aranda, E. M. (2003). Global care work and gender constraints. The case of Puerto Rican transmigrants, *Gender and society, 17*(4), 609–626; Wendy, C. (2004, December). Gendered religious organizations: The case of Theravada Buddhism in America. *Gender Society, 18,* 777–793; Carolyn, C. (2005, June). A self of one's own: Taiwanese immigrant women and religious conversion. *Gender Society, 19,* 336–357; Itzigsohn, J. (2000). Immigration and the boundaries of citizenship: The institutions of immigrants' political transnationalism, *International Migration Review, 34*(132), 1126–1154; Lowell, L., & Gerova, S. G. (2004). *Diaspora and economic development: State of knowledge,* Working paper of the Institute for the Study of International Migration, Georgetown University; Vertovec, S. (2004). *Trends and impacts of migrant transnationalism,* Working Paper no. 3, Centre on Migration, Policy and Society, University of Oxford; Fox, J., & Salgado, G. R. (2005). Building civil society among indigenous migration. *US-Mexicao Policy Bulletin,* Vol. 7, August.

14. The initial appearance of this phenomenon can be found already at the start of European colonial rule in the 19th century. An active civil society existed even under oppressive colonial rule, and continued to do so in the independent states, even where civil freedom was limited by a dictatorial regime. See: Sabar, G. (2002). *Church, state and society in Kenya — From mediation to opposition, 1963–1993.* London: Frank Cass; Sabar-Friedman, G. (1996). The power of the familiar: Everyday practice in the Anglican church of Kenya, *Church and State, 38,* 377–397.

15. Although these studies dealt mainly with immigrants, some of them residents or citizens with full rights who acquired an advanced profession in that country before returning home, their perception of the profession as the main means to a successful return was the same as that of the women migrants in Israel. Ammassari, S., & Black, R. (2001). From Nation-building to enterpreneurship: the impact of elite return migrants in Cote d'Ivioire and Ghana. Paper presented at the International workshop on migration and poverty in West Africa, March, 2005; "Home, sweet home — for some, How can Africa move from brain drain to brain gain?" *The Economist,* August 11, 2005; Ammassari, S., & Black, R. (2001). Harnessing the potential of migration and return to promote development: Applying concepts to West Africa. Geneva IOM, *Migration Research Series* 5; Diatta, M. A., & Mbow, N. (1999). Releasing the development potential of return migration: the case of Senegal. *International Migration, 37*(1), 243–266; OECD. (2001). *International Moblity of the Highly Skilled.* Paris: OCED.

16. Virginia, W. (1981). *A Room of one's own.* Tel Aviv: Shocken (translated into Hebrew); Yisraeli, D. (1999). Gender relations in the world of work. In: D. Israeli, A. Friedman, H. Dahan Caleb, H. Hertzog, M. Hassan, H. Naveh, & S. Fogiel-Bijaoui (Eds), *Sex, gender and politics.* Tel aviv: Hakibbutz Hameuhad; Friedan, B. (1997). *Beyond gender: The new politics of work and family.* In: B. O'Farrell (Ed.), Washington, D.C.: Woodrow Wilson Center Press; Friedan, B. (1963). *The feminine mystique.* New York: W. W. Norton. See: Pessar, P. (1995). Introduction. In: *A visa for a dream: Dominicans in the United States.* New York: Allyn & Bacon.

17. On financial strategies adopted by migrant women see for example: Carolyn, C. (2005). A self of one's own: Taiwanese immigrant women and religious conversion. *Gender Society, 19,* 336–357; Pei-Chia, L. (2003). Maid or madam? Filipino migrant workers

and the continuity of domestic labor. *Gender Society*, *17*, 187–208; Raijman, R., Schammah-Gesser, S. & Kemp, A. (2003). International migration, domestic work, and care work: Undocumented Latina migrants in Israel. *Gender Society*, *17*, 727–749; Zentgraf, K. M. (2002). Immigration and women's empowerment: Salvadorans in Los Angeles. *Gender Society*, *16*, 625–646; Predelli, L. N. (2004). Interpreting gender in Islam: A case study of immigrant Muslim women in Oslo, Norway. *Gender Society*, *18*, 473–493; Killian, C. (2003). The other side of the veil: North African women in France respond to the headscarf affair. *Gender Society*, *17*, 567–590.

18. Raijman, R., Schammah-Gesser, S., & Kemp, A. (2003). International migration, domestic work, and care work: Undocumented Latina migrants in Israel. *Gender Society*, *17*, 727–749; Zentgraf, K. M. (2002). Immigration and women's empowerment: Salvadorans in Los Angeles. *Gender Society*, *16*, 625–646; Hondagneu-Sotelo, P. (2001). *Domestica, immigrant workers cleaning and caring in the shadows of affluence.* Berkeley, CA: University of California Press; Pessar, P. (1999). Engendering migration studies. *American Behavioral Scientist*, *42*, 577–600; Salazar Parrenas, R. (2000). Migrant Filipina domestic workers and the international division of reproductive labor. *Gender and society*, *14*(4), 560–581; Salazar Parrenas, R. (2001). *Servants of globalization: Women, migration and domestic work.* Stanford, CA: Stanford University Press.

19. Spitzer, D., Neufeld, A., Harrison, M., Hughes, K., & Stewart, M. (2003). Caregiving in a transnational context — My wings have been cut: where can I fly? *Gender and Society*, *17*(2), 267; Toro-Morn, M. I. (1995). Gender, class family and migration: Puerto Rican women in Chicago. *Gender and Society,* *9*(6), 712–726.

20. Interviews conducted with Michael, in Kumasi Ghana Jan. 2005 and Atto Bayo in Kumasi Jan. 2005 and with Chief, Accra Ghana, Jan. 2005. See: Kamir, O. (2004). Lecture given at Tel Aviv University, April.

21. De Jong, G. F. (November, 2000). Expectations, gender, and norms in migration decision-making. *Population Studies*, *54*(3) 307–319; Yang, X., & Guo, F. (Winter, 1999). Gender differences in determinants of temporary labor migration in China: A multilevel analysis. *International Migration Review*, *33*(4), 929–953; Hoy, C. (1999). Gender preference for children and its consequences for migration in China. *Geografiska Annaler. Series B, Human Geography*, *81*(1), 41–53; Kanaiaupuni, S. M. (June, 2000). Reframing the migration question: An analysis of men, women, and gender in Mexico. *Social Forces*, *78*(4), 1311–1347; Tacoli, C. (Autumn, 1999). International migration and the restructuring of gender asymmetries: Continuity and change among Filipino labor migrants in Rome. *International Migration Review*, *33*(3), 658–682; Boyle, P., Cooke, T. J., Halfacree, K., & Smith, D. (May, 2001). A cross-national comparison of the impact of family migration on women's employment status. *Demography*, *38*(2), 201–213.

Image 29.1. African migrant laborer with child, on the streets of Tel Aviv.

Image 29.2. Migrant laborer at her temporary home with her child.

Chapter 30

Humanitarian Care in Haiti and Rwanda

Anne E. McCarthy

Many health-care providers seek out international or global health activities. These activities may be undertaken early in their medical career while still in training, or during their peak career years, often increasing at the time of retirement. Most of these people have a desire to use their medical expertise to give back to those most in need, hopefully this service includes strengthening of the local healthcare delivery in their host countries. During my 20-year career with the Canadian Military (Canadian Forces, Department of National Defence), I had the privilege of deploying for a month or more on two very memorable occasions, to Rwanda and Haiti. The following pages will outline some of my experiences and lessons learned. I hope that these words may encourage others to explore beyond their own borders and comfort zones, qualities that are often an intimate part of international health activities.

In 1995, I went to Kigali, Rwanda where I worked with the Australian Military on a medical/surgical ward at the Central Hospital of Kigali. Our main assignment was to look after the ill United Nations personnel serving in Rwanda. In truth, much of our time was spent looking after children brought in from the many area orphanages as well as civilian and military trauma victims. I had been sent to fill the position of the Tropical Medicine Specialist, but spent a lot of time providing medical and other care that had little to do with the management of infectious diseases, and was remarkably different from my regular Canadian employment.

Trauma is an important cause of morbidity and mortality in the developing world, and an important cause of death in travelers, mostly due to motor vehicle-related mishaps. We certainly saw our share of motor vehicle-related trauma, whether it was pedestrians being hit by poorly maintained vehicles or numerous people being thrown from the back (or the top) of an overcrowded vehicle. There was however, one day of trauma that sticks out from the rest. It was the rainy season; 9 months after the war ended and 12 months after the president had been shot down. The population of Kigali was in flux, with estimates that it was increasing substantially (some claimed doubling) each week. People were returning to their land, or else they were laying claim to the land that others had deserted. The population was trying to get back to more normal life activities including farming. Unfortunately, the

Travel Medicine: Tales Behind the Science
Copyright © 2007 by Elsevier Ltd.
All rights of reproduction in any form reserved.
ISBN: 0-08-045359-7

recent war had made a lot of farmland unsafe. What was worse, because of the heavy rains, some areas thought to be safe a couple of weeks earlier were no longer safe as the rains washed away soil and at times unearthed wartime souvenirs. During the war there were many mines planted and never retrieved, as well there were grenades and unexploded arsenal all around. On an otherwise sunny morning we received our first mine victims, a pair of 20-year-old cousins who found a mine close to their home and decided to bring it into the kitchen to explore it further. One cousin walked outside the front door to retrieve something when he heard the explosion — he was lucky. His cousin, seated in front of the explosive when it went off did not fair as well; he expired in the hospital resuscitation room. Within a couple of hours we received a 29-year-old lady who was 29-weeks pregnant, having endured three previous unsuccessful pregnancies. She was working on the family land when she stepped on a mine — one leg was blown off and the other was severely damaged. She also lost her index and 5th fingers on the right and 2nd, 3rd, and 4th digits on her left hand. That night she went into premature labor and lost the baby. She did survive, with severe deficits and little hope of having a productive life with her degree of disability. While we were carrying out the initial resuscitation of the lady above, we heard AND felt the next mine go off, indicating that it was in close proximity to the hospital. A thirty-two-year-old man had stepped on a land mine and had severe injuries to both of his feet, necessitating bilateral amputations. Otherwise he had relatively minor injuries and recovered. Later that evening there were a group of children rushed to the hospital, they had been playing with a grenade that they had found close to home, when it went off. Surprisingly, none were killed, but one boy lost most of one hand and had wounds to his trunk and face, the three other children had less severe injuries.

There were many infectious and vaccine-preventable diseases that we saw in the UN troops and in the local population. These included malaria, respiratory tract infections (tuberculous and nontuberculous), meningitis, and lots of complications of HIV/AIDS. There were two cases of tetanus during my short stay. The first, admitted just before I arrived, required intubation, ventilation, and paralysis for 6 weeks, a treatment not readily available in any other hospital in the country. In fact, this treatment put a drain on the military medical resources, and forced my anesthesia colleague to acquire and use curare as a paralytic agent; he had no previous experience with this historical agent. Infectious diseases were common, and despite the availability of a relatively well-equipped laboratory by African standards, we often did not have a definitive diagnosis, and relied on syndrome management.

The courage and fortitude of the human spirit is always something to be admired, and is demonstrated daily by those embracing life at times of strife. There was one 8-year-old boy, who walked with his Dad for eight days to come to Kigali because of fever and abdominal pain. At surgery he was found to have a ruptured appendix and quite severe peritonitis. He received a course of antibiotics postoperatively and then he and his Dad, who slept under his bed to provide him basic care during the perioperative course, set out for the long walk home. For a couple of weeks on the medical ward we had a young girl who sang like an angel. She had an often devastating but common childhood injury in Africa; she was burned by the household cooking fire, resulting in severe burns to her neck and chest. Because this injury occurred just as the war broke out she was unable to get any medical attention. This resulted in severe scarring and adhesions — with her chin scared down onto her chest. She had surgical release of her contractures with good results, but would likely require further surgery as she grows and matures, and there is no guarantee that she will be able to get that surgery.

Some of the best health intervention that I was part of in Rwanda was actually spear headed by the deployed soldiers, who were experts in engineering and logistics, and had no formal medical training. These individuals spent their infrequent hours of leisure visiting local orphanages and finding out and providing what was needed. They found and delivered water bladders, built latrines, screened windows and doors (were they existed), and repaired or created plumbing. They also dragged along any medical people they could find to assess the children. On one Sunday morning we visited an orphanage run by two young nursing graduates from France, with the help of a local lady who volunteered her time. It was during visits like these that I really had to take off my doctor's hat and look at things from a public health and preventive perspective — was there safe food and water, minimization of injury potential, protection from preventable diseases? It was amazing and very humbling to see what they were accomplishing, and how much benefit they were providing to the 200 or so children in their care, with minimal resources. The children were clothed and slept safely, often more than a few to a bed, with bed nets to prevent malaria. They received at least one balanced meal per day, with meat available usually twice weekly. The older children acted as extended family to the young. Older children were being given vocational training — using sewing machines and tools purchased from donations from our troops. There was school activity going on and attention to preventive medical care, including a make shift infirmary where children received minor medical care and routine vaccines, with records kept for each child. For a number of orphanages that we visited, it became obvious over time that, fortunately, many of the children had surviving relatives to whom they could be returned. This proved a fine balancing act for a number of children perceived themselves far better-off in the orphanage rather than at home where resources were even more limited. Most of those in charge of these orphanages were very cognizant of this potential and worked hard to empower the children to thrive at home as well.

In Haiti, I worked with a handful of Canadian colleagues along with the U.S. Army, Navy, and Marines, where we were responsible for looking after the military troops and foreign police assisting the government. We also provided humanitarian care through outpatient clinics in Port-aux-Prince and throughout the countryside. These clinics were often carried out in conjunction with local healthcare providers and included a "surgical" clinic each Saturday at the port. This clinic was run by the Sisters of Charity, continuing to look after the poorest of the poor. We provided general medical care, as well as minor surgical care, including dental extractions, to the hundreds of people who lined up each Saturday morning. The severely ill would be transferred to the local hospital and ill young children would be admitted for a night or two to the ward in the orphanage run by the Sisters. Near the end of the clinic one Saturday, an 18-month-old was carried into the clinic by his mother — he was severely dehydrated, lethargic, and unresponsive due to a diarrheal illness. As well, the mother had noted that he had stopped wetting his diaper in the past 12 hours. We were not really set up for acute resuscitation in the clinic, but did have IVs and fluid so we found a flat surface to lay him down and one of our nurses with extensive pediatric experience tried unsuccessfully to put in an IV. We lacked an interosseous needle and did not have the capability of placing central line, so we improvised. I grabbed an 18-gauge needle, cleaned off his leg and placed it into his tibia. We started resuscitating fluid to the child and had the most gratifying experience when he opened his eyes and actually urinated on me! Our Lazarus child (picture) was watched for a couple of days at the convent orphanage and later discharged home.

So what had all this taught me, besides the ongoing desire to help internationally and to help prepare and mentor those taking on international health challenges? There is no doubt that these experiences have been of far greater benefit to me than to the countries that I visited, providing me with life experience and personal growth that far exceeds any little bit of help that I may have provided. These privileged experiences have taught me about the resourcefulness and the strength of the human spirit. Observing the aftermath of some well-meaning individuals who come in and provide unsustainable healthcare without strengthening the local healthcare services, it taught me repeatedly about the "First do no harm" part of the Oath I took at medical school graduation. These and my ongoing international health activities teach me to be prepared to provide any type of help that may be required, and that may mean carrying beams to help build or refurbish a school or latrine. I undertook my activities in Rwanda and Haiti at a time when I was working as an infectious diseases and tropical medicine consultant at a Canadian academic center, far removed from my days in the trenches as an intern or general practitioner carrying out trauma resuscitation, yet those were the skills that were perhaps utilized most, especially in Rwanda.

These and other international health experiences continuously emphasize, at least to me, the need to provide the help that is required and requested locally and ideally to do it by strengthening local resources and skill so that they can provide the ongoing care that is needed. When planning for such activities it is important to anticipate what you may be faced with, and to make certain that you update any expected skills that might be a little rusty PRIOR to your trip. Always remain flexible and be aware that perhaps the most important thing that you will do is provide training for local healthcare providers or to take off your acute care hat and provide advice on prevention/public health interventions of benefit to the whole community. In the words of Eleanor Roosevelt:

> "You gain strength, courage and confidence by every experience in which you must stop and look fear in the face… you must do the things you think that you cannot do."

Image 30.1. Children admitted to central hospital of Kigali, the older child on the left is actually a caregiver for the little girl on the bed who underwent months of antibiotic therapy and repeated operations for severe tibial osteomyelitis.

Chapter 31

Muslim Pilgrimage

Ziad A. Memish

Introduction

Logistically, the Hajj, the most monumental mass migration of humanity today, would challenge the most highly industrialized nations in the world. Saudi Arabia, a relatively young economy, has fostered the most enormous growth in this religious pilgrimage history has yet seen, with aggressive and rapid modernization in all aspects of Hajj planning: Hajj facilities, procedures, healthcare and policy making are all comprehensive and on an immense scale. Still, there is no sign of slowing in the growth of pilgrim attendance. As Hajj congregations grow in the order of millions, the Kingdom of Saudi Arabia rises to new challenges on colossal scales with relentless drive, challenges that are the focus of this chapter discussion.

The Growth of the Overseas Pilgrimage to Makkah

Hajj is the greatest assembly of humankind on earth. More than 2.5 million Muslims attended Hajj this year (Figure 31.1). Of these, 1.5 million were overseas visitors, 89% of whom arrived by air. The majority of the remainder (10%) arrived by land and 1% by sea. We can expect the Hajj to become bigger: Islam now is a growing religion with 1.3 billion followers of diverse ethnicity from communities within 140 countries.

Over the years, not only has there been growth in numbers, but also resulting demands on planning have also increased. Umrah, a 'mini-pilgrimage' (which the Muslim can undertake at any time of the year) also involves traveling to Makkah and circumambulating the Ka'aba. The steady increase in numbers participating in Umrah throughout the calendar year demonstrate both the increased numbers of Muslims and their growing ability and willingness to travel to Makkah.

Travel Medicine: Tales Behind the Science
Copyright © 2007 by Elsevier Ltd.
All rights of reproduction in any form reserved.
ISBN: 0-08-045359-7

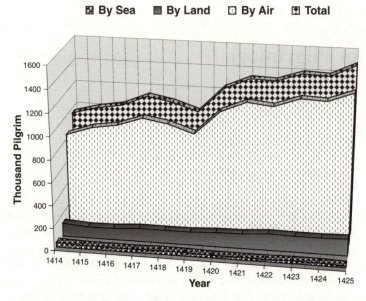

Figure 31.1. The number of overseas pilgrims according to modes of arrival to Hajj between 1414 and 1425H (1994–2005).

The Rites of Hajj

Religious pilgrimage is described in all faiths to a varying degree, but while most are voluntary, the Hajj is considered a mandatory requirement for all Muslims who are eligible. Millions of Muslims make a visit to the Ka'aba, (the house of God) and surrounding holy sites. Over a number of days, their struggle becomes both literal and metaphysical: the pilgrim struggles in a surging current of the faithful as he struggles to absolve his sin through holy rituals. While he seeks to offer prayer, the pilgrim must also struggle against distinct environmental and public health hazards throughout the journey. These hazards have been repeatedly reported for over a hundred years when scientific insights were once limited because few Muslim physicians lived or published in the West.

Each pilgrim, on arrival to Makkah performs an initial circumambulation (*Tawaf*) around the Ka'aba seven times. He then leaves for the Plain of Arafat, a dozen miles east of Makkah, where Hajj culminates in the Day of Standing when all two million stand, supplicating together en masse. Mount Arafat is where the Prophet Mohammed gave his final sermon to his followers and many pilgrims ascend the summit believing prayers here to be most blessed. En route, the pilgrim makes overnight stops for prayer and contemplation in Mina on the way toward Arafat and in Muzdaliffah on return.

After Arafat, pilgrims return through the heaving jams to Muzdaliffah where they gather small stones for the next day's stoning of pillars. On return to Mina, the pilgrimage is complete, and the new Hajjee (a pilgrim who has completed the Hajj) makes an animal sacrifice (often by proxy) as thanks to God for accepting his Hajj. After a final farewell Tawaf of seven circuits around the Ka'aba, the pilgrim leaves Makkah immediately.

Figure 31.2. Extraordinary congestion during the Hajj.

Today we can learn much from Hajj. Pilgrimage presents a unique opportunity to study health issues in a mobile population. Due to massive scale and singular focus on one city, Hajj affords insights no other migration can yet offer (Figure 31.2). Substantial hazards accompany such extraordinary congestion; both health hazards of performing Hajj and the public health concerns relating to the returning pilgrim. Health hazards could be infectious and noninfectious problems encountered during Hajj.

Communicable Hazards at the Hajj

The congestion and the mass migration of the pilgrims bring a number of infectious processes to the fore. Meningococcal disease (MCD), respiratory tract infections, blood-borne, diarrheal and zoonotic diseases all are frequently encountered problems for the pilgrims, either during Hajj or following Hajj. Unique occupational infections affect the abattoir worker at the Hajj and the pilgrims from the barbers, areas that are now firmly addressed by the Saudi authorities. Most concerning are emerging infectious diseases (including SARS/avian influenza) and their devastating potential to spread.

Meningococcal Disease

During Hajj, carrier rates for MCD rise as high as 80% due to intense overcrowding, high humidity and dense air pollution. When carrier rates become so abnormally high, outbreaks are a real public health threat. Additionally, the risk of invasive infection in carriers is compounded by a loss of upper airway epithelial integrity in the setting of upper respiratory tract infection (URTI), which is very common among pilgrims. Many outbreaks of MCD occurred over the years. It started in 1987 with a large outbreak of meningococcal meningitis serogroup A that affected many pilgrims in Makkah and internationally. Bivalent serogroups (A and C) polysaccharide meningococcal vaccine became mandatory requirement for all pilgrims (local and international) and was successful in eliminating future large outbreaks of serogroup A MCD. In the years 2000 and 2001, two large outbreaks of meningococcal meningitis serogroup W135 occurred among hajjis and their family members. A shift in the vaccine requirements for hajj from bivalent to quadrivalent (serogroups A, C, Y, W135) polysaccharide vaccine was successful in eliminating future outbreaks. Continuing concerns with the lack of efficacy of the polysaccharide meningococcal vaccine in children less than 5 years, the lack of efficacy of the polysaccharide vaccine in eliminating nasopharyngeal carriage and the need for repeat dosing every 3 to 5 years have led to greater interest in investigating the role of the newly licensed conjugated quadrivalent meningococcal vaccine (Menactera) during future hajj seasons, since the conjugated meningococcal vaccine is suppose to address all the shortcomings of the polysaccharide vaccine.

Respiratory Tract Infection at the Hajj

Acute respiratory tract infections are very common during the Hajj, particularly so when the pilgrimage falls in the winter season. In this years Hajj and subsequent Hajjs to follow, the influenza season will begin to eclipse the Hajj season, coinciding with one another for some time, magnifying concern for community-acquired pneumonia (CAP).

The close contact among pilgrims during periods of intense congestion, their shared sleeping accommodations (chiefly in tents) and the dense air pollution all combine to increase the risk of airborne respiratory disease transmission. Acute respiratory tract infections are normally very common at the Hajj, with the majority affecting the upper respiratory tract. Involvement of the lower respiratory tract is also seen and specific pilgrim hosts, many of whom will be elderly, are at increased risk due to preexisting comorbidities such as diabetes, renal disease, age, cardiopulmonary disease or underlying immunosuppression.

A viral etiology of URTI is most commonly implicated at the Hajj but bacterial superinfection often follows. More than 200 viruses can cause URTI but at the Hajj the main culprits are respiratory syncytial virus (RSV), parainfluenza, influenza and adenovirus.

Undoubtedly, the intense congestion, living in close proximity with vast crowds and the aging pilgrims constituting so much of the congregation, are all factors magnifying TB risk. Additionally many Muslims travel from countries of high TB endemicity. Air travel must also be considered as a magnifying risk factor for infection since the bulk of pilgrims now enter the Kingdom by air, often after long-distance plane journey. Any infection acquired or incubating not only may be transported to the pilgrim's home country but actually transmitted to fellow passengers. Confined space, long journey time, recirculated air and limited ventilation all compound the risks of transmission of airborne or droplet-spread infection.

As a result, the Ministry of Health (MOH) endeavors to minimize risk of transmission of respiratory illness by modifying high-risk behavior. Pilgrims are encouraged to wear facemasks in order to reduce airborne transmission. Many also wear facemasks to combat air pollution during times of extreme traffic jams.

Influenza vaccine is highly advisable for all pilgrims embarking on Hajj, particularly those over 60 or those with comorbidities to limit complicating bacterial respiratory tract infection. This will become an even more pressing need as the influenza season eclipses Hajj in the lunar years to come.

Skin Infections

Hajj involves long walking, heaving crowds in often hot and humid weather and constant need to perform rituals barefoot when in the Haram mosque. Bacterial skin infections have been well described in the literature in the Hajj pilgrim. Primary pyoderma, including impetigo, carbuncles, furuncles and folliculitis occurred more frequently than secondary pyoderma. Secondary pyoderma complicates eczema most often followed by intertrigo and tinea pedis.

Long rituals of standing and walking, chafing garments, heat, diaphoresis and perhaps obesity in the pilgrim are all factors promoting skin infection. Many reports exist linking pyoderma to heat and physical congestion, so perhaps the findings are unsurprising. Feet and other exposed areas should be protected if necessary, and if the pilgrim notices a new wound, he must seek attention of one of the myriad medical posts at the holy sites. Any pre-existing skin condition should be protected and medicated as appropriate — pilgrims should travel with their usual medications and ointments, which are all permissible during Hajj.

Zoonotic Disease

The proximity of cattle, the massive slaughter of beasts and the intense congestion and chaos of the Hajj period behooves zoonotic disease by a major consideration.

Despite excellent abattoir facilities (Figure 31.3), animals continue to be predominantly slaughtered by laypersons caught up in the joy of ending their Hajj successfully.

Risks of contracting brucellosis, Rift Valley fever (RVF), Crimean-Congo hemorrhagic fever (CCHF) and Orf are significant.

Brucellosis is endemic to Saudi Arabia but to date no outbreak has occurred during Hajj. Imported animals account for about 85% of sacrificed animals, exceeding 6 million in recent years at a cost of $4 billion annually.

A new flavivirus was isolated in 1995 from six patients from south of Jeddah. Patients presented with dengue-like VHF (viral hemorrhagic fever) and the pathogen has been identified as Alkhumra virus. This virus is closely related to Kyasanur forest disease virus. During the 2001 Hajj season four cases of classical VHF were diagnosed in Makkah. To date there have been 37 cases in total. Patients present with an acute febrile illness with hepatitis (100%), hemorrhagic manifestations (55%) and encephalitis (20%). Any role for arthropods, animals or rodents in transmission of Alkhumra virus is unknown.

Hazards Related to Illegal Barbers at the Hajj

Muslim men observe completion of a successful Hajj by shaving their heads. Head shaving is an important means of transmission of blood-borne disease, including Hepatitis B, C and HIV. Illegal unlicensed barbers continue to operate at the Hajj, shaving hair at the

Figure 31.3. State of the art automated abattoir facilities at the Hajj.

roadside with nonsterile blades, which are reused on multiple scalps (Figure 31.4). Hepatitis B virus (HBV) and Hepatitis C virus (HCV) transmission is increased by the ingress of pilgrim barbers from regions with endemicity for both pathogens.

The MOH continues to take an aggressive legislative stance to eliminate unlicensed barbers from operating during the Hajj. Licensed and approved barbershops/government-related head shaving areas are stationed along the Hajj routes where the rites terminate. Nevertheless, enforcing this restriction continues to be a problem in crowds in excess of a million.

New Hazards: Emerging Diseases

Severe Acute Respiratory Syndrome (SARS)

SARS spread was undoubtedly facilitated by air travel, not in as much as transmission aboard aircraft but the speed at which index cases traveled, often while in their incubating period and arrived at new destinations ready to infect, for it was an American businessman traveling from China to Hong Kong who exported the disease to Vietnam. Still without specific treatment and carrying a high mortality, SARS spreads the specter of a sinister epidemiological threat to Hajj planners and the pilgrims themselves, capable of igniting an epidemic of unprecedented scale. Saudi authorities have issued recommendations concerning SARS and the Hajj following the formation of a scientific taskforce immediately after

Figure 31.4. Illegal unlicensed barbers operating at the Hajj.

the WHO announcement of SARS. A number of strategies were acutely implemented in 2003 to prevent the ingress of SARS into the Kingdom.

Clearly, prevention of entry for SARS is a feasible strategy for the Hajj. Even one case of SARS during the Hajj would carry cataclysmal implications. So far no cases of SARS have been reported in the Kingdom and regionally only one case in Kuwait in 2003 was documented.

Noncommunicable Hazards at the Hajj

Noncommunicable hazards are probably the best known dangers of Hajj in this current era of continuous news feed. Hajj is now a widely televised event and a stable news bulletin for audiences across the globe. Even with the best intentions, crowd behavior engenders specific risks, which continue to generate causalities and even fatalities.

Stampede Trauma at the Hajj

The unparalleled congestion during all stages of Hajj compounds risks of traumatic injury to pilgrims enormously. Stampede is perhaps the most feared trauma hazard. Once established, little can be done to abort ripples of panic spreading through crowds, contributing rapidly to casualties and all too often fatalities. Even several pilgrims losing their footing, falling can precipitate a mass stampede. In the confusion, others fall, the 'blind' crowd continues to surge forward and people are lost in the subsequent crush. Crush and trauma injuries are worst at points of exit where huge crowds bear down in a panic to escape. Fatalities result from asphyxiation or head injury, neither of which can be attended to quickly in the mass crowds.

Those at risk of stumbling or falling (the elderly or less surefooted) should be advised to avoid the worst times of Hajj rites and to be clear of the most congested areas. For instance, when making the Tawaf (circuits around the Ka'aba), the pilgrims should be advised to circumambulate on the higher levels of the Mosque rather than in the center of the Mosque next to the Ka'aba. As each circuit commences and finishes at a specific corner of the Ka'aba, crowd densities focus there foremost. Close to the Ka'aba, though the circuits are shorter (and therefore of shorter duration), the jam of humanity pulls individuals inward like a current forcing them into the congestion and unable to break free or assume a slower pace. Pedestrian cross traffic constituted by those who have completed seven circuits or are embarking on their Tawafs is significant and adds to the congestion and delays feasible exit from the tightening spiral. Inward movement towards the confined center of this dense crowd is therefore inevitable and pilgrims can do little to avoid this. A single stumble here, therefore, could be disastrous.

Particularly dangerous for stampedes is the Jamarat area where mass stoning of effigies symbolizing Satan occurs.

Trauma risks also present themselves outside of the immediate holy sites. For a major part of the Hajj, pilgrims move about either on foot in dense traffic or in vehicles themselves. Extreme traffic buildup and poor compliance with seatbelts together with disordered traffic flow contribute to trauma risk. Motor vehicle accidents are inevitable and contribute to trauma casualties and even fatalities during the Hajj.

Fire-Related Injury

Fire has caused substantial loss of life at the Hajj in recent years. Risk increases with the increased scale of the Hajj, which has followed modern travel. In 1997 fire devastated the Mina area, where tents were set ablaze by open stoves, since banned at Hajj. The loss of life was significant, with 343 deaths and over 1500 estimated casualties. Since then all the makeshift tents, which had been in place at the time of the blaze, have been replaced by permanent fiberglass installations. At the time of Hajj, Teflon-coated awnings are added providing accommodations for the migrant millions at the Hajj. The aluminum frames remain in place the rest of the year. These simple though costly measures have ensured that fire of this scale has since never been repeated.

Occupational Hazards of the Abattoir Worker

Islam stipulates three specific occasions for animal sacrifice, of which one is an offering during the Hajj. The true meaning of sacrifice is submission to the will of God. The sacrificer (who may be male or female) invokes the name of God at the time of slaughter, and killing the animal quickly and mercifully and in doing so demonstrates that God has power to give and take life of all His creatures and that the Muslim is obedient to His will.

Annually, therefore, Hajj sees the slaughtering of millions of sheep, cows, camel and goat for which a sophisticated system of abattoirs has developed. The scale of slaughter is colossal, with over one million heads of cattle slaughtered each Hajj.

The MOH advises against slaughtering of animals by laypersons and encourages the use of accredited and monitored facilities in designated areas for the slaughtering of animals.

The five abattoirs cover an area of 42.3 hectares; the largest, Al-Badilla, is the only unit to slaughter all four permitted species (cows, goat, camel and sheep). Wadi-al-Nahr is the smallest and most efficient slaughtering on an industrial scale. Revolving conveyor belts remove carcasses to incinerators. At The Trial Unit Slaughterhouse hydraulic scissors cut the neck and legs of the sheep and modern facilities dispose of the resulting blood and other fluids. At all slaughterhouses, blood and animal fluids drain into an underground collecting system into storage tanks. In 1983 quick freezing equipment was installed, which allowed 69,000 sheep to be frozen and immediately exported to the needy Muslims overseas. Fleets of planes await this frozen cargo to transport out of the Kingdom of Saudi Arabia immediately.

For the abattoir worker, Hajj is an unimaginably busy time and even the most experienced butcher can sustain injury. Seasonal orf has been reported in this population in association with the slaughter of sheep. Orf is a viral disease of sheep and goats, caused by the parapox virus. Human infection results from direct contact with infected animals and produces skin lesions.

Environmental Heat Injury

Heat exhaustion is a leading cause of morbidity and occasional mortality during the Hajj, particularly when Hajj falls in summer. Heat stroke (HS) is a medical emergency characterized by hyperpyrexia, altered mentation and even multiorgan failure. HS can be exertionally related.

Makkah lying at 20 degrees north of the equator routinely achieves ambient air temperatures in excess of 45°C during summer months. With the oppressive congestion of humanity during the Hajj, HS is an anticipated complication. Lack of acclimatization and the arduous physical rituals, exposed spaces with limited or no shade and the turmoil of Hajj all combine to produce HS in many pilgrims.

Heat-related illness accounts for 70% of all hospital admissions. Adequate fluid intake and seeking shade is essential to combat heat stroke, but often caught in the emotional turmoil of Hajj, the distracted and supplicating pilgrim may not notice the dangers of extreme heat exposure until symptoms are pronounced.

Though pilgrims can perform rituals at night in the darkness, sun exposure is a major problem. Sunburn, though seemingly trivial, is a serious risk. Umbrellas, especially white umbrellas are highly advisable and, to our understanding, permitted without invalidating Hajj.

Seeking shade and wearing high-SPF sunblock creams is highly recommended even for those with the darkest skins. Children who may be accompanying their parents must be especially protected. Nighttime rites are to be encouraged whenever possible and pilgrims must know that timings of rites are flexible and acceptable at the pilgrim's convenience.

The heat in Makkah is such that even full thickness foot burns have been documented. Walking barefoot in holy sites precipitates foot injury, and one report documenting a pilgrim who sustained full-thickness burns to the sole of both feet during Hajj points to the extreme environmental temperatures a pilgrim has to face. Though shoes are forbidden in the holy mosque, footwear is permitted in Arafat, Mina and Muzdaliffah. Also, socks may be worn within the Mosque to protect feet.

The Future of Hajj

Hajj has become, for an intense, brief period, the epicenter of mass migration of millions Muslims of enormous ethnic diversity. No other mass migration can compare, either in scale or in regularity, or at this stage, in 2006, there are no signs of Hajj growth slowing.

Travelers to Makkah face specific environmental hazards, both through the physical environment, and through the unique microbiological milieu created at Makkah.

With the prevailing influence of globalization and an increasing, previously unequalled, mobility of the Hajj pilgrim, infectious disease 'hoofbeats' will increasingly signal less well-recognized processes rippling in the transmission envelope the Hajj produces. Not only the scale, but also the massive global migration involved in Hajj magnifies public health risk. Hajj presents a unique infection control challenge that impacts the international public health arena, which is continually expanding as the globe becomes more mobile.

Clinicians everywhere must be aware of potential risks and suggest appropriate strategies, which can be both applied before departure and implemented in the field. Practitioners must also be aware of the risks presented by the returned pilgrim, and be alert to reporting any post-Hajj illness.

Increasingly, international collaboration (in planning vaccination campaigns, developing visa quotas, arranging rapid repatriation, managing health hazards at the Hajj and providing care beyond the holy sites) has become essential. Planning and supporting Hajj has become a forum for collaboration crossing any political considerations.

References

Ahmed, Q. A., & Memish, Z. A. (2002). Mecca bound: The challenges ahead. *Journal of Travel Medicine, 9*, 202–210.

Ahmed, Q. A., Arabi, Y., & Memish, Z. A. (2006). Health risks at the Hajj. *Lancet, 367*, 1008–1015.

Gatrad, A. R., & Sheikh, A. (2005). Hajj: Journey of a life time. *British Medical Journal, 330*, 133–137.

Memish, Z. A. (2000). Infection control in Saudi Arabia: Meeting the challenge. *American Journal of Infection Control, 30*, 57–65.

Memish, Z. A., Venkatesh, S., & Ahmed, Q. A. (2003). Travel epidemiology: The Saudi perspective. *International Journal of Antimicrobial Agents, 21*, 96–101.

Shafi, S., Memish, Z. A., Gatrad, A. R., & Sheikh, A. (2005, Dec. 15). Hajj 2006: Communicable disease and other health risks and current official guidance for pilgrims. *Euro Surveillance, 10*(12), E051215.2.

Chapter 32

The Pilgrimages of Christianity

Michel J. Deprez

Introduction

The desire to leave home to go and honor God in a holy site has been a feature of mankind since our origins. Historians find the tradition of pilgrimage in all the world's civilizations, even those farthest away in time. People are born pilgrims, their lives are a voyage, their second births happen in a holy land where their walking leads, and they discover that their real origin is not their place of birth.

   Christian pilgrimages find their roots in the Bible:

> God says to Abraham, "Leave your land ... to the land that I would have you see" (Genesis XI, 1 and 4)
> and Moses, what a pilgrimage as that of the exodus of the Hebrews to the Promised Land, and David, "I am full of joy when one says to me," "We will go to the house of Eternity". Our feet stop on your thresholds, O Jerusalem, Jerusalem which is built like a city of harmonious unity. For it is there that the tribes come, the tribes of Eternity, according to the charter of Israel, to celebrate the name of the Lord. (Psalm 122, 1–4)

   St. Luke the evangelist shows us that the adolescent Jesus accompanied his parents for the annual pilgrimage to Jerusalem, this city which had 30,000 inhabitants and which welcomed 15,000 pilgrims each year. On reaching adulthood, he mingled with the masses that went to river Jordan to receive the baptism of penitence bestowed by John. The last pilgrimage of Christ was the path towards Jerusalem, to the Passion, and to the Resurrection.

A Short History

As soon as the persecutions of the first three centuries A.D. ceased, the Christians, henceforth free to practice their religion, built churches and sanctuaries.

Travel Medicine: Tales Behind the Science
Copyright © 2007 by Elsevier Ltd.
All rights of reproduction in any form reserved.
ISBN: 0-08-045359-7

In the Orient, the Holy Places, witness to the episodes of Jesus' life, were marked by chapels and churches to which the faithful became accustomed to coming for prayer, sometimes from far away. The most venerated site is the tomb of Christ in Jerusalem. In the Occident, Rome appeared early as a very busy pilgrimage site. From Britain, Gaul (now France), and Ireland, people came to worship the tombs of the Apostles Peter and Paul, and visit the catacombs, memorials to early Christian persecutions.

The golden age of pilgrimage in the West was the Middle Ages. Soon after the year 1000, social and economic life was reborn, as were the exchanges and the contacts between the regions of the former Roman Empire after an eclipse of six centuries.

The "Marcheurs de Dieu" (literally, "Walkers for God") shared in this renaissance and played a fundamental role in it, both by tracing new routes across Europe and the Near East, and by deepening the spiritual meaning of pilgrimage.

Temporarily eclipsed by Islam's invasion of the Holy Land, the pilgrimage to Jerusalem, by the end of the 10th century, had an increased number of pious visitors coming from the Occident. The trip had become easier. The Italians, notably the Venetians, organized a maritime transport service.

Overland a new route was opened, thanks to the recapture of Sicily, and above all, the conversion of the Hungarians, which permitted the walkers to reach Jerusalem by the Danube valley, the Balkans, Constantinople, Asia Minor, and Antioche.

The crusades themselves, despite their political and military motives, nevertheless managed to maintain their character of pilgrimage.

In Rome, faced with progressively fewer pilgrims, Pope Boniface VII felt it necessary to relaunch the pilgrimage. He decided to make the year 1300 a Holy Year and inaugurate the first Roman jubilee. All the Christians who would visit the Basilicas of St. Peter and St. Paul, for 15 consecutive days during the year, would benefit from plenary indulgence, that is, a lifting of the torment in Purgatory occasioned by their sins. There was thus a vigorous awakening of the Italian pilgrimage, which brought in its wake a renewing of religious nomadism in all of Europe.

However, the most illustrious, the most frequented, and the most popular of the medieval pilgrimages is Santiago de Compostela, in Galicia, in the extreme north-west part of Spain. There lies, according to a very ancient tradition, the body of the Apostle Santiago Magor, decapitated on the orders of King Herod in the year 44 A.D.

All during the year, by the tens of thousands, pilgrims of every origin and social class arrive at this sanctuary at the extreme limit of the couchant. Four routes "Chemin de St. Jacques" lead them there — these cross France and converge near the Pyrenees to make one route on Spanish territory. The four starting points of these four routes — Tours, Vezelay, le Puy-en-Velay, and Arles — are themselves sanctuaries.

Rome and Santiago de Compostela are not the only large pilgrimages in Europe. At the Mont St. Michel, in Normandy, people have come from afar since the 8th century, by routes called "Chains of Paradise or the Pilgrims' Way," to honor the Archangel, protector of the French monarchy.

In Canterbury, England, pilgrims worship Tomas Becket, assassinated in the cathedral December 29th, 1170, for political reasons by the knights of the court of Henry II, Plantagenet, a crime that earned the indignation of all Christianity.

Numerous sanctuaries dedicated to Virgin Mary have also been the places of pilgrimages. Notre Dame de Chartres was one of the first; pilgrims worshiped the "Chemin de la Vierge," a relic brought back from Jerusalem.

Notre Dame de Rocamadour was, since the 12th century, the most important pilgrimage dedicated to Mary in the West. At Notre Dame du Puy, also in France, pilgrims also worship a Black Virgin brought back from the crusades by Saint Louis (Louis IX) — 200,000 pilgrims came and celebrated the jubilee in 1407.

We can also cite, without being exhaustive, in Belgium, Notre Dame de Hal (a Black Virgin given by St. Elizabeth of Hungary), in Austria, Notre Dame de Moriazell, in England, Notre Dame de Walsingham...

Towards the year 1500, there were hardly any regions in Europe where it was necessary to walk for more than a day before reaching a sanctuary dedicated to Mary.

After the shine of the medieval centuries, the pilgrimages went through three centuries of decline, until about the year 1830.

The humanists and the Reformed Christians of the 16th century denounced and criticized — often quite severely — the practice of pilgrimage, mostly for the sale of indulgences and the excessive worship of relics. During the 17th century, the Devotion becomes more individual, and there is less taste for the pilgrimage and its noisy crowds. The great migrations dried up, disdained by the "devout" intellectuals soon reinforced by the "enlightened" spirits of the Siècle des Lumières (the Enlightenment).

Of course, the great sanctuaries such as Rome, Lorette, and Santiago de Compostela continued to attract travelers throughout the 17th and 18th centuries; but there was nothing like the medieval crowds. However, Jerusalem was reserved, in practice, for rich pilgrims.

In parallel, popular Catholicism was concentrated in the regional sanctuaries, where the local saints continued to have the favor of the poor people who paid no heed to Voltaire's sarcasm. For him, the pilgrimages were nothing but "ignoble manifestations of superstition, stupidity and shamelessness".

The French revolution of 1789, fiercely opposed to the cult of the relics and the worship of holy objects, dealt a mortal blow to numerous traditional pilgrimages — the sale of chapels as national goods, treasures confiscated, sanctuaries pillaged, pious objects destroyed. At the beginning of the 1800s, all the great machinery of the Middle Ages seemed to have disappeared forever.

Around the 1830s, an unexpected and spectacular renewal took place, following the repeated apparitions of the Virgin, in Paris, rue du Bac in 1830, in La Salette in 1846, and in Lourdes in 1858. At the same time, the Curé d'Ars in Ain, France, gathered around himself some 120,000 people in a village of 230 inhabitants. Teresa Martin, a Carmelite nun in Lisieux (Normandy), who died in 1897 at the age of 24 years, gained immediate worldwide celebrity with the posthumous publication of her autobiography. This large movement has mysteriously continued throughout the 20th century, with apparitions of the Virgin in Fatima (in Portugal) in 1917, then at Beauraing and in Banneux (in Belgium) in 1932–1933, and more recently, in 1981, in Medjogorje, a previous Croatian commune in Yugoslavia, now Bosnia-Herzgovinia.

This great movement of popular devotion is still ongoing. It is estimated that some 50 million Christians travel each year in order to visit a sanctuary. We have to acknowledge that for the last hundred and seventy years, the practice of pilgrimage has returned with a surprising force. The holy year 2000, which started on Christmas Eve 1999, and ended during Epiphany 2001, has shaken the Christian world. Thousands and thousands of people struck out on the century-old routes, wanting to put their feet in the footsteps of the pilgrims of the Middle Ages.

Today the number of sanctuaries that have been counted, only in France, are over a thousand, and the crowds flow, each year in growing numbers to the most important. Lourds has more than 4 million pilgrims, Le Sacré Coeur de Montmartre welcomes more than 3 million pilgrims and tourists, Chartres and Notre Dame de la Garde, in Marseille, 2 million, 140 rue du Bac in Paris, and the Basilica of Lisieux, 1 million, 850,000 at Sainte Anne d'Auray, 350,000 at Paray-le-Monial, etc.... etc....

Logistics

We should also look, in broad-brush strokes, at the daily side of this great collective adventure of popular devotion. A history of pilgrimage would need to review in detail their functions, the ways that they are done, and their hazards.

In those times, being itinerant was an adventure and a risk. The rich pilgrim could be robbed, and had to travel with his armed guard. The poor beggar was protected by his lack of treasure, but the brigands could suspect him of hiding a few pieces of gold in reserve.

Since the Carolingiens, the law protected the pilgrims and handed down heavy penalties to those who robbed or killed them. Gregory VII, the creator of the first Roman Jubilee, in the year 1300, threatened to excommunicate whoever dared to stop or seize a pilgrim. Pilgrimages to other countries aggravated the risks; border crossings in particular were dangerous, and often controlled by racketeers. No concessions were made for linguistic problems.

The travels of pilgrims, like those of armies, propagated microbes into new territories and previously unexposed populations. The risk was reciprocal, and the pilgrims were often victims (such as in plague epidemics). Many would get sick and die.

One German preacher, working in Rome, claimed to have buried 3500 pilgrims during the single jubilee year of 1450. And so those welcoming points, multiplied at the destination as well as on the roads of the pilgrimage, were used as hospices (hospitals) as well — the 18th century kept them only for this purpose.

Finding a place to sleep was another adventure, both on the road, and on arrival. Early on, the city of Rome dealt with this problem, as simple fraternal improvisation could not suffice for the scale of the masses.

A comparison with our time shows the size and severity of the problem. For instance, Lourdes (19,000 inhabitants) has become a city that is only bested by Paris in terms of hotel numbers, and has the greatest hotel density on the planet, with about 50,000 beds.

It is thus that still today, a pilgrimage of 100,000 people to Lourdes can only be an exception, with vast camping grounds and bus services to assure comings-and-goings between all the hotels in the region. One of the last military pilgrimages, grouping almost 100,000 soldiers of all nationalities, found itself confronted by the insoluble problem of pilgrims without food or lodging, for whom it was necessary to improvise, as well as one could, but not without long waits and frustrations.

In Rome, during the Middle Ages, the Jubilee years kept the pilgrims longer, in terms of a longer voyage, not just 1–7 days as in Lourdes, but weeks or months.

The witnesses of the time measured the flow of great jubilees at an average of 200,000 pilgrims per day. However much this number was an exaggeration; we can guess the amplitude of the problem in a city that had no more than 100,000 inhabitants at the time. We can imagine the crowding, the dramas surrounding food, camping, and health care, and the extent that it was necessary to organize relief for a Christian generosity that was always overwhelmed.

To cross customs and the borders, the pilgrims equipped themselves with recommendations from their bishops or with "laissez-passer" (passports). It was on this basis that recipient states, fearful of being overwhelmed, controlled the pilgrims by requiring that their papers were in order. On the other hand, this system was still used, only 20 years ago, by Poland, in order to limit the number of pilgrims going to Rome.

Numerous border crossings of medieval pilgrims on the road to Jerusalem have given rise to difficult negotiations, where pilgrims were extorted, if they were not to find themselves a clandestine and dangerous passage.

All of this is forgotten at the time when pilgrimages are organized on the basis of tourism — an enviable boon for the economy of the recipient countries. Pilgrims can become demanding and fussy about the comfort of their lodging, in direct relation to the price that they have paid for the trip.

The renaissance of pilgrimages during the age of tourism by train, boat, then plane, is not a mere consequence of improved services. On the contrary, the pilgrims have been leaders in this domain. They have widened the horizons of the travel agents.

In 1872, the city of Lourdes arranged the chartering of 178 trains for 119,000 pilgrims and invented the voyages of the sick in 1874.

These new means of making pilgrimages have not extinguished, but rather stimulated, the heroic pedestrian form. On the eve of the First World War, Charles Peguy restored the pedestrian pilgrimage to Notre Dame de Chartres, motivated by an evangelical thirst and a popular living tradition. This tradition is perpetuated in the form of an annual Students' Pilgrimage, which continues to this day.

Chapter 33

Hindu Pilgrimages

Santanu Chatterjee

> There is no happiness for him who does not travel! Therefore wander! The
> fortune of him who is sitting, sits; it rises when he rises; it sleeps when he
> sleeps; it moves when he moves. Therefore wander! (Aitreya Brahamanan,
> the Rigveda, 800–600 B.C.)

Pilgrimages are a strong tradition within Hinduism. This remains an integral aspect of the
religious practices and is deeply embedded in the cultural psyche of the people. Places of
spiritual power were the focus of earlier pilgrimages. Shrines and temples are situated where
the flow of positive energy is most beneficial. Architecture was considered a divine science,
and temples were constructed conforming to certain sacred geometric principles. This ensured
well-being through harmony of mind, body and spirit.

India as a confluence of different religions has always attracted pilgrims from all over
the world. Though Hinduism continues to be the oldest religion in the country, the subcontinent has been the birthplace of various religions like Buddhism, Jainism, Sikhism and
Sufism. The religious geography is therefore complex and incorporates a unique ethnic
mosaic, given the constant influx of differing racial, cultural and social influences, especially from the Northwest and Southeast regions in the Peninsula. Travel for the purposes
of learning, pilgrimage and trade have always been an integral part of the social fabric of
this vast subcontinent. Carrying on with this long tradition, pilgrim tourism in the country
today has attained unprecedented levels and is an important segment of domestic tourism
market.

The religion identified as Hinduism did not actually appear until the centuries preceding
the Christian era. The word comes from the Farsi word *Sindhu*, which describes the people
living east of the river Indus, one of the great rivers that is home to an ancient civilization.
Hinduism encompasses the myriad beliefs originating in the subcontinent. The religion is
an aggregation of the beliefs and practices derived from the Vedism and fertility cults of
the Harappan peoples, which existed since 3000 B.C. This later incorporated both the
shamanistic and devotional practices of the indigenous cultures of the South and the tribal
rituals from the aboriginals of Central and Northeastern India. A marriage of philosophy and

Travel Medicine: Tales Behind the Science
Copyright © 2007 by Elsevier Ltd.
All rights of reproduction in any form reserved.
ISBN: 0-08-045359-7

doctrine, Hinduism is essentially monotheistic and encourages selfless living. Its origins cannot be traced to one historical founder nor does it follow any particular creed. Conceptually, all Hindus believe in an eternal encompassing principle of ultimate reality called *atman* or self. Many deities abound, and worship of a particular personal deity is always done with the awareness that all deities are either simply manifestations or represent different aspects of one Infinite Being, known as Brahman. Of the many forms, Brahma the Creator, Vishnu the Preserver and Shiva the Destroyer are the central Trinity of the Divinity. *Devi* or *Mahadevi* is the name for the great goddess and personifies the energy of the gods. She is seen by her followers as the ultimate, the supreme Creator of the Universe. The Goddess tradition in India has a rich and vibrant history. She is often seen as being ambivalent; on the one hand benevolent and forgiving and on the other terrifying and fierce. Another component in Hinduism is Tantrism, an esoteric mystical ritual in which female symbolism predominates. There are innumerable gods, each with his or her own character and attributes. Each of the greater and lesser deities is accepted as a sort of window through which the Creator glimpsed and lived life. In addition, sacred writings in the form of epic poems and philosophical texts are the basis of the religious doctrines and teachings, the oldest and one of the most revered of these holy books being a collection of magical chants and hymns known as the *Rig Veda*.

The subcontinent offers a vast network of scared destinations. For practical purposes, to be considered a true pilgrimage, a temple must have a long-term history of attracting pilgrims from a geographic area much beyond its immediate region. Given this condition, conservative estimates of the number of pilgrimage sites in India today are around 1820 shrines. Today, most Hindus, who constitute the largest number of travelers in India, cherish worldly values and often also undertake pilgrimages for material gain (money, fertility and other personal bonus) and recreation. It is this orientation, among other factors, that has led to the tremendous increase in pilgrimage tourism. Hindus call the sacred places to which they travel *tirthas* and the pilgrimage as *tirtha-yatra*. This place is often located at the confluence or *sangam* of physical and mythical rivers or at the top of a hill (*mala*). *Tirtha* is a place where an important event, either caused by nature or through the efforts of a man, has occurred leaving an enduring impact on the human society. Varanasi, for example, was a place where most of Brahman Granthas were written or the temple town of Somnath, in the Western state of Gujarat, is a place of great seismological and celestial events that caused permanent changes in the earth's topography. The Vedas normally associate *Tirthas* along the banks of famous rivers as these were the places where the art of cultivation of land was born and the science of agriculture was developed. For the devout, these places are not merely physical locations but represent crossings through which their rites, offerings and prayers can help them attain salvation and thereby provide release from the endless cycle of birth, death and rebirth. There is another reason perhaps for certain places to be accorded sanctity in the Hindu tradition. Pious individuals who lead exemplary lives infuse their environments with their holiness and virtues that accrues from their spiritual practices. Devotees who had earlier visited the saints while they were alive often continue to seek inspiration in the same places after the saint had died. Over many centuries, folk tales about the lives of the saints attain legendary proportions, attracting pilgrims from all over the country. If miracles were reported at the shrine, the saint's legends spread across the entire country, attracting still more pilgrims.

Our earliest sources of information on pilgrimages come from the Vedas where some of the mountain valleys and confluences of rivers are spoken of with great reverence. After this period in history, pilgrimages became popular as is evident from the writings of the great epic, the Mahabharata (350 B.C.), which documents up to 300 sacred pilgrimage sites. By the time the *Puranas* (sacred texts from 2nd to 15th century A.D.) were written, pilgrimages had increased considerably in numbers. However, the *Puranas* speak of other types of *tirtha*. The *Skanda Purana* says that holy deeds and divine words are also *tirtha*. So, a person need not travel to attain salvation, according to Hindu religious philosophy. Simple meditation and prayers and pious deeds at a particular place can also help earn religious merit. Holy deeds included such acts as propitiating ancestors, giving food, clothes and money to the poor, planting trees and abstaining from cutting trees and killing animals unless very necessary. This philosophy shows that travelers were introduced beforehand to the 'true spirit of travel', where one proceeds humbly and with great concern for the social and natural environment.

Pilgrimages have at least two elements in common: the journey and the desire to experience a source of awe and divinity. The greater the challenge of the travel, the stronger is its allure. Traditionally, the seven sacred rivers, the seven sacred cities and the four divine abodes or *dhams* situated at four corners of the land constitute the essential pilgrimage circuits. The most well known however are probably the *Shakti Pithas* or the places of power. The *Pithas* provide a powerful basis to understand Mother India as identified with the Goddess herself. The main intention for such journeys is viewing the deity, a process known as *darshan*. This spiritual communion is one of the most important aspects in pilgrimages. The image of the deity could either be iconic when it has some semblance or aniconic when it merely symbolizes the main deity.

There is certainly a difference between tourism and pilgrimage, but, on our personal journeys, we are always both pilgrim and tourist. Tourism is considered as a leisurely fun-filled activity whereas pilgrimage is somehow sacred and therefore more serious. In truth, there is always some overlap. Even on a spiritual quest, one may at times feel like a tourist. On the contrary, a tourist might suddenly find something that he considers sacred, he may come in contact with a piece of history or feel a spiritual presence, causing new insights and challenges to his original perceptions. Many of us go on pilgrimages but not all our experiences are similar. Every individual has a different experience to relate. All perceptions and reactions stem, however, from our common desire to forge a close relationship with the Divine. And it is this personal experience that makes a pilgrimage so different from a holiday or business trip.

Each year millions of men and women go on pilgrimages. According to the Domestic Tourism Study 2006, 80 million Indians travel every year to religious destinations. The Lord Venkateshwara temple in Tirupati, Andhra Pradesh attracts over 15 million pilgrims every year and is most popularly visited temple. Every day there are over 5000 pilgrims within the temple complex and during peak season (October–December) the numbers can rise to around 100,000. The shrine of Mata Vaishno Devi, which draws over 6.5 million pilgrims annually, is India's second most visited temple. Situated at a height of 5300 ft, it is located inside a cave within the Trikuta Bhagwati hills in Jammu and Kashmir. The cave temple is accessible only by foot with a 12.5 km trek to the summit. Numerous large pilgrimages abound ranging from the Kumbh Mela in the flat dusty Indo-Gangetic plains of Northern India to the Sabarimala *yatra* in the Kerala state of South India. The population movements in such large religious gatherings have a tremendous and wide-ranging health impact. From heat illness to high altitude sickness, pilgrimages offer all possibilities for morbidity. The elderly and the infirm are a high-risk group. These places are all the more sacred and that they are inaccessible, involving long distance travel under harsh physical conditions. Crossing mountains and forests is the price to pay to obtain the blessing or *darshan* of the deity. This reinforces the value and experience of the pilgrimage.

There is no typical profile of a pilgrim in India — they come from as diverse a background as the country itself, whether from the upper, middle or poorer classes. Most take a short break from their normal life and then return home following the completion of their pilgrimage. Others may wander around for many years visiting many of the sacred shrines all over the subcontinent. Such journeys can therefore be either a single journey or a series of wanderings among the holy places. Philosophically, they represent the nodes of an intricate pilgrimage pattern. These shrines are scattered all over the subcontinent and offer simple food and accommodation to the wandering pilgrims in exchange of cleaning and cooking services. Pilgrims usually participate in either the daily ritual, *Puja,* or devotional worship with chanting and singing of hymns or in silent prayer and meditation. Pilgrims on such long journeys generally fall into two distinct groups. First are the *Sadhus* or hermits. They are wandering ascetics who are members of numerous different semi-monastic orders and have renounced family life. Second are elderly men and women, who having completed the responsibilities of family life have chosen to lead their final years practicing *Bhakti Yoga* or love of the divine at the shrines of the deities. Thus, these travels are not simply a way to obtain salvation but to understand and appreciate the diversity of the subcontinent, its many cultures, its varied flora and fauna and its myriad people.

The Kailash Manasarovar pilgrimage is unique in many senses. Mount Kailash, believed by Hindus to be the abode of Lord Shiva and his consort Parvati, is situated in Tibet about 835 km from Delhi at a height of 6690 m. Lake Manasarovar at 4550 m has a circumference of 88 km with an area of 320 km and is situated near the mountain. Now there are two standard routes followed by Indian pilgrims to Mt. Kailash. One is organized by the Government Of India, in cooperation with the Chinese government, which takes the pilgrim directly from Uttar Pradesh to Tibet. It is an arduous trek of 26 days where pilgrims are taken across from early June to September in 16 batches with a maximum of 60 people per batch. This is possibly the only one pilgrimage in the world where it is mandatory to undergo a full physical examination for medical fitness prior to undertaking the journey. Another medical examination is conducted 6 days into the trek at an altitude of 3500 m. Those suffering from high blood pressure, asthma, heart disease, diabetes and epilepsy are excluded from the journey. The other route is via Nepal, which is an easier route and takes 16 days. Use of four-wheel drive vehicles to the Manasarovar and the Kailash base camp at Tarchen via the Tibetan plateau makes this journey much shorter and more comfortable. Acclimatization can be a problem if one gets quickly transported by helicopter from the low-lying plains to the altitudes of the Tibetan plateau especially during the *parikrama.*

For many pilgrims, the process of getting to their destination involves preliminary vows and fasting, intensive cooperative efforts among different families and groups, extensive traveling on foot, fleet-footed mountain horses, yaks or being carried across on wooden frames or shoulders of porters. The constant singing of devotional songs and fervent prayers provide for constant encouragement, as the groups trudge along. On arrival, pilgrims often make contact with priests, and for a fee plan the group's schedule and ritual activity in the temple premises. At some of the major sites, the families of the priests have served as hereditary guides for groups of pilgrims over many generations and this relationship between priest and pilgrim has continued over the years. Devotees often circumambulate the buildings and wait in line for long hours just for a glimpse of the deity's image. At auspicious bathing sites, pilgrims may have to wade through the crush of other devotees to dip into the sacred waters of a river or a tank. Worshipers engaged in special vows or in praying for the cure of a loved one may purchase shrine amulets to give to the god and obtain the blessed food called *prasad*, sanctified by the god's presence, to take back home to friends and family. Once, the *darshan* is complete, the temple bell rung, devotees break their fast by partaking the *prasad*. The premises around the temples usually have many stalls with souvenir hawkers, shopkeepers and sometimes even amusement parks contribute to a lively *mela* or village fair atmosphere. This is certainly part of the attraction of many pilgrimage sites. Among the faith healers and quacks, genuine practitioners of indigenous systems of medicine set up stalls in these *melas* and offer holistic cures. Such gatherings therefore are also an opportunity to experience the practice of the Indian system of medicine. The *Atharva Veda* is the most important source of information on ancient Hindu medicine and is the origin of Ayurveda or the science of living. Indians used the 'Snake root plant' or *Rauwolfia serpentina* about 3000 years ago to treat several diseases from mental disorders to insomnia and snake bite. They also used the poppy juice (*Papavar somniferum)* to relieve pain and anxiety. Tribal healers use medicinal plants for a wide variety of diseases, ranging from rheumatism, paralysis, leprosy, jaundice, diabetes and malaria to syphilis, chronic constipation, and diarrhea. Several of the medicinal plants, which were being used by the tribal people of India for centuries, have found wide acceptance and application in other systems of Indian medicine like Ayurveda, Siddha and Unani, and even in modern medicine.

Certain important sites are well known throughout India and attract hundreds of thousands of pilgrims annually. Probably the most significant is Varanasi. Situated on the north bank of the Ganges river, Varanasi or Kashi is the one of the most visited pilgrimage destinations. One of the seven holy cities, it is the most favoured place for Hindus to die and be cremated in. Hindus believe that cremation at the holy city ensures instant *moksha* or liberation of the soul. It is sacred to Buddhists and Jains too who flock to the *ghats* or steps, leading from temples down to the banks of the sacred Ganges. Though this city had been subjected to repeated attacks from Muslim invaders during the 11th century and its buildings demolished, there are records to prove more than 3000 years of continuous habitation, making Varanasi one of the oldest living cities. Encircling the city is a sacred path of 50 miles touching 108 shrines called the *Panchakroshi Parikrama*. Such circumambulation is an essential part of most pilgrimages. However, one can do this symbolically too by visiting the Panchakroshi temple that has the 108 wall reliefs of the temples, especially for those pilgrims who are unable to complete the circle due to illness and infirmity. The particular riverside location of Varanasi is considered especially potent because, in less than 10 km the Ganges is met by two other rivers, the Asi and the Varana. Winding 1560 miles across northern India, from the Himalaya Mountains to the Indian Ocean, the Ganges is a sacred river. The river supports a staggering 400 million people along its 2510 km course. If one, however, considers the Sunderbans delta, which the Ganges shares with the Brahmaputra river at the mouth of the Indian ocean, the number of people it supports is nearly half a billion or nearly one-tenth of all humanity, making it the most populous river basin in the world. Known as *Ganga Ma* or Mother Ganges, the river is revered as a goddess whose purity cleanses the sins of the faithful. But while her spiritual purity has remained unchallenged, her physical purity has deteriorated as India's booming population imposes an ever-growing burden upon her. The river is now polluted with human and industrial waste. The majority of the Ganges' pollution is organic waste consisting of sewage, trash, food, and human and animal remains. Over the past century, city populations along the Ganges have grown at a tremendous rate, while waste-control infrastructure has remained relatively unchanged. Antiquated sewage-system channels add to this problem. Some 300 million gallons of waste pour into the river each day. The effects are alarming. Recent water samples collected in Varanasi reveal fecal-coliform counts of about 50,000 bacteria per 100 milliliters of water, approximately 10,000% higher than the government standards for safe river bathing. The result of this pollution is an array of water-borne diseases including cholera, hepatitis, typhoid and amoebic dysentery.

Historically, people have traveled both knowingly and unknowingly regarding risks of such travels. In this context, it is that an estimated 80% of all health problems and one-third of deaths in India are attributable to water-borne diseases, given the complex interactions between agent, host and environment. Diarrheal diseases are a major cause of mortality and morbidity in large gathering outbreaks. Studies have shown that they contribute to between 25 to 50% of all deaths in rural settings. The impact of such a disease is influenced by changes in human ecology and socioeconomic status. Overcrowding, improper sewage disposal and poor personal hygiene are intimately linked in the chain of events leading to disease causation. Large-scale interstate movement of pilgrims also offers an ideal oppor-tunity for the spread of vector-borne diseases and tuberculosis. Falciparum malaria infection has been brought by travelers from malarious to non-malarious areas. Cholera has been the focus in pilgrimages. This disease has spread from the subcontinent, following the trade and pilgrimage routes, initiating epidemics on its way. The cholera epidemics of northern India between 1867 and 1895 started at pilgrimage sites along the banks of the Ganges in the North-Western Provinces. These sites were hotbeds of cholera and the colonial authorities had varying quarantine policies. In 1783, British historians estimated that cholera accounted for 20,000 pilgrim deaths in the Indian holy site of Hardwar. Within months the bacilli spread outwards towards China, north to Russia and southwest to the Middle East. It did not reach Europe until 1826, having travelled along these trade routes. By 1831, cholera infected nearly half of the Hajj faithful making the annual pilgrimage to sacred sites in Mecca and Medina. Dehydrated, and shedding vibrios, dying pilgrims returned home depositing bacteria along key transportation routes. The great ports of Alexandria and Istanbul were soon staggering under a cholera epidemic that subsequently radiated outwards throughout North Africa and into the Balkans, up the Danube and onwards towards Hungary and Germany. In this global situation, following another cholera outbreak among 3 million pilgrims at the Hardwar *Mela*, the officiating sanitary officer of the British Indian government, James McNabb Cuningham (1829–1905) ruthlessly and efficiently established cordons and emergency isolation hospitals. Any pilgrim suspected of harbouring the disease was quarantined. The outbreak was con-trolled in due course. Then in mid-1868, on the eve of the opening of the Suez Canal and consequently the direct and faster sea route from India to West Europe, Cuningham was persuaded by those in authority in London to adopt a new cholera ideology, which was completely at variance with policies he himself had used in 1867. Cholera was seen in a 'new light' as a locally generated disease, which was not caused by population or pilgrim movements, and hence there was no need for quarantine of the shipping from Bombay. This radical alteration in policy and ideology was a political decision and was based on commercial considerations. This new official British doctrine on cholera in India was announced in the middle of 1868, and put into effect by the end of the year, just prior to the opening of the Suez Canal. As stated by officials in England and by J. M. Cuningham in India, it was now hotly denied that cholera was caused by a living germ, that it was carried from place to place by human beings or that it was carried from place to place by people traveling by railways or on ship. This led to a disastrous tragedy with nearly a million dying from cholera in 1900 in the subcontinent.

Sacred site festivals in India called *melas* are another interesting part of the pilgrimage tradition. Celebrating a mythological event in the life of a deity or an auspicious astrological period, the *melas* attract enormous numbers of pilgrims from all over the country. The origins are shrouded in mix of myths, mysteries, legends and astrological considerations. Traditionally, Shankarcharya the 9th century philosopher was associated with the *Mela* in Prayag. He considered Prayag to be the centre point of his four monasteries in the four geographical corners of the subcontinent. This periodic festival during 9th to 12th century provided a contact between the reclusive monks, ascetics and their devotees, and provided opportunities for religious discourses and exchange of philosophical thoughts. Also, meetings occurred between various religious sects for better understandings and mutual cooperation. This festival developed over a period of time, assumed greater heights and came to be known as the *Kumbha Mela*. According to the *Puranas* however, Brahma, the Creator, advised the celestial Gods to obtain the *Kumbh* or pot containing the nectar of immortality known as *amrit* to help them regain the strength and overcome their weakness brought about by a previous Curse. The Gods sought help from the demons and together they churned the primordial ocean depths to retrieve the *Kumbh*. As Dhanwantari, the divine healer, appeared from the bottom of the Ocean with the *Kumbh* containing nectar, a great fight ensued between the Gods and demons to wrest control of the pitcher. During this fierce battle which lasted for 12 days and nights, a few drops of nectar spilled and fell in four different places on earth: Prayag in Allahabad, Haridwar, Nasik and Ujjain. Since then, whenever the planets align in the same astrological configuration, pilgrims and devotees converge to commemorate this divine event. This riverside festival is therefore held every 3 years in each of the four different locations, rotating between Prayag near the city of Allahabad, situated at the confluence of the rivers Ganges, Yamuna and the mythical Saraswati, Nasik on the Godavari river, Ujjain on the Sipra river and Hardwar on the Ganges, returning to each of these four places once every 12 years. In practice, the four-city cycle may take eleven or thirteen years, given the difficulties and controversies in astrological calculations. In 2001, at the last *Purna Kumbh Mela* in Allahabad, nearly 24 million participated in the ritual bathing and prayers making this the largest religious gathering in the world. An *Ardh* or half *Mela* takes place 6 years after the *Maha Kumbh* in each location. The next *Ardh Mela* will be held in January 2007 at Allahabad. The auspicious dates are thus predetermined astrologically and coincide with one round of Jupiter through the zodiac. In Allahabad, it takes place with Jupiter in *Vrishabh* (Taurus) while the Sun enters *Makara* (Capricorn) coinciding with the northerly course of the Sun. The major bath takes place when the Moon enters Makara. *Prayag Snan* or ritual bathing in this confluence of the rivers is of great importance. For the devout, bathing in these rivers during the *Kumbha Mela* is considered an endeavour of great religious significance, cleansing both body and spirit. It is believed that it washes away all the sins and ends the cycle of rebirth and death, as the soul becomes one with the Almighty. Many thousands of naked holy men from various sects immerse themselves in the river for a ceremonial bath. Following the bathing of the *sadhus*, millions of other devotees attempt to enter the river. The great religious fervour of so many people focused on a small area of land adjoining the river had frequently resulted in hundreds of pilgrims being trampled to death in the past, as the masses surge towards the riverbanks during the auspicious hour. In recent times, unprecedented planning, improved infrastructure and efficient ground coordination between the various governmental agencies have ensured a smoother and safer functioning of this festival.

In South India, another pilgrimage has attained significance in recent times, attracting several million pilgrims to its abode. This is the Sabarimala shrine in Kerala. Located at a height of 1200 m amidst 18 hills in the Sahyadri mountain of the Western Ghats region of south-central Kerala and structured around the cult of Ayyappan. This pilgrimage presents some geographical and anthropological characteristics. Lord Ayyappan is a symbol of religious unity and communal harmony and the temple to all, irrespective of caste, creed, religion, social status or nationality. From the anthropological point of view, this pilgrimage stands out through its ritual initiation ceremony to the cult (*mala puja*), its essentially male-dominated attendance justified by the preservation of the ritual purity of the site and the period of austerity and regulations (*vratam*) of 41 days (vegetarianism, prayers and chastity), which is strictly observed by all pilgrims. Geographically, Sabarimala, is a hilly forest area and part of the journey needs to done on foot, with a major part of this terrain lying within the Periyar Tiger Reserve. There are three routes and the pilgrimage symbolizes the journey to heaven. In spite of cardiac care units, 31 pilgrims died in 2006, 29 of them being between 25 and 49 years of age. Besides, air and water pollution caused by the pilgrims during the season, progressive deforestation has caused a negative impact on the biodiversity of the region. The wildlife is losing their natural habitat and is getting pushed further into the forest reserve. The Sabarimala Master Plan incorporates satellite pilgrim facilities; efficient crowd management systems that when implemented will handle maximum number of pilgrims with minimum environmental impact.

In a contemporary context of pilgrimage and health, the annual pilgrimage to Deogarh deserves mention. Deoghar and Sultanganj are two ancient holy spots in the eastern State of Bihar. During the rainy monsoon season at a particular time, on their way to the 'Shravani Mela', thousands of pilgrims walk the 105 km stretch between the two places. Most wear saffron-coloured clothes and having collected water from the river in Sultanganj, trek their way through the Suia Pahad, or the 'mountain of needles' with the water in vessels suspended at either end of a bamboo staff balanced on their shoulders. Most walk slowly and many travel this route with their children and grandchildren. With nearly 200,000 people coming in everyday, and many staying on to rest and recuperate before starting their return journey on foot, the capacity to meet the water and sanitation needs of Deogarh town was fully stretched. Facilities on the route are almost nonexistent and many use fields for defecation. Hygiene is compromised since all are barefoot. In 2002, the poliovirus had been active along this pilgrims' route. UNICEF undertook a month-long polio immunization campaign along the paths leading to the annual pilgrimage and at Deogarh itself. Around 25,000 children were immunized in the first fortnight of the polio campaign in such a novel approach.

Hindu pilgrimages today have wide-ranging environmental and socio-cultural consequences. Accelerated consumption of food, water and land resources for uncontrolled pilgrimage tourism development has considerable influence on the health and welfare of the local population. Moreover, accident prevention is a prime concern since fires, injuries, drowning and stampedes during the ritual bathing are common occurrences. Provision for safe temporary housing, ensuring adequate potable water and providing a hygienic waste disposal system are priority issues.

The key to finding the optimum balance between the pilgrims, their intentions and their health lies in developing socially responsible tourism initiatives, which minimize any negative impact. Therefore, apart from providing for basic medical facilities catering to medical emergencies, adequate measures to control infectious diseases constitute an important public health exercise.

References

Arnold, D. (1986). Cholera and colonialism in British India. *Past and Present, 113*, 118–151.

Bhardwaj, S. M. (1973). *Hindu places of pilgrimages in India: A study in cultural geography.* Berkeley: University of California Press.

Bhardwaj, S. M. (1989). *Hindu places of pilgrimage in India: A study in cultural geography.* New Delhi: Surjeet Publications/University of California Press.

Brown, T. (1824). *On cholera, more especially as it appeared in India.* Edinburgh.

Clift, J. D., & Clift, W. B. (1992). *The archetype of pilgrimage: Outer action with inner meaning.* New York: Paulist Press.

Cousineau, P. (1998). *The art of pilgrimage.* Conari Press.

Cohen, E. (1979). A phenomenology of tourist experiences. *Sociology, 13*, 179–201.

Cohen, E. (1992). Pilgrimage and tourism: Convergence and divergence. In: A. Morinis (Ed.), *Sacred journeys: The anthropology of pilgrimage* (pp. 47–61). Westport, CT: Greenwood Press.

Eck, D. L. (1999). *Banaras, city of light,* Columbia University Press.

Gurukkal, R., & Raju (2001). *Report on Sabarimala enclave management* (p. 158). Kottayam: School of Social Sciences, Mahatma Gandhi University.

Harrison, M. (1992). Quarantine, pilgrimage and colonial trade: India 1866–1900. *Indian Economic and Social History Review, 29*, 299–318.

Kayastha, S. L., & Singh, S. N. (1977). A study of preferences and behaviour pattern of tourists in Varanasi. *National Geographical Journal of India (Varanasi), 23*(3–4), 143–150.

Khalid, A. (2004). Disease and Pilgrimage in Northern India, 1867–1894. Paper presented during the BASAS Annual Conference, School of Development Studies, University of East Anglia, 5–7th April 2004.

MacNamara, C. (1876). *A history of Asiatic cholera.* London: Croom Helm.

Morinis, E. A. (1984). *Pilgrimage in the Hindu tradition: A case study of West Bengal.* New Delhi: Oxford University Press.

Rana, P. S., & Singh, R. P. B. (2004). Behavioural perspective of pilgrims and tourists in Banaras. In: A. Raj (Ed.), *The tourist — A psychological perspective* (pp. 187–206). New Delhi: Kanishka Publication.

Watts, S. (1997). Cholera and civilization: Great Britain and India, 1817–1920, and 'Afterword: To the epidemiologic transition?'. In: S. Watts (Ed.), *Epidemics and history: Disease, power and imperialism* (pp. 167–212, 269–279). London: Yale University Press.

Watts, S. (2001). From rapid change to stasis: Official responses to cholera in British-ruled India and Egypt: 1860–1921. *Journal of World History, 12*(2), 321–374.

Watts, S. (2001). 'Review' of David Arnold, The New Cambridge History of India (Vol. 3, Pt. 5), Science, technology and medicine in Colonial India. Cambridge University Press. *Bulletin of the History of Medicine, 78,* 337–340.

Chapter 34

Pilgrimages in the High Himalayas

Ken Zafren

The lofty mountains of the Himalayas and the great rivers they spawn are the cradle of many religions. Hinduism and Buddhism both arose in India in the shadow of the Himalayas, but they are not the only religions with roots and pilgrimage sites in the highest mountain range of the world.

Many pilgrimage sites are sacred to more than one religion. For example, Mt. Kailas in Tibet, the holiest site of Buddhism, is also a pilgrimage site for adherents of at least three other ancient religions — Bon, the original religion of Tibet, Hinduism and the Jain religion of India. Hemkund Lake in the Indian Himalayas, at an altitude of 4329 meters, is another pilgrimage site for devotees of several religions, including Hindus and Sikhs. There are dozens of pilgrimage sites throughout the Himalayas, many above 3000, 4000 and even 5000 meters.

The opening of Nepal and Tibet to foreign tourism has also given rise to a modern generation of secular pilgrims. The most popular pilgrimages of the Trekker sect are the circuit of Annapurna and the ascent of Kala Patar in the Everest region, both in Nepal. Adherents of the smaller but no less enthusiastic Climber sect regularly set up a number of temporary pilgrimage sites, most frequently during the pre- and postmonsoon seasons. The largest of these sites is Everest Base Camp in Nepal. It is the usual practice for climbers to consecrate a base camp with a Buddhist ceremony, known as a puja, prior to beginning the ascent, in order to assure good luck for the climb.

The concept of pilgrimage is inherent in the roots of many religions. The Buddha was raised in luxury as a prince, but then learned about suffering. He renounced his royal home and took to wandering. The story is told in many places, including the book, 'Siddharta', by Hermann Hesse. Buddhism itself was imported into Tibet by pilgrims who went to India to receive Buddhist teachings.

Tibet's great yogi, Milarepa, like the Buddha, renounced his comfortable origins and lived alone. He was naked until his sister convinced him to wear clothes. He didn't have to worry about hypothermia, because he practiced the yoga of vital heat. This skill of Tantric yoga involves the would-be-adept visualizing an internal fire. For the final examination, the student is wrapped in wet sheets and sits on a frozen lake while meditating overnight.

Travel Medicine: Tales Behind the Science
Copyright © 2007 by Elsevier Ltd.
All rights of reproduction in any form reserved.
ISBN: 0-08-045359-7

By morning, the sheets must be dry. Milarepa ate nettles that he found near his cave, high in the Himalayas. Some hungry hunters came to his cave after failing in their hunt and asked him for food. Milarepa offered to share his nettle soup with them, but they preferred to remain hungry.

Tantric yoga originated with the Hindus and is still practiced among ascetics of Hinduism and related religions. One scientific expedition in the Himalayas described a pilgrim who arrived at their camp. He was from the plains of India and had never before been to high altitude or seen snow. Nevertheless, he was able to sleep outdoors lightly clad during a night with subfreezing temperatures and also demonstrated an ability to eat glass.

Buddhist pilgrims consider Mt. Kailas, which they know as Kang Rinpoche — precious snow mountain — to be the center of the earth. They circle the mountain clockwise, a distance of about 50 kilometers. Each circumambulation takes 3 days. Tibetans may make 3, 5, 13 or more circuits. Some prostate themselves, stand up and then prostrate themselves again, measuring the trail with the length of their bodies. One circuit takes as much as a month using this method. The physical demands of such pilgrimages can be quite rigorous.

Near the high point of the circuit, the Drolma La, at about 5600 meters, is a cave created by Milarepa during a climbing contest with Naro Bonchung of the Bon religion. This contest was held to determine which would be the primary religion of Tibet. According to the Buddhist version, Milarepa meditated at the base of the mountain until just before sunrise, while Naro Bonchung toiled up the mountain. At the moment of sunrise, Milarepa flew to the summit and won the contest. The Bonpo, who follow the earlier Tibetan religion, which was largely supplanted by Buddhism, have a different version of this story. They circle the mountain, which they consider the 'Nine-Story Swastika Mountain', counterclockwise.

The Hindus consider Mt. Kailas to be the abode of Shiva. Four great rivers — the Brahmaputra, Indus, Sutlej and Karnali (a tributary of the Ganges) — originate from the four faces of Mt. Kailas as waters which flow from the heavens through Shiva's matted hair. The Jain religion uses the name Mt. Ashtapada. Its founder, Rishabanatha, achieved spiritual liberation on the summit. Access to Mt. Kailas has become more difficult for Hindus and Jains because of political tensions in border regions. Prospective pilgrims from India are required to pass a pretrip medical examination and are further examined at high altitude while en route.

Guru Rinpoche, whom the Sherpas of Nepal consider to be the founder of the unreformed order of Tibetan Buddhism, traveled to the Khumbu region at the base of Mt. Everest long ago to open this area for his followers. Whether the Khumbu is actually one of the reserves, which were hidden for use in times of trouble, is controversial outside of Sherpa circles. These valleys were to be uninhabited. If someone tried to find one of them before the appropriate time, it would prove impossible, as they were guarded by high mountain walls. This description certainly fits the Khumbu region, which the Sherpas first reached about 400 years ago when it was almost, if not completely, without inhabitants. The access route was the Nangpa La, a formidable pass, the summit of which is over 5700 meters and covered by a glacier.

Guru Rinpoche eschewed the difficult terrestrial access in favor of an aerial approach. He flew from Tibet, as a bird would fly, having acquired the same skill as Milarepa. By doing so, he avoided travel problems such as altitude illness as well as problems of conventional air travel such as deep venous thrombosis and airline food. The latter is of mostly historical interest. However, when he arrived at the site of the present-day monastery of

Thyangboche, he landed so hard that his footprints are still visible in a rock, which is located behind the monastery. Apparently he was not injured.

Guru Rinpoche must have wandered widely in Khumbu. On walks with Sherpa friends, even in unlikely places, one finds spots that he visited. One such spot, above the tiny village of Dughla is marked only by a set of ruined stone walls and is not to be found in any guidebook. Here, Guru Rinpoche camped and meditated for a week. There was no water there when he arrived, but he solved this problem by producing a spring nearby. The spring can still be seen today. One can hope that he did not suffer, as many modern pilgrims do, from waterborne diseases such as giardia.

Sherpas follow the unreformed order of Tibetan Buddhism, in contrast to the more popular reformed order, whose spiritual leader is the Dalai Lama. However, they also revere the Dalai Lama. Before it was destroyed by the Chinese, the monastery at Rongbuk was the spiritual center for the Sherpa people. The current Thyangboche Rinpoche (reincarnate lama) was educated there and many older Sherpas remember trekking to Rongbuk via the Nangpa La. These days, the Nangpa La is a route for Tibetan refugees escaping to Nepal or India, many of whom have died of hypothermia or suffered frostbite. For many years, there have been Tibetan guides whose goal is to smuggle children across this pass so that they can be educated in Tibetan Buddhism at Dharamsala in India, by the government in exile of the Dalai Lama, a very difficult and dangerous 'pilgrimage'.

From the perspective of travel health, pilgrimages in the Himalaya present a number of potential medical problems. The most obvious difficulties are those of altitude and cold. In August 1996, over 200 Hindu pilgrims and their local porters died of hypothermia in a blizzard on the trek to the Amarnath Cave in the Indian Himalayas. Over 160,000 pilgrims made the trek during the months of July and August that year. In more recent years, some pilgrims on the 'Amarnath Yatra' have been killed by Muslim militants. There were an estimated 40 victims in the years 2001 and 2002, in spite of the presence of thousands of Indian soldiers. A few deaths of porters and their clients also occur due to fall from the narrow trails each year.

Easier access and a shorter trail has made it possible to reach the Amarnath Cave from the trailhead and return in one day, rather than spending two nights camping along the trail. The result has been to attract an increasing number of out-of-shape pilgrims from urban areas in India. Some are carried or use ponies, although many expect divine help for the unaccustomed exertion.

Problems of sanitation and disease transmission in large groups put pilgrims at high risk from gastrointestinal and respiratory illnesses, and the sheer number of pilgrims in a single place has led to deaths by stampede. These problems are hardly unique to the high Himalayas.

Altitude illness is not the exclusive province of trekkers and climbers, although most studies involve those groups rather than religious pilgrims. Hindu pilgrims from Nepal and India visiting Gosainkunda Lake in Nepal (elevation 4300 meters) usually make the trek from Kathmandu at 1300 meters in two nights. Most reach Dunche (2000 meters) by bus. They ascend in one day from Dunche to the lake and sleep by its shores. In the morning they pray, take a quick ritual dip and descend back to Dunche.

The majority of the pilgrims suffer from altitude illness. In their paper, "Disoriented and ataxic pilgrims: an epidemiological study of acute mountain sickness and high-altitude cerebral edema at a sacred lake at 4300 m in the Nepal Himalayas", Basnyat et al., (2000) describe a 68% incidence of acute mountain sickness (AMS) and a 31% incidence of high altitude cerebral edema (HACE). In a subsequent paper, Cumbo et al., (2002) studied the role of dehydration. Some of the pilgrims are fasting and dehydrated, especially the pilgrims whose fasting includes not drinking water and some have become severely dehydrated. It is fortunate that the pilgrims descend early in the morning before more severe altitude illness can develop. Otherwise, there would be a significant death toll.

The pilgrims believe that Gosainkunda Lake was formed when Shiva (the Creator and Destroyer) swallowed some poison from the ocean in order to protect the other gods. He became quite ill and sought the snows of the Himalayas for relief. He stuck his trident into a mountainside, releasing three streams, which formed the lake.

The pilgrims generally ascribe their illness to the scent of flowers along the trail. Indeed, the illness and hallucinations may be part of the "attraction" of the trek to Gosainkunda. The pilgrims are said to expect to attain an altered state in which they can commune with the Lord Shiva. Many trekkers may also be seeking an altered state, but generally consider AMS to be an undesirable condition rather than part of the experience.

The proximity of Kala Patar induces a sense of urgency in many trekkers. Kala Patar, from which can be seen a fantastic panorama including the summit of Mt. Everest, is a shoulder of the famous and beautiful peak, Pumori. It has two summits, at about 5550 and 5700 meters. It has existed in its present form for many thousands of years, since the last retreat of the Khumbu Glacier, and is likely to persist for many more thousands of years. By the time trekkers arrive at Pheriche or Dingboche which is about two-days walk away, this fact is forgotten and the rush to the top is foremost in many minds. The potential consequences of this are summarized in the expression: "See Everest and die." More commonly, the consequences are merely a miserable bout of AMS.

The Himalayan Rescue Association (HRA) has for years recommended an itinerary of gradual ascent in order to allow for acclimatization to take place and to minimize the occurrence of AMS, HACE, and high altitude pulmonary edema (HAPE). For those trekkers who fly to Lukla (2800 meters), this involves one night at about that altitude (a few hours walk toward Namche Bazar), two nights at Namche Bazar, a night at Thyangboche, two nights at Pheriche or Dingboche and a night at Lobuje, before ascending to the top of Kala Patar. Even this itinerary is too fast for some people. The doctors who have worked at the HRA aid post over the years have a number of stories involving patients whose main goal is to reach the summit of Kala Patar sooner rather than later. Mostly these pilgrims pay for their haste by having a miserable experience with breathlessness and headaches.

I remember all of my walks to the summit of Kala Patar, but I have met many trekkers who were so hypoxic and ill at the time they ascended that they have no real memory of the event or would prefer to forget it. They could have had a much more enjoyable experience by waiting an extra day or two. Especially in the fall trekking season, the weather is usually so stable that there is little risk of waiting a day or two. One wife was told by a doctor at Pheriche that her husband was too ill with AMS to ascend further for a day or two and that she must wait in the lodge with him to help him and to make sure he wasn't getting worse. She was observed a bit later sneaking out the back window of the lodge on her way to Kala Patar. I don't know how their marriage held up.

Whether they visit the Himalayas for religious reasons or just to seek the mountains and get their good tidings, pilgrims seldom return unchanged. I am convinced that most are spiritually enriched by their experiences.

References

Basnyat, B., Subedi, D., Sleggs, J., Lemaster, J., Bhasyal, G., Aryal, B., & Subedi, D. (2000). Disoriented and ataxic pilgrims: an epidemiological study of acute mountain sickness and high-altitude cerebral edema at a sacred lake at 4300 m in the Nepal Himalayas. *Wilderness and Environmental Medicine, 11*(2), 89–93.

Cumbo, T. A., Basnyat, B., Graham, J., Lescano, A. G., & Gambert, S. (2002). Acute mountain sickness and bicarbonate clearance: preliminary field data from the Nepal Himalayas. *Aviation, Space, and Environmental Medicine, 73*(9), 898–901.

Jinpa, G. G., Ramble, C., & Dunham, C. (2005). *Sacred Landscape and Pilgrimage in Tibet*. New York: Abbeville Press.

Johnson, R., & Moran, K. (1989) *The Sacred Mountain of Tibet: On Pilgrimage to Kailas*. Rochester, Vermont: Park Street Press.

Rohde, D. (2002, August 5). Braving nature and militants, Hindus trek for a peek at God's icy symbol. *New York Times*.

SECTION 8:

WHEN DISEASES TRAVEL

Chapter 35

Cholera: A Travel History of the First Modern Pandemic

Eyal Meltzer and Eli Schwartz

Preface

No book on travel medicine can be complete without considering the other side of the travel disease equation: for while our usual concern is with people that travel to areas of endemic diseases, these illnesses can occasionally begin in their own form of travel.

This "travel of diseases" has of course been a feature of human illness since antiquity. Throughout history, it was mostly associated with that most disruptive form of human travel — military campaigns. The association of war and pestilence was noted in biblical times,[1] throughout classical and medieval times (the Black Death for instance followed in the footsteps of the destruction caused by the Mongol invasions in Eurasia), and right up to the present era of World Wars.

Nonviolent forms of human travel, such as commerce and tourism, had a less publicized role in the travel of diseases although this potential was well recognized by the late middle ages. This led to the inception of early forms of quarantine in the Levant and Europe, but these approaches were far from comprehensive.

The first "traveling disease" to have its travel history documented fully by modern scientific methods was undoubtedly the great "Asiatic Cholera" pandemic of the 19th century. Its successive waves prompted the birth of modern epidemiology, the first international agreements concerning health and travel, as well as innovations, such as medical cartography, intravenous fluid therapy, and a Victorian passion for sanitation.

Origins

The term "cholera" is medieval in origin and was used to describe a flux or acute diarrheal illness. The term most likely originates from the medieval association of diarrhea with a flow of bile — one of the four bodily humors. Such acute gastroenteritis-like illnesses were of course as ubiquitous in the past as they are today. To this can be attested the many "local patriotic" designations such as "English" and "American" cholera in England and its North American colonies, and "Cholera *nostras*" in Germany. However, except among infants, this simple "Cholera morbus" was rarely fatal. In the words of the American physician Dr. Austin Flint (1812–1886): "It is remarkable that an affection involving so much disorder should leave the effected organs in a condition to resume so speedily the execution of their function (Flint, 1866)".

Up until the 19th century, European patients and doctors had no experience with a diarrheal disease that could kill within hours. For them, the "Asiatic Cholera" — henceforth to be referred to simply as cholera — was a new and frightening experience.

Vibrio cholerae, the causative agent of the disease, has probably existed in Bengal for many years. A hardy bacterium, it favors aquatic including marine habitats, and can remain dormant in seafloor sludge for decades. Attaching itself to copepods — tiny marine invertebrates — it can infect their predators such as shellfish. Infected food and water are the usual modes of transmission of cholera.

The reason for the sudden transformation from a localized waterborne scourge to a rapidly spreading pandemic is not clear. If lessons learned during the latest pandemic apply to the first, a genetic transformation with the emergence of new epidemic strains may have helped to foment the explosive spread of the disease (Morris, 2003).

The First Pandemic: Cholera Begins its Journey

What drove cholera to commence its travels? It was certainly not a new disease, and in its ancestral home of Bengal it has undoubtedly existed for several millennia. It surely was not a case of an unknown disease spreading from an isolated human community. In fact, the rich and the populous Bay of Bengal has been a regional hub of commerce for thousands of years, and an international one for at least two centuries.

Be that as it may, when epidemic cholera first raised its head in the period of 1817–1826 (Table 35.1), the geopolitical situation in South and Southeast Asia was certainly conducive to the rapid spread of disease. The Indian subcontinent was ravaged by armed conflict. The recently ended Maratha war had wrought a lot of destruction and caused the movement of populations in Bengal and the Deccan. To the north, the expansion of the Newar state of Nepal caused the first Anglo-Nepalese war and internecine strife in Afghanistan to the northeast was the reason behind the fleeing of exiles. To the East, repeated Burmese incursions into Assam caused a mass movement of refugees, and brought about the first Anglo-Burmese war. On the other hand, commerce was booming after the end of the Napoleonic Wars. Calcutta, the headquarters of the largest trading empire then in existence, the East India Company, was at the hub of a maritime network, running throughout major ports in Asia and Europe.

It is not surprising therefore that when cholera erupted in Bengal in 1817 it rapidly gained a foothold in China, Southeast Asia, the Malay Archipelago, and the Philippines. Transported by moving British garrisons, it moved to Ceylon, and to Muscat in the Persian Gulf.

The western limit of its maritime expansion at this time however was Mauritius, where the disease was brought in by the ship Topaze (Great Epidemics, 1856). Cholera's maritime travels at this time were curtailed, and it did not spread to Europe or the Americas. It should be

Table 35.1: Timeline in cholera history.

1816–1826	First pandemic
1829–1851	Second pandemic
1852–1860	Third pandemic
1854	John Snow investigates the cholera in Soho, London
1863–1875	Fourth pandemic
1881–1896	Fifth pandemic
1883	Cholera bacillus identified by Koch in Egypt
1893	Haffkine tests the first cholera vaccine in India
1899–1923	Sixth pandemic
1961–1970s	Seventh pandemic
1991	Outbreak and reestablishment of cholera in South America

remembered that the average traveling time from Europe to Bengal by sea was about 90 days and in a very crowded vessel of the time, the cholera epidemic would have run its course by the time the infected ship reached Europe.

While overland travel was certainly slower, the disease had the advantage of incremental growth and spread from station to station. Through land routes cholera spread in Afghanistan, and in the wake of the Persian army returning from besieging Baghdad, it spread in Iran as well. For reasons that remain obscure, cholera apparently ceased its westward travels by 1823 in the Asiatic part of the Russian empire. The fact that cholera did not cross from the great trade hubs on the Volga to the main cities in western Russia, may explain why it failed to infect Europe at this time.

The Second Pandemic: Cholera Resumes its Travels

It is not at all clear if the apparent lull in cholera activity signified a true cessation of transmission. This will be an ongoing question since the distinction made between the seven pandemics/epochs of disease activity is somewhat arbitrary. It is certain that data about disease activity from many regions of Asia during this period are sparse. However, the occasional obituaries of Europeans in India during this period as well as reports of small outbreaks in Southeast Asia suggest that the first pandemic was still active. For example, cholera outbreaks on HMS Alligator and HMS Boadicea (involved in the British military campaign in Burma) were reported to have made "dreadful ravages among the crew".[3,4]

Academic interest was undoubtedly created by the first wave of cholera. European physicians reported on cases encountered in India, and several monographs were published. Epidemic/Asiatic cholera was the thesis subject of at least four graduates of Edinburgh University in the year 1827 alone.[5]

In 1826, cholera resumed its travels. Erupting with great severity in Bengal, it spread throughout the subcontinent over the next 2 years, and at the same time retraced its former route through Afghanistan and central Russia. This time however, as though crossing an invisible mercantile watershed within the Russian empire, it rapidly spread throughout the larger Russian cities.

From these centers, with their extensive northern and western trading networks, an explosive epidemic of cholera began. Within a year, most Baltic ports and countries reported extensive epidemics. Rapidly, cholera spread throughout Eastern Europe to Vienna, and by 1831 to France and Britain.

At this phase of its travels, cholera was a confirmed illegal immigrant as it infiltrated every land border and dodged every quarantine service. Cordoning the borders with foot soldiers, which was done in Prussia, isolating affected villages with troops with orders to shoot all those attempting to leave, which was done in Russia, were all ineffective means to arrest the spread.

When news of the affliction in eastern and central Europe reached Britain, a strict quarantine was maintained at first, with the airing of all imported Baltic goods to exclude any pestilential miasmata. However, the extent of trade was enormous, and the traveling time by sea was short — as little as 2–3 days from cholera-stricken Hamburg, for instance, to northern England. By late 1831, cholera indeed had crossed from Germany to Sunderland, and within a few months to London, as well as to other mercantile centers and ports that were devastated. By 1832, Ireland was invaded.

Unlike the protracted travel required from India to Europe, transatlantic journeys were a matter of mere 4 weeks or so. And as was indeed feared and expected in the Americas, cholera "skipped the puddle" in 1832, probably brought over by Irish immigrants. Canada and the United States were affected first, and the Caribbean and Latin America a year later. Cholera was not averse to shorter journeys by sea and Portugal, Spain, and Marseille in southern France were all affected.

In addition to its European Grand Tour, cholera went on pilgrimage and journeyed from Mesopotamia (which it had reached earlier) to Mecca. This nexus of travelers from all over the Islamic world was first hit during the Hajj season of 1831, and continued to be a source of infection for the next 80 years. Within a few months of Muslim pilgrims returning home from Mecca, cholera spread to Syria and Palestine, Egypt, Tunis, and subsequently, throughout North Africa, and sub-Saharan Africa. The true extent of its ravages in these poorly documented regions will probably never be known.

Popular Response to the Second Pandemic

A reader of the cholera travelogue of the 19th century today would find it perhaps difficult to understand and identify with the popular responses to the epidemic. An inkling of understanding of the panic associated with the spread of cholera was perhaps gained by the recent SARS epidemic. Still, armed as we are with germ theory, vaccinations, and antimicrobials, and above all, with modern public health, safe water, and effective sewage treatment — can we truly identify with the victims of cholera?

"The inhabitants of Gateshead fell asleep on the 25th December in perfect security and devoid of panic, but before the sun rose on the 26th 55 individuals had been seized, 32 of whom were destined not to see it set … from one o'clock on Sunday (Christmas Day) to ten o'clock this day (45 hours) 119 persons had been seized and 52 died".[5] Families and neighbors had thus to contend with a fiend that emerged suddenly, carrying them to the grave one after another. The disease itself was not only often fatal, but also caused immense suffering and pain until its final comatose phase, leaving its victims horribly changed and discolored.

For the unfortunate hosts of cholera, helplessness and uncertainty prevailed. What caused the disease? Was it an illness or perhaps a poisoning — first used by the British on the natives of India and now imported to Europe? Was it contagious or perhaps caused by atmospheric conditions? How could it be that a person could become ill without coming into contact with the already sick?

Some truths however were crystal clear to all. The unwelcome guest was certainly an inverted snob, affecting preferentially the poorest, lowest orders of society, but sparing the affluent. Were the rich or the noble causing the disease? Was this a Malthusian plot to eliminate the swarming poor of Europe? These were the fears that caused such scenes as the shutting up of nobles within their castles in Hungary, and burning them alive.

The affluent segment of the society certainly had its interests in mind or preferred to ignore the problem; how else could the poor explain such farcical scenes as the public declaration of the town council of Sunderland — the first place to be affected in Britain — that Asiatic Cholera was certainly not present in the town (making quarantine unnecessary) even while people were dying? (Longmate, 1966)

If the poor found only limited help from their "betters," they had even less to expect from the national governments (their response in some of the absolute monarchies of the time was harsh in the extreme). Affected loci of disease were cordoned of and left to fend for themselves, their people killed if they tried to leave. Parliamentary Britain was no better, with the government first trying to shift all responsibility of the management of the epidemic to local authorities.

Another issue was that the medical profession was a poor source of comfort. Doctors seemed unable to agree about what caused the scourge, and were certainly ineffectual in treating the afflicted. Physicians were eager to study the disease, and traveled throughout the continent in the wake of cholera. But was all this medical travel innocent, or perhaps were the doctors causing the disease? Did they infect people in order to have fresh corpses to dissect, or perhaps to augment their income? Such fears were voiced from Moscow to Liverpool. Riots with attacks centered on hospitals and doctors occurred in many places. In fear and ignorance, even the patients were sometimes assaulted (Burrell & Gill, 2005)! In many places, the most basic social contracts became void, and with it all charity. Patients were driven out from villages and left to die on the roadside, while their houses were burnt. Hospitals refused to admit cholera patients, and even a decent burial was not to be had.

Eventually, after more than 10 years on the road, cholera apparently returned home to gather fresh forces. The national death toll across Europe ranged from less than one percent in Britain to as high as 20 percent in Russia. In most places, life returned to its former order; in France the carefree Orléan government even coined a special medal to mark the occasion. But not all were as complacent — cholera's impact set many people thinking.

On the Road Again: The Third Pandemic, Snow and Scientific Breakthrough

The bitter argument within the medical profession between the contagionists and the miasmatists was to rage for two more generations;[2] both sides however were united in associating the prevalent filth and squalor, and the horrible living conditions of the working classes with the spread of cholera. The idea of "sanitary reform" was born and was to bring about the greatest improvement in the health of any medical innovation, since the time of Jenner.

However, when cholera returned to call on its unwilling hosts, things were as bad as they had ever been. The disease proved to be rather conservative in its tastes, revisiting its previous haunts with the utmost regularity. Indeed, the divisions to distinct pandemics are somewhat arbitrary; since the second pandemic onwards, new waves of cholera occurred even while previous outbreaks still resonated on the same continent.

It was, however, in London that a great breakthrough was made in the fight against cholera. It was here that the road to improving public health took a new turn; instead of targeting filth ("nuisances" was the term used at the time) in general, water came into focus. John Snow was a physician and surgeon who from a humble beginning, was carving a place for himself in the British capital. He was a pioneer in the use of "ether" — the earliest form of anesthesia. Living in London during the 1840s, he could not help but be aware of the disease, and in 1847 he first published a monograph, suggesting that the noxious element of the disease was introduced to the body through eating and drinking, completely unrelated to the air or atmospheric conditions.

In 1853 London was again hit with a severe outbreak of cholera. For the residents of the region of Golden Square in Soho, the outbreak began explosively with more than 50 cases occurring during the last night of August 1853. During the next 10 days approximately 500 persons had lost their lives. It was, in the words of John Snow "The most terrible outbreak of cholera which ever occurred in this kingdom". He was at hand not only in the role of physician but also as an investigator. His detailed enquiry showed clearly that those inhabitants that took their water from the Broad street pump were struck by cholera. The removal of the pump handle was a simple measure that caused the outbreak to abate.

Another meticulous investigation by Snow proved to be even more decisive: a few years earlier in the south of London, a new water company had begun its operation, drawing its water from an upstream segment of the Thames. The district was therefore divided into two arbitrary populations, differing only in the source of their water. The experiment "… was on the grandest scale. No fewer than three hundred thousand people of both sexes, of every age and occupation, and of every rank and station, from gentlefolk down to the very poor, were divided into two groups without their choice, and, in most cases, without their knowledge; one group being supplied with water containing the sewage of London, and, amongst it, whatever might have come from the cholera patients, the other group having water quite free from such impurity". The results of the experiment were conclusive: those who consumed sewage-laced water were affected by cholera, while those who drank pure water were protected. It must be emphasized that these observations were made a generation prior to the identification of the cholera bacillus, and in fact prior to any knowledge of bacteria at all!

Unfortunately, these discoveries were dismissed by the authorities at the time, and Dr Snow himself was not to see his theory being adopted (having died from stroke a few years after its publication). The sanitary idea however continued its growth.

Wherever proper sanitation took hold, cholera's visitations decreased or ceased completely. Local successes led to more ambitious attempts to halt the traveling disease. A series of international conferences in the latter third of the 19th century led to replacing the old quarantine system with a system of inspection, disinfection, medical supervision of the exposed, and with cross-border reporting.

At the same time, cholera had lost its anonymity. Although the bacillus was already described in Florence in 1854 by Filippo Pacini, it was largely ignored until the 1880s. Through the efforts of Robert Koch working at the time in Egypt, the "coma-like" bacillus was identified as the causative agent of the disease. Some of Koch's colleagues were still vehemently opposed to the idea (notably Max von Pettenkoffer of the University of Munich, who swallowed a broth culture of vibrios and suffered only mild diarrhea, thus "disproving" Koch). A decade later, however, Koch's discovery was put to good use by the brilliant work of Haffkine, who, having first tested the vaccine's efficacy on himself, went on to vaccinate tens of thousands in India in the midst of the ongoing epidemic, saving countless lives.

It was through these measures that cholera found itself banished from the comforts of travel in the developed/industrialized world: cholera was becoming a backpacker.

The Latter Day Travels of Cholera

It was the growing "sanitary divide" between industrialized countries and their colonies (rather than the introduction of cholera vaccines) that probably caused cholera to restrict its travels during the sixth pandemic to areas such as Egypt, sub-Saharan Africa, Mecca, and parts of the Balkan. In fact, from 1923 and for nearly 40 years cholera rarely left its home. When it broke out in 1961 it spread rapidly but selectively, always affecting poorer nations. Its worst affects were probably in Africa, where the disease hopped from one refugee crisis to another. Its most spectacular growth however was in the Americas (Guthmann, 1995). After nearly a century of absence, in 1991 cholera jumped ship (literally — being in all probability introduced in bilge and ballast water) in Peru. Having caused several thousand deaths, it spread to nearly all of South and Central America. Here, as in Africa and its Asian homeland, cholera should be regarded as a resident rather than as a traveler. But are cholera's perambulations really over?

It is highly unlikely that large-scale epidemics of cholera will occur in any nation that maintains adequate water and sewage treatment standards. However, new epidemic strains of cholera can certainly cause havoc in less fortunate countries. The recent experience with the O139 cholera strain in India has demonstrated this potential.

The most recent cases and outbreaks are reported from Africa (Table 35.2), with many cases occurring among displaced populations.

Could cholera be eradicated completely? The answer is unfortunately no — at least not with the tools that are currently available. With its known ability to remain dormant for years in the environment, its often subclinical or mildly symptomatic course that is usually undiagnosed; and especially with the absence of effective vaccines, cholera will be a fact of life in many developing countries during the 21st century as well.

According to UN sources, at least 20% of world population does not have access to clean and adequate drinking water. Indeed, providing people in the Indian subcontinent with sanitary conditions at a level enjoyed by late Victorian Europe can do more towards the goal of cholera eradication than any vaccine.

For today's traveler, cholera is fortunately an insignificant hazard. There are virtually no case reports among travelers from the developed world. New cholera vaccines that have been developed during the last decades are usually not recommended therefore to the routine

Table 35.2: List of cholera outbreaks in the 21st century.

Date of WHO report	Country
28 January 2000	Madagascar
2 May 2000	Somalia
6 July 2000	Federated States of Micronesia
12 September 2000	Afghanistan
13 October 2000	South Africa
22 November 2000	Somalia
26 July 2001	Tanzania
26 July 2001	Afghanistan
26 July 2001	Chad
14 August 2001	India
27 November 2001	Nigeria
5 March 2002	Democratic Republic of Congo
28 June 2002	Mozambique
19 July 2002	Burundi
24 July 2002	Niger
13 August 2002	Côte d'Ivoir
6 September 2002	Malawi
13 September 2002	Liberia
16 September 2002	Democratic Republic of Congo
8 January 2003	Côte d'Ivoire
8 May 2003	Iraq
9 May 2003	Zambia
19 May 2003	Uganda
21 May 2003	Mozambique
23 May 2003	South Africa
13 June 2003	Democratic Republic of Congo
3 July 2003	Liberia
20 November 2003	Benin
25 November 2003	Mali
28 January 2004	Chad, Mozambique and Zambia
2 June 2004	Niger
15 June 2004	Cameroon
3 December 2004	Nigeria
21 June 2005	Afghanistan
24 February 2006	Southern Sudan
10 May 2006	Angola
4 October 2006	Ethiopia

travelers. However, it is well to remember that the famous slogan of travel medicine: *"Boil it, cook it, peel it or forget it"* is rooted back to the sanitary measures taken against cholera.

Epilogue

Cholera was certainly not the first "traveling disease," but in the industrialized world it was the first disease to have its travels recorded, in detail, through the various pandemics. The disease has always been an astute social scientist; observing class distinctions in 19th century Europe, it always affected the poor rather than the rich, workers more than their employers, and women rather than men.

In the world of the 21st century, its travels follow the fault line between developed and developing, affluent and poor, and it is always at hand to accommodate the occasional war or refugee crisis. As long as poor sanitary conditions and endemic transmission coexist, there is the possibility of cholera resuming its travels.

Notes

1. Jeremiah, chapter 21 lines 4–6: "Thus saith the LORD God of Israel; Behold, I will turn back the weapons of war that are in your hands, wherewith ye fight against the king of Babylon, and against the Chaldeans, which besiege you without the walls, and I will assemble them into the midst of this city. And I myself will fight against you with an outstretched hand and with a strong arm, even in anger, and in fury, and in great wrath. And I will smite the inhabitants of this city, both man and beast: they shall die of a great pestilence."
2. The "contagionist-miasmatist controversy": this bitter controversy raged among medical circles for the better part of the 19th century. The "miasma theory" of infection related the occurrence of epidemics to unspecified environmental–atmospheric conditions, an airborne "impurity" that induced infection. The contagionists favored the transfer of an infectious agent or "virus" through contact with the sick or via food and water. In the case of cholera, the disease was prevalent in locales that were often close to impure, stinking bodies of water, with refuse everywhere and effective sewage nowhere. These data apparently lent support to both sides; the fortunate fact was that all concurred that the solution was the adoption of sanitary measures. More than 50 years were required to finally convince the medical profession, that it was not the stinking "miasma" that conferred the disease but the ingestion of infected water.
3. The Edinburgh Advertiser 1826-07-14.
4. The Edinburgh Advertiser 1826-04-18.
5. The Edinburgh Advertiser 1827-08-03.

References

Burrell, S., & Gill, G. (2005). The Liverpool cholera epidemic of 1832 and anatomical dissection — medical mistrust and civil unrest. *J Hist Med Allied Sci., 60*, 478–498.

Flint, A. (1866). *A Treatise on the Principles and Practice of Medicine*. Philadelphia: Henry C. Lea.

Great Epidemics. (1856). Harper's new monthly magazine, *13*(75), 359–367.

Guthmann, J. P. (1995). Epidemic cholera in Latin America: Spread and routes of transmission. *Journal of Tropical Medicine and Hygiene, 98*, 419–274.

Longmate, N. (1966). *King Cholera: The biography of a disease*. London: H Hamilton.

Morris Jr., J. G. (2003). Cholera and other types of vibriosis: A story of human pandemics and oysters on the half shell. *Clinical Infectious Diseases, 37*, 272–280.

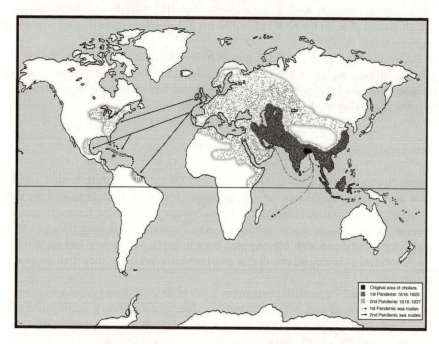

Figure 35.1. Map of the first two cholera pandemics.

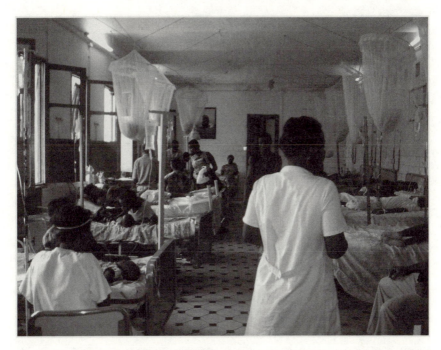

Image 35.1. Busy pediatric ward during a cholera epidemic in Equatorial Guinea.

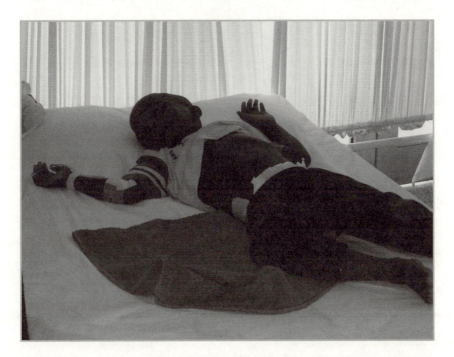

Image 35.2. Local hospital's intensive care unit; Child being treated for severe cholera.

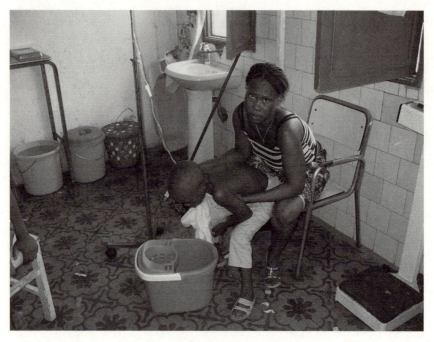

Image 35.3. "Rice Water" excretion of a child with cholera.

Chapter 36

The Role of Armies in Spreading Epidemics: Vector and Victim

Eran Dolev

The association between war and epidemics has been known for centuries. Since ancient times it has also included a third party — famine. 'The sword is without, and the pestilence and the famine within: he that is in the field shall die with the sword; and he that is in the city, famine and pestilence shall devour him'.[1] A lot of literature concerning the association between war and disease has been published. Since the Biblical plague that smote the Assyrian army of Sennacherib to the modern battles fought recently in Africa, the relationship between war, famine and disease has been well established.[2,3] Many battles in history have been lost or won due to outbreak of epidemics. Armies have been destroyed not by their enemies but rather by various germs. Some of these, presumably inevitable military disasters, which decided who would be the victor and who would be the victim, could have been avoided by simple sanitary measures known at the time. Or, as Hans Zinsser has asked why 'the epidemics get the blame for defeat, the generals the credit for victory' when actually it should be the opposite.[4]

However, one aspect of this relationship has not been emphasized enough: the role of the armies themselves, victors or vanquished, in spreading diseases. No doubt war times have always been characterized by ill-nutrition, overcrowding, insanitation and misery — all these factors are known to be an adequate background for outbreak of epidemics. Several historical events could not be properly explained without the understanding of the military factor as a vector in spreading diseases. It is the purpose of this article to throw some light on the problem through historical examples.

Malaria and the Fall of Rome

During the 5th century A.D., the Western Roman Empire came to its end: it was conquered and torn to pieces by various Barbarian tribes. One of the great empires in history, which had developed its war machine almost to perfection, disappeared from the stage of history.

Travel Medicine: Tales Behind the Science
Copyright © 2007 by Elsevier Ltd.
All rights of reproduction in any form reserved.
ISBN: 0-08-045359-7

No doubt the sinking of Rome was a long process: the Roman Empire did not collapse in a short time. It took at least two centuries for the large empire to disintegrate. Historians could identify several causes for the collapse of Rome. There had been economic, military, religious and other reasons. Yet, none of them, alone or combined with other reasons could give an adequate and comprehensive explanation for the process.

It was then that a medical theory was proposed: it seemed that there were enough data to assume that during the 4th century A.D., an unidentified epidemic hit Rome. That pestilence decimated the population of Rome to a large extent and eventually brought about the decay of the Empire. The problem was the identification of the pest. Several etiologies have been suggested as the epidemic, which, together with other factors, led to the end of the empire. However, the identity of none of them could be established.

One etiology in particular was considered reasonable for the devastating epidemics: it was lead poisoning. Several historians were impressed by the developed Roman system of aquaducts. When lead was identified as a component of various water pipes, the theory of lead poisoning through drinking water was suggested: it could explain the massive effect of the poison and its various effects. The lead poisoning theory was definitely abandoned about twenty-five years ago.[5]

It was during 2001 when Dr. David Soren and his international team of archaeologists were excavating a Roman villa near the town of Lugnano, some 70 miles north of Rome, near the Tiber river. They found 49 children's skeletons, among them babies and neonates. It looked as if all the children had died and had been buried during a very short period of time about 450 A.D. It could be assumed that all the buried children had died as a result of an epidemic. The skeletons of several children showed signs of hyperostosis, which is a typical sign for severe anemia. DNA examinations of the skeletons revealed the presence of *Plasmodium falciparum*.[6]

The DNA finding provided evidence to the theory that an outbreak of malignant form of malaria was the lethal epidemic that hit Roman Italy during the 5th century A.D. and contributed to the downfall of the Roman Empire. One question has remained still unanswered: why and how the falciparum malaria reached Rome during the 4th and the 5th centuries A.D.? What had been the origin of the disease and what had been the mechanism that had brought it to Roman Italy.

Malaria is among the oldest diseases that have infected the human race. It causes high morbidity in the affected populations. Malaria caused by *Plasmodium falciparum* has been a main factor in children's mortality. As such, it served as an evolutionary power that has influenced the human genome. Disorders such as Thalassemia, G6PD deficiency and various other hemoglobinopathies are considered to be the outcome of the malarial influence on the affected human populations, creating a better protection against the malaria parasites. G6PD deficiency, as well as Thalassemia and other conditions are found mainly in areas where malaria has been prevalent. On the other hand, it is assumed, that populations who lack this traits, which give the erythrocytes an advantage over the malaria parasite, have not suffered from malaria during the process of evolution. Thus, while Greek population was influenced very much by malaria in Greece itself, the Greek islands, modern Turkey and other parts of the Mediterranean, Italian Rome, though covered with marshes and infested by mosquitoes, anophelines among them, did not suffer from malaria.

During the 1st century B.C., the Roman Empire reached the Middle East. Roman legions conquered Syria and gradually captured the whole Middle East. That area was and until recently has been, a malarial zone. It is easy to assume that the Roman legions began to suffer from malaria. When the veterans began to return home, to Rome, they brought with them the Plasmodia in their blood. Then, malaria came to Rome: there were marshes, anopheles and malaria parasites — everything that was needed to create an epidemic in a population who had not encountered the disease.

It took the disease about two centuries to create a real problem. The number of malaria-carriers among the veterans of the Legions was most probably quite low. Then, when the local population had become a large reservoir for the plasmodia, the epidemic began to expand, and maybe, also to be more lethal. *Plasmodium falciparum* malaria, the most malignant form of malaria, affected Roman society by causing high morbidity among adults and a disease manifested by high mortality among newborn and young children. This epidemic decimated the population of Rome. The malaria epidemic incapacitated the Roman ability to cope with all problems, domestic and foreign, that the Roman Empire had to face, and brought about the destruction and fall of the Western Roman Empire.

The Conquest of the Aztec Empire

It is assumed that at the beginning of the 15th century, the Aztec Empire in Mexico consisted of twenty-five million inhabitants. This cultured, prosperous and wealthy empire was conquered by Hernan Cortez who commanded a Spanish force of a little more than five hundred soldiers. Historians have faced a problem: how to explain this unprecedented conquest.

Various theories have tried to explain the Spanish success by technological superiority. However, these theories could not explain the fact that during several decades since the conquest of Tenochtitlan (Mexico City), the local population decreased by more than eighty percent. Even those who believed that the Spaniards committed genocide of the Aztec population, could not explain the pace in which the local population was decimated, in the urban as well as in the rural areas.

The story of the conquest of Mexico was the story of the encounter between Europe, the Old World and the recently discovered New World. The encounter of the Europeans with the New World included also the transoceanic transmission of diseases. One of these diseases was smallpox, which reached the Caribbean Islands in 1507. While the Spaniards, who had been exposed to the disease during childhood and later were all immune to it, for the native population, the encounter with smallpox was devastating. The outcome was that the disease caused high morbidity with high mortality among the natives while the Spaniards were not affected by it at all.

In April 23, 1520, smallpox was introduced into Mexico itself via Veracruz by a black soldier who suffered from smallpox, a member of the Spanish delegation of Panfilio de Narvaez. The disease rapidly spread into the inland and killed million on its way. When Cortez burst into Tenochtitlan, the Aztecs' capital on 13 August 1521, after three months of siege, he could capture the city quite easily as the local population had been devastated by smallpox epidemic.

William McNeill was then right when he wrote: 'Clearly, if smallpox had not come when it did, the Spanish victory could not have been achieved in Mexico'.[7]

During 1530–1531, an epidemic of measles reached Mexico. What used to be a children's disease in Europe had a terrible effect on the local population, the survivors of the smallpox epidemics. In 1546, the Mexican population encountered a third major epidemic, imported from Europe: this time it was epidemic typhus.

In the meantime smallpox spread southwards and reached the Inca domain in 1525. Its effect on the local population was again devastating. Starting by killing the Inca ruler and about 200,000 others, the empire's institutions ceased to exist. Francisco Pizarro and his Spanish force did not face any real resistance when they conquered the Inca Empire.

The Thirty Years' War (1618–1648)

A prelude to the understanding of this war may be found in the story of the invasion of the army of the Roman Holy Empire into Hungary in 1542. When the army entered Hungary, the troops began to suffer from typhus epidemics. The toll was very high: during a short period of time the army lost 30,000 soldiers. Since then Hungary would be remembered as 'the graveyard of Germans' and typhus would be called in Germany 'the Hungarian Disease'. However, the most important outcome of the encounter of the German army with typhus was realized much later: the retreating units, sick with typhus, spread the disease along their route of retreat.[8]

The Thirty Years' War, which was fought on different battle fields during different times, involved practically all European countries for quite a long time. It is difficult to identify the various epidemics that devastated the European population during these series of battles. It is accepted that the two major pestilences that caused most of the morbidity and the mortality, among both soldiers and civilians, were typhus and bubonic plague. The various populations were also affected by minor ailments as dysentery, influenza and scurvy. However, the important phenomenon was not the outbreaks of diseases by themselves but the mode of their spread.

Most of the outbreaks were initiated by the military movements around Europe:

> The war began in Bohemia. After the battle on White Hill, near Prague (8th November, 1620), the soldiers of Count Mansfeld, who were already infected with typhus fever, marched down the Main to the Palatinate and to Alsace, devastating the country as they passed and leaving severe pestilences behind them.[9]

Such was the mechanism by which the various diseases were spread around Europe. Or in the words of Hans Zinsser:

> The Thirty Years' War was the most gigantic natural experiment in epidemiology to which mankind has ever been subjected. Europe was a spot map of constant small outbreaks of every conceivable infectious disease; and through this area, for a little over twenty-nine years, armies marched and countermarched, and disbanded soldiers, fugitives and deserters vagabonded far and

wide. Famines resulted and populations wandered in fugitive hordes toward food and protection. Wherever men traveled, disease followed them.[10]

Napoleon's Army Retreat from Moscow (1812–1813)

The retreat of Napoleon's French army from Moscow, during an extremely cold winter, under permanent pressure from the following Russian Army, was one of the most enduring military experiences in history:

'The French soldiers, almost naked, or clothed in torn and half-burned rags, without shoes, their feet covered with straw, and their frozen limbs covered with festering sores, they marched through Poland and Germany. Typhus fever and other disease associated with it marked their course'.[11]

The local population, along the French army routes of retreat, were ordered to host at their homes the exhausted, sick and miserable soldiers. Later 'many people stated positively, that they contracted the disease almost immediately after they had occupied small, narrow rooms in company with infected French soldiers, or after they had washed their clothes or waited upon them'.[12]

Recently, a mass grave of Napoleon's soldiers was found near Vilnius, one of the main stations along the route of the French retreat from Russia. DNA studies that were performed on the corpses showed that louse-borne infectious diseases affected nearly one-third of the buried soldiers.[13,14] These findings confirm the stories and memoirs of the surviving soldiers as well as the testimonies of the local population. The findings also identify the French soldiers' ailments as louse-borne diseases and contribute to the understanding of the spread of typhus in Europe during 1813.

The Crimean War

This war is well remembered in the collective memory due to the charge of the British Light Brigade at Balaclava. However, it should be remembered as a typical example of an unnecessary war, where nothing was achieved by all participating countries. It should also be remembered as a campaign that brought about two severe epidemics which could be prevented.

In 1853, a cholera epidemic appeared in several places in France. During the year 1854 it spread through the whole country, mainly southward. When the French army, whose main camps were located in southern France, was ordered to embark for the Crimea, several soldiers had already been suffering from cholera. Wherever the French troops went, they spread cholera with them. The outbreak of cholera in Bulgaria during 1854 was the outcome of the French troops movements in that country.

All the participating armies, British, French, Russian and Turkish, suffered from various ailments during the Crimean War. Typhus epidemic appeared among the troops during the winter of 1855–1856. Several months later, when the war was over and the British soldiers returned home, they brought with them epidemic typhus back to England. It caused several outbreaks in various parts of the country.[15,16]

Thus, the losses of the Crimean War had begun in France, several months before it was waged in the Crimea itself and continued in England for long months after the last British soldier had left the Russian soil. It was a typical example to what Prinzing would write about sixty years after the Crimean War:

> In countries which have the misfortune to be the scene of protracted wars, the mortality regularly undergoes a considerable increase. This is caused chiefly by the infectious diseases, which in war times so often appear in the form of epidemics. These diseases, moreover, not only afflict the country in which the war is waged, but are also carried by prisoners, returning soldiers, and in other ways, into the land of the victor, where it is possible for them to spread over a large territory.[17]

Notes

1. *The Old Testament, The book of Ezekiel*, Chapter 7, 15.
2. Prinzing, F. (1916). *Epidemics resulting from wars*. Oxford, London: Clarendon Press.
3. Smallman-Raynor, M. R., & Cliff, A. D. (2004). *War epidemics*. London: Oxford University Press.
4. Zinsser, H. (1963). *Rats, lice and history* (p. 153). Boston: Little, Brown & Co. (Originally published in 1934).
5. Scarborough, J. (1984). The myth of lead poisoning among the Romans. *Journal of the History of Medicine, 39*, 469–475.
6. Abbot, A. (2001). Earliest malaria DNA found in Roman baby graveyard. *Nature, 412*, 847.
7. McNeill, W. H. (1977). *Plagues and peoples* (p. 207). Oxford, London: Blackwell.
8. Zinsser, H. (1963). pp. 267–268.
9. Prinzing, F. (1916). p. 27.
10. Zinsser, H. (1963). pp. 272–273.
11. Prinzing, F. (1916). p. 124.
12. Prinzing, F. (1916). p. 107.
13. Raoult, D., Dutour, O., Mouhamdi, L., Jankauskas, R., Fournier, P. E., Ardagna, Y., et al. (2006). Evidence for louse transmitted diseases in soldiers of Napoleon's Grand Army in Vilnius. *Journal of Infectious Diseases, 193*, 112–120.
14. Vasold, M. (2004). The epidemic typhus of 1813/14. *Wurzburger Medizinhistorische Mitteilungen, 23*, 217–232.
15. Prinzing, F. (1916). pp. 170–174.
16. Smallman-Raynor, M. R., & Cliff, A. D., pp. 417–452.
17. Prinzing, F. (1916). p. 1.

Chapter 37

The Spread of Disease in the 20th Century and Lessons for the 21st Century

Stephen M. Ostroff

Movement and the emergence of infectious diseases have always gone hand-in-hand. One needs only to think back to the spread of plague from Asia to Europe in the 14th century (ushering in the concept of quarantine), the introduction of smallpox to the Americas with the voyages of discovery in the late 1400s, the transfer of syphilis back to the old world on those same voyages, and theories regarding emergence of tuberculosis in sub-Saharan Africa via European colonization. Movement is probably a better term for this phenomenon than travel. The latter usually refers only to people, whereas the former includes goods, animals, and insects in addition to people. All have played a role in the spread of infectious diseases.

The tendency for diseases to move took off in the 20th century as movement itself accelerated. Not only did the variety of conveyances increase (e.g., automobiles, trucks, buses, aircraft, and spacecraft) but also everything got bigger and faster, even trains and ships. These modes of transportation allowed us to probe places we had never been to before: remote terrestrial locations, the oceans, and aerospace. In some instances, microbes came along for the ride.

Examples of movement-associated emerging disease from the early 20th century include the introduction of plague into the Americas and the Spanish flu. *Yersinia pestis* came ashore with rodents from a ship, which had traveled from Hong Kong to San Francisco at the dawn of the 20th century, sparking a plague outbreak in the city in 1900 (Kinyoun & Wyman, 2006). From that single introduction, the organism has gradually but relentlessly extended its range in animals and conveyances until today it is found throughout large portions of the western half of North America. Fortunately the human disease impact of plague in North America remains small (Centers for Disease Control and Prevention, 2006).

The 1918 Spanish flu is entirely another matter, proving to be the single most devastating epidemic the world has ever seen. This event is estimated to have killed 50 million people globally over a period of only a few short months, devastating whole communities virtually overnight (Taubenberger & Morens, 2006). With the current growing interest in avian

Travel Medicine: Tales Behind the Science
Copyright © 2007 by Elsevier Ltd.
All rights of reproduction in any form reserved.
ISBN: 0-08-045359-7

influenza, images of the 1918 pandemic have resurfaced, including makeshift hospitals in gymnasiums and armories, masked security personnel, and corpses littering the streets. As a result of this epidemic, life expectancy temporarily plummeted all over the world; in the United States life expectancy decreased from 51 to 39 years. Although no one knows for sure how the Spanish flu spread, travel surely contributed. We were in the midst of World War I. Mass displacements and malnutrition among civilian populations affected by the war were common. Ships carried thousands of soldiers back and forth from the Americas to Europe, and troops were moving all around the continent. This was the perfect recipe for a disease explosion. Many accounts suggest that the 1918 virus first appeared in the United States Midwest, moved to the east coast, then from America to Europe along with the troops, alit in Spain, and spread exponentially from there. All this was at a time when travel was still relatively slow. In 1918, that journey took months; today it would take hours.

Like its filovirus cousin Ebola, Marburg virus is an African pathogen that causes severe hemorrhagic fever. Yet in 1967 it was first identified not in Africa, but in a small university town in Germany (which is how the virus got its name) (Slenczka, 1999). How did it get there? The virus hopscotched from Africa to England to Germany, in a group of African monkeys whose kidneys were to be used for tissue culture purposes. A strange disease then occurred among workers who handled the monkeys or their tissues in both Germany and Yugoslavia, killing almost a fourth of those infected. A similar episode in the late 1980s in Washington DC (involving an Ebola virus variant of no obvious pathogenicity to humans) occurred in cynomolgus monkeys and their handlers originating from the Philippines (Jahrling et al., 1990). It prompted the international best seller *The Hot Zone* by Richard Preston, vaulting emerging infectious diseases to the forefront of public consciousness (Preston, 1994).

In 1976, a new cause of pneumonia was recognized among those who traveled to an American Legion convention in Philadelphia, Pennsylvania (Fraser et al., 1977). This illness, known ever since as Legionnaires disease, had as its source the cooling system of an upscale, downtown hotel named the Bellevue Stratford. Apropos for a disease that got its start at a convention, many subsequent Legionnaires disease outbreaks have been associated with travel settings. Among the more common are hotels; others include spas, cruise ships, and flower shows (Fields, Benson, & Besser, 2002).

Travel has played a prominent role in the second devastating epidemic of the 20th century. This, of course, is acquired immune deficiency syndrome (AIDS) caused by the human immunodeficiency virus. This disease was first identified in 1981 (Gottlieb et al., 1981). While the origin of AIDS is considered to involve a virus that jumped the species barrier from great apes to humans, its subsequent spread was greatly assisted by human movement. Although details remain murky, the disease clearly spread from its origins in central Africa by road, hitch hiking with long-haul truckers. Movement to the western hemisphere may have been facilitated through persons who went to Africa like workers from Haiti and soldiers from Cuba. North American visitors to Haiti, which was then a popular tourist destination, carried the disease from the Caribbean back home with them. Once HIV emerged in places like Thailand, its global spread was furthered by the large-scale sex tourism industry of the 1980s and 1990s in that country. The international spread of HIV could be documented because of clades (or subtypes) of the virus, which appeared in different locations (McCutchan, 2000). In a number of small, isolated locations like Pacific island countries, the first appearance of HIV was often linked to locals who had traveled abroad for school or work. The long latency of HIV before the appearance of symptoms gave ample opportunity for this virus to spread undetected via population movements and tourism. Unfortunately, the disease burden of HIV continues to mount. At last count, more than 65 million persons have been cumulatively infected and more than 25 million have died (UN AIDS, 2006).

South America was cholera-free for almost the entire 20th century. But in 1991, the disease suddenly appeared in several areas of coastal Peru almost simultaneously (Swerdlow et al., 1992). From there, cholera quickly spread throughout the entire continent of South America, into Central America, and as far north as Mexico, over a brief period of less than two years. Almost 1.3 million cases were recorded over the next decade, with close to 13,000 fatalities (Pan American Health Organization, 1991–2002). It took many years and billions of dollars in sanitation improvements to bring the disease under control in affected areas. Although some have suggested that this outbreak was a natural event related to movement of the organism on sea-currents, a more likely explanation is that it was introduced in ballast released from a ship traveling from a cholera-endemic area. Its subsequent spread was aided by the absence of population immunity, but it was travelers and movement of goods that rapidly spread the organism. Infections linked to air travel and to foods were well documented.

The last major infectious disease event of the 20th century, and the first naturally occurring ones of the 21st century, illustrate the powerful role movement and travel now play in the emergence of infectious diseases. In August of 1999, a cluster of encephalitis cases was identified in New York City. This human cluster occurred at the same time bird die-offs were reported in the region. Investigations found that the human and avian outbreaks were linked and the causative agent was identified as West Nile virus, an arbovirus never previously seen in the western hemisphere (Asnis, Conetta, Texeira, Waldman, & Sampson, 2000). Over the next five years, the virus methodically marched across North America, reaching the Pacific coast in 2004. In its wake, it has caused hundreds of thousands of infections, almost 25,000 illnesses, and close to 1,000 deaths in the United States and Canada. It has reappeared annually in all areas that it has invaded, suggesting it is a permanently entrenched part of the microbial flora in North America. It has also progressively moved south and has been identified in Central America, the Caribbean, and as far south as Argentina.

How West Nile virus moved from its natural range (Africa, the Middle East, Europe, and Western Asia) to North America remains a mystery. Studies showed that the virus found in New York City was closely related to one identified a year earlier in the Middle East, suggesting this as the source of introduction (Lanciotti et al., 1999). All subsequent West Nile viruses in North America have been clonal descendants of the 1999 New York strain, suggesting a single discreet introduction. Possible explanations include movement of infected mosquito vectors on a plane or in cargo or movement of an infected bird (intentionally or naturally), animal, or human. The latter two explanations are less likely, as mammalian West Nile viremias tend not to be high enough to allow back-transmission to biting mosquitoes. Regardless, movement of something from the Old World to the New World was surely involved. Bird movement is thought to explain the steady westward migration of the virus. Travel-associated disease has been a feature of West Nile since 1999, being reported in persons traveling to North America and in North Americans traveling from uninfected to infected areas. This episode serves as a stark reminder of how easy it now is for vector-borne pathogens considered to be geographically specific to move to new locations.

In the spring of 2000, the annual pilgrimage (Hajj) to Mecca took place. This event is the single largest annual gathering in the world; millions of travelers from throughout the Muslim world participate. Pathogens have been known to also make the pilgrimage, causing outbreaks during the event and disseminating from the event. The 2000 and 2001 Hajjs were no exception. The pathogen was *Neisseria meningitidis* W135. As a result of previous episodes of meningococcal disease at the Hajj, the Saudi government required all pilgrims to be vaccinated. However, while the U.S. vaccine produced immunity against four types (A,C,W135, and Y), the European vaccine only protected against types A and C. After the event, pilgrims returned home carrying the Hajj-specific W135 strain and sparked outbreaks (in themselves or in contacts) in at least 11 countries, mostly locations where the pilgrims had not been protected against W135. These outbreaks resulted in more than 300 cases of disease in both 2000 and 2001, with a mortality rate of approximately 25% (World Health Organization, 2002). There is strong evidence that the dissemination of W135 from the Hajj into a number of locations, especially the African meningitis belt, altered the usual distribution of circulating meningococcal types over the next several years (Traore et al., 2006).

Severe acute respiratory syndrome (SARS), which was recognized in early 2003, was through-and-through a travel-related disease. The pivotal event occurred on the weekend of February 21st, when a medical professor from Guangdong China, and his wife, traveled to Hong Kong to attend a family wedding. This professor had been caring for persons with a mysterious new disease, and despite not feeling well, elected to attend the wedding. The couple stayed on the 9th floor of the Metropole Hotel in Hong Kong. Although the professor attended the wedding, he was otherwise too sick to do much else while in the hotel. He died in a Hong Kong hospital shortly after the wedding (Centers for Disease Control and Prevention, 2003).The majority of subsequent SARS outbreaks can be directly linked back to ten other guests who stayed at the hotel (all but one on the 9th floor) that same weekend. After they were exposed in unknown fashion, these guests flew to Canada, the United States, Ireland, Singapore, and Vietnam, while some remained in Hong Kong. In several instances, prolonged chains of transmission involving hundreds of cases were the result. Movement of infected persons resulted in a small outbreak in Thailand and of diagnosed illness in Germany. Air travel from Hong Kong caused the spread of disease to locations in Mainland China and Taiwan. Beijing was hit especially hard. Ultimately 8,096 cases and 774 fatalities were diagnosed in 30 different countries (World Health Organization, 2003a). Transmission was documented on several transportation modes, including commercial planes, taxis, and trains. Absent specific medical interventions, the disease was eventually brought under control through a concerted global public health effort that included intensive surveillance and screening procedures, isolation and quarantine, travel restrictions, and barrier precautions. The outbreak resulted in severe disruptions to the global economy, to travel, and to commerce (World Health Organization, 2003b). Every part of the world was affected, either directly or indirectly. The last documented SARS case was in 2004; the potential for reintroduction and subsequent spread through travel is unknown.

Among today's infectious disease threats, none has engendered more concern than the potential for a pandemic due to the emergence of human disease related to avian influenza subtype A (H5N1). Human infection was first recognized in 1997 in Hong Kong, when 18 cases and six fatalities occurred (Yuen et al., 1998). At that time, the poultry and human outbreaks were aborted through the destruction of all poultry in the territory. In 2003, H5N1 reemerged in Vietnam and China. Since then, the virus has spread widely, mostly through poultry movement and in migratory birds. Movement of the virus in smuggled birds has been documented (Van Born et al., 2005). Avian disease due to H5N1 has now appeared in more than 50 countries in Asia, Europe, and Africa (World Health Organization, 2006a), either killing or requiring the destruction of hundreds of millions of birds.

In humans, H5N1 has caused a severe disease marked by fulminate respiratory failure and pneumonia (WHO, 2005). More than 250 human cases have been confirmed by the World Health Organization in 10 countries, with the largest numbers in Vietnam, Indonesia, Thailand, China, and Egypt (World Health Organization). The median age of affected persons has been 20 years (range 3 months to 75 years), and overall mortality has been close to 60% (World Health Organization, 2006b).These factors qualify this virus as one with high pandemic potential. It has already met two of the three criteria generally associated with a pandemic strain. First, it is an unusual influenza subtype, never having been associated with human disease prior to 1997. Second, it causes unusually severe disease. To date, the third criterion, that the virus easily spreads from person-to-person, has not been met. Virtually all human cases have had direct or close contact with sick and dying poultry. Although several clusters either confirmed as, or strongly suggesting, person-to-person transmission have been identified, none have shown sustained human-to-human spread (Wong & Yuen, 2006). If this occurs through virus mutation or recombination, a pandemic would be virtually assured, since there is virtually no population immunity in humans against the H5 subtype. Although no one knows how severe the pandemic would be, H5N1 human disease presently exhibits some of the characteristics seen with the 1918 Spanish flu, especially its predilection to affect healthy young adults.

Health authorities around the world have voiced concern that H5N1 could trigger a 1918-type pandemic, even though we have tools at our disposal like antiviral drugs and vaccines that were unavailable a century ago. However, the ability for rapid global dissemination of an easily transmissible strain (a la SARS) through travelers also did not exist a century ago. While to date travelers have not figured in the epidemiology of H5N1 human disease, this situation is unlikely to continue, even given the present limited person-to-person spread. Should the virus acquire the capacity for such spread, travel will without question be a critical factor in its dissemination.

In spite of the medical and technologic advances of the last century, there is every reason to think that the patterns of infectious disease emergence seen in the 20th century will continue to be replicated in the 21st century. If anything, movement will play an even more prominent contributing role to this phenomenon, resulting in widespread, multinational outbreaks *a la* meningococcal disease from the Hajj and SARS. This is because the number of people traveling, the volume of international commerce, the size of conveyances, and their speed, will continue to rise. Microbes will continue to be unwitting hitch-hikers on this global (and may be even extra-terrestrial) merry-go-round. How we deal with these trends, whether through improved global monitoring of travelers, improved detection methods, and better prevention and control measures, will in large part determine whether we humans are able to maintain our equilibrium with the ever-changing microbes that cohabit our world.

References

Asnis, D. S., Conetta, R., Texiera, A. A., Waldman, G., & Sampson, B. A. (2000). The West Nile Virus outbreak of 1999 in New York: The Flushing Hospital experience. *Clinical Infectious Diseases*, *30*, 413–418.

Centers for Disease Control and Prevention. (2003). Update: Outbreak of severe acute respiratory syndrome — worldwide, 2003; *Morbidity and Mortality Weekly Report*, *52*, 241–248.

Centers for Disease Control and Prevention. (2006). Human plague four cases, 2006. *Morbidity and Mortality Weekly Report*, *55*, 940–943.

Fields, B. S., Benson, R. F., & Besser, R. E. (2002). Legionella and Legionnaires' disease: 25 Years of investigation. *Clinical Microbiol Reviews*, *15*, 506–526.

Fraser, D. W., Tsai, T. R., Orenstein, W., Parkin, W. E., beecham, H. J., Sharrar, R. G., et al. (1977). Legionnaires' disease: Description of an epidemic of pneumonia. *The New England Journal of Medicine*, *297*, 1189–1197.

Gottlieb, M. S., Schroff, S., Schanker, H. M., Weisman, J. D., Fan, P. T., Wolf, R. A., et al. (1981). *Pneumocystis carinii* pneumonia and mucosal candidiasis in previously health homosexual men: Evidence of a new acquired cellular immunodeficiency. *The New England Journal of Medicine*, *305*, 1425–1431.

Jahrling, P. B., Giesbert, T. W., Dalgard, D. W., Johnson, E. D., Ksiazek, T. G., Hall, W. C., et al. (1990). Preliminary report: Isolation of Ebola virus from monkeys imported to USA. *Lancet*, *335*, 502–505.

Kinyoun, J. J., & Wyman, W. (2006). Plague in San Francisco, 1900. *Public Health Reports*, *121*(Suppl 1), 17–37.

Lanciotti, R. S., Roehrig, J. T., Deubel, V., Smith, J., Parker, M., Steele, K., et al. (1999). Origin of the West Nile virus responsible for an outbreak of encephalitis in the northeastern United States. *Science*, *286*, 2333–2337.

McCutchan, F. E. (2000). Understanding the genetic diversity of HIV-1. *AIDS (London, England)*, *14*(Suppl. 3), S31–S44.

Pan American Health Organization. *Cholera: Number of cases and deaths in the Americas* (1991–2002, by country by year). Available at: www.paho.org/english/ad/dpc/cd/cholera-1991-2002.htm

Preston, R. (1994). *The Hot Zone*. New York, NY: Random House.

Slenczka, W. G. (1999). The Marburg virus outbreak of 1967 and subsequent episodes. *Current Topics in Microbiology and Immunology*, *235*, 49–75.

Swerdlow, D. L., Mintz, E. D., Rodriguez, M., Tejada, E., Ocampo, C., Espejo, L., et al. (1992). Waterborne transmission of epidemic cholera in Trujillo, Peru: Lessons for a continent at risk. *Lancet*, *340*, 28–33.

Taubenberger, J. K., & Morens, D. M. (2006). 1918 Influenza: the mother of all pandemics. *Emerging Infectious Diseases*, *12*, 15–22.

The Writing Committee of the World Health Organization (WHO). (2005). Consultation on Human Influenza A/H5. Avian influenza A(H5N1) infection in humans. *The New England Journal of Medicine*, *353*, 1374–1385.

Traore, Y., Njanpop-Lafourcade, B. M., Adjogble, K. L. S., Lourde, M., Yaro, S., Nacro, B., et al. (2006). The rise and fall of epidemic *Neisseria meningitidis* serogroup W135 meningitis in Burkino Faso, 2002–2005. *Clinical Infectious Diseases*, *43*, 817–822.

UNAIDS. (2006). *Report on the global AIDS pandemic* (a UNAIDS 10th anniversary special edition). Geneva, Switzerland. Available at : www.unaids.org/en/HIV_data/2006globalreport/default.asp

Van Born, S., Thomas, I., Hanquet, G., et al. (2005). Highly pathogenic H5N1 influenza virus in smuggled Thai eagles. Belgium. *Emerging Infectious Diseases*, *11*, 702–705.

Wong, S. S., & Yuen, K. Y. (2006). Avian influenza virus infection in humans. *Chest, 129*, 156–168.

World Health Organization. (2002). Emergence of W135 Meningococcal Disease. Report of a WHO Consultation, Geneva 17–18 September 2001. World Health Organization, Geneva, Switzerland.

World Health Organization. (2003a). *Cumulative number of reported cases of severe acute respiratory syndrome (SARS)*. Geneva: World Health Organization. Available at http://www.who.int/csr/sarscountry/en/

World Health Organization. (2003b). *The World Health Report 2003: Shaping the future*. Geneva: World Health Organization.

World Health Organization. (2006a). *World: Areas reporting confirmed occurrence of H5N1 avian influenza in poultry and wild birds since 2003*. Geneva: World Health Organization. Available at: http://gamapserver.who.int/mapLibrary/app/searchResults.aspx

World Health Organization. (2006b). Epidemiology of WHO-confirmed human cases of avian influenza A(H5N1) infection. *Weekly Epidemiological Record, 81*, 249–260.

World Health Organization. (2007). Cumulative number of confirmed human cases of avian influenza A/(H5N1) reported to WHO. Geneva: World Health Organization. Available at: http://www.who.int/csr/disease/avian_influenza/country/

Yuen, K. Y., Chan, P. K., Peiris, M., et al. (1998). Clinical features and rapid viral diagnosis of human disease associated with avian influenza A(H5N1) virus. *Lancet, 351*, 467–471.

Chapter 38

As Travel Medicine Practitioner during the SARS Outbreak in Singapore

Annelies Wilder-Smith

Severe Acute Respiratory Syndrome, or SARS, was responsible for the first pandemic of the 21st century. It changed history, and it changed my life.

I happened to be working as travel medicine practitioner in Singapore at the time of the national SARS outbreak. Singapore was one of the places that became affected early on in the epidemic when there was no awareness of the disease.

As it transpired, Singapore was the fifth most severely SARS-afflicted country, with 238 cases. I happened to be not only working in Singapore, but was working at Tan Tock Seng Hospital — the hospital that was to be designated the SARS hospital — and was responsible for the Travelers' Health & Vaccination Centre.

The day was March 6, 2003, on our usual Friday grand rounds: A young colleague (Dr. L) in our infectious diseases department presented a 23-year-old woman (let's call her Elly), who had recently traveled to Hong Kong and was now suffering from a progressively worsening pneumonia. No causative pathogen had yet been identified. Dr. L was not so much concerned about the absence of a causative pathogen (as this is often the case in community acquired pneumonia), but was rather concerned about the rapid progression despite her young age. It was noted that she had recently returned from a shopping trip to Hong Kong.

During our discussions, it was noted that her traveling companion had also been admitted to another hospital with the same symptoms. And then there were these rumors about an unusual cluster of 'respiratory tract infectious' cases in Vietnam. We decided to initiate full infection control measures for this patient. There was a problem with this, however, and it was that she had already been in hospital for 6 days without isolation and she had been in contact with many friends, visitors and fellow patients, as well as the hospital staff. The consequences of these 6 days ultimately led to the epidemic in Singapore, and most cases could eventually be traced back to her.

Meanwhile, Dr. L, who had cared for our index patient left for New York to attend an infectious diseases conference. He traveled together with his pregnant wife and mother-in-law. After arrival in New York he felt unwell. He suspected that he had contracted dengue — a

Travel Medicine: Tales Behind the Science
Copyright © 2007 by Elsevier Ltd.
All rights of reproduction in any form reserved.
ISBN: 0-08-045359-7

common problem in Singapore. He consulted a physician in New York. Indeed, leukopenia and thrombocytopenia was noted, thus confirming his suspicion of dengue. However, his chest X-ray also showed pneumonia. There was no way he could have connected his symptoms with that of his patient he had seen in the previous week. This all occurred in the couple of days before the term 'SARS' was coined and before the WHO sent out the alert on 13 March. Dr. L felt so unwell that he decided to cut short his stay in New York and he embarked on the next Singapore Airlines flight to return to Singapore. Just before he departed, he called a doctor friend in Singapore to announce that he was diagnosed with pneumonia and was returning home.

Meanwhile, back in Singapore, 'all hell' had broken loose. On Friday after our morning grand rounds, several nurses, friends and visitors came down with the same symptoms — and all had been in contact with Elly in the preceding week. They were admitted and immediately isolated. By the end of the weekend, we had numerous admissions and we knew that something really unusual was happening.

We had staff working around the clock, we had huge media attention and atop this we received a visit by the Minister of Health. By early Monday morning, the first list of the most common symptoms and laboratory findings was put together. I will never forget the staff meeting on that Monday morning. The Director of the Communicable Diseases Center announced, "We have an outbreak at hand, and it appears to be bigger than we thought". We had no clue how big it was going to be, or what sinister effects it would have...

The next two weeks, we lived with great uncertainty. These were the worst two weeks of the epidemic, for we neither knew what the causative agent was nor its mode of transmission nor its treatment. We were horrified to see one medical or nursing colleague after the other coming down with the disease. By now, the first patients that we had seen were starting to die.

In the first week after our first cases, the WHO named the disease "SARS", and they sent out global alerts. Meanwhile Dr. L was on his flight back to Singapore, unaware of what was going on in Singapore. His friend, whom he had contacted just prior to his departure, was astute enough to conclude, however, that the symptoms Dr. L displayed, and his recent contact with the index case, were highly suggestive of this new disease and he alerted the Ministry of Health. The Ministry in turn alerted Singapore Airlines and this led to the halt of the flight in Frankfurt. To his amazement, Dr. L was escorted from the airport in full protective gear, admitted to a Frankfurt hospital. Within hours, his name was in all the news media around the world. His pregnant wife also fell ill, but his mother-in-law for some mysterious reasons did not, although all three of them had been in close contact over a prolonged time. The passengers and crew were debriefed about SARS, the recognition of its symptoms and signs, and they were given advice to seek care if they developed any such indications.

Four days later, a 22-year-old stewardess of that flight sought help at our clinic when she developed a fever and cough. During the flight, Dr. L was kept isolated in the back of the plane. The stewardess had only brief contact with him while serving food, picking up trays, and the like. She kept as much distance as possible and this included minimal communication. SARS was confirmed in the stewardess making her the first reported case of in-flight transmission.

Let me go back to the first few days when the outbreak started to unfold. As you can imagine, my travel clinic was swamped by the public demanding the flu vaccine and any other information about SARS. Our Communicable Diseases Centre turned into a major screening hub. We screened hundreds of contacts in made up tents using portable X-rays. It soon became clear that as a sole department, we would not be able to cope with all the screening. The screening was therefore moved to the main building of Tan Tock Seng Hospital under the auspices of the Accident & Emergency Department. My travel clinic was closed and my staff had a change of job: from advising travelers and administering vaccines to taking their temperatures and asking about any respiratory symptoms.

22 March, the hard decision. Close down our hospital completely. It became the designated SARS hospital, admitting only probable and suspect SARS cases. Large numbers were seen and although we were a 1,400 bed hospital, we were soon short of isolation rooms....

Fear

SARS came suddenly and caught us unaware. It's novelty, ease of transmission, and the speed of its spread, put us all in a state of fear. The epidemic progressed rapidly, and it was tragically associated with high death rates. One after another of Elly's relatives and friends died: first her father, then her pastor, her mother and finally her uncle. Her grandmother was also in the ICU, but mysteriously she survived. Elly herself survived. We kept her in hospital for a very long time, partly because we were unsure how long she would be able to transmit the disease to others, partly also to protect her from all the media attention. I often wondered how she was coping.

Characterized by a high rate of transmission to healthcare workers, SARS struck deep and hard and affected every one of us with varying degree. The constant fear of getting infected was felt throughout. This fear intensified, as colleagues became patients and young patients died. More distressing was the fear of inadvertently transmitting the infection to loved ones, especially children. Many moved out of their usual abode and did not touch their children or spouses for weeks. We became also suspicious of each other. I remember vividly how one colleague wanted to whisper something into my ear, and I jumped away out of fear of getting infected. Fear of death became a daily reality.

Pains and Frustrations

N95 masks soon became a shortage, and we had to learn how to use the same mask for one whole day. N95 masks muffled speech, hid expressions of your face, and worse, if one quickened the pace of walking, then we ended up gasping breathlessly for air. In the smouldering humid heat of Singapore, the sweat would drop underneath our hair covers, soak the masks and slowly droop down our faces, leaving us in doubt whether the masks were still working. We also had to rationalize our gowns and gloves. Frustrations abounded as policies were changed almost daily. We wrote so many guidelines; and every day seemed to bring up a new revision of those from the previous day. Although Singapore was exemplary in its transparency and abundance of information, as healthcare workers we felt we were scrambling for information. I was literally glued to the websites to gain more up-to-date information of the global outbreak.

In the view of the public, the outbreak was mainly associated with our hospital. Healthcare workers were shunned by the public. There were stories of nurses not being allowed to return to their rented apartments. Buses would not stop at our hospital so that transportation home was not possible. Taxis refused to come by. We felt stigmatized. Instead of the moral support that we craved for, we felt left alone. My children were not invited to birthday parties anymore. Our neighbors did not let their children play with ours.

I became infuriated about the way the press dealt with Elly. The media also obtained information on patient's names that were eventually published.

Despair

The atmosphere in the hospital was eerie. Instead of the usual buzz with visitors, restaurants and coffee shops, the hospital was empty. I only met masked healthcare workers. Movements within the hospital were restricted. Visitors were not allowed. Every minute of the day, we were geared up. In one of my e-mails, I wrote to my friends back home: "I am masked, gloved, gowned — but not yet cloned". The end time atmosphere in the hospital was accentuated by the TV sets that aired the start of the war in Iraq. In April, the previously hidden large number of SARS cases in China was suddenly revealed to the world. This news made me loose all hope. I imagined that the epidemic would now turn into global proportions sweeping the world, thereby killing 15% of its population. I imagined my life as a doctor from now to be a life geared up physically in masks and gowns, psychologically geared for death.

In Singapore, the outbreak was initially only hospital based, but in April the news was out that SARS had affected a large vegetable market. Overnight, thousands of people had to be quarantined. The market was closed. That evening I went shopping and realized that there were no more vegetables in supply!

Many patients had died, but death struck really home when a young medical officer died on 7 April. His mother, a doctor, who had cared for him initially during his illness, was also struck by the disease. She eventually died. One of my infectious disease colleagues was admitted to hospital because of fever. Fortunately, her fever turned out to be due to the flu that she had caught from her kids, and she was discharged. Not long after, I started feeling unwell myself. I wondered "Am I going to be the next?" I was afebrile, but I decided to separate myself from my family, said farewell to my children and my dear husband from the distance, and spent the night isolated in a room. I measured my temperature every hour, ready to get myself admitted if it reached the threshold. Alone like this, I reflected over my life and wondered whether I was ready to die. That night was a life-changing experience.

The news of the death of Carlo Urbani, the Italian WHO doctor who was instrumental in the control of SARS in Vietnam, sent our hospital staff into depression. There was both grief and shock in the air. The final blow came when the husband of a friend of mine contracted SARS. He was a surgeon in his mid-thirties, a very bright and popular consultant. He deteriorated rapidly and because of the strict isolation regulations in practice, there was no time for adequate farewell. From his isolation room, he communicated with his wife via text messages. I was grief stricken when I later heard that he had succumbed to SARS. Even worse, there was no funeral, only a rushed cremation the very next day, as these were the rules for SARS-related deaths.

With this tragedy, my facade crumbled and I broke down, the first time during all these weeks. I sobbed. I grieved for his widow, a friend and colleague with whom I still teach in community medicine, often finding myself wakening up at night and praying for her.

The worst about dying during SARS was the fact that this was a lonely death. In total, we lost a total of five healthcare workers to SARS in Singapore: 2 doctors, 1 nursing officer, 1 nursing aide and 1 hospital attendant.

The Turning Point

There was a strong group spirit of commitment and determination amongst us, and this enabled us to continue working. Voices to quit were few; almost everyone stayed on. Dr. Carlo Urbani's words were a reality for us: "Health and dignity are in-dissociable in human beings. It is a duty to stay close to victims and guarantee their rights". After the initial stigmatization, and ostracization, against healthcare workers, there was a turning point in public opinion.

All of a sudden, we became the heroes of the nation. We were in a battle against SARS together. We were showered with thank you cards, gifts, vitamins and herbal medicine. The walls of our hospital were plastered with well wishers comments and 'thank you' posters sent by companies, institutions, schools, churches, non-government organizations, individuals, etc. Almost every day, the media highlighted a healthcare worker with a full story and pictures in the newspapers. Emotional support and positive affirmations were morale boosters. The hospital management under the leadership of Dr. Lim Suet Wuen arranged frequent staff updates; and the transparency increased our trust in the authorities. Our status as healthcare workers was elevated, and with it our morale. Progressively stricter infection control measures were put in place. Our temperatures were measured three times per day. Audits were made to ensure compliance with all the measures. Infection control was now part of our daily lives.

Two to three weeks into the epidemic it became clear, that infection control measures were effective; no more new cases occurred amongst the staff of our hospital. We started feeling safe at work. In fact, we became the safest hospital to work in as new cases continued to arise in the other hospitals in Singapore. It may sound strange but because of the implemented strict infection control measures I even felt safer in the hospital than outside. Never did I think that I should leave Singapore. There was only one moment when I seriously considered it: the newspaper suddenly announced that doctors whose spouses were also doctors but working in different hospitals should be separated. My husband is indeed a doctor in another hospital. I thought "if they separate us, then I will separate myself from Singapore". Luckily, the plan was never put in action, as it turned out that a vast majority of Singapore's doctors are married to other doctors who often happen to work in different hospitals or practices.

By May, it became evident that SARS was under control in Singapore. On 31st May we were declared SARS free. Worldwide, also, cases were diminishing. My despair had turned into hope — a hope that SARS will not continue to have a deathly grip on our daily lives.

Research: SARS and Travel

Once we had hope, life at the SARS hospital now also meant facing up to the scientific challenges of this newly emerging coronavirus. The operation center at our hospital became a large center where dozens of people sat long hours every day, even weekends, to do data entry, to analyze data and interpret new findings.

I was tasked to do a seroepidemiological cohort study among healthcare workers exposed to SARS in the first month of our nosocomial outbreak. The goal of the study was to investigate the incidence of and factors associated with asymptomatic SARS-CoV infection. While I took blood samples from the more of 100 study subjects, I listened to heartbreaking stories. The findings were interesting. Of all exposed (before infection control measures were instituted) healthcare workers, 7.5% had asymptomatic SARS (SARS serology positive). Multivariate analysis showed that asymptomatic SARS was associated with lower SARS antibody titers and higher use of masks compared to SARS that presented with pneumonia.

This was an interesting study, however, my main interest circled around SARS and its relationship to travel. SARS, travel and travel medicine were intricately interlinked. Travelers belonged to those primarily affected in the early stages of the outbreak, travelers became vectors of the disease, and finally, travel and tourism themselves became the victims. In fact, travelers not only turned a newly emergent local virus into a global outbreak, but travelers were also the first to unmask the mysterious disease in Southern China.

I followed up all imported cases of SARS, and all incoming flights to Singapore with SARS cases on board. Of the six imported cases, which all occurred before screening measures were implemented at the airport, only the first resulted in extensive secondary transmission. None of these cases resulted in in-flight transmission. Of 442,973 air passengers screened after measures were implemented, 136 were sent to our designated hospital for further SARS screening; none was diagnosed as having SARS. The SARS outbreak in Singapore can be traced to the first imported case. The absence of transmission from the other imported cases was most likely a result of relatively prompt identification and isolation of cases.

New imported SARS cases therefore need not lead to major outbreaks if systems are in place to identify and isolate them early. Screening at entry points is costly, has a low yield and is not sufficient in itself. However, the costs and efforts may be justified in light of the major economic, social and international impact, which even a single imported SARS case can have.

Acknowledgements

This article is dedicated to my friend and colleague, Dr. Woon Puay Koh, who lost her surgeon husband to SARS.

References

Wilder-Smith, A., Earnest, A., & Paton, N. I. (2004). Use of simple laboratory features to distinguish the early stage of severe acute respiratory syndrome from dengue fever. *Clinical Infectious Diseases*, *39*(12), 1818–1823.

Wilder-Smith, A., Goh, K. T., & Paton, N. I. (2003). Experience of severe acute respiratory syndrome in Singapore: Importation of cases and defense strategies at the airport. *Journal of Travel Medicine*, *10*, 259–262.

Wilder-Smith, A., Paton, N. I., & Goh, K. T. (2003). Low risk of in-flight transmission of severe acute respiratory syndrome: The Singapore experience. *Journal of Tropical Medicine and International Health*, *8*(11), 1035–1037.

Wilder-Smith, A., Teleman, M. D., Earnest, A., Heng, B. H., Ling, A. E., & Leo, Y. S. (2005). Asymptomatic SARS coronavirus infection among health care workers, Singapore. *Emerging Infectious Diseases*, *11*(7), 1142–1145.

Chapter 39

What Does the Travel Medicine Practitioner Need to Know About the International Health Regulations?

Max Hardiman

The travel medicine practitioner is primarily concerned to provide advice and other services aimed at maintaining and protecting the health of individual travelers who consult with them. The International Health Regulations (IHR) have a rather different role; that of seeking to protect the world against the spread of disease from one population to another and address travelers only as one possible means by which such disease spread can occur. Despite this distinction in their respective roles, the internationally binding nature of the Regulations and the inclusion within them of specific requirements for certain travelers, makes it important for clinicians in travel medicine to be familiar with some aspects of the legal provisions.

The IHR have been around for more than 50 years although they were originally called International Sanitary Regulations in 1951. They are an agreement between almost all of WHO's 192 Member States about certain international actions to prevent the international spread of disease. The Regulations currently in force have rules that apply to three infectious diseases: cholera, plague and yellow fever. Their current significance to travel medicine is that in respect of the three above-mentioned diseases, they mandate national authorities to carry out certain public health measures in respect to travelers and conveyances. Some of these measures may be routinely applied such as the requirement for proof of yellow fever vaccination through a valid vaccination certificate from specified groups of travelers and the disinfection of aircraft flying on certain routes, other measures are related to the discovery of actual cases of illness such as the placing under surveillance or isolation of suspects among the passengers or crew following a case of cholera on board an international conveyance.

The IHR have recently undergone an extensive revision and re-negotiation between WHO's Member States, and the revised Regulations (IHR) (2005) will enter into force in international law in June 2007. The text of the revised Regulations is divided into ten parts; Part 1 deals with definitions and purpose, Parts 2 and 3 deal with the identification and response to public health emergencies, Parts 4 to 7 cover public health actions at international points of entry and exit, including documentation and charges levied, while the remaining parts deal with procedural and legal aspects of the agreement. Some more technical detail, including model certificates and declarations, are found in a series of nine Annexes.

In overview, the most significant change to the Regulations has been to broaden their scope of application from three diseases to any event with the potential to be a public health emergency of international concern, including events that do not have an infectious etiology. In circumstances where chemical or radiological events pose a serious risk to public health and of spreading internationally, much the same mechanisms for rapid identification, investigation, public health response and co-ordination are applicable. The mechanisms for providing co-ordinated international support to States experiencing outbreaks or other public health risks requiring urgent intervention are given much greater emphasis in the revised Regulations.

In respect of travel medicine it is perhaps the changes to the provisions for different health measures, particularly those applying to persons, that are of most direct relevance. The Regulations contain provision for health measures for application on a routine basis and which may be either generic measures that can impact on the risk of spread for a variety of disease entities or specific measures relevant to one particular disease. There are also provisions for further measures to be recommended during emergency situations, which are tailored to the specific emergency context.

The generic measure includes the permission for State authorities to require certain information from travelers and perform preliminary, non-invasive, medical examinations when indicated. Further examination and investigation may be carried out when justified by the findings of the initial measures. The issues of safety, consent and information provision to travelers subjected to these measures are also covered. Further provisions deal with the circumstances in which a State may deny entry and/or compel a traveler to undergo certain health measures to prevent the spread of disease.

Of the disease-specific measures for routine application, it is the requirements for yellow fever vaccination that are of greatest interest to the travel medicine practitioner. It is important to stress that the basic principle of requirements are unchanged by the revision, and what follows is a description of the changes to some of the details. Although States will continue to identify specific yellow fever vaccination centers, the Article in the current Regulations restricting the issuance of yellow fever vaccination certificates to such centers has been omitted from the revision. It should be clear that the vaccination requirement under the Regulations is not a measure for individual protection but to prevent a person leaving an area where they could have become infected with yellow fever from transporting the infection to another country where onward transmission could take place. In order to identify which travelers may be required to provide proof of vaccination, WHO will maintain a list of countries where it has determined that a risk of yellow fever transmission is present. This list will be broadly similar to, but not necessarily identical with, the list of counties to which visitors are advised to undergo vaccination for their own personal protection.

The broader scope of the IHR (2005) is reflected in changes to the certificate of vaccination; while maintaining the basic structure and data elements of the current yellow fever vaccine certificate, it also allows for the possibility of being used to certify additional types of vaccination or prophylaxis, should such certification become necessary in the future. Similarly the areas for which vector control measures are recommended in respect of international conveyances will maintain the existing focus on the vectors of yellow fever as a starting point but would permit the extension of such measures to the vectors of other diseases in accordance with recommendations under the Regulations made in the future.

Beyond the measures for yellow fever the IHR (2005) have moved away from the definition of fixed maximum measures relating to specific diseases and in their place focus on the development of context specific recommendations, made either on a temporary emergency basis or established for routine application in respect of ongoing risks of disease spread. Although States will not have legal obligations to follow these recommendations, experience has shown that there is a high degree of compliance with timely and relevant guidance issued by WHO in respect to preventing international disease spread. The indicative list of health measures that may be considered in such recommendations includes many that would impact significantly upon international travelers, such as health screening on arrival or departure, certification requirements and restrictions on travel. It will therefore be important for those giving health advice to travelers to ensure that they are kept informed of any new recommendations that may be issued under the IHR.

A number of provisions are included to protect the international traveler from unjustified health measures. While states are permitted to apply measures in addition to those provided for under the Regulations, there are a series of requirements in relation to such measures aimed at ensuring that they are scientifically valid and that information about their application is available. Specific articles seek to restrict unjustified medical examination, interruption of voyages, denial of entry, forced vaccination, documentation requirements and unreasonable charges. In addition there is reference to the dignity, human rights and fundamental freedom of persons and specifically to the treatment of international travelers during the application of health measures including quarantine or isolation.

It is the responsibility of the individual governments to notify WHO of events that qualify as potential public health emergencies of international concern, however travel medicine practitioners will be interested in the provision that requires States to report concerns regarding emergencies that may be developing elsewhere in the world on the basis of imported cases of disease, as it may well be in travel clinics where such imported cases are first detected.

In summary, the two topics covered in the IHR that are of most practical importance to the travel medicine practitioner are the yellow fever vaccination requirements including the modified international certificate and the issuance of any recommendations under the IHR after they enter into force in June 2007. While much of the IHR addresses topics outside of the scope of clinical practice, there are significant areas of common interest and both approaches can work synergistically to make the experience of international travel safer for both the travelers and for the world at large.

References

Summary of IHR in Annex 3 of International Travel and Health. Available at: http://www.who.int/ith/en/
The text of the revised Regulations is found in "Revision of the International Health Regulations", WHA58.3 — a resolution of the World Health Assembly. Available at: http://www.who.int/csr/ihr/IHRWHA58_3-en.pdf

SECTION 9:

EPILOGUE

Chapter 40

A Look into the Future: Space Travel

Larry DeLucas

As early as 1903, the year the Wright brothers proved that man could fly, scientists wrote about the possibility of space travel. The Russian space pioneer Konstantin Tsiolkovsky wrote about the requirements for space flight in his book, 'Beyond the Planet Earth' where he discussed a space station that would eventually lead to orbiting platforms that would grow in number and lead to future expeditions to the Moon, Mars and beyond our solar system. These early visions became reality with the advent of Russia's Mir, the United States' Skylab and most recently the International Space Station. Each of these orbiting facilities demonstrated that humans can indeed live and work in space for prolonged periods of time. Almost all exploration requires significant risk and financial commitment. Thus, exploration generally begins with government-sponsored programs. In this case aerospace companies are involved as subcontractors to the government-led initiatives. However, as risks are quantified and reduced via experience and technology development, commercial entrepreneurs naturally become involved, provided there is an opportunity to establish a profitable business. Today, government-sponsored space programs have led to a burgeoning new industry called "space tourism".

Once just outlandish imaginations of science fiction writers, space tourism is now a reality for the wealthy. Passengers will have their own personal spacesuits and be able to experience several minutes of weightlessness. First proposed by Richard Branson's Virgin Galactic, Inc., the first test flights are scheduled in less than twelve months. By 2015 the price of space flight is expected to drop precipitously with weeklong vacations in orbiting hotels costing less than two hundred thousand dollars. Tourists are already signing up, using their credit cards to partake in this unique travel adventure. The earliest adventures will most likely involve 2.5-hour suborbital flights (68 miles above Earth) on a space plane that seats less than ten passengers. As a former astronaut, I am convinced that the general public will want to experience the wonders of this travel adventure, even if it means they would not be able to afford any other vacations for ten years. It begins with the ride of a lifetime (dwarfs anything ever experienced at the amusement park), followed by the emotional thrill of looking at Earth and the heavens to the background music of Pachelbel, Strauss or Mozart while sipping a glass of finest wine. Sleep approximates a state of suspended animation

Travel Medicine: Tales Behind the Science
Copyright © 2007 by Elsevier Ltd.
All rights of reproduction in any form reserved.
ISBN: 0-08-045359-7

without any back pain (remember tourists are weightless) they simply float in the middle of a coffin-like cubical. Upon awakening there is no need to stretch and limber up before proceeding to the bathroom, instead one simply floats over to it. Oh! another added perk, everyone is at least one inch taller in space since gravity is not compressing the spine. So anyone who is a little overweight with a slightly enlarged midsection, can enjoy a trip back to past glory days and will look much thinner. So now what's in store for that lean-looking body each day while orbiting the Earth at 17,500 miles/hr? Well, the sky is not the limit! Imagine playing soccer, football, basketball, tennis and more in a weightless environment. Hang time in basketball could be forever and anyone, even the short guys, could slam dunk the ball! Guests could relax in zero-gravity suits with opportunities to work in the on-board gardens that produce food eaten onboard, or perhaps visit the ballroom after dinner for a night of dancing under the stars (with everyone light on their feet). Who knows, there may even be casinos up there, but of course the roulette wheels would need some special modifications.

One group of entrepreneurs, Space Island Group (SIG), led by Mr. Gene Myers has already begun planning for a large orbiting commercial space station that would provide the infrastructure to support scientific research and also provide a number of large pods for space tourism. Competition is fierce, with another group, Bigelow Aerospace of Las Vegas developing an inflatable Earth-orbiting module, which would be able to function as a single hotel suite. Mr. Robert Bigalow, owner of Budget Suites of America hotel chain, is investing $500 million of his own money in the project. The prospect of space travel is certainly gaining momentum; the Rochester Institute of Technology is currently offering a class in space tourism that involves thinking about the business aspects such as finding creative ideas that provide unique opportunities for tourists as well as the challenges of hospitality management in space.

There are a number of manageable health-related challenges associated with space travel to low Earth orbit (i.e. altitudes of 200–400 miles above Earth), especially if mission durations extend beyond one month. But the challenges associated with space travel to distances further than low Earth orbit (i.e. the Moon, Mars and beyond) are particularly daunting. Low Earth orbit missions include all missions where the space vehicle simply circles the Earth (i.e. space shuttle, Mir, Skylab and International Space Station). The duration for these varies from as little as 5 days to more than 1 year (two cosmonauts stayed on the Mir space station more than a year). To date, more than 375 people have flown in space, most for less than 30 days. My only space shuttle flight, STS-50, lasted 14 days with the Columbia shuttle circling the Earth 221 times at an altitude of 220 miles above Earth. As soon as the orbit is reached the weightless environment causes bodily fluids to begin to shift upward, producing facial edema. For several astronauts the shift in fluid and most likely, its affect on the vestibular system, produces what is known as space adaptation syndrome (SAS). SAS is believed to be responsible for headaches, malaise and vomiting. More than 75% of the humans flown in space experience some or all of these effects. In addition, fluid shift causes swelling or fluid in the sinus regions, typically making it more difficult to breath through the nose and altering the smell and taste senses. The fluid shift also places additional pressure on the brain, impairing the ability to think quickly (personal opinion based on my experience for one flight). Within three days many of these symptoms improve remarkably but a totally normal state is never reached. Movement in a gravity-free environment requires some acclimation. First-time travelers will have difficulty becoming used to the fact that although they have no weight, momentum continues to exist. Thus, flying through the cabin and grabbing a handle to stop puts travelers at risk of twisting an arm or shoulder. It would be easy for you to cause a rotator cuff tear. During the first few days the bowels shut down for the most part. Stomach muscles must be used to move fecal matter through the gut, a process that is easy for some and difficult for others. Nutrition in space continues to be a problem with the typical astronaut experiencing weight loss, dehydration and reduced appetite. The normal sleep cycle is disrupted with duration and depth of sleep decreased. If a mission in low Earth orbit lasts more than one month, fairly severe orthostatic hypotension will be experienced upon return to Earth. Landing a space shuttle after a one-month stay in space would be impossible (today the astronauts who stay on the space station for more than one month are returned to Earth by other astronauts who fly the shuttle to the station to exchange crews, returning to Earth within one week with the previous crew (thus the commander and pilot are very expensive taxi drivers). After returning to Earth, neurological recovery of balance and mobility requires 1–3 days for short missions and 10–30 days for longer missions. I stayed in space for 14 days and was not allowed to drive a car for 10 days after we landed. The immune system is compromised and wound healing delayed, eye–hand coordination is degraded with both fine and gross motor skills diminished.

Now to the big problems — the skeletal muscle deteriorates with significant atrophy observed in some astronauts after only 5 days in space. After only 14 days in space, I had lost more than 10% of my muscle mass in several of my weight-bearing muscles (I did not exercise but even if I had, the reduction still would have been significant). This is compounded by a 1% loss of bone density for each month in space. Thus, upon return from extended space stays of 1 year or longer, post-travel pathologies such as muscle fatigue, weakness, loss of coordination and delayed onset muscle soreness are often experienced. Exercise (i.e. cycle ergometry) is somewhat effective in reducing cardiac aerobic deconditioning but it does not prevent muscle deterioration.

But to travel to the Moon or to Mars exposes more problems and considerations that must be addressed. Once beyond low Earth orbit, travelers are exposed to harmful high-energy charged solar and cosmic particles (ranging from protons to iron nuclei). There is little information regarding the effect of this radiation on humans but there is a strong possibility that there would be significant damage to cellular DNA, causing a significant risk of cancer and other problems. A trip to Mars would generally require six-months travel each way and at least a one-year stay on the surface (during which time fuel would be produced from the Martian soil and atmosphere for the return trip). By the time the spacecraft arrived, the crew would not be strong enough to land it but even if they could, standing up and walking on the surface would be impossible. There are other considerations that must be planned for, such as the fact that the trip itself will require an optimum functioning spacecraft and crew. There would be little possibility of returning to Earth if equipment malfunctions or the craft's environment becomes off-nominal. Imagine if one of the crew requires surgery for appendicitis, a tooth extraction or a fractured limb. Communication with experienced medical personnel on Earth will be delayed 20 minutes or more depending on the position of the craft as it journeys to Mars. As an eye doctor, I have always worried about crew experiencing a corneal abrasion due to the dust and dirt that floats in the vehicle. Corneal abrasions are extremely painful, rendering an astronaut virtually helpless without medical attention.

To have a physician on-board would be necessary but what if the physician was the one injured? Finally, the psychological factor is also of concern. Crews must be carefully chosen based on a number of factors related to their ability to work well with others, perform under pressure and the ability to tolerate isolation. There are obviously a number of concerns that prohibit trips with humans to Mars in the foreseeable future. However, low Earth orbit commercial travel is certainly on its way to becoming a reality in this decade. As the customer base grows and we continue to advance our understanding and treatment for the medical problems associated with space travel, I am confident that we will continue to increase the duration and distances of future trips to space.

Subject Index